Aho-Girl

\ˈahôˌgərl\ *Japanese, noun.*
A clueless girl.

3 | Hiroyuki

WITHDRAWN

CHARACTER PROFILES

AHO-GIRL's Cast of Characters

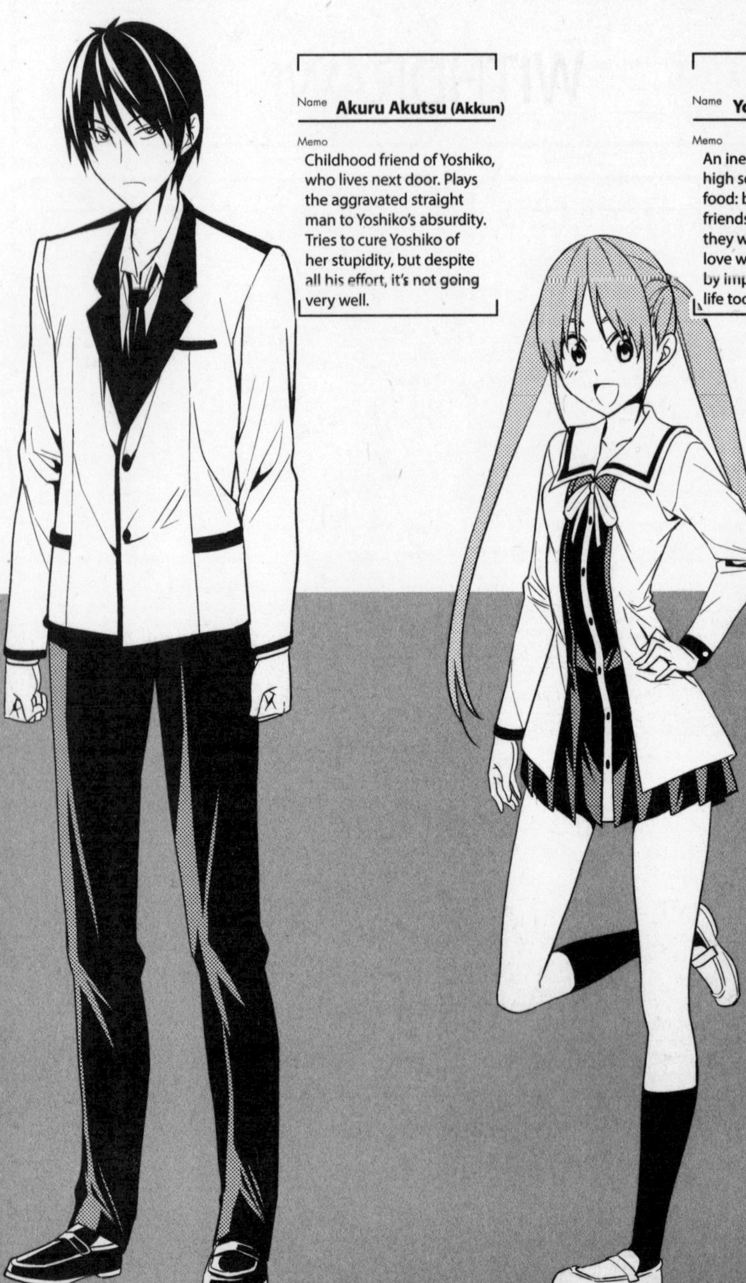

Name **Akuru Akutsu (Akkun)**

Memo
Childhood friend of Yoshiko, who lives next door. Plays the aggravated straight man to Yoshiko's absurdity. Tries to cure Yoshiko of her stupidity, but despite all his effort, it's not going very well.

Name **Yoshiko Hanabatake**

Memo
An inexpressibly clueless high school girl. Favorite food: bananas. Has been friends with Akkun since they were kids and is in love with him. Lives entirely by impulse. Tends to enjoy life too much.

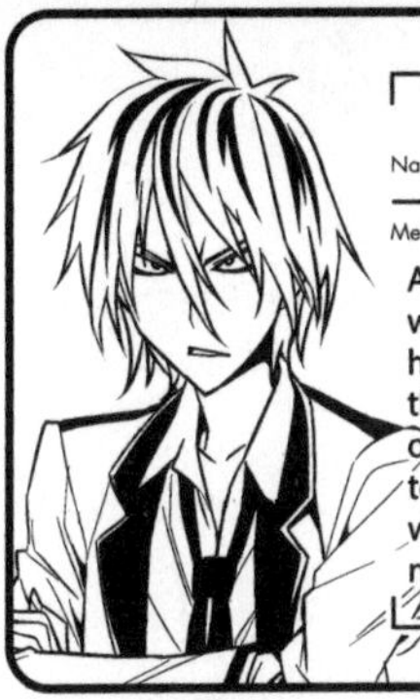

Name **Ryuichi Kurosaki**

Memo

An unfortunate hooligan who knows nothing of human kindness and therefore was easily won over by Yoshiko. Seems to want to be friends with Akkun, but there's not much hope for that.

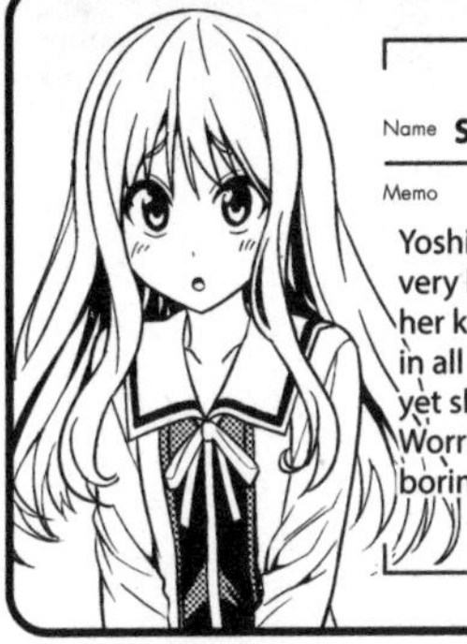

Name **Sayaka Sumino**

Memo

Yoshiko's friend. She's a very kind girl. She knows her kindness lands her in all sorts of trouble, yet she remains kind. Worries about being boring.

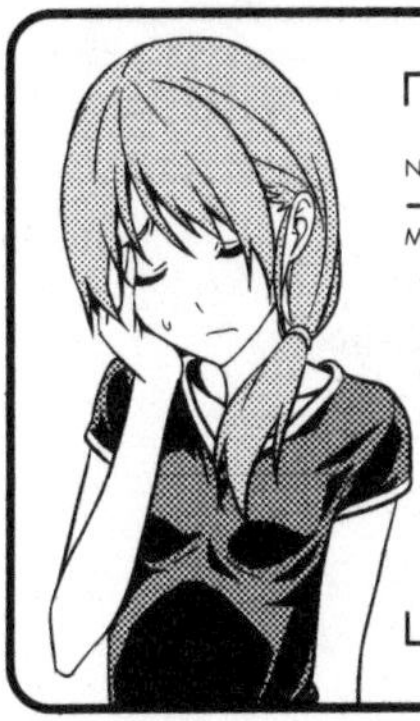

Name **Yoshie Hanabatake**

Memo

Yoshiko's mother. While she does worry about Yoshiko, she's far more worried about her own sunset years. Will use any means necessary to fix Yoshiko up with Akkun.

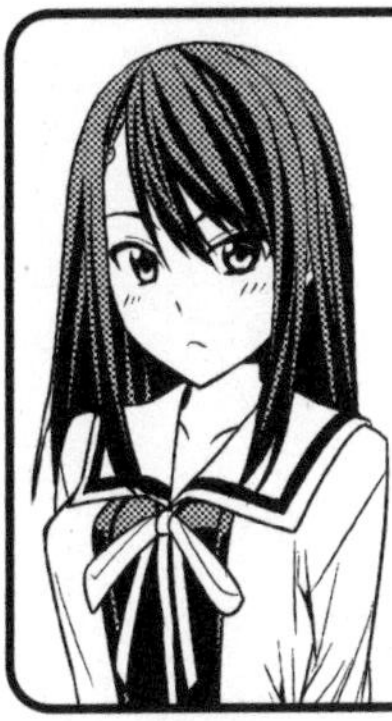

Name **Head Monitor**

Memo

An upperclassman at Yoshiko's school. Has fallen head over heels for Akkun and begun to stray from the moral path, but she doesn't realize it. G cup.

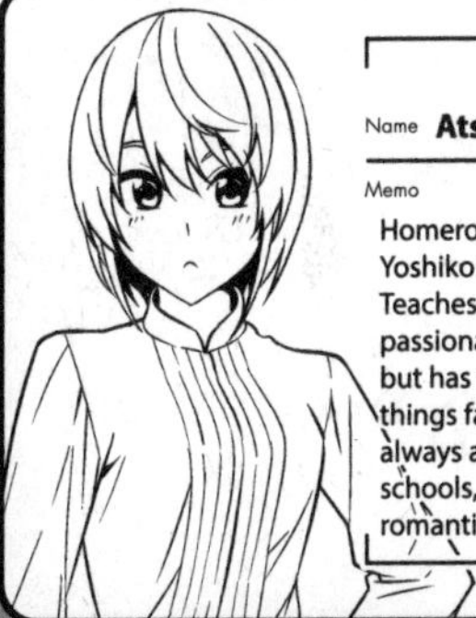

Name **Atsuko Oshieda**

Memo

Homeroom teacher for Yoshiko and Akkun's class. Teaches math. She is passionate about education, but has a tendency to treat things far too seriously. Has always attended all-girls schools, and so has no romantic experience.

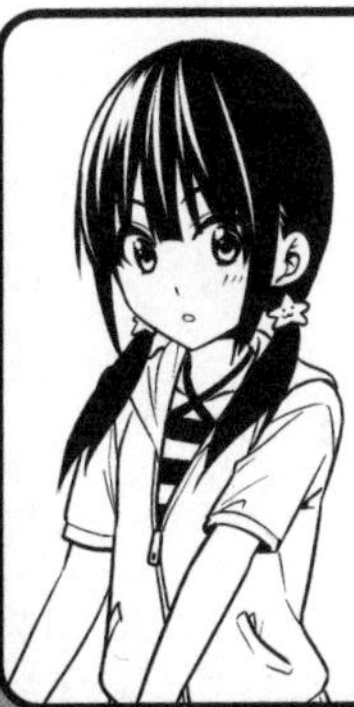

Name **Ruri Akutsu**

Memo

While her brother Akkun is an overachiever, Ruri's not quite so fortunate. She is constantly dismayed by her terrible grades. Perhaps the day will come when all her hard work pays off. Hates Yoshiko.

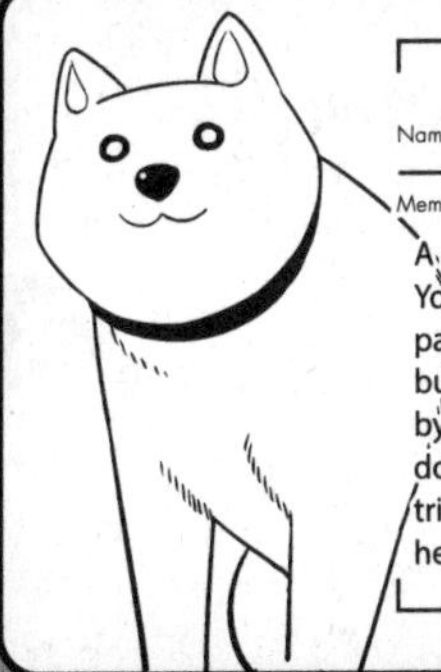

Name **Dog**

Memo

A ridiculously big dog Yoshiko found at the park. Started out vicious, but once vanquished by Yoshiko, has become docile. Is quite clever and tries to stop Yoshiko from her wilder impulses.

HIROYUKI
PRESENTS
AHO-GIRL
VOLUME.3

AHO-GIRL 3

CONTENTS

+ + = AHO-GIRL

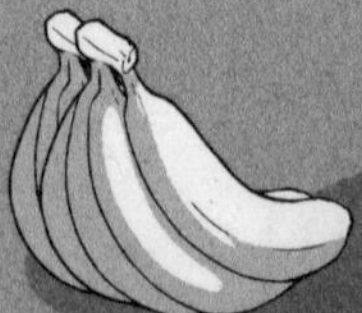

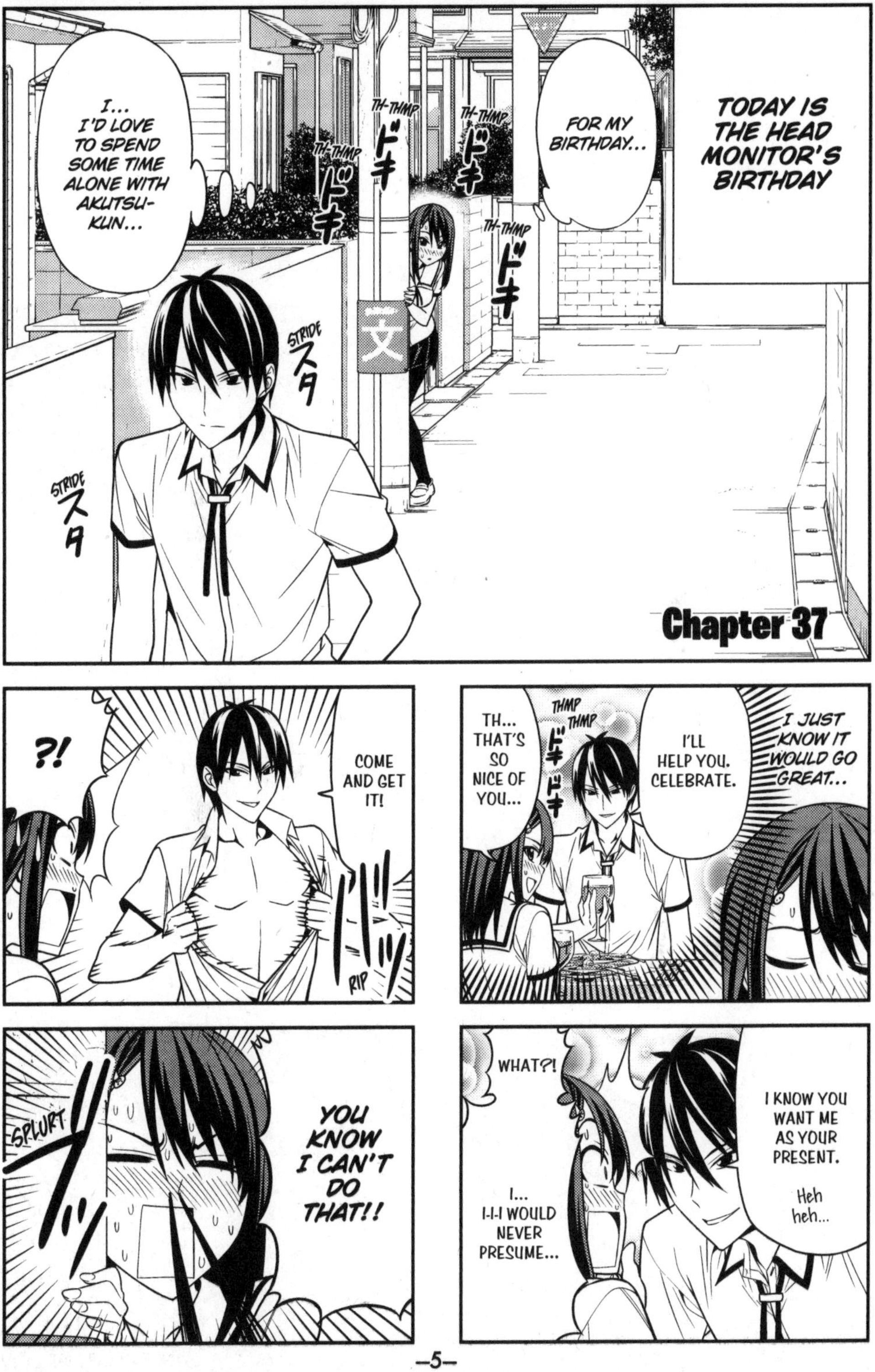
TODAY IS THE HEAD MONITOR'S BIRTHDAY
FOR MY BIRTHDAY...
TH-THMP ドキ
TH-THMP ドキ
TH-THMP ドキ
TH-THMP ドキ
I... I'D LOVE TO SPEND SOME TIME ALONE WITH AKUTSU-KUN...
STRIDE スタ
STRIDE スタ
Chapter 37
I JUST KNOW IT WOULD GO GREAT...
I'LL HELP YOU. CELEBRATE.
THMP THMP ドキドキ
TH... THAT'S SO NICE OF YOU...
COME AND GET IT!
?!
RIP
I KNOW YOU WANT ME AS YOUR PRESENT.
Heh heh...
WHAT?!
I... I-I-I WOULD NEVER PRESUME...
YOU KNOW I CAN'T DO THAT!!
SPLURT

When I Think about You, I...

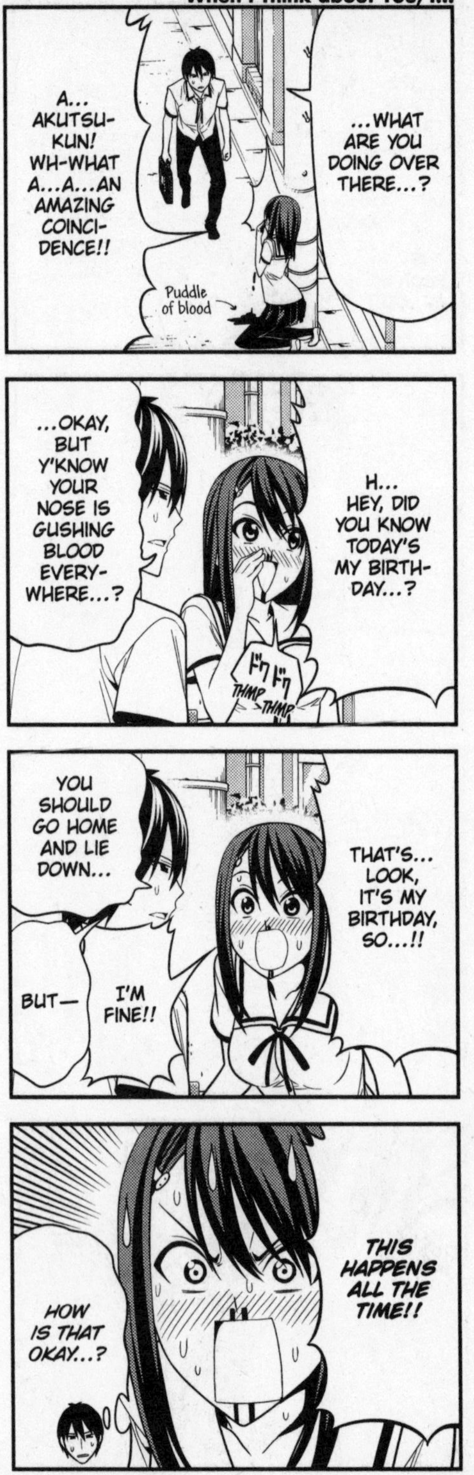
...WHAT ARE YOU DOING OVER THERE...?
A... AKUTSU-KUN! WH-WHAT A...A...AN AMAZING COINCIDENCE!!
Puddle of blood
H... HEY, DID YOU KNOW TODAY'S MY BIRTHDAY...?
...OKAY, BUT Y'KNOW YOUR NOSE IS GUSHING BLOOD EVERYWHERE...?
ドクドク THMP THMP
THAT'S... LOOK, IT'S MY BIRTHDAY, SO...!!
YOU SHOULD GO HOME AND LIE DOWN...
I'M FINE!!
BUT—
THIS HAPPENS ALL THE TIME!!
HOW IS THAT OKAY...?

Why Are You Here?

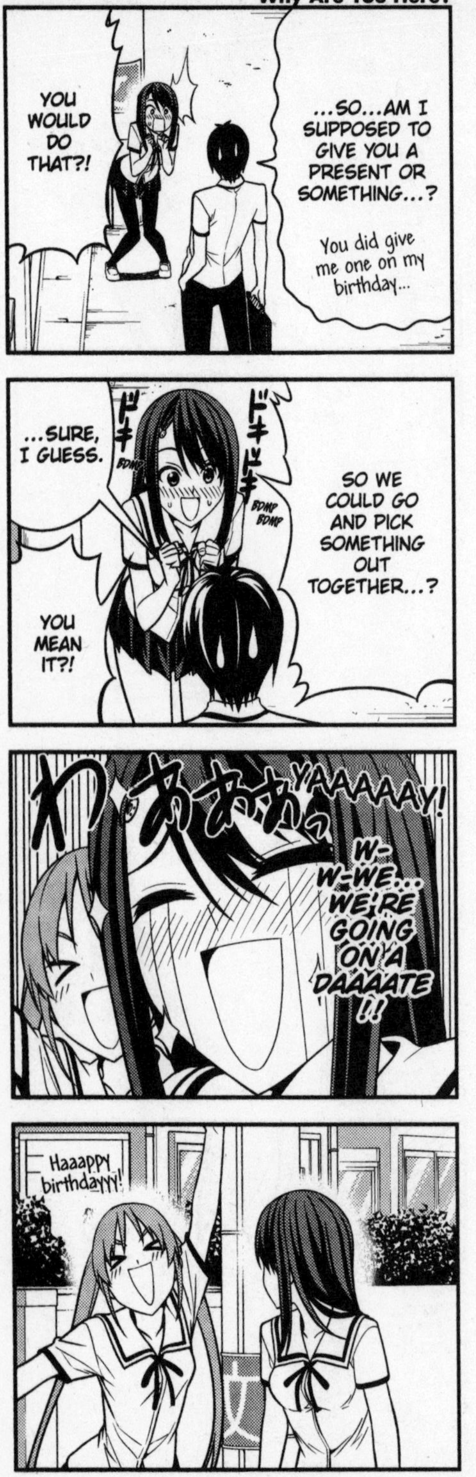
...SO...AM I SUPPOSED TO GIVE YOU A PRESENT OR SOMETHING...?
You did give me one on my birthday...
YOU WOULD DO THAT?!
ドキッドキ BDMP BDMP
SO WE COULD GO AND PICK SOMETHING OUT TOGETHER...?
...SURE, I GUESS.
ドキ BDMP
YOU MEAN IT?!
わあああっ YAAAAAY!
W- W-WE... WE'RE GOING ON A DAAAATE!!
Haaappy birthdayyy!

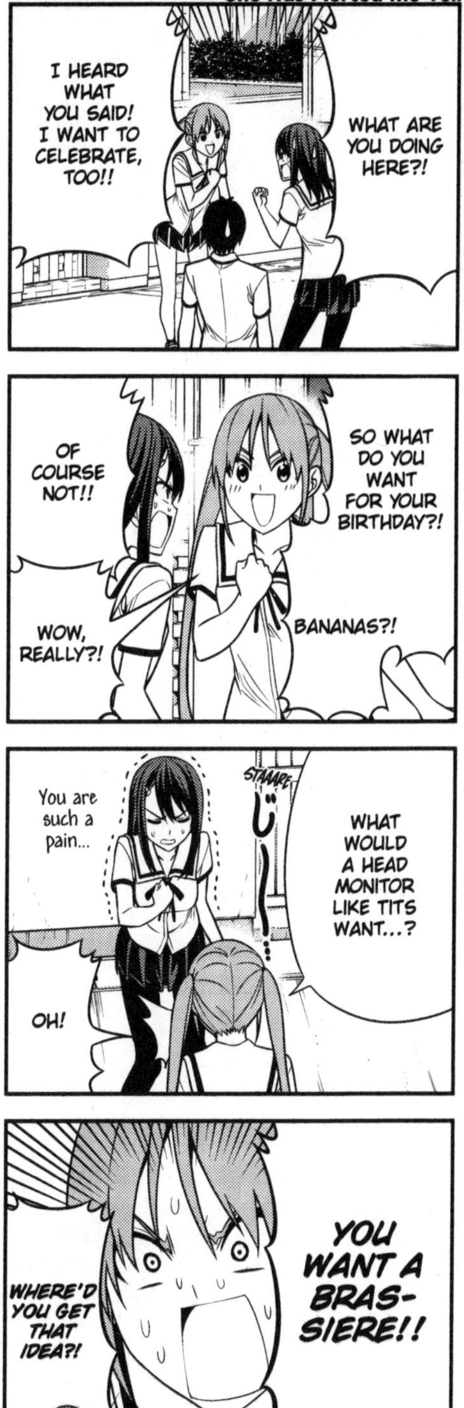
WHAT ARE YOU DOING HERE?!
I HEARD WHAT YOU SAID! I WANT TO CELEBRATE, TOO!!
SO WHAT DO YOU WANT FOR YOUR BIRTHDAY?!
OF COURSE NOT!!
BANANAS?!
WOW, REALLY?!
STAAARE
じー
WHAT WOULD A HEAD MONITOR LIKE TITS WANT...?
You are such a pain...
OH!
YOU WANT A BRAS-SIERE!!
WHERE'D YOU GET THAT IDEA?!

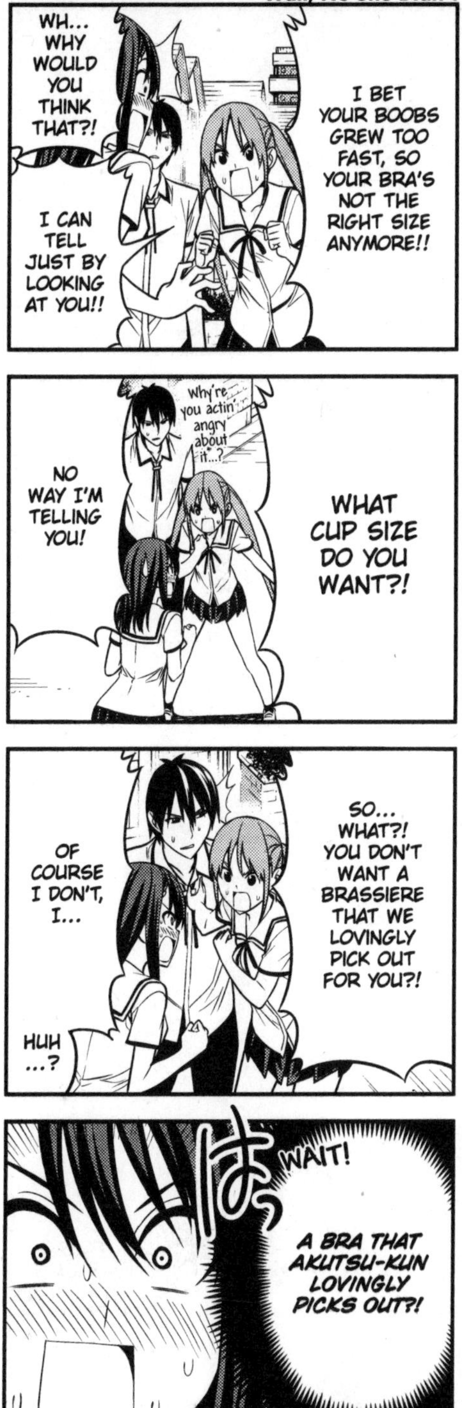
I BET YOUR BOOBS GREW TOO FAST, SO YOUR BRA'S NOT THE RIGHT SIZE ANYMORE!!
WH... WHY WOULD YOU THINK THAT?!
I CAN TELL JUST BY LOOKING AT YOU!!
WHAT CUP SIZE DO YOU WANT?!
Why're you actin' angry about it...?
NO WAY I'M TELLING YOU!
SO... WHAT?! YOU DON'T WANT A BRASSIERE THAT WE LOVINGLY PICK OUT FOR YOU?!
OF COURSE I DON'T, I...
HUH ...?
は
WAIT!
A BRA THAT AKUTSU-KUN LOVINGLY PICKS OUT?!

Honey Trap

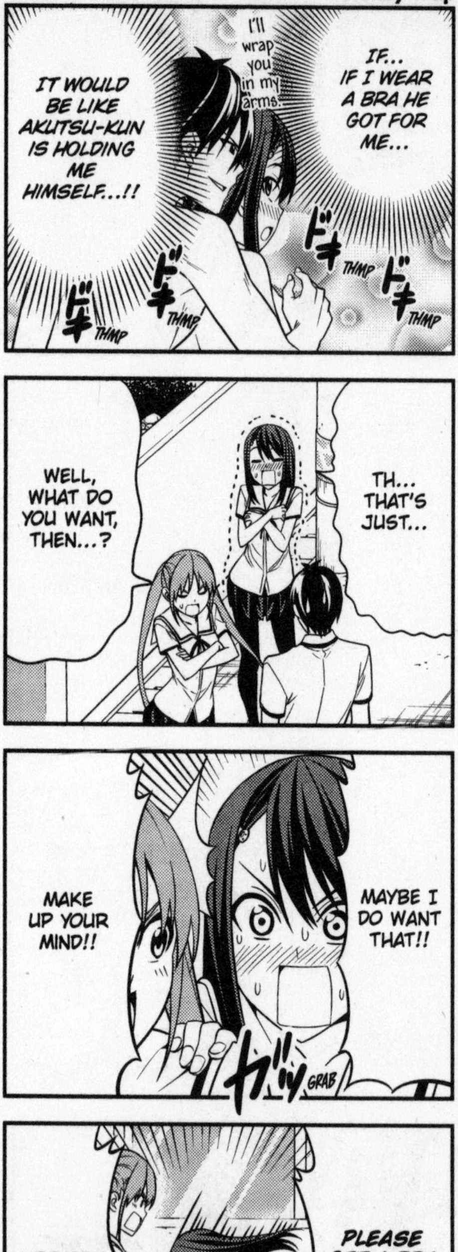
IF... IF I WEAR A BRA HE GOT FOR ME...
I'll wrap you in my arms.
IT WOULD BE LIKE AKUTSU-KUN IS HOLDING ME HIMSELF...!!
ドキ THMP
ドキ THMP
ドキ THMP
ドキ THMP
TH... THAT'S JUST...
WELL, WHAT DO YOU WANT, THEN...?
MAYBE I DO WANT THAT!!
MAKE UP YOUR MIND!!
ガッ GRAB
PLEASE GET A BRA FOR ME!!
HRRMPH. AGREED!!
バッ VWIP

But You're a Boy

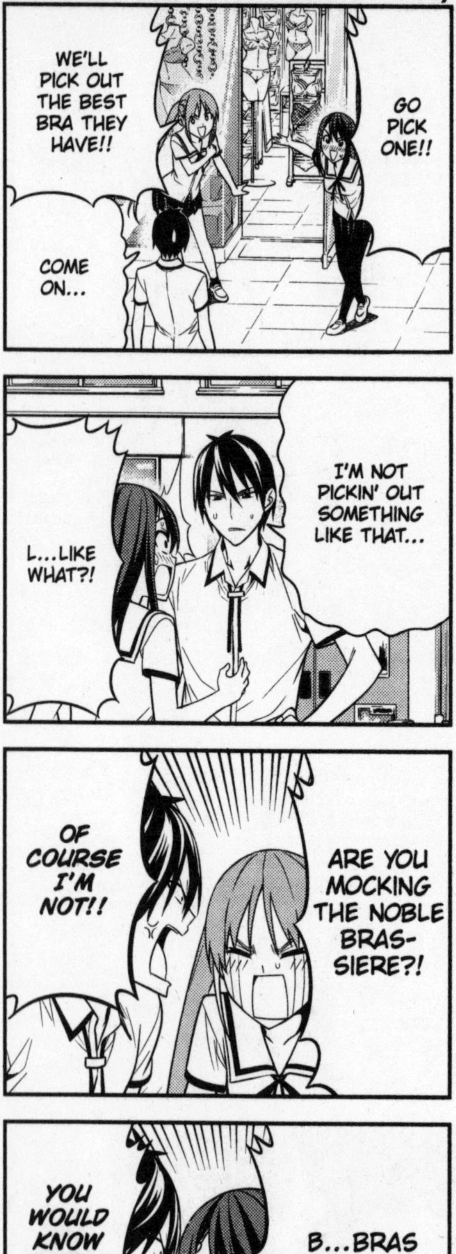
GO PICK ONE!!
WE'LL PICK OUT THE BEST BRA THEY HAVE!!
COME ON...
I'M NOT PICKIN' OUT SOMETHING LIKE THAT...
L...LIKE WHAT?!
ARE YOU MOCKING THE NOBLE BRAS-SIERE?!
OF COURSE I'M NOT!!
B...BRAS ARE VERY IMPORTANT TO GIRLS ...!!
YOU WOULD KNOW BETTER THAN ANY-ONE!!

A Risky Argument

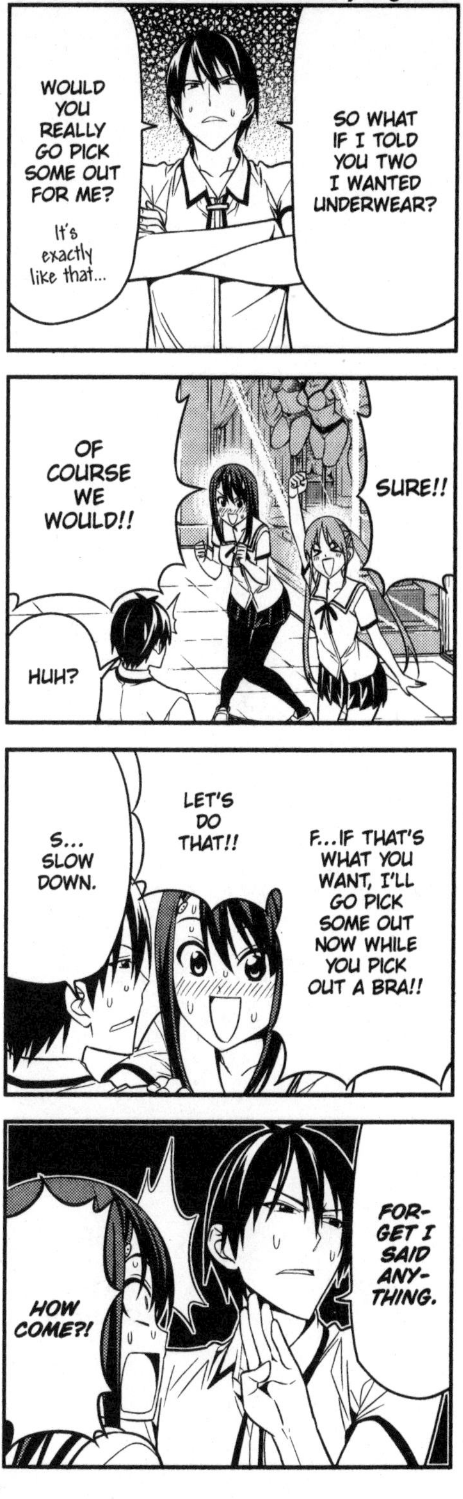
SO WHAT IF I TOLD YOU TWO I WANTED UNDERWEAR?
WOULD YOU REALLY GO PICK SOME OUT FOR ME?
It's exactly like that...
SURE!!
OF COURSE WE WOULD!!
HUH?
F...IF THAT'S WHAT YOU WANT, I'LL GO PICK SOME OUT NOW WHILE YOU PICK OUT A BRA!!
LET'S DO THAT!!
S... SLOW DOWN.
FOR-GET I SAID ANY-THING.
HOW COME?!

Hardly an Exemplar of Public Decency

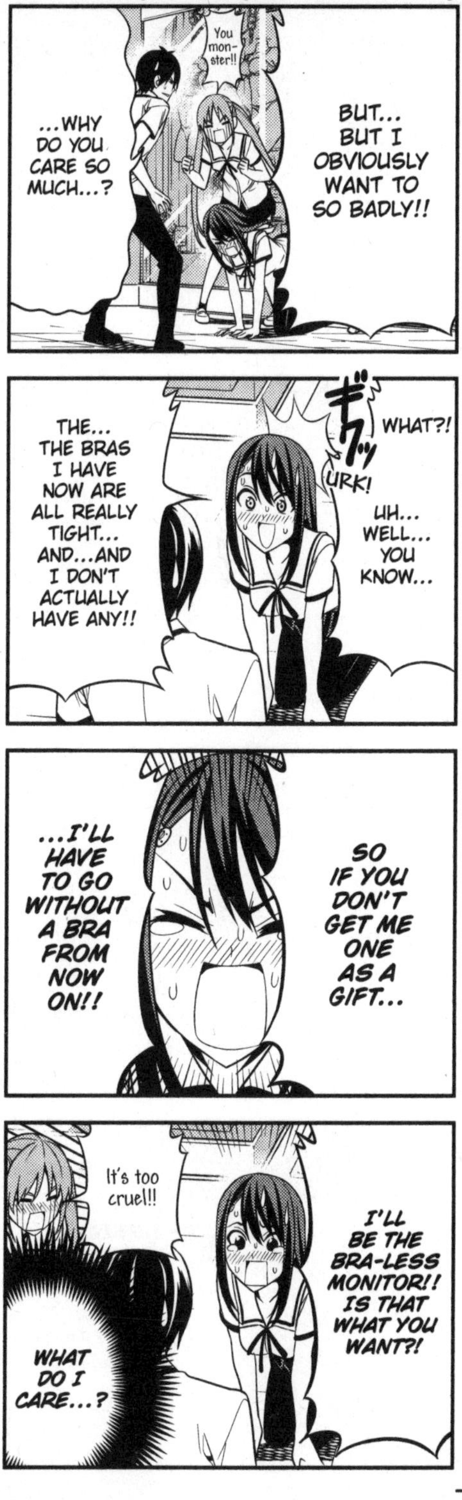
BUT... BUT I OBVIOUSLY WANT TO SO BADLY!!
You mon-ster!!
...WHY DO YOU CARE SO MUCH...?
WHAT?!
ギクッ
URK!
UH... WELL... YOU KNOW...
THE... THE BRAS I HAVE NOW ARE ALL REALLY TIGHT... AND...AND I DON'T ACTUALLY HAVE ANY!!
SO IF YOU DON'T GET ME ONE AS A GIFT...
...I'LL HAVE TO GO WITHOUT A BRA FROM NOW ON!!
I'LL BE THE BRA-LESS MONITOR!! IS THAT WHAT YOU WANT?!
It's too cruel!!
WHAT DO I CARE...?

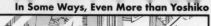

She Told the Sales Clerk Her Size

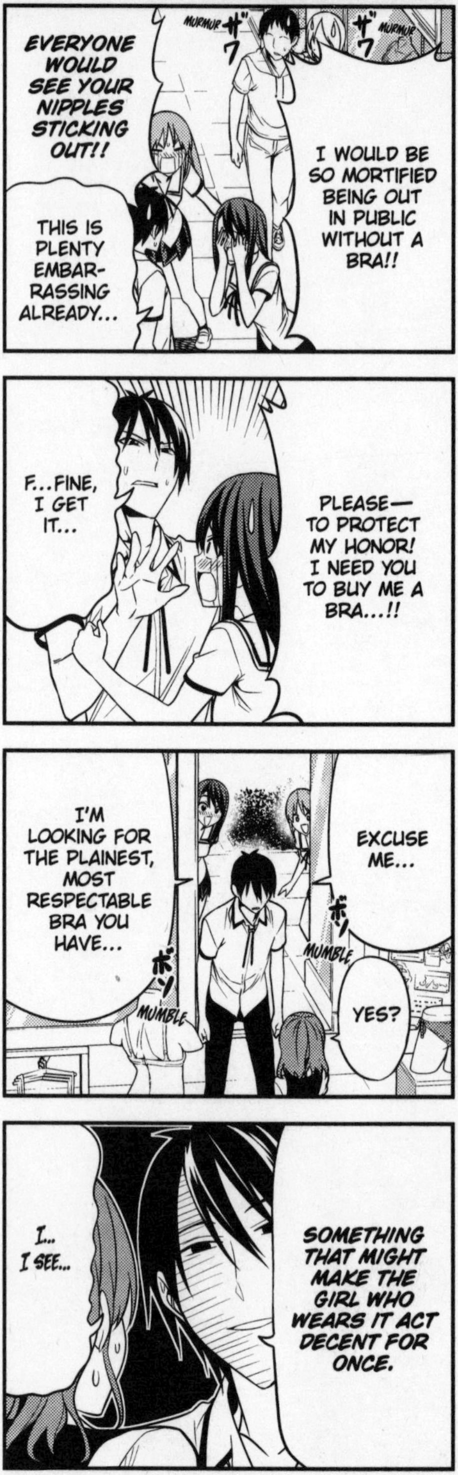
MURMUR ザワ
MURMUR ザワ
I WOULD BE SO MORTIFIED BEING OUT IN PUBLIC WITHOUT A BRA!!
EVERYONE WOULD SEE YOUR NIPPLES STICKING OUT!!
THIS IS PLENTY EMBARRASSING ALREADY...
PLEASE— TO PROTECT MY HONOR! I NEED YOU TO BUY ME A BRA...!!
F...FINE, I GET IT...
EXCUSE ME...
ボソ MUMBLE
YES?
I'M LOOKING FOR THE PLAINEST, MOST RESPECTABLE BRA YOU HAVE...
ボソ MUMBLE
SOMETHING THAT MIGHT MAKE THE GIRL WHO WEARS IT ACT DECENT FOR ONCE.
I... I SEE...

In Some Ways, Even More than Yoshiko

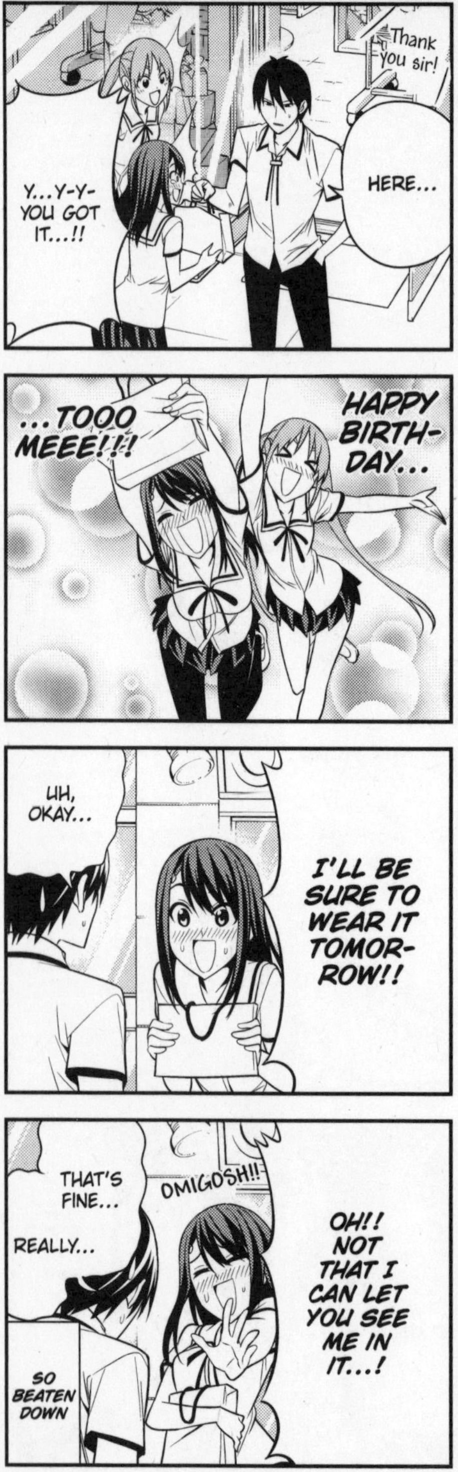
Thank you sir!
HERE...
Y...Y-Y-YOU GOT IT...!!
HAPPY BIRTHDAY...
...TOOO MEEE!!!
I'LL BE SURE TO WEAR IT TOMORROW!!
UH, OKAY...
OH!! NOT THAT I CAN LET YOU SEE ME IN IT...!
OMIGOSH!!
THAT'S FINE...
REALLY...
SO BEATEN DOWN

What a Cruel Man

THE NEXT DAY
...MAN, BRAS ARE EXPENSIVE...
Receipt→
MUST BE A LOT EASIER IF YOUR CHEST NEVER GETS ANY BIGGER.
?
WHY ARE YOU LOOKING AT ME, AKKUN-SAN?

(Today once again, we'll carry, fight, multiply and then be)

Aho-Girl

\ˈahôˌgərl\ *Japanese, noun.*
A clueless girl.

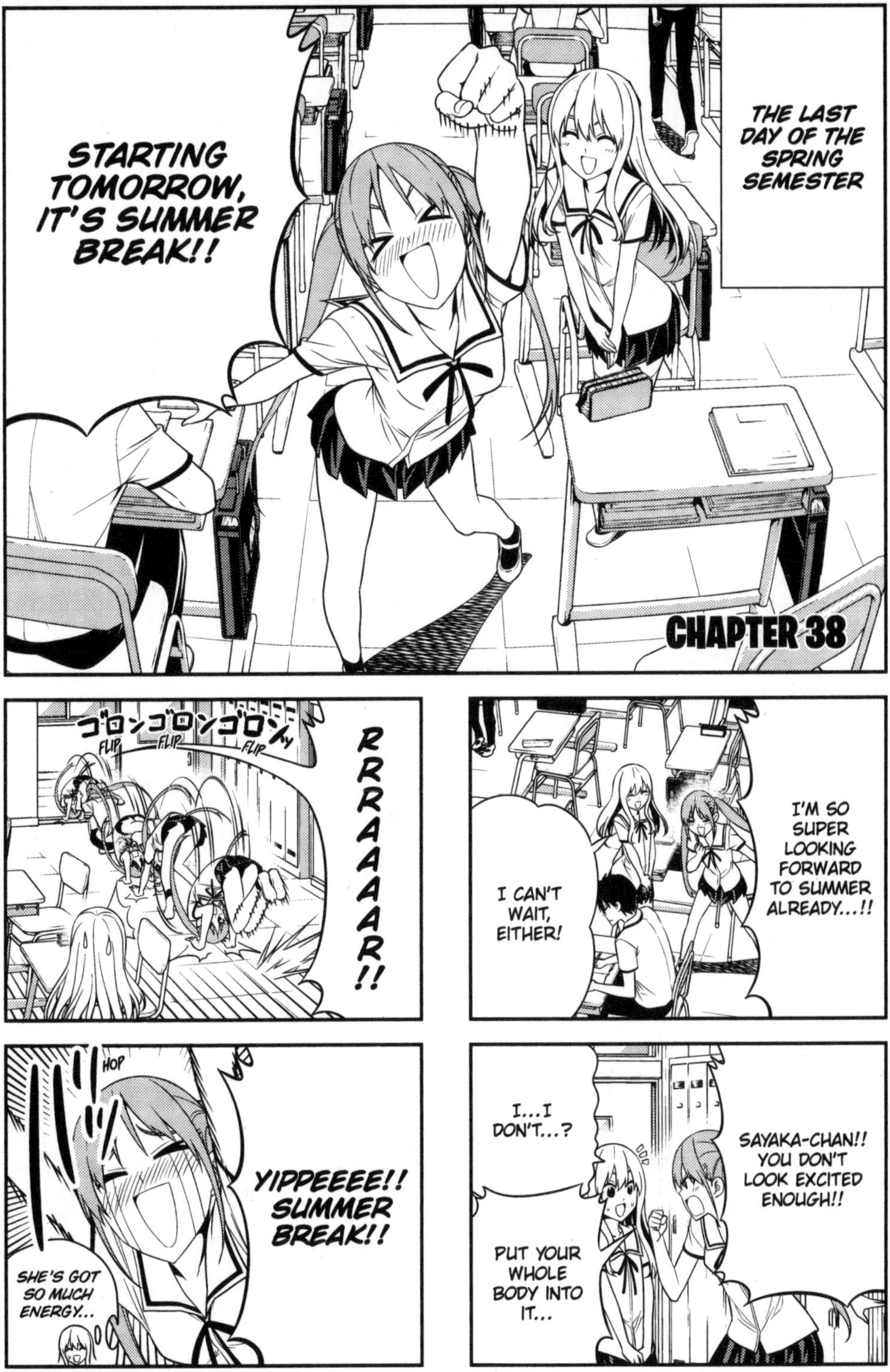
THE LAST DAY OF THE SPRING SEMESTER
STARTING TOMORROW, IT'S SUMMER BREAK!!
CHAPTER 38
I'M SO SUPER LOOKING FORWARD TO SUMMER ALREADY...!!
I CAN'T WAIT, EITHER!
RRRAAAAAR!!
ゴロンゴロンゴロン
FLIP FLIP FLIP
SAYAKA-CHAN!! YOU DON'T LOOK EXCITED ENOUGH!!
I...I DON'T...?
PUT YOUR WHOLE BODY INTO IT...
HOP
YIPPEEEE!! SUMMER BREAK!!
SHE'S GOT SO MUCH ENERGY...

Call and No Response

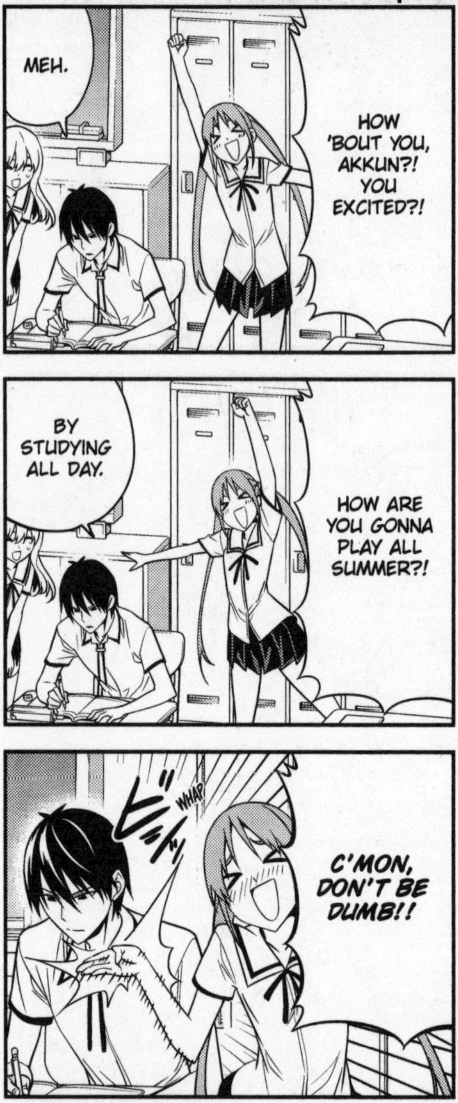
HOW 'BOUT YOU, AKKUN?! YOU EXCITED?!
MEH.
HOW ARE YOU GONNA PLAY ALL SUMMER?!
BY STUDYING ALL DAY.
WHAP
C'MON, DON'T BE DUMB!!
THWHACK

It's a Little Different

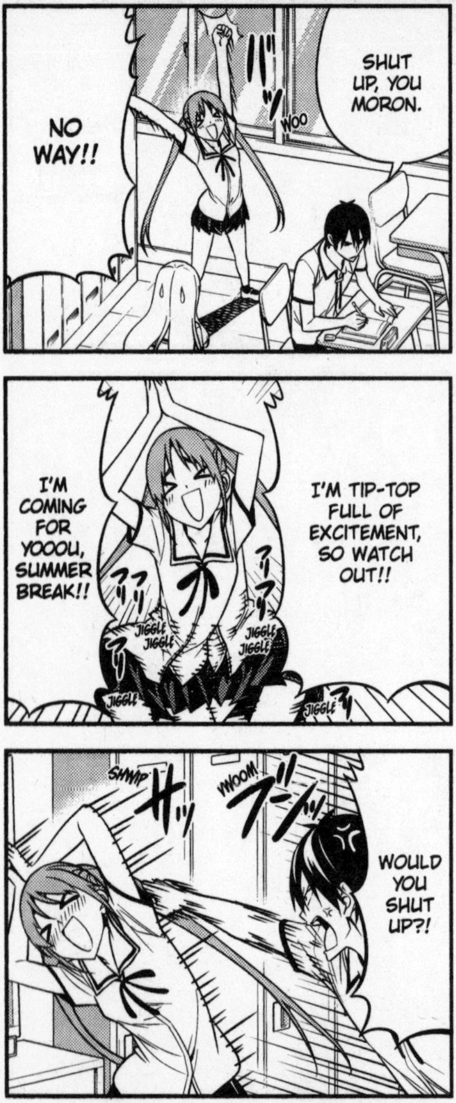
SHUT UP, YOU MORON.
WOO
NO WAY!!
I'M TIP-TOP FULL OF EXCITEMENT, SO WATCH OUT!!
I'M COMING FOR YOOOU, SUMMER BREAK!!
JIGGLE JIGGLE
JIGGLE JIGGLE
JIGGLE
JIGGLE
WOULD YOU SHUT UP?!
VWOOM
SHWIP
I'M A LITTLE DIFFER-ENT...
...DURING SUMMER BREAK.
TWINKLE

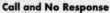

What Is This, a Game?

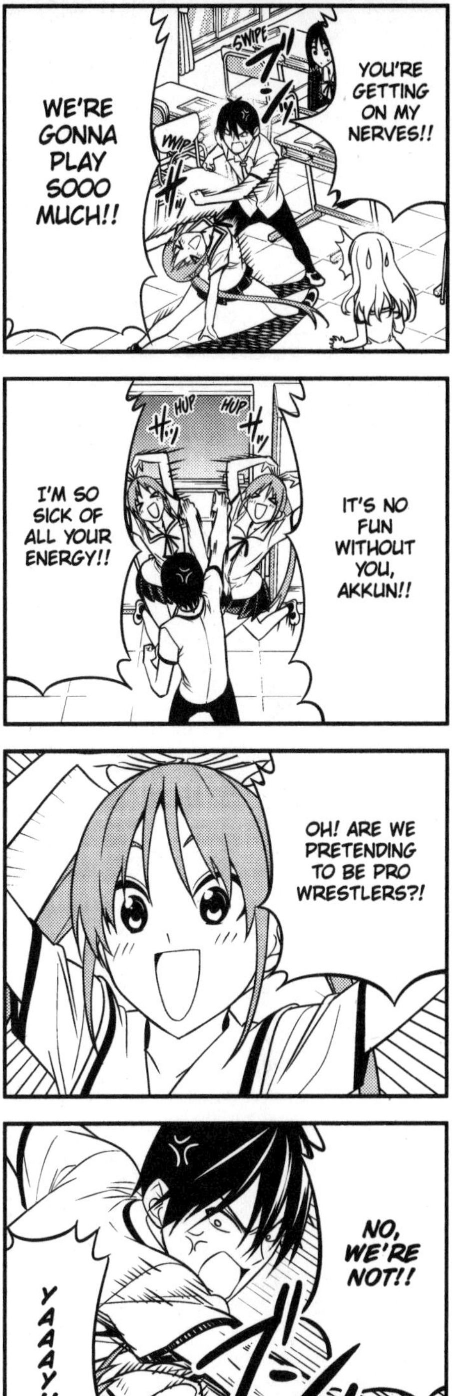
YOU'RE GETTING ON MY NERVES!!
SWIPE
WE'RE GONNA PLAY SOOO MUCH!!
VWIP
HUP
HUP
IT'S NO FUN WITHOUT YOU, AKKUN!!
I'M SO SICK OF ALL YOUR ENERGY!!
OH! ARE WE PRETENDING TO BE PRO WRESTLERS?!
NO, WE'RE NOT!!
YAAAAY!!
VWOOSH

It's Just Getting Started

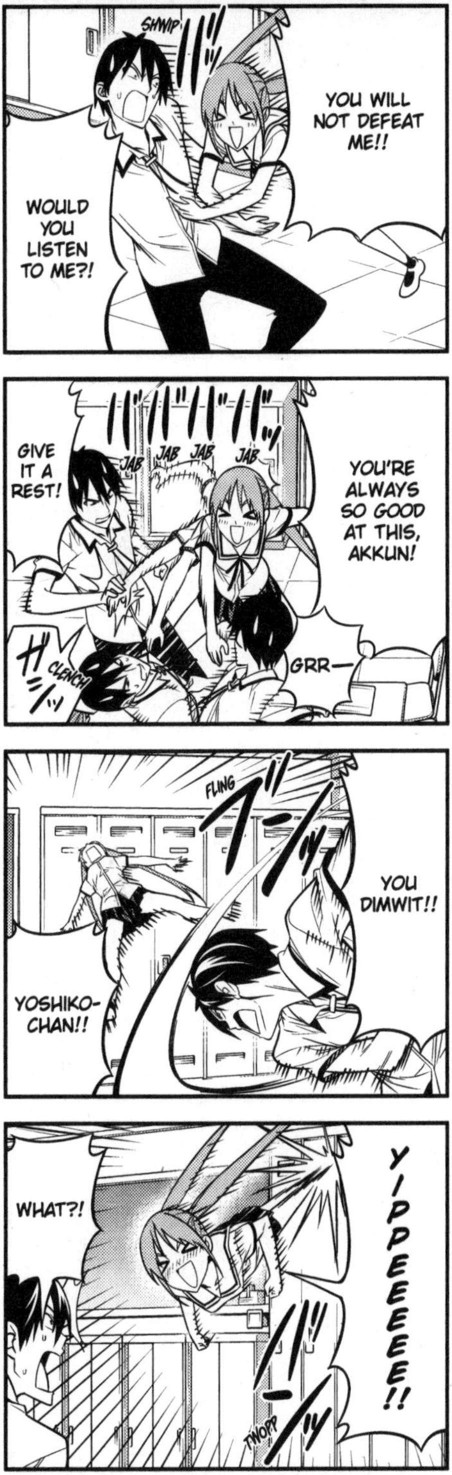
YOU WILL NOT DEFEAT ME!!
SHWIP
WOULD YOU LISTEN TO ME?!
YOU'RE ALWAYS SO GOOD AT THIS, AKKUN!
JAB JAB JAB JAB
GIVE IT A REST!
GRR—
CLENCH
YOU DIMWIT!!
FLING
YOSHIKO-CHAN!!
YIPPEEEEEE!!
WHAT?!
TWOPP

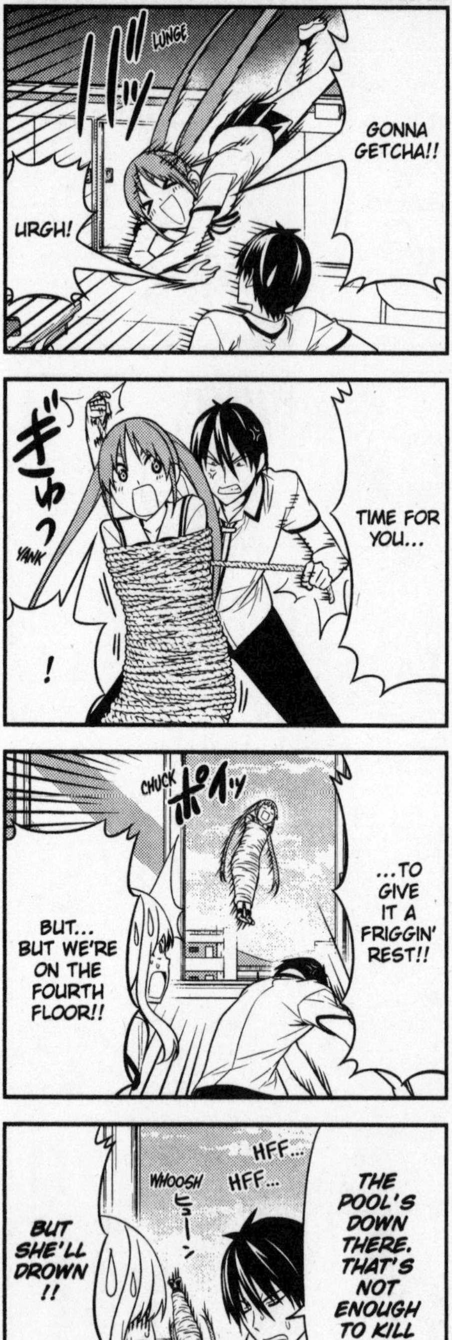
LUNGE
GONNA GETCHA!!
URGH!
TIME FOR YOU...
ぎゅっ
YANK
!
...TO GIVE IT A FRIGGIN' REST!!
ポイッ
CHUCK
BUT... BUT WE'RE ON THE FOURTH FLOOR!!
THE POOL'S DOWN THERE. THAT'S NOT ENOUGH TO KILL HER.
HFF... HFF...
WHOOSH
BUT SHE'LL DROWN!!

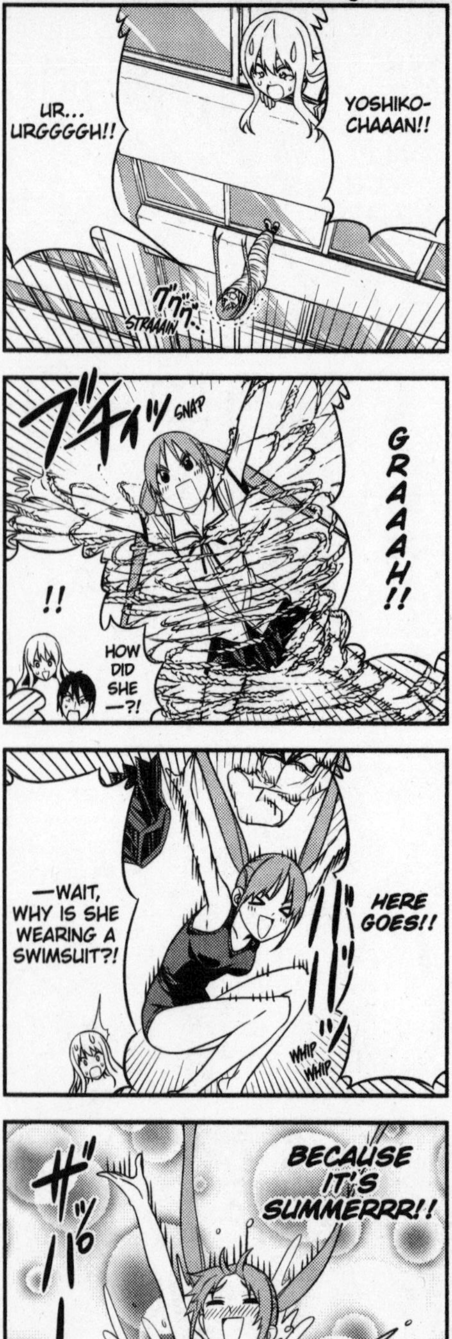
YOSHIKO-CHAAAN!!
UR... URGGGGH!!
STRAAAIN
GRAAAAH!!
ブチィッ
SNAP
!!
HOW DID SHE—?!
HERE GOES!!
WHIP WHIP
—WAIT, WHY IS SHE WEARING A SWIMSUIT?!
BECAUSE IT'S SUMMERRR!!
SKLASSSH

That's Kid(?)napping

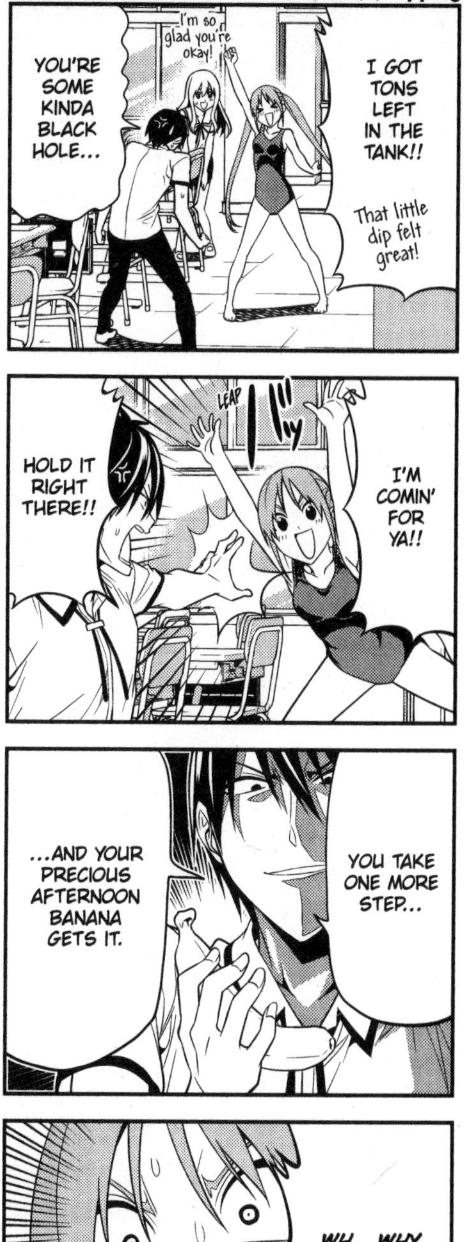
I GOT TONS LEFT IN THE TANK!!
That little dip felt great!
I'm so glad you're okay!
YOU'RE SOME KINDA BLACK HOLE...
I'M COMIN' FOR YA!!
LEAP
HOLD IT RIGHT THERE!!
YOU TAKE ONE MORE STEP...
...AND YOUR PRECIOUS AFTERNOON BANANA GETS IT.
WH...WHY WOULD YOU MAKE SUCH A TERRIFYING THREAT?!

Unwitting Participation

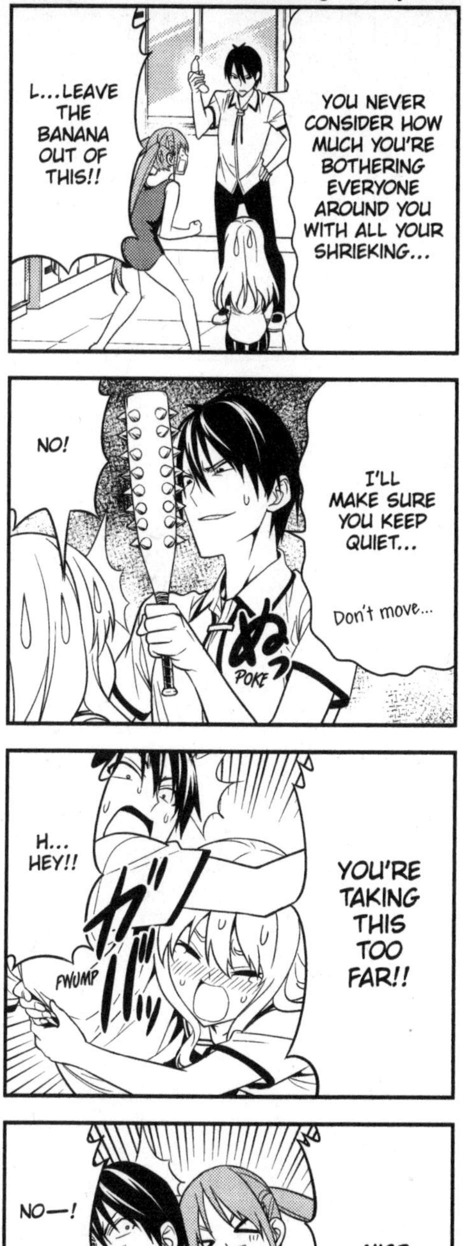
YOU NEVER CONSIDER HOW MUCH YOU'RE BOTHERING EVERYONE AROUND YOU WITH ALL YOUR SHRIEKING...
L...LEAVE THE BANANA OUT OF THIS!!
I'LL MAKE SURE YOU KEEP QUIET...
Don't move...
POKE
NO!
YOU'RE TAKING THIS TOO FAR!!
H... HEY!!
FWUMP
NICE ASSIST, SAYAKA-CHAN!!
SNATCH
NO—!
Wait, what?!

She Went a Little Too Crazy

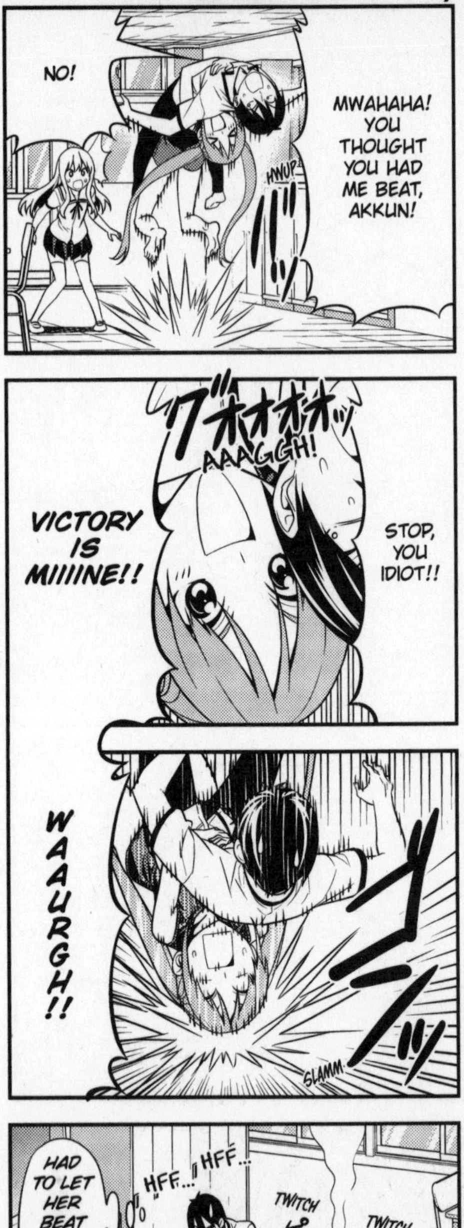
MWAHAHA! YOU THOUGHT YOU HAD ME BEAT, AKKUN!
NO!
HNUP
グオオオオッ
AAAGGH!
STOP, YOU IDIOT!!
VICTORY IS MIIIINE!!
WAAAURGH!!
SLAMM
HFF... HFF...
TWITCH
ピクッ
TWITCH
ピクッ
HAD TO LET HER BEAT HERSELF, I GUESS...

A Premonition of Suffering

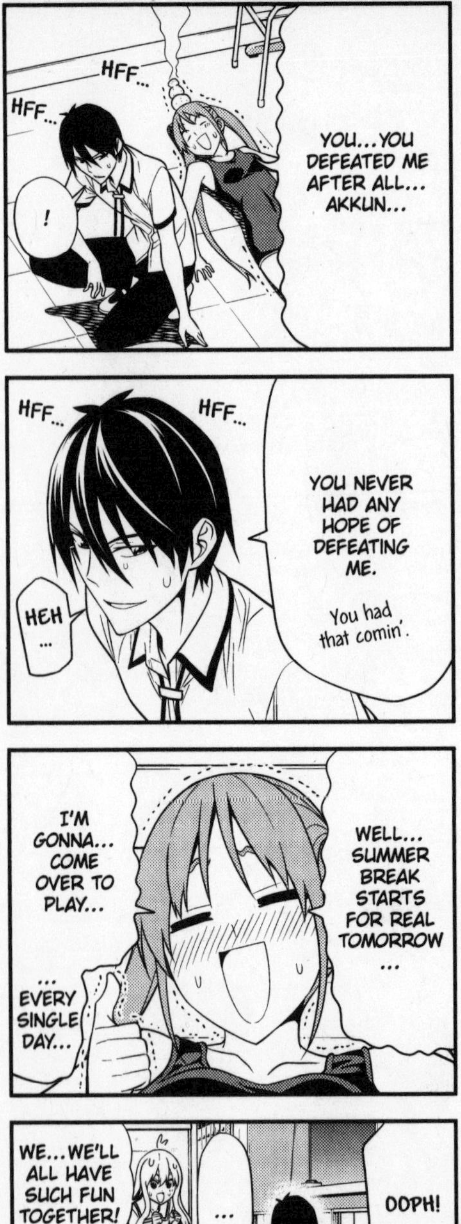
HFF...
HFF...
YOU...YOU DEFEATED ME AFTER ALL... AKKUN...
!
HFF...
HFF...
YOU NEVER HAD ANY HOPE OF DEFEATING ME.
You had that comin'.
HEH...
WELL... SUMMER BREAK STARTS FOR REAL TOMORROW...
I'M GONNA... COME OVER TO PLAY...
...EVERY SINGLE DAY...
OOPH!
...
WE...WE'LL ALL HAVE SUCH FUN TOGETHER!
A THRILLING SUMMER BREAK... STARTS NOW...

Miscellaneous Thoughts

I HOPE... AKUTSU-KUN AND I CAN GROW CLOSER THIS SUMMER...!!

MEAN-WHILE...

YOSHIKO IS NOT THE ONLY ONE GETTING PSYCHED UP.

I HOPE AKUTSU-KUN AND I CAN GROW CLOSER THIS SUMMER...!!

(We're messing around too much; we're children of summer)

Aho-Girl

\'ahô,gərl\ *Japanese, noun*.

A clueless girl.

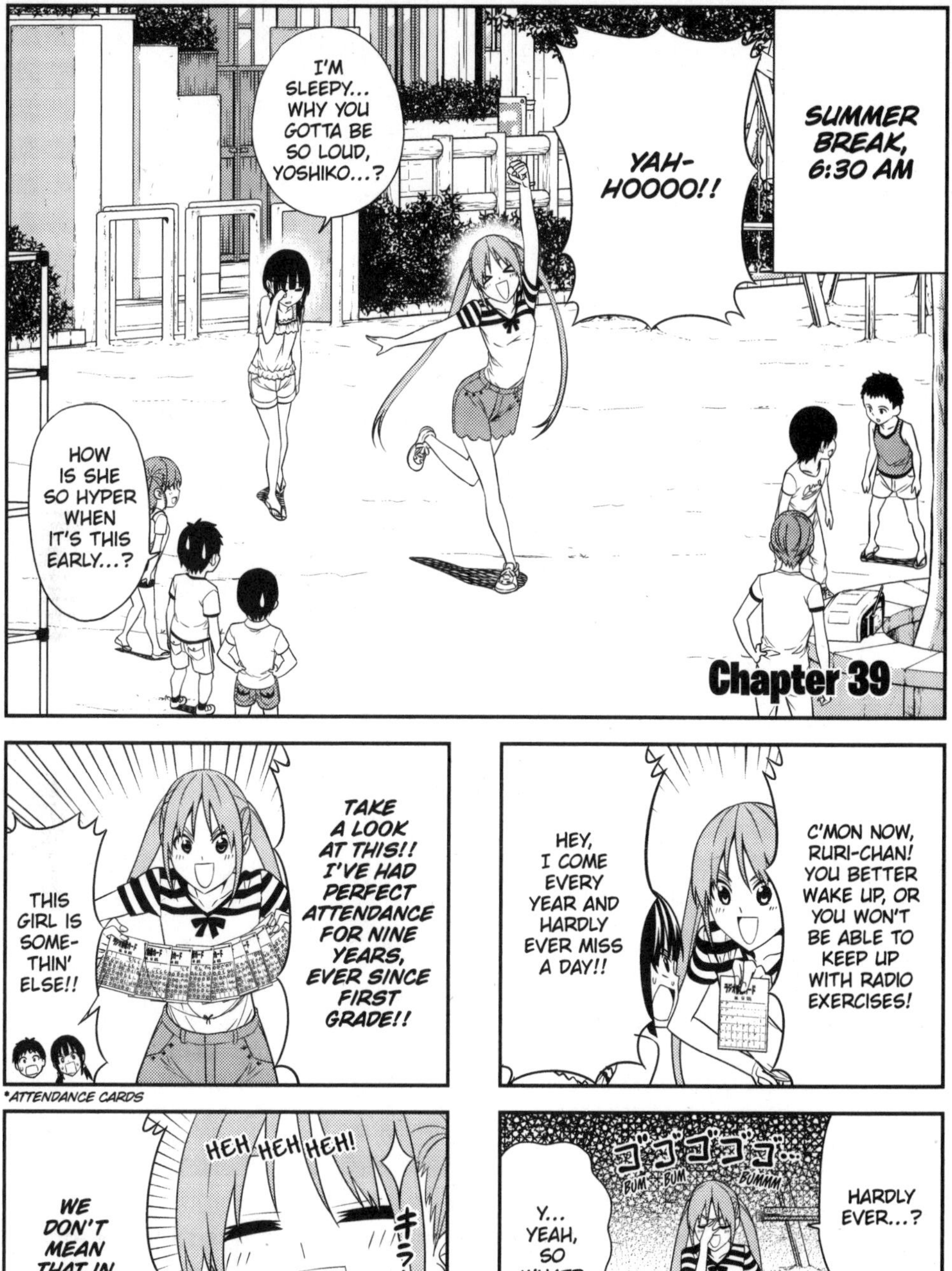
SUMMER BREAK, 6:30 AM
YAH-HOOOO!!
I'M SLEEPY... WHY YOU GOTTA BE SO LOUD, YOSHIKO...?
HOW IS SHE SO HYPER WHEN IT'S THIS EARLY...?
Chapter 39
C'MON NOW, RURI-CHAN! YOU BETTER WAKE UP, OR YOU WON'T BE ABLE TO KEEP UP WITH RADIO EXERCISES!
HEY, I COME EVERY YEAR AND HARDLY EVER MISS A DAY!!
TAKE A LOOK AT THIS!! I'VE HAD PERFECT ATTENDANCE FOR NINE YEARS, EVER SINCE FIRST GRADE!!
THIS GIRL IS SOME-THIN' ELSE!!
*ATTENDANCE CARDS
HARDLY EVER...?
ゴゴゴゴゴ…
BUM BUM BUMMM
Y... YEAH, SO WHAT?
ゴソゴソ…
RUSTLE RUSTLE
HEH HEH HEH!
キラーン
GLEAAAM
WE DON'T MEAN THAT IN A GOOD WAY!!

Let the Emotion Take You Over

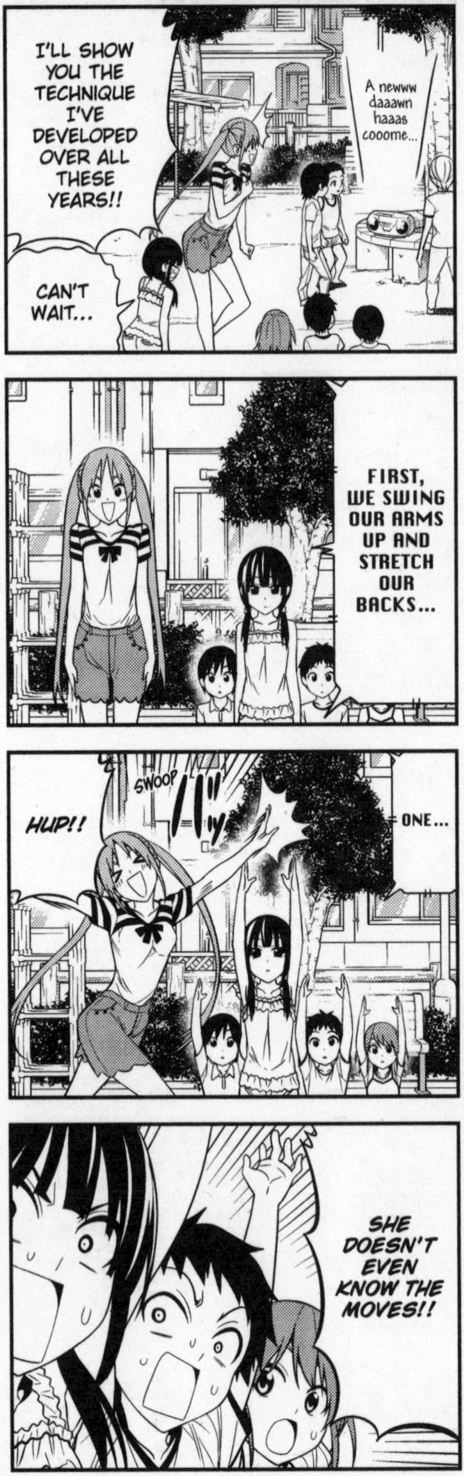
A newww daaawn haaas cooome...
I'LL SHOW YOU THE TECHNIQUE I'VE DEVELOPED OVER ALL THESE YEARS!!
CAN'T WAIT...
FIRST, WE SWING OUR ARMS UP AND STRETCH OUR BACKS...
ONE...
SWOOP
HUP!!
SHE DOESN'T EVEN KNOW THE MOVES!!

She Sounds Like Hayashi-sensei

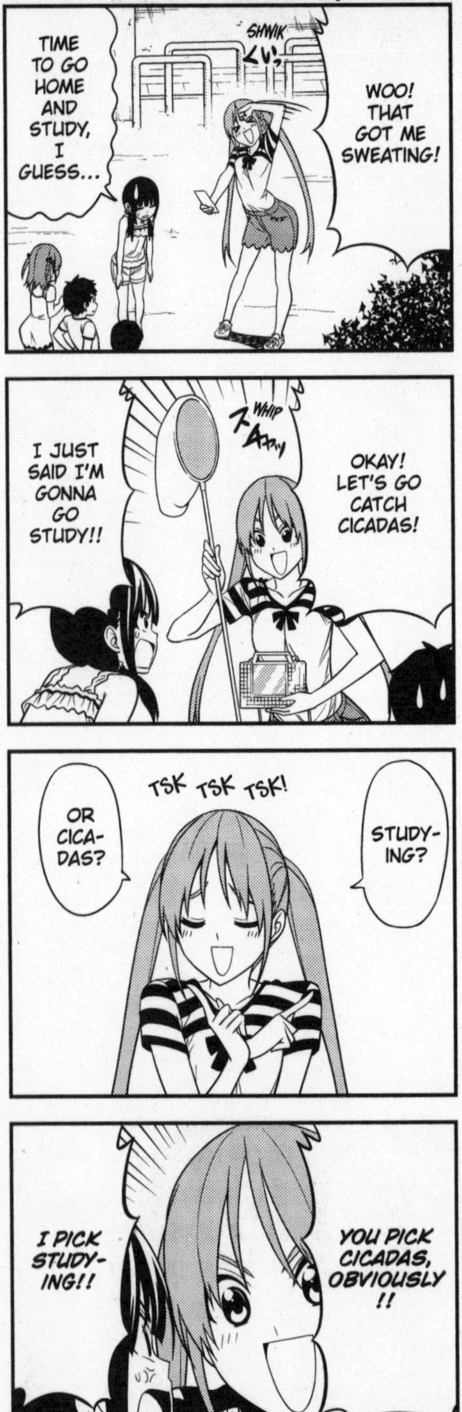
WOO! THAT GOT ME SWEATING!
SHWIK
TIME TO GO HOME AND STUDY, I GUESS...
OKAY! LET'S GO CATCH CICADAS!
WHIP
I JUST SAID I'M GONNA GO STUDY!!
STUDYING?
TSK TSK TSK!
OR CICADAS?
YOU PICK CICADAS, OBVIOUSLY!!
I PICK STUDYING!!

Such Innocence

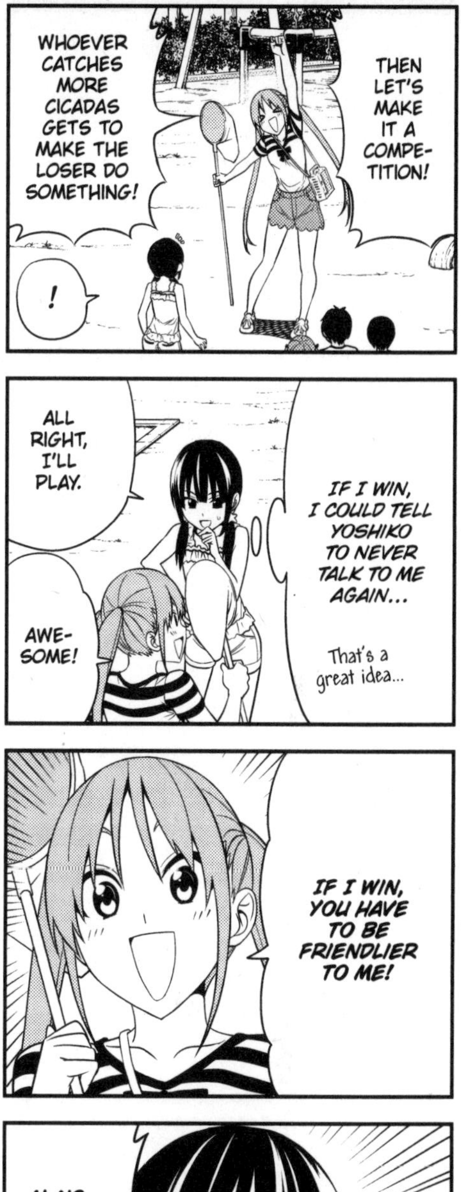
THEN LET'S MAKE IT A COMPE-TITION!
WHOEVER CATCHES MORE CICADAS GETS TO MAKE THE LOSER DO SOMETHING!
!
IF I WIN, I COULD TELL YOSHIKO TO NEVER TALK TO ME AGAIN...
That's a great idea...
ALL RIGHT, I'LL PLAY.
AWE-SOME!
IF I WIN, YOU HAVE TO BE FRIENDLIER TO ME!
N-NO... PICK SOME-THING ELSE!!

I Hear Something

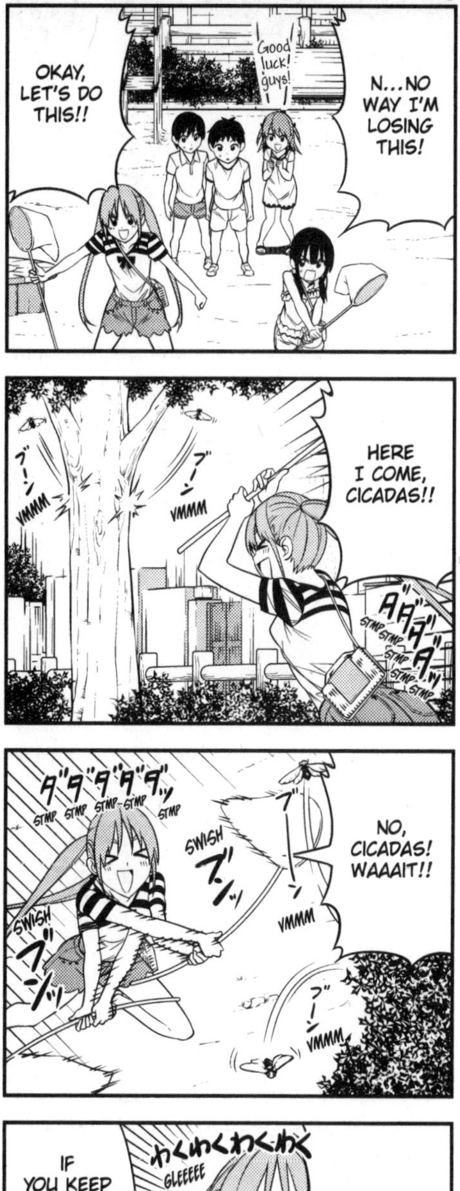
N...NO WAY I'M LOSING THIS!
Good luck! guys!
OKAY, LET'S DO THIS!!
HERE I COME, CICADAS!!
ダダダダ
STMP STMP STMP STMP STMP
ブーン
VMMM
ブーン
VMMM
NO, CICADAS! WAAAIT!!
ブーン
VMMM
ブーン
VMMM
ダダダダダッ
STMP STMP STMP STMP STMP
SWISH
ブンッ
SWISH
ブンッ
THEY'RE SO FAST!!
わくわくわくわく
GLEEEEE
IF YOU KEEP SHOUTING AT THEM, THEY'RE GONNA KEEP FLYING AWAY...

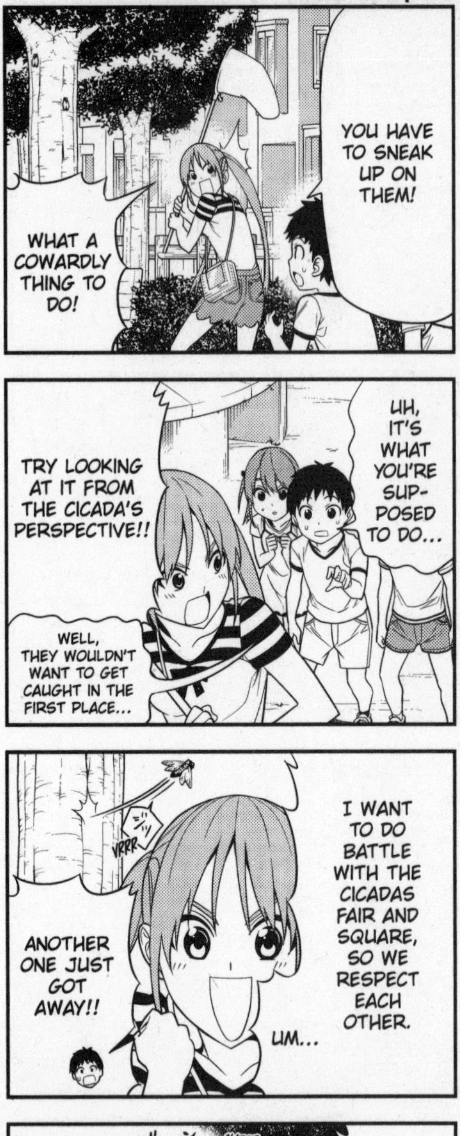
YOU HAVE TO SNEAK UP ON THEM!
WHAT A COWARDLY THING TO DO!
UH, IT'S WHAT YOU'RE SUP-POSED TO DO...
TRY LOOKING AT IT FROM THE CICADA'S PERSPECTIVE!!
WELL, THEY WOULDN'T WANT TO GET CAUGHT IN THE FIRST PLACE...
I WANT TO DO BATTLE WITH THE CICADAS FAIR AND SQUARE, SO WE RESPECT EACH OTHER.
UM...
ジジッ VRRR
ANOTHER ONE JUST GOT AWAY!!
HYAAAAH!!
ドタドタ CLATTER
ドタドタ CLATTER
ブン SWISH
ブン SWISH
ブ〜ン VMMM
SHE'S TERRIBLE AT THIS...

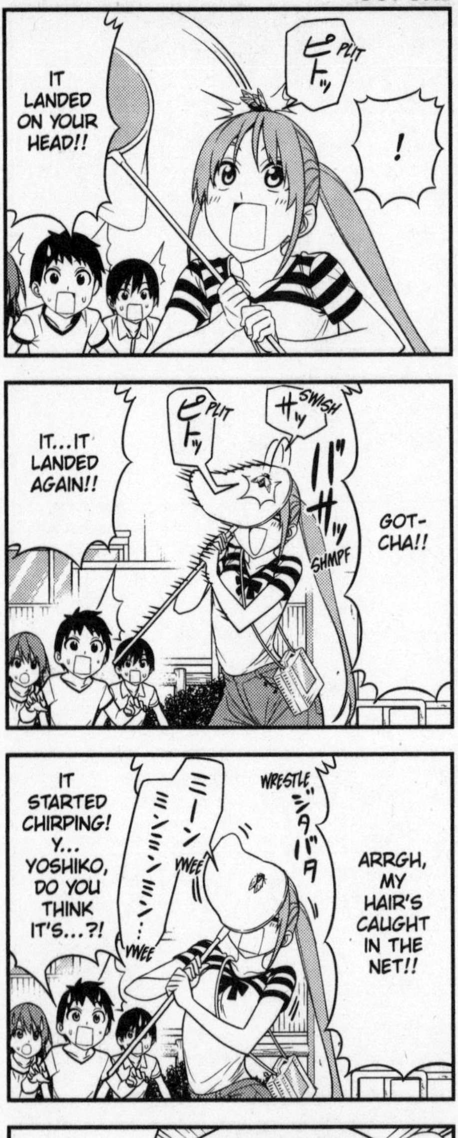
ピトッ PLIT
!
IT LANDED ON YOUR HEAD!!
GOT-CHA!!
バサッ SHMPF
サッ SWISH
ピトッ PLIT
IT...IT LANDED AGAIN!!
ARRGH, MY HAIR'S CAUGHT IN THE NET!!
ジタバタ WRESTLE
ミーンミンミンミン... VWEE VWEE
IT STARTED CHIRPING! Y... YOSHIKO, DO YOU THINK IT'S...?!
ジョボジョボ DRIBBLE
シー PSSSS...
THAT CICADA'S TOTALLY MOCKING YOU!!

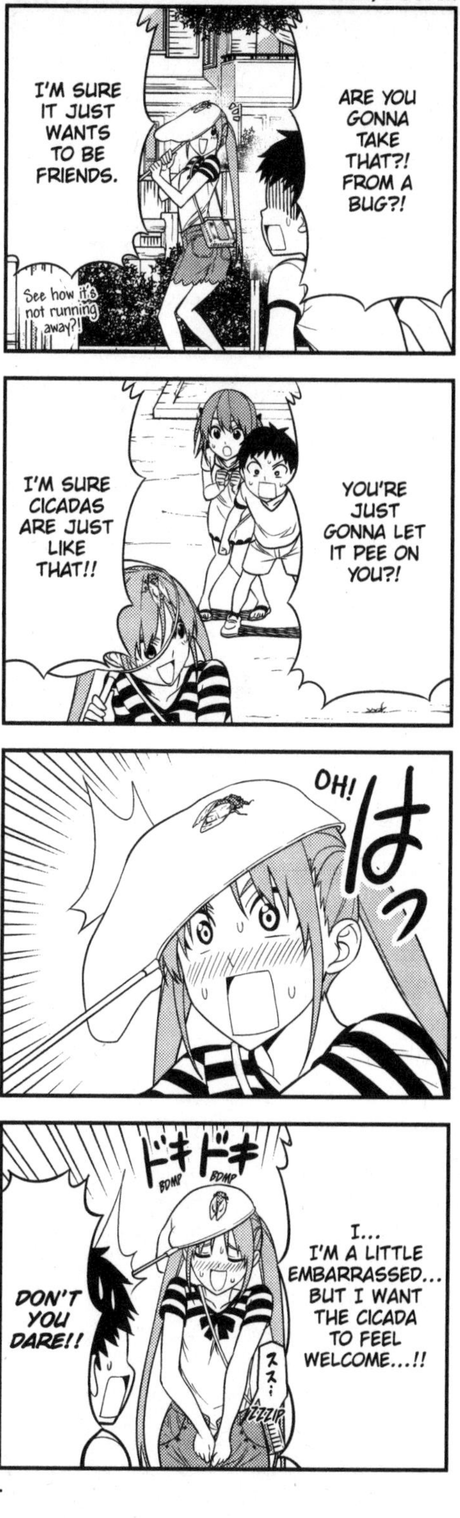
ARE YOU GONNA TAKE THAT?! FROM A BUG?!
I'M SURE IT JUST WANTS TO BE FRIENDS.
See how it's not running away?!
YOU'RE JUST GONNA LET IT PEE ON YOU?!
I'M SURE CICADAS ARE JUST LIKE THAT!!
OH!
はっ
ドキドキ
BOMP BOMP
I... I'M A LITTLE EMBARRASSED... BUT I WANT THE CICADA TO FEEL WELCOME...!!
スス…
ZZZZIP
DON'T YOU DARE!!

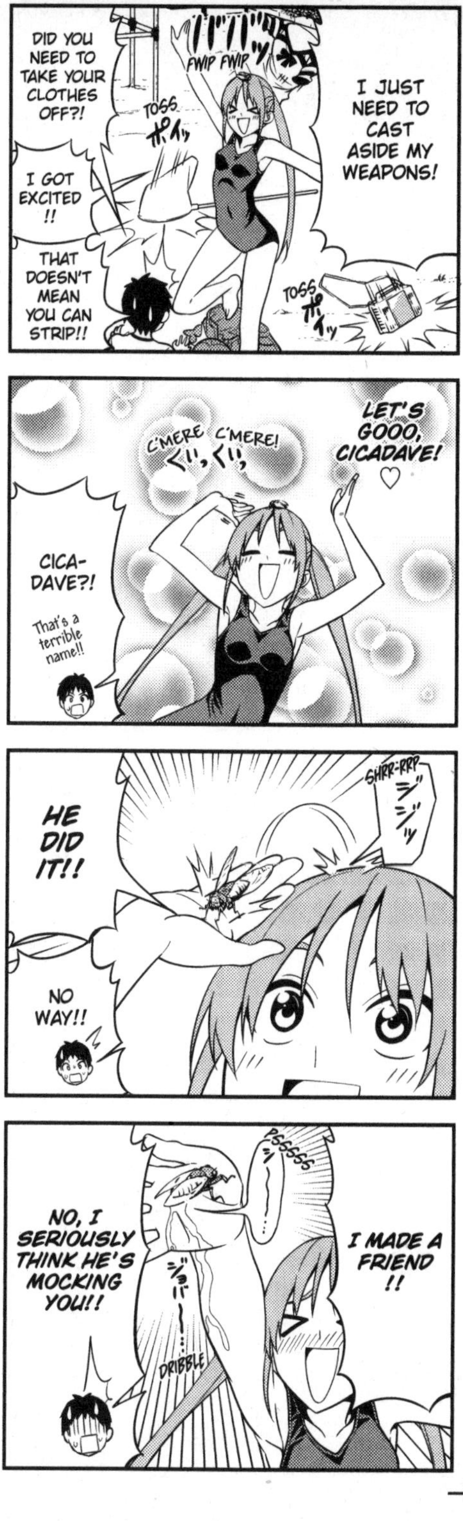
I JUST NEED TO CAST ASIDE MY WEAPONS!
FWIP FWIP
DID YOU NEED TO TAKE YOUR CLOTHES OFF?!
TOSS
ポイッ
I GOT EXCITED !!
THAT DOESN'T MEAN YOU CAN STRIP!!
TOSS
ポイッ
LET'S GOOO, CICADAVE! ♡
C'MERE C'MERE!
くい、くい
CICA-DAVE?!
That's a terrible name!!
SHRR-RRP
ジジッ
HE DID IT!!
NO WAY!!
I MADE A FRIEND !!
PSSSSS
NO, I SERIOUSLY THINK HE'S MOCKING YOU!!
DRIBBLE

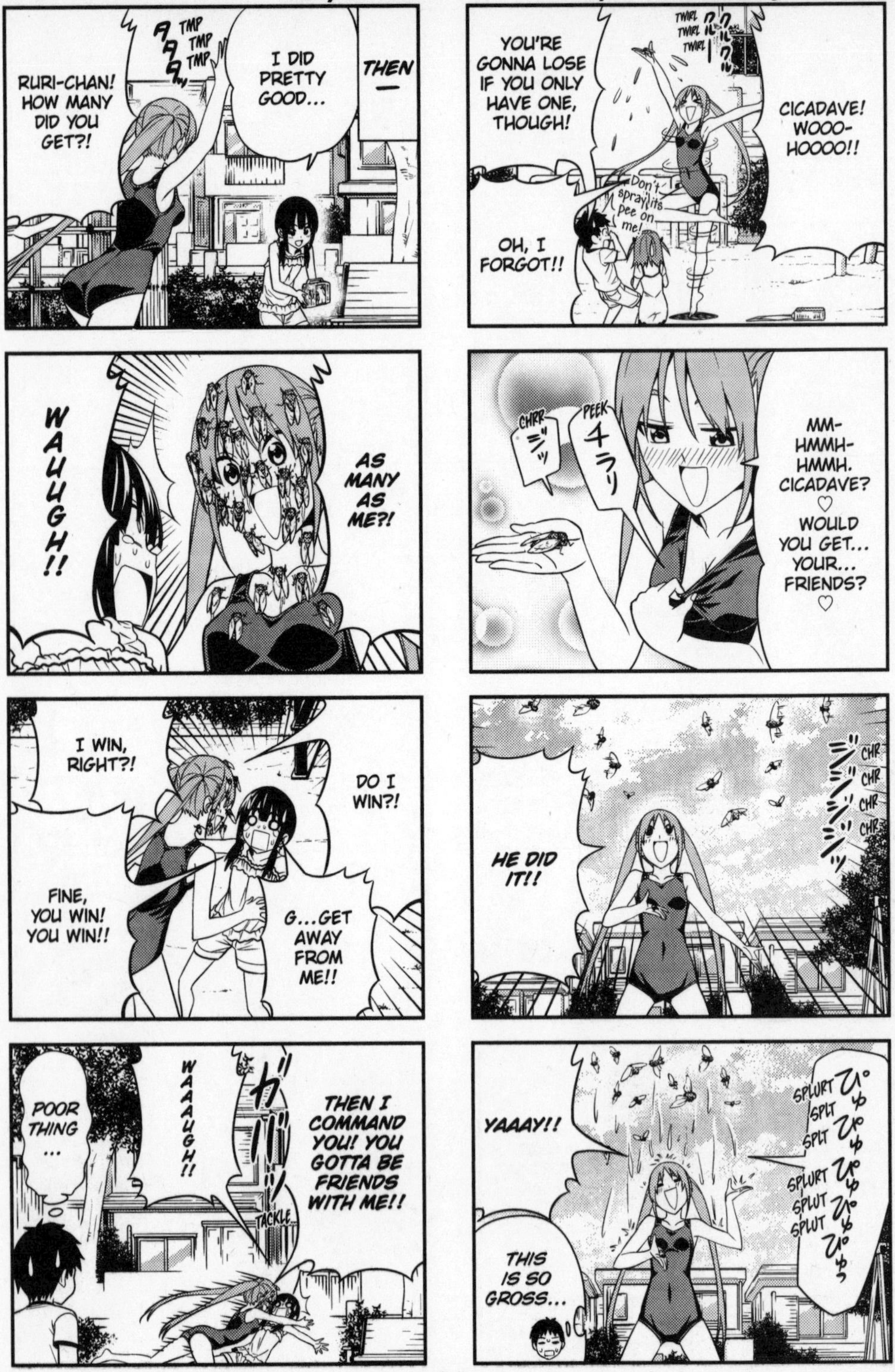
CICADAVE! WOOO-HOOOO!!
TWIRL TWIRL TWIRL
YOU'RE GONNA LOSE IF YOU ONLY HAVE ONE, THOUGH!
Don't spray its pee on me!
OH, I FORGOT!!
MM-HMMH-HMMH. CICADAVE? ♡ WOULD YOU GET... YOUR... FRIENDS? ♡
PEEK チラリ
CHRR ジッ
CHR CHR CHR CHR
HE DID IT!!
SPLURT SPLT SPLT SPLURT SPLUT SPLUT
YAAAY!!
THIS IS SO GROSS...
THEN—
I DID PRETTY GOOD...
TMP TMP TMP
RURI-CHAN! HOW MANY DID YOU GET?!
AS MANY AS ME?!
WAUUGH!!
DO I WIN?!
I WIN, RIGHT?!
G...GET AWAY FROM ME!!
FINE, YOU WIN! YOU WIN!!
THEN I COMMAND YOU! YOU GOTTA BE FRIENDS WITH ME!!
TACKLE
WAAAAUGH!!
POOR THING...

Raptures

MEAN-WHILE

I'M MAKING SO MUCH PROGRESS STUDYING TODAY!

THROUGH THE SACRI-FICES OF HIS LITTLE SISTER.

(Swing your arms up, stretch as tall as you can)

Aho-Girl

\'ahô,gərl\ *Japanese, noun*.

A clueless girl.

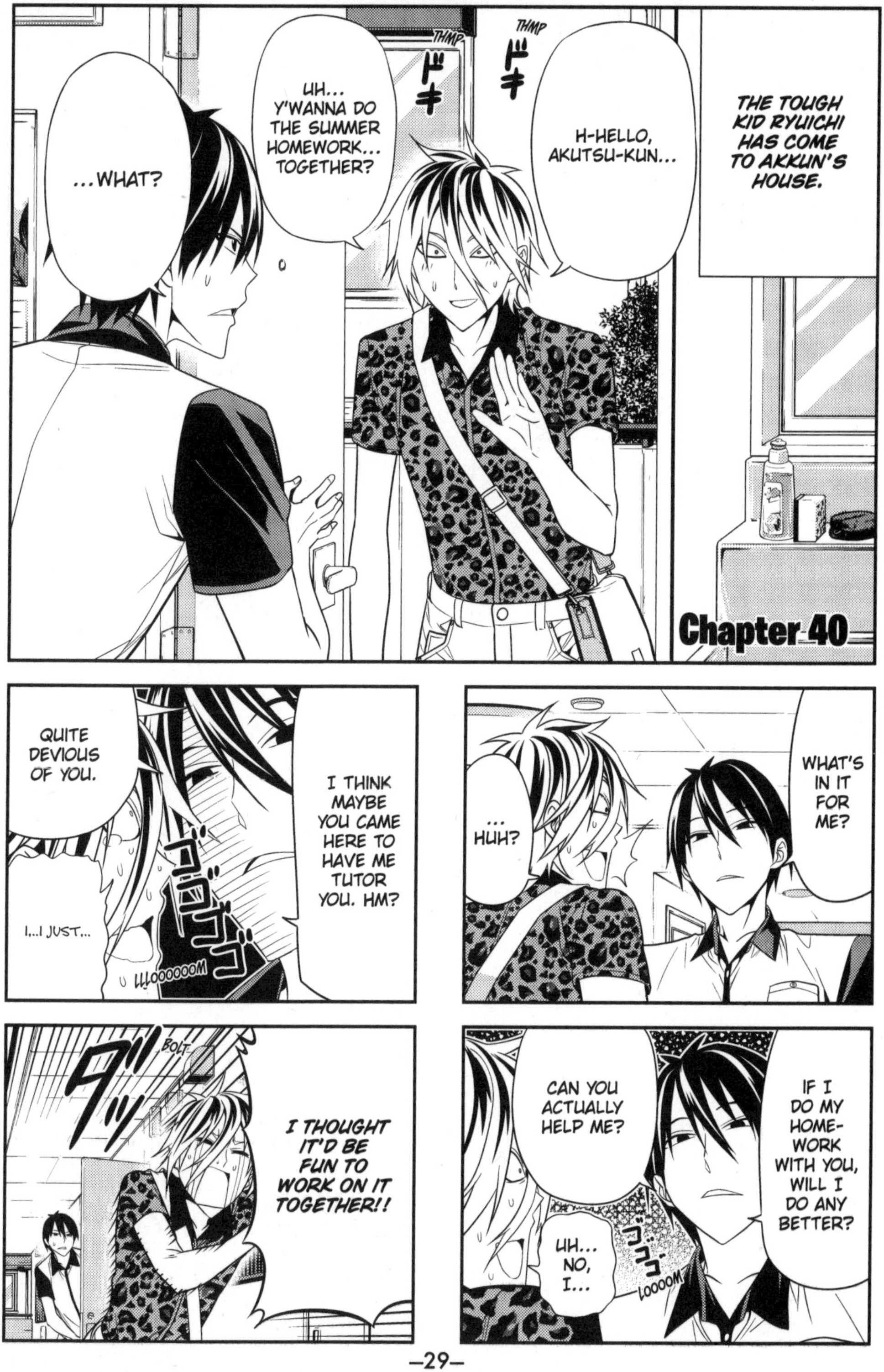
THE TOUGH KID RYUICHI HAS COME TO AKKUN'S HOUSE.
Chapter 40
THMP
H-HELLO, AKUTSU-KUN...
THMP
UH... Y'WANNA DO THE SUMMER HOMEWORK... TOGETHER?
...WHAT?
WHAT'S IN IT FOR ME?
...HUH?
I THINK MAYBE YOU CAME HERE TO HAVE ME TUTOR YOU. HM?
QUITE DEVIOUS OF YOU.
WOOOOOOM!!!
I...I JUST...
IF I DO MY HOMEWORK WITH YOU, WILL I DO ANY BETTER?
CAN YOU ACTUALLY HELP ME?
UH... NO, I...
BOLT
I THOUGHT IT'D BE FUN TO WORK ON IT TOGETHER!!

Nothin' But a Flunky. We're Not Friends.

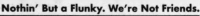

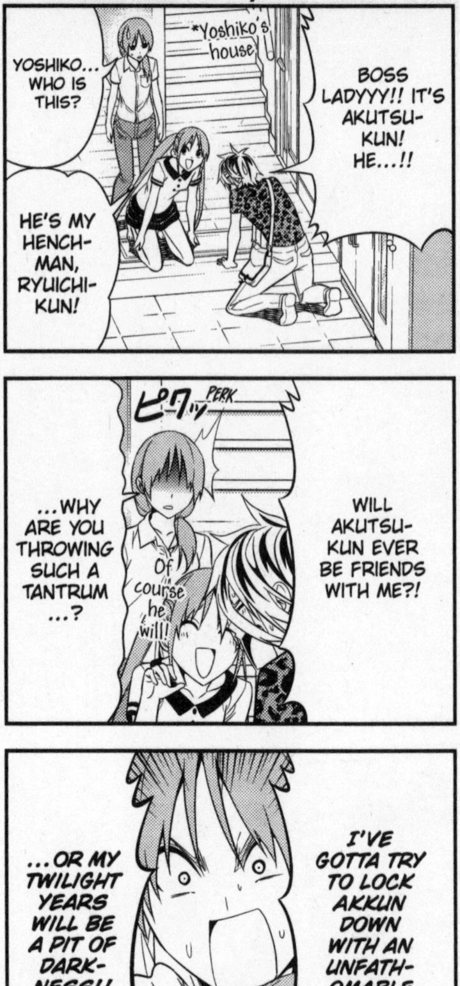
*Yoshiko's house
BOSS LADYYY!! IT'S AKUTSU-KUN! HE...!!
YOSHIKO... WHO IS THIS?
HE'S MY HENCH-MAN, RYUICHI-KUN!
ピクッ PERK
WILL AKUTSU-KUN EVER BE FRIENDS WITH ME?!
Of course he will!
...WHY ARE YOU THROWING SUCH A TANTRUM ...?
I'VE GOTTA TRY TO LOCK AKKUN DOWN WITH AN UNFATH-OMABLE IDIOT...
...OR MY TWILIGHT YEARS WILL BE A PIT OF DARK-NESS!!
← THE UNFATHOMABLE IDIOT
TREMBLE TREMBLE プルプル
WHAT'S MAKING FRIENDS, COMPARED TO THAT?! YOU EXPECT EVERYTHING IN LIFE TO BE EASY?!
I...I'M SORRY...

It's a Trap

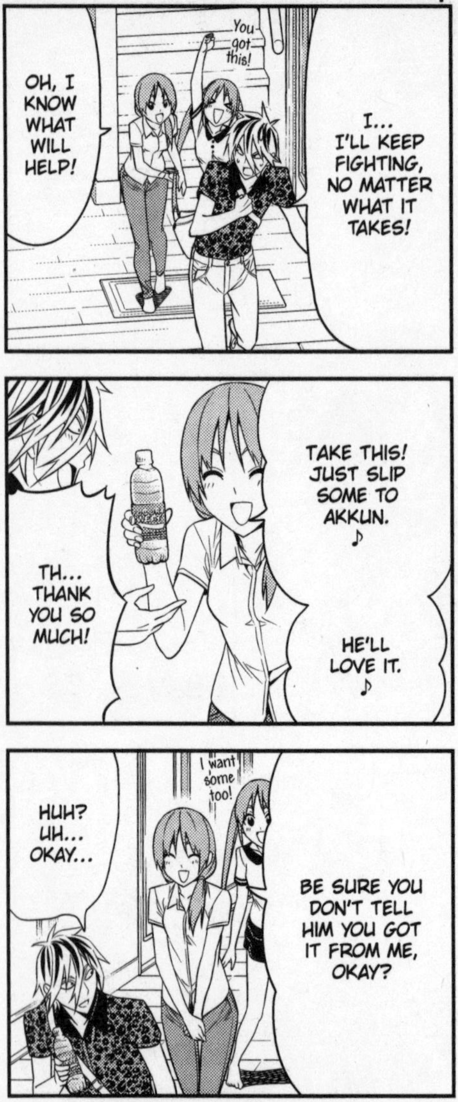
I... I'LL KEEP FIGHTING, NO MATTER WHAT IT TAKES!
You got this!
OH, I KNOW WHAT WILL HELP!
TAKE THIS! JUST SLIP SOME TO AKKUN. ♪
HE'LL LOVE IT. ♪
TH... THANK YOU SO MUCH!
BE SURE YOU DON'T TELL HIM YOU GOT IT FROM ME, OKAY?
I want some too!
HUH? UH... OKAY...
NO, I MEAN IT. DON'T TELL HIM...
UM... GOT IT...

Fill 'Em up! A Drink to Friendship!

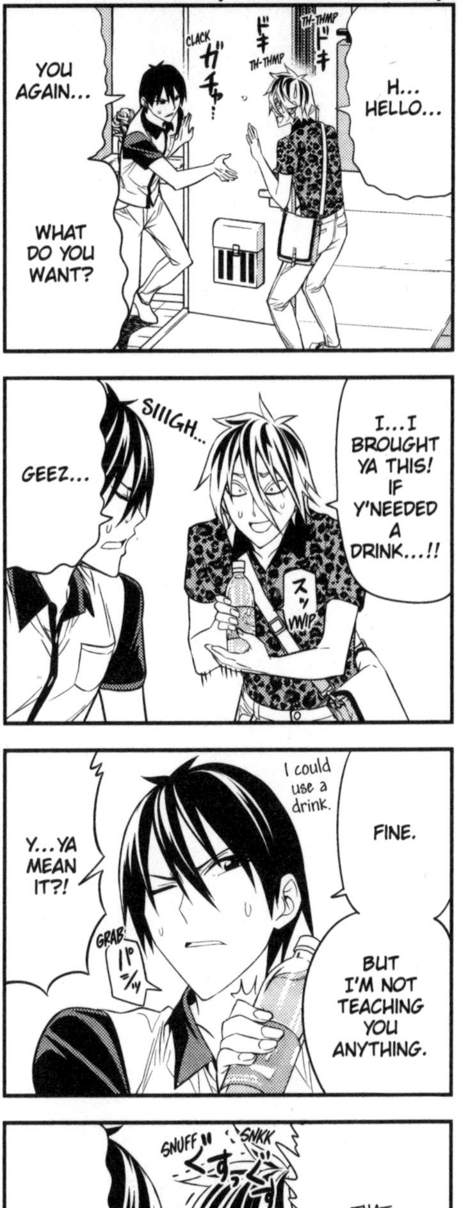
H... HELLO...
TH-THMP
ドキ
TH-THMP
ドキ
CLACK
ガチャ...
YOU AGAIN...
WHAT DO YOU WANT?
I...I BROUGHT YA THIS! IF Y'NEEDED A DRINK...!!
スッ
VWIP
SIIIGH...
GEEZ...
FINE.
I could use a drink.
BUT I'M NOT TEACHING YOU ANYTHING.
Y...YA MEAN IT?!
GRAB
パシッ
THAT... THAT'S GREAT...!! I BEEN WANTIN' TO BE FRIENDS WITH YA FOR SO LONG...!!
SNKK
ぐすっ
SNUFF
ぐすっ
THIS GUY'S SO CREEPY...
ゴクッ...
GLP

The Perfect Crime

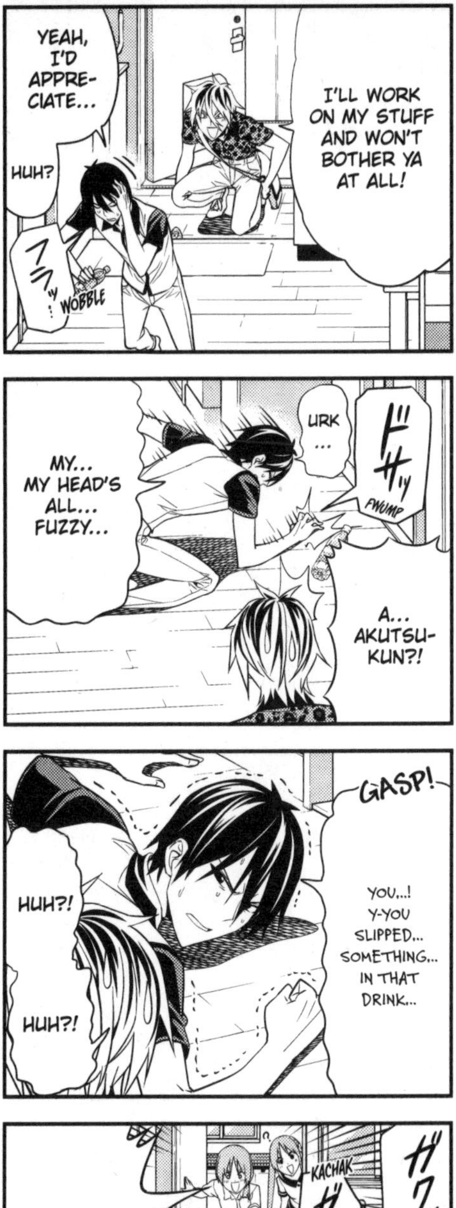
I'LL WORK ON MY STUFF AND WON'T BOTHER YA AT ALL!
YEAH, I'D APPRECIATE...
HUH?
フラッ...
WOBBLE
ドサッ
FWUMP
URK...
A... AKUTSU-KUN?!
MY... MY HEAD'S ALL... FUZZY...
GASP!
YOU...! Y-YOU SLIPPED... SOMETHING... IN THAT DRINK...
HUH?!
HUH?!
ガクッ
SLUMP
KACHAK
ガチャッ
JOLT
ビクッ
IT WORKED!!

An Evil Philosophy

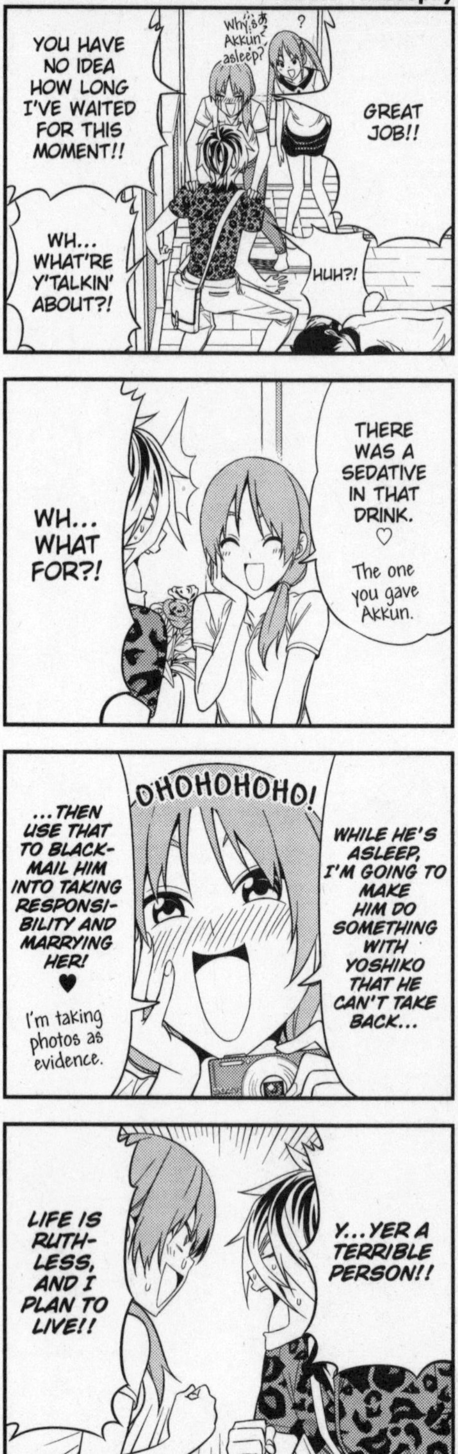
?
Why is Akkun asleep?
GREAT JOB!!
YOU HAVE NO IDEA HOW LONG I'VE WAITED FOR THIS MOMENT!!
HUH?!
WH... WHAT'RE Y'TALKIN' ABOUT?!
THERE WAS A SEDATIVE IN THAT DRINK. ♡
The one you gave Akkun.
WH... WHAT FOR?!
WHILE HE'S ASLEEP, I'M GOING TO MAKE HIM DO SOMETHING WITH YOSHIKO THAT HE CAN'T TAKE BACK...
OHOHOHOHOHO!
...THEN USE THAT TO BLACKMAIL HIM INTO TAKING RESPONSIBILITY AND MARRYING HER! ♥
I'm taking photos as evidence.
Y...YER A TERRIBLE PERSON!!
LIFE IS RUTHLESS, AND I PLAN TO LIVE!!

I'll Protect Him!

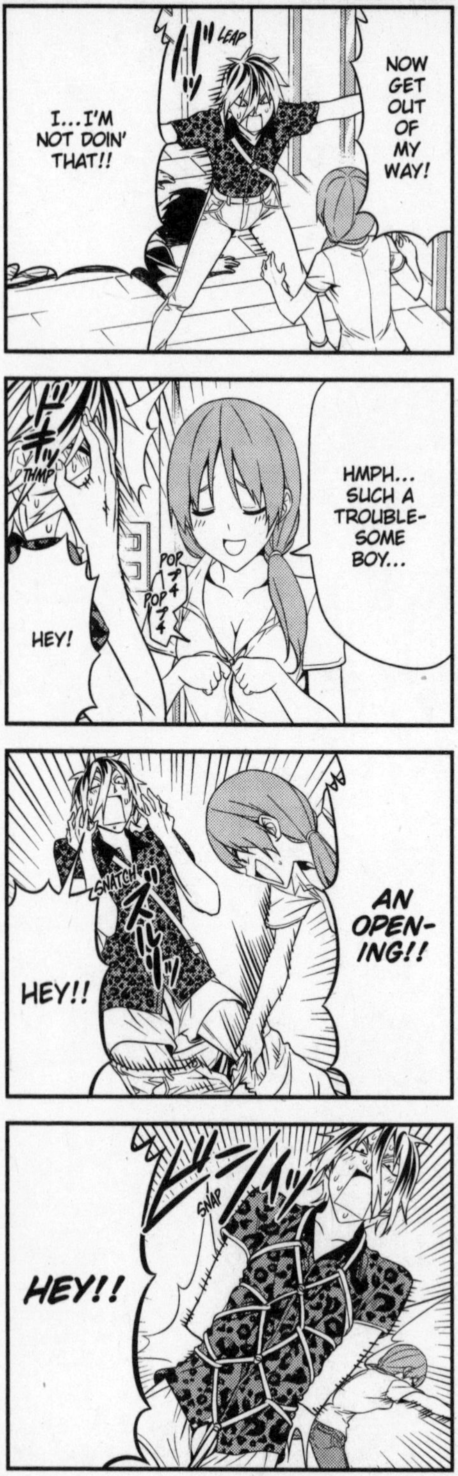
NOW GET OUT OF MY WAY!
LEAP
I...I'M NOT DOIN' THAT!!
HMPH... SUCH A TROUBLESOME BOY...
POP
POP
THMP
HEY!
AN OPENING!!
SNATCH
HEY!!
SNAP
HEY!!

Coming from Behind

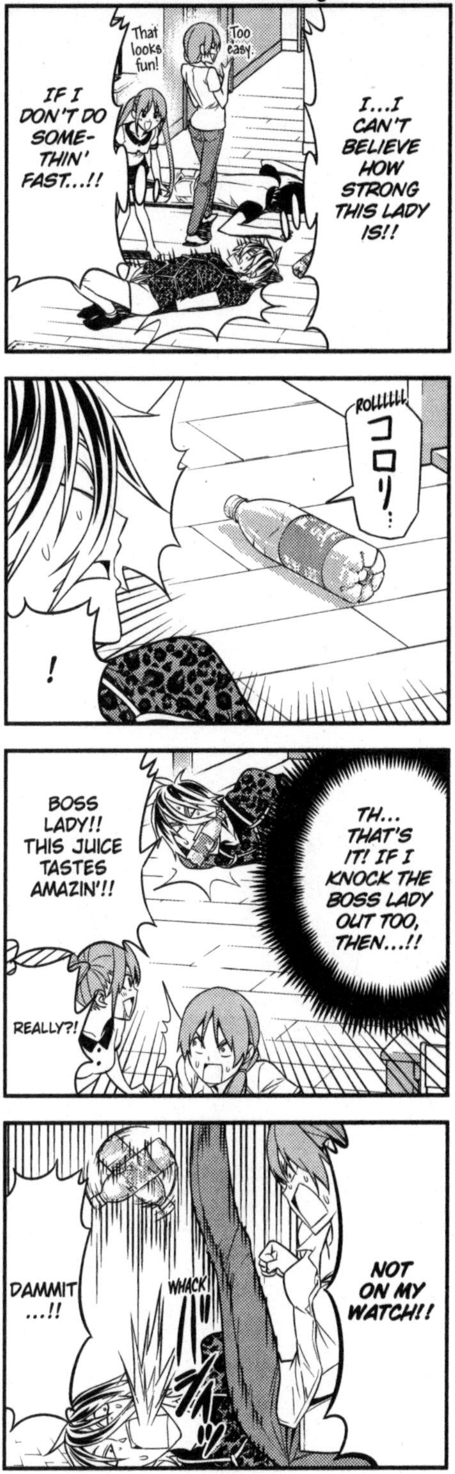
I...I CAN'T BELIEVE HOW STRONG THIS LADY IS!!
Too easy.
That looks fun!
IF I DON'T DO SOME-THIN' FAST...!!
ROLLLLLL
コロリ...
!
TH... THAT'S IT! IF I KNOCK THE BOSS LADY OUT TOO, THEN...!!
BOSS LADY!! THIS JUICE TASTES AMAZIN'!!
REALLY?!
NOT ON MY WATCH!!
WHACK
DAMMIT ...!!

A Terrible Threat

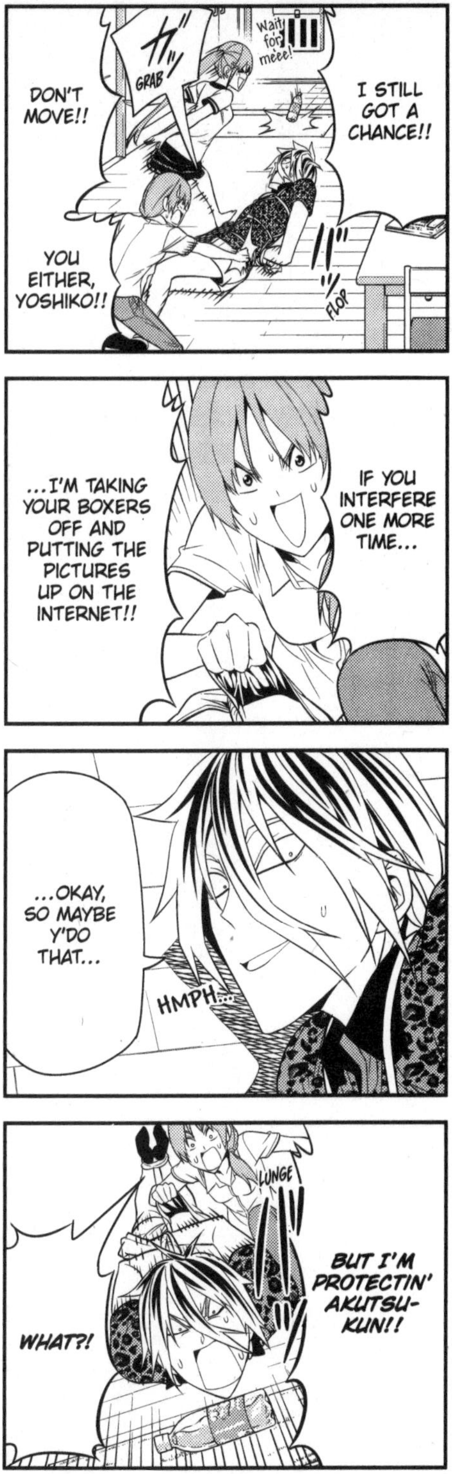
I STILL GOT A CHANCE!!
Wait for meee!
GRAB
DON'T MOVE!!
YOU EITHER, YOSHIKO!!
FLOP
IF YOU INTERFERE ONE MORE TIME...
...I'M TAKING YOUR BOXERS OFF AND PUTTING THE PICTURES UP ON THE INTERNET!!
HMPH...
...OKAY, SO MAYBE Y'DO THAT...
LUNGE
BUT I'M PROTECTIN' AKUTSU-KUN!!
WHAT?!

My Bro's in Trouble...!!

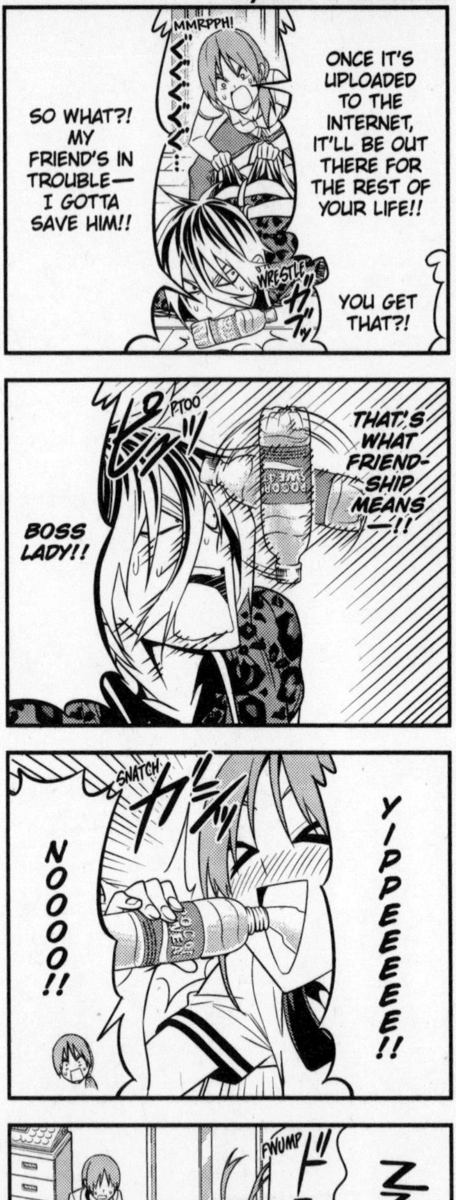
MMRPPH!
ONCE IT'S UPLOADED TO THE INTERNET, IT'LL BE OUT THERE FOR THE REST OF YOUR LIFE!!
YOU GET THAT?!
SO WHAT?! MY FRIEND'S IN TROUBLE— I GOTTA SAVE HIM!!
WRESTLE
THAT'S WHAT FRIEND-SHIP MEANS—!!
PTOO
BOSS LADY!!
YIPPEEEEEE!!
SNATCH
NOOOOO!!
ZZZZZZZZZZZZ...
FWUMP
HFF... HFF...
H... HOW COULD YOU...

Goodbye. Goodbye. Goodbye.

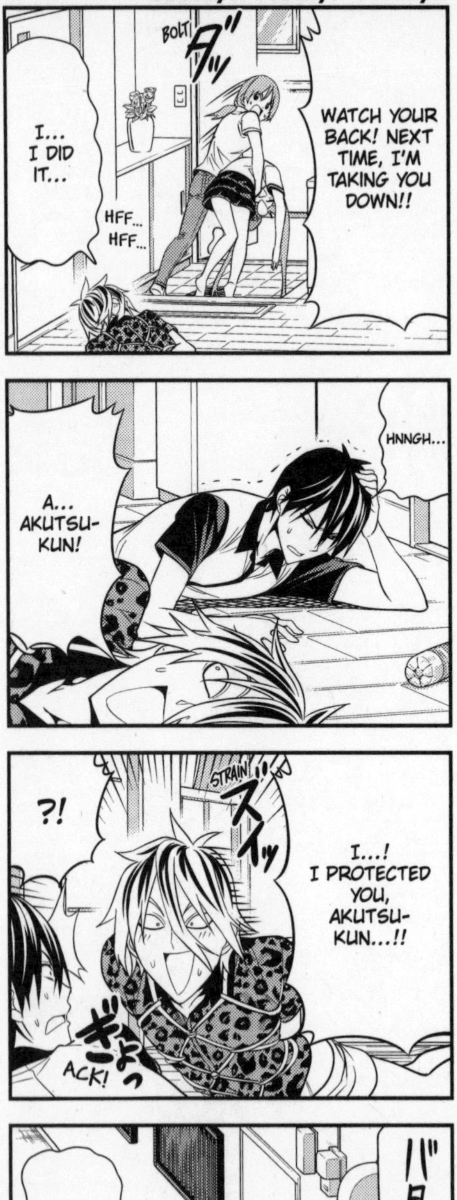
WATCH YOUR BACK! NEXT TIME, I'M TAKING YOU DOWN!!
BOLT
I... I DID IT...
HFF... HFF...
HNNGH...
A... AKUTSU-KUN!
I...! I PROTECTED YOU, AKUTSU-KUN...!!
STRAIN
?!
ACK!
SLAM
UM... HEY...
AKUTSU-KUN...?

You've Got a Mouth, Don't You?

HEY... UM...? YOU...YOU PLANNIN' TO LEAVE ME LIKE THIS...?

HUH?

HUH?

TOSS

BUT I CAN'T USE MY HANDS!!

(I don't give an)

Aho-Girl

\\ˈahôˌgərl\\ *Japanese, noun.*
A clueless girl.

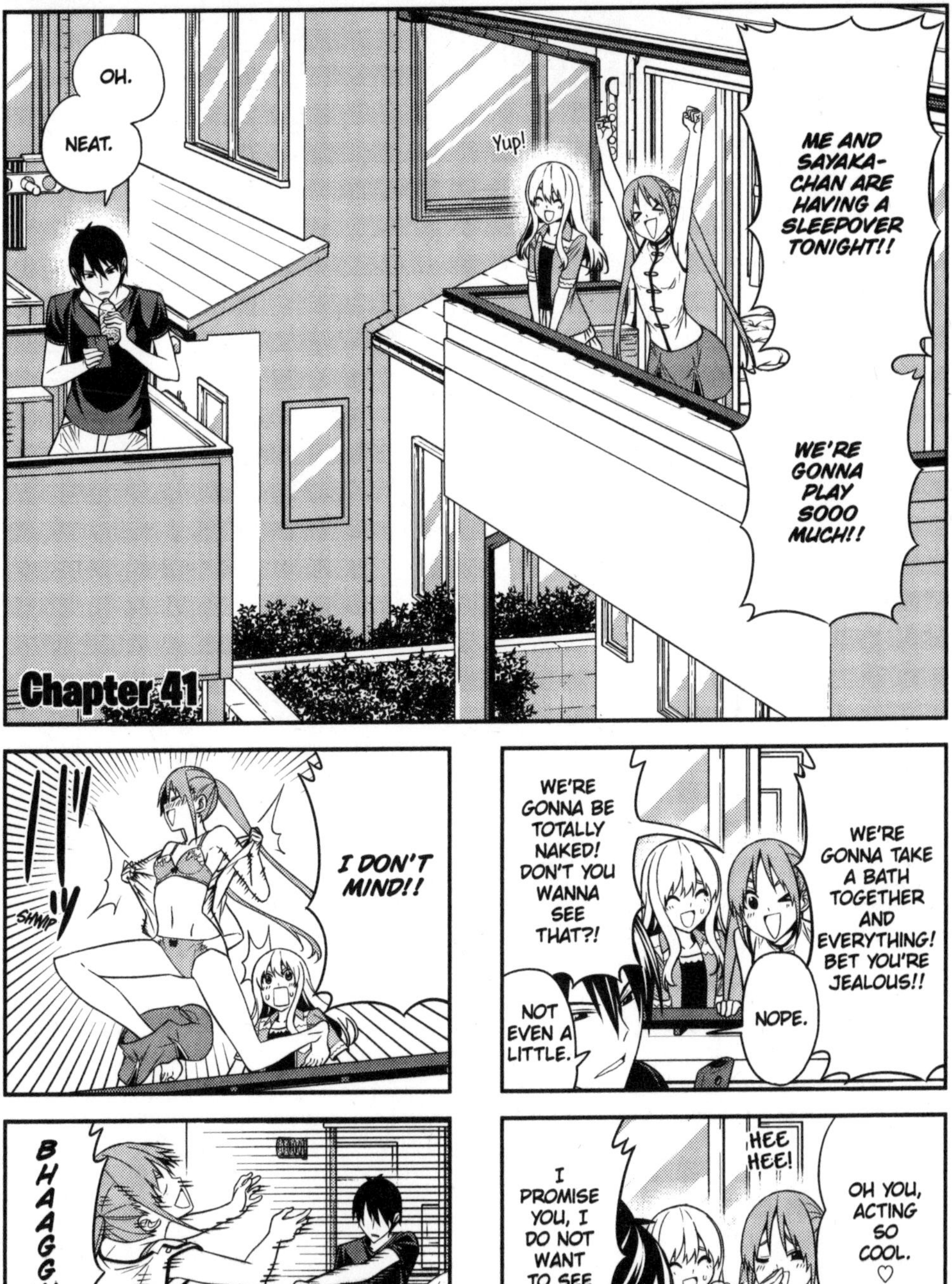
ME AND SAYAKA-CHAN ARE HAVING A SLEEPOVER TONIGHT!!
Yup!
WE'RE GONNA PLAY SOOO MUCH!!
OH.
NEAT.
Chapter 41
WE'RE GONNA TAKE A BATH TOGETHER AND EVERYTHING! BET YOU'RE JEALOUS!!
WE'RE GONNA BE TOTALLY NAKED! DON'T YOU WANNA SEE THAT?!
NOPE.
NOT EVEN A LITTLE.
I DON'T MIND!!
SHWIP
OH YOU, ACTING SO COOL. ♡
HEE HEE!
I PROMISE YOU, I DO NOT WANT TO SEE THAT!!
BHAAAGGHH!!
THWAKK

There's Something Disgusting about Animals...

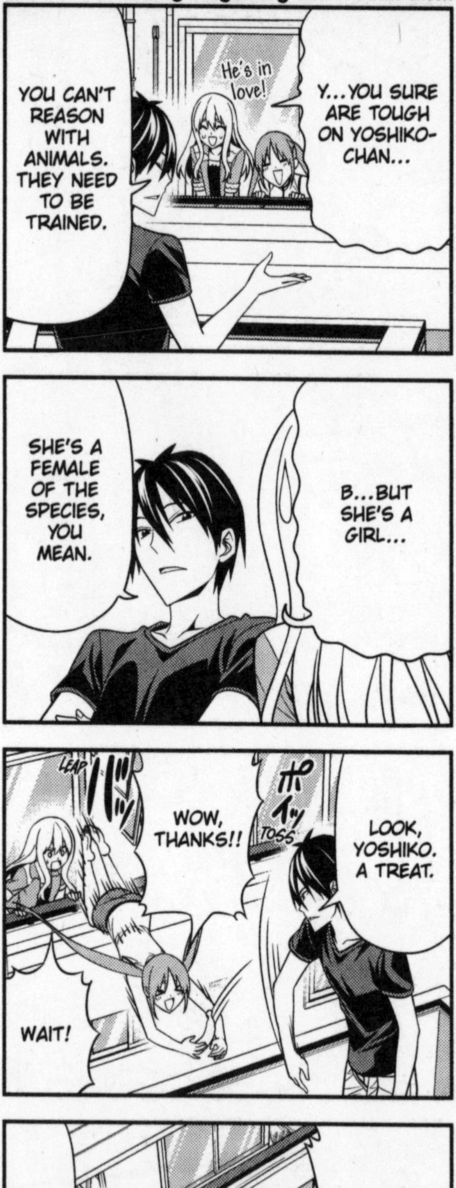
Y...YOU SURE ARE TOUGH ON YOSHIKO-CHAN...
He's in love!
YOU CAN'T REASON WITH ANIMALS. THEY NEED TO BE TRAINED.
B...BUT SHE'S A GIRL...
SHE'S A FEMALE OF THE SPECIES, YOU MEAN.
LOOK, YOSHIKO. A TREAT.
ポイッ TOSS
WOW, THANKS!!
バッ LEAP
WAIT!
YUMMY BANANA!!
SSHF SSHF
...
SHE REALLY IS AN ANIMAL.

Sayaka-chan Planned This

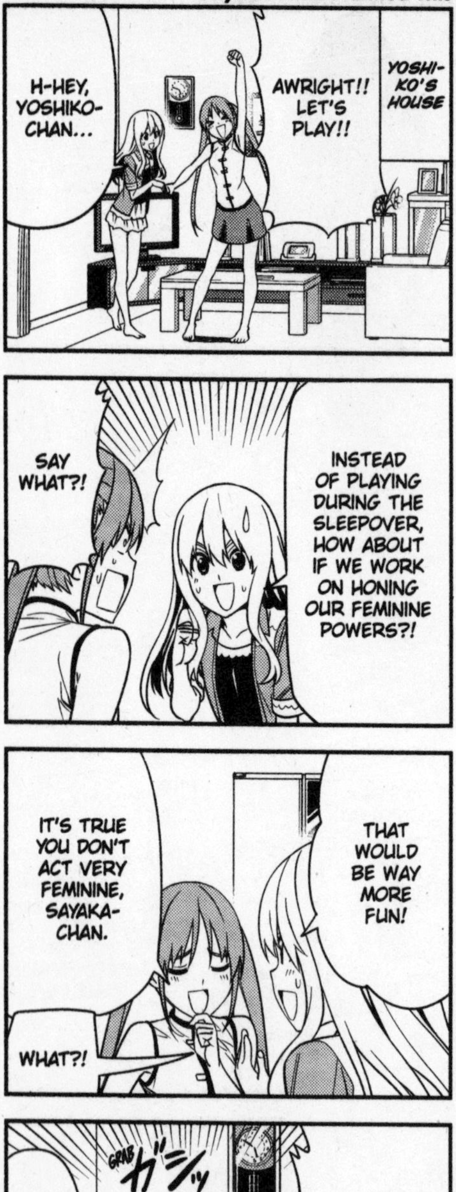
YOSHI-KO'S HOUSE
AWRIGHT!! LET'S PLAY!!
H-HEY, YOSHIKO-CHAN...
INSTEAD OF PLAYING DURING THE SLEEPOVER, HOW ABOUT IF WE WORK ON HONING OUR FEMININE POWERS?!
SAY WHAT?!
THAT WOULD BE WAY MORE FUN!
IT'S TRUE YOU DON'T ACT VERY FEMININE, SAYAKA-CHAN.
WHAT?!
ガシッ GRAB
OKAY! LET'S DO THIS! ♪
WH... WHAT JUST HAPPENED?

Old Proverb

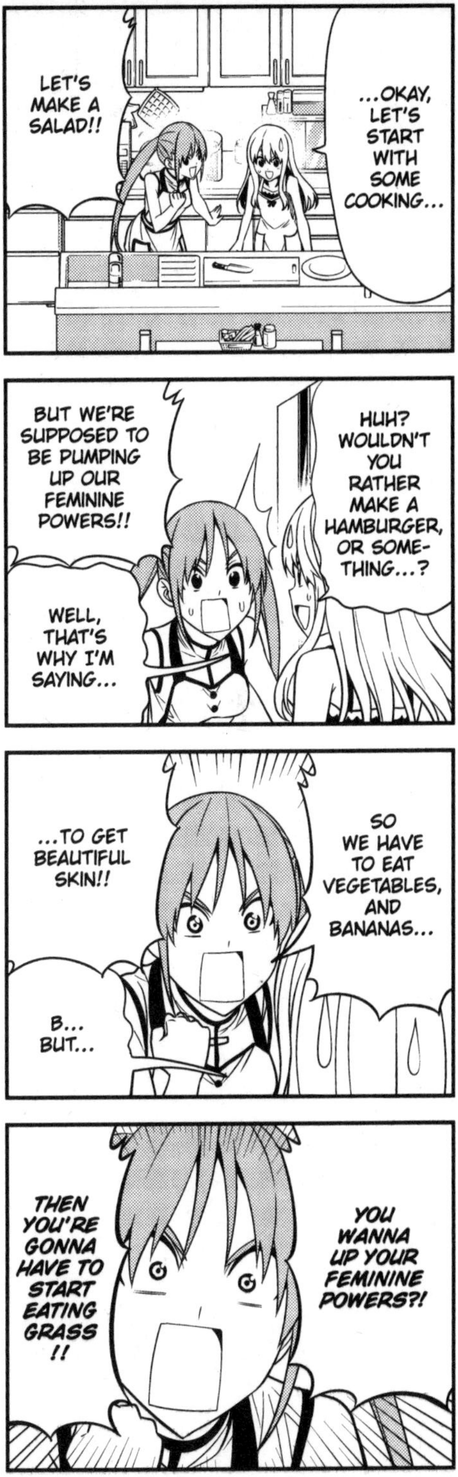
...OKAY, LET'S START WITH SOME COOKING...
LET'S MAKE A SALAD!!
HUH? WOULDN'T YOU RATHER MAKE A HAMBURGER, OR SOME-THING...?
BUT WE'RE SUPPOSED TO BE PUMPING UP OUR FEMININE POWERS!!
WELL, THAT'S WHY I'M SAYING...
SO WE HAVE TO EAT VEGETABLES, AND BANANAS...
...TO GET BEAUTIFUL SKIN!!
B... BUT...
YOU WANNA UP YOUR FEMININE POWERS?!
THEN YOU'RE GONNA HAVE TO START EATING GRASS !!

Living Example

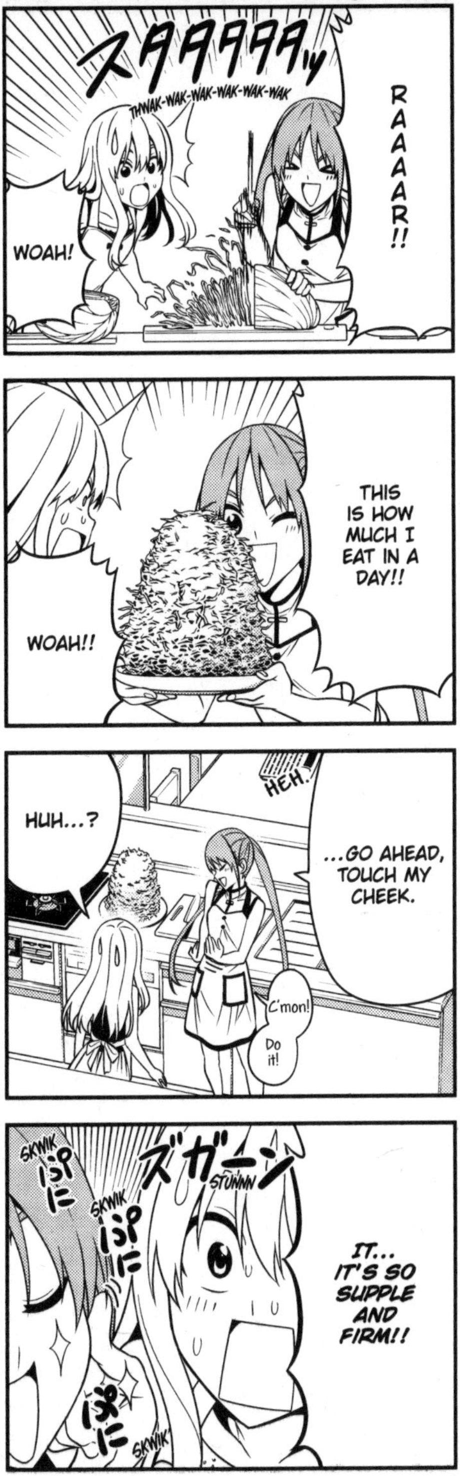
RAAAAAR!!
スタタタタタッ
THWAK-WAK-WAK-WAK-WAK-WAK
WOAH!
THIS IS HOW MUCH I EAT IN A DAY!!
WOAH!!
HEH.
...GO AHEAD, TOUCH MY CHEEK.
C'mon!
Do it!
HUH...?
IT... IT'S SO SUPPLE AND FIRM!!
ズガーン
STUNNN
ぷに
SKWIK
ぷに
SKWIK
ぷに
SKWIK

Don't Give up!

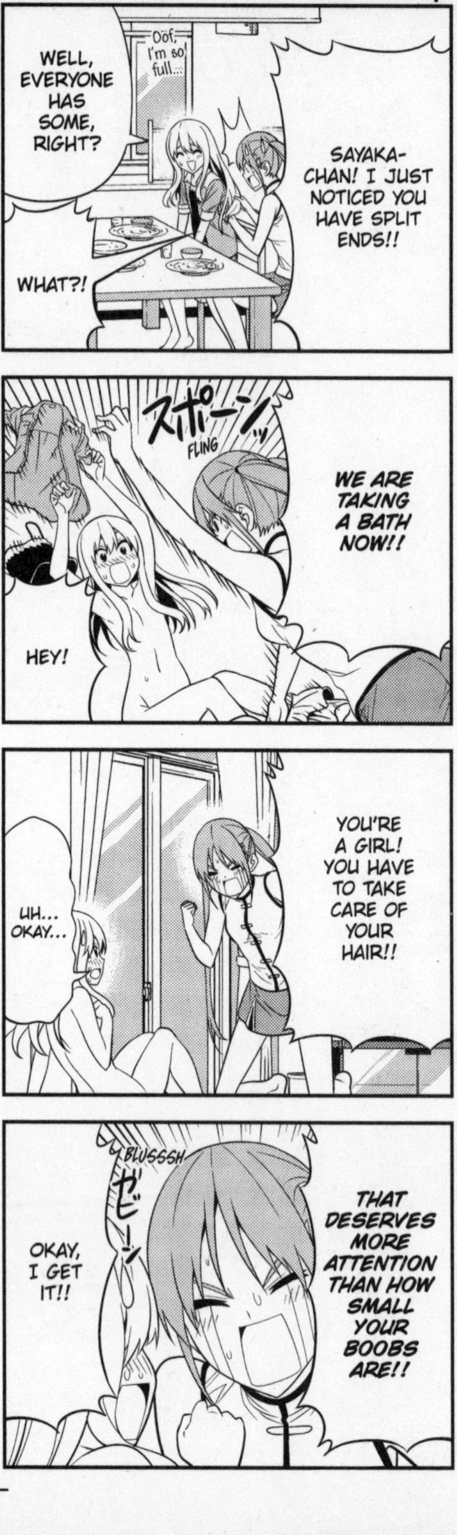
SAYAKA-CHAN! I JUST NOTICED YOU HAVE SPLIT ENDS!!
WELL, EVERYONE HAS SOME, RIGHT?
Oof, I'm so full...
WHAT?!
スポーン
FLING
WE ARE TAKING A BATH NOW!!
HEY!
YOU'RE A GIRL! YOU HAVE TO TAKE CARE OF YOUR HAIR!!
UH... OKAY...
ゼーン
BLUSSSH
THAT DESERVES MORE ATTENTION THAN HOW SMALL YOUR BOOBS ARE!!
OKAY, I GET IT!!

My Feminine Power is 530,000

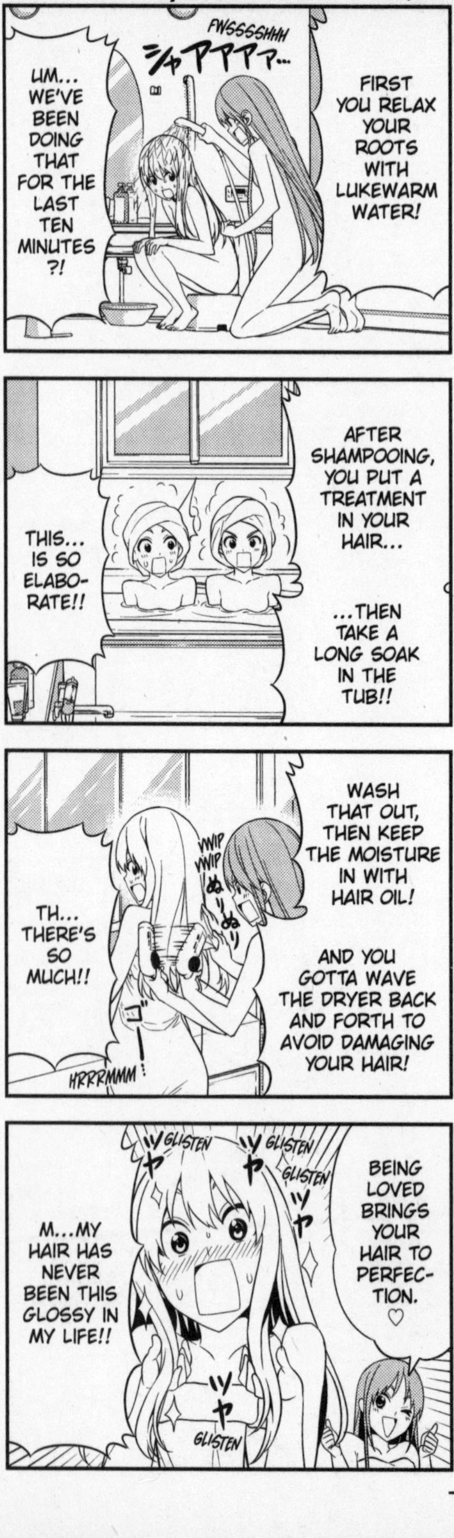
FWSSSSHHH
シャアアアァ...
FIRST YOU RELAX YOUR ROOTS WITH LUKEWARM WATER!
UM... WE'VE BEEN DOING THAT FOR THE LAST TEN MINUTES ?!
AFTER SHAMPOOING, YOU PUT A TREATMENT IN YOUR HAIR...
...THEN TAKE A LONG SOAK IN THE TUB!!
THIS... IS SO ELABO-RATE!!
WASH THAT OUT, THEN KEEP THE MOISTURE IN WITH HAIR OIL!
AND YOU GOTTA WAVE THE DRYER BACK AND FORTH TO AVOID DAMAGING YOUR HAIR!
ぬりぬり
VWIP VWIP
TH... THERE'S SO MUCH!!
ゴー
HRRRMMM
ツヤ GLISTEN
ツヤ GLISTEN
ツヤ GLISTEN
BEING LOVED BRINGS YOUR HAIR TO PERFECTION. ♡
M...MY HAIR HAS NEVER BEEN THIS GLOSSY IN MY LIFE!!
ツヤ GLISTEN

Appreciation

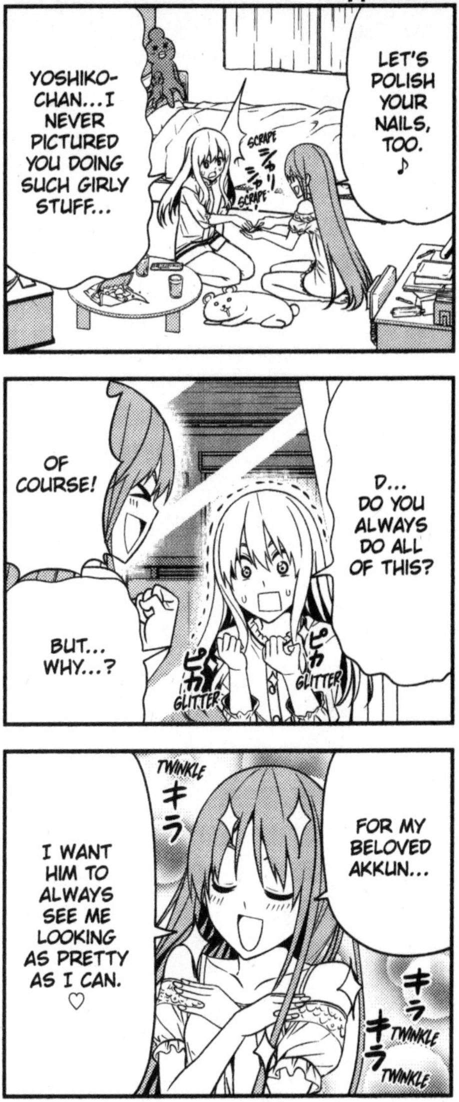
LET'S POLISH YOUR NAILS, TOO. ♪
YOSHIKO-CHAN...I NEVER PICTURED YOU DOING SUCH GIRLY STUFF...
SCRAPE
SCRAPE
D... DO YOU ALWAYS DO ALL OF THIS?
OF COURSE!
BUT... WHY...?
GLITTER
GLITTER
FOR MY BELOVED AKKUN...
TWINKLE
I WANT HIM TO ALWAYS SEE ME LOOKING AS PRETTY AS I CAN. ♡
TWINKLE
TWINKLE
YOU'RE THE GIRLIEST GIRL OF US ALL!!
BWAAAH?!

Second Try

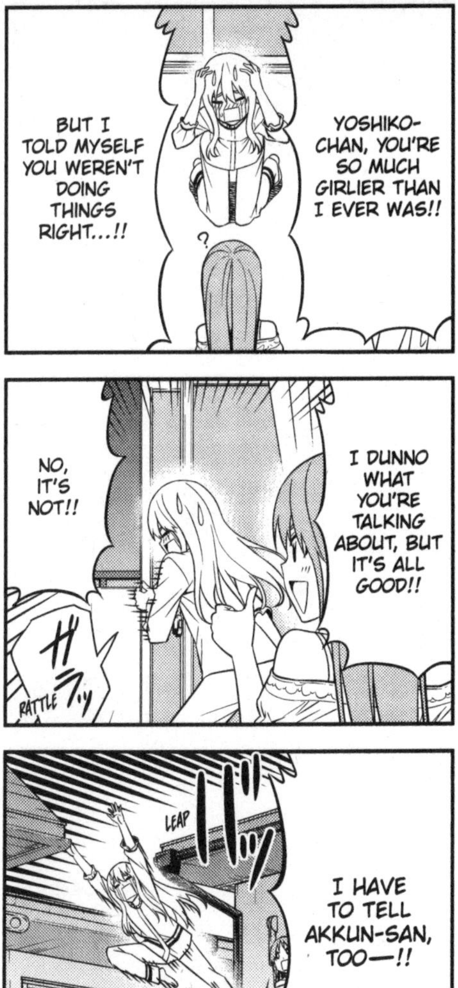
YOSHIKO-CHAN, YOU'RE SO MUCH GIRLIER THAN I EVER WAS!!
BUT I TOLD MYSELF YOU WEREN'T DOING THINGS RIGHT...!!
?
I DUNNO WHAT YOU'RE TALKING ABOUT, BUT IT'S ALL GOOD!!
NO, IT'S NOT!!
RATTLE
I HAVE TO TELL AKKUN-SAN, TOO—!!
LEAP
QUIVER
QUIVER
P... PLEASE HELP ME!

Akuru Refuses to Understand

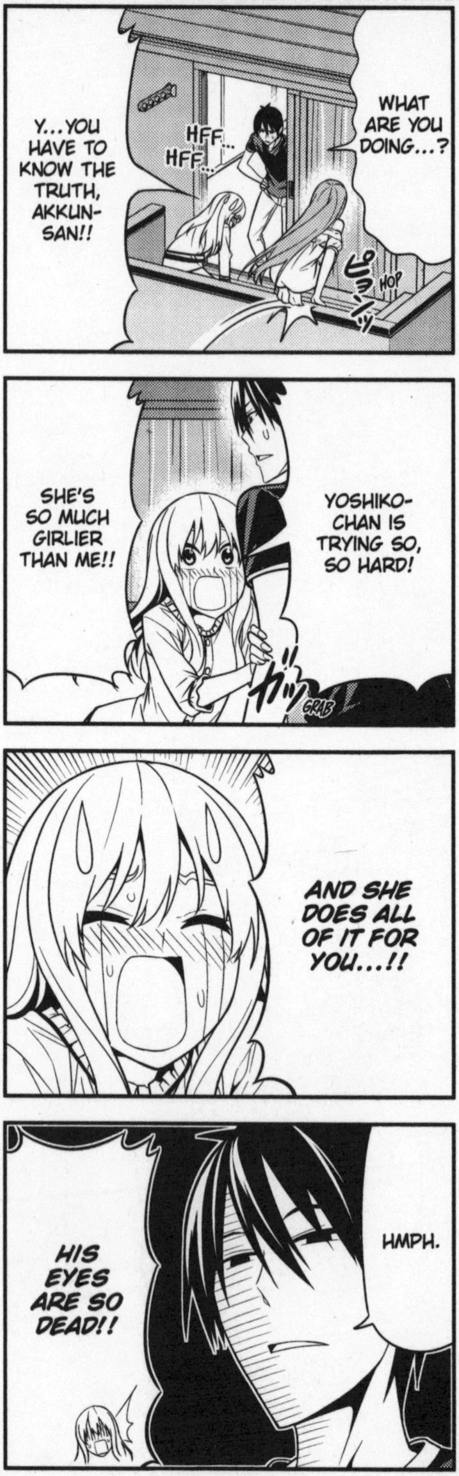
WHAT ARE YOU DOING...?
HFF... HFF...
Y...YOU HAVE TO KNOW THE TRUTH, AKKUN-SAN!!
HOP
YOSHIKO-CHAN IS TRYING SO, SO HARD!
SHE'S SO MUCH GIRLIER THAN ME!!
GRAB
AND SHE DOES ALL OF IT FOR YOU...!!
HMPH.
HIS EYES ARE SO DEAD!!

That's Not What She Meant

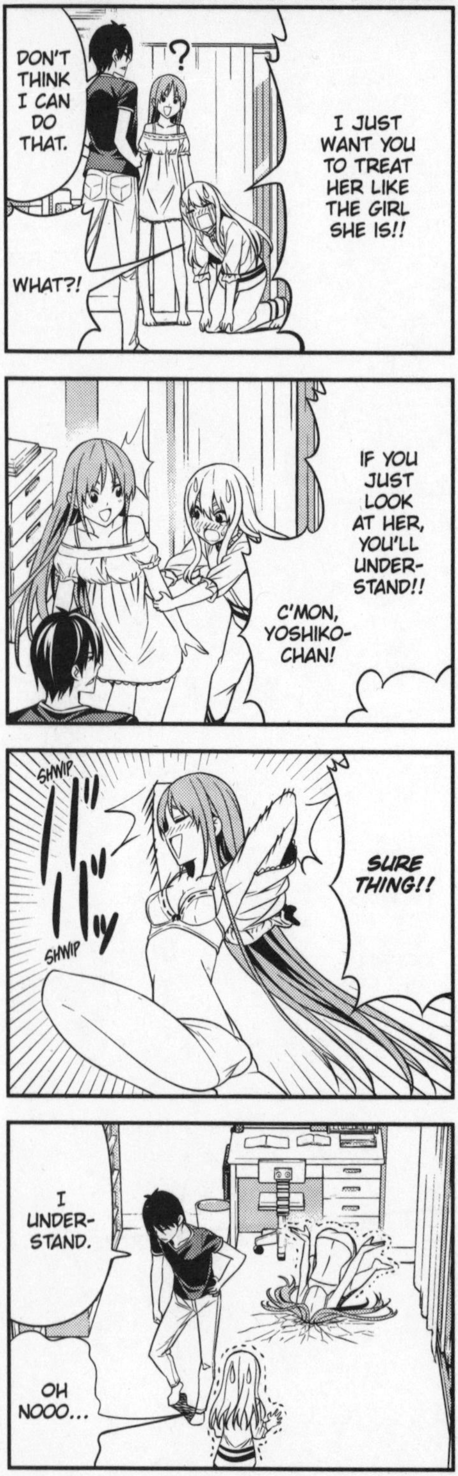
I JUST WANT YOU TO TREAT HER LIKE THE GIRL SHE IS!!
?
DON'T THINK I CAN DO THAT.
WHAT?!
IF YOU JUST LOOK AT HER, YOU'LL UNDER-STAND!!
C'MON, YOSHIKO-CHAN!
SURE THING!!
SHWIP
SHWIP
I UNDER-STAND.
OH NOOO...

He Completely Refuses to Understand

SUMINO...

SHE DOES SO MUCH WORK... TO MAKE HER SKIN...AND HER HAIR...SO BEAUTIFUL...

NNGH—

IT DOESN'T MATTER IF AN ANIMAL IS DIRTY OR WELL-GROOMED—

IT'S STILL AN ANIMAL.

Aho-Girl

\ˈahôˌgərl\ *Japanese, noun.*
A clueless girl.

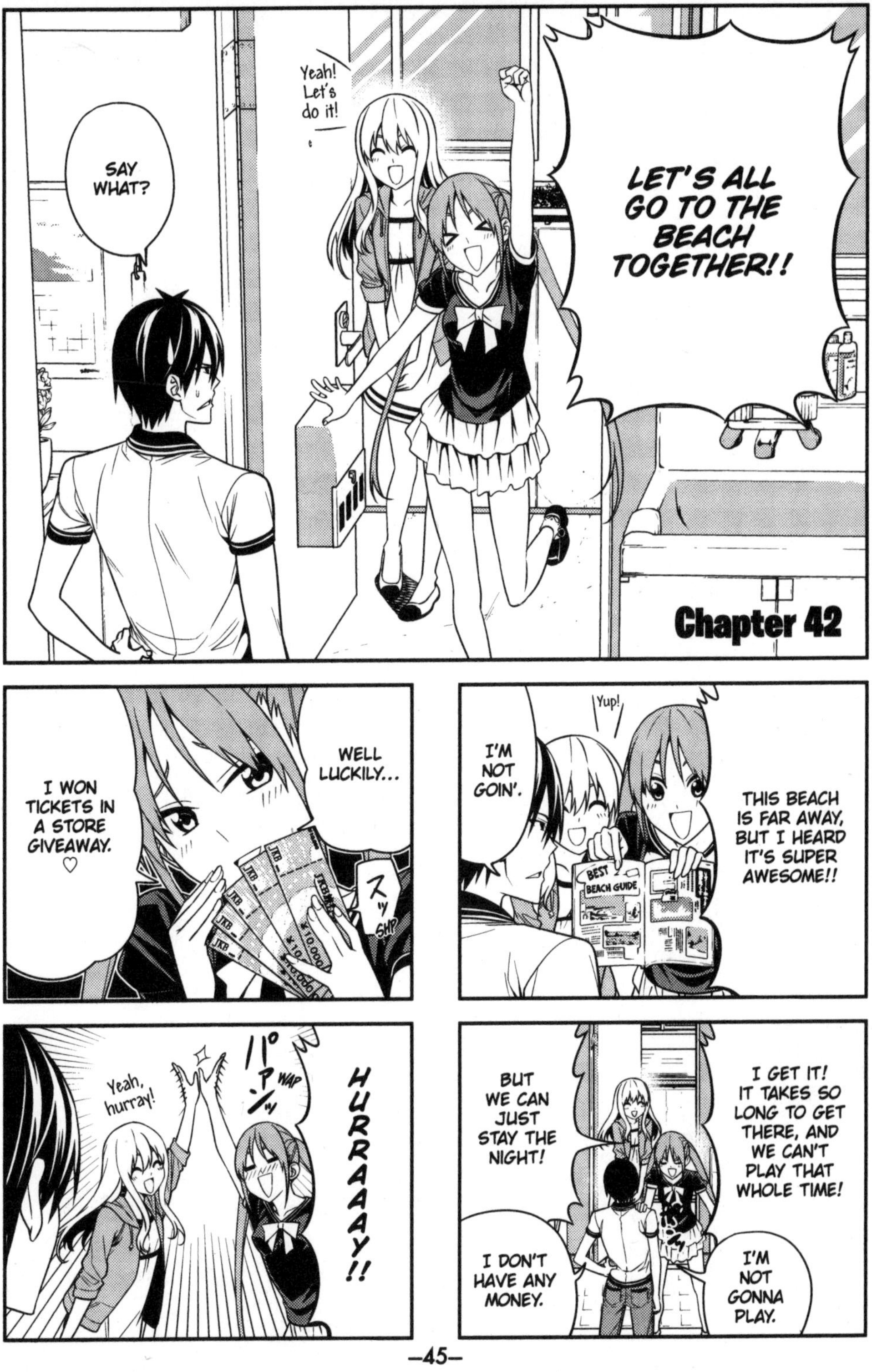
LET'S ALL GO TO THE BEACH TOGETHER!!
Yeah! Let's do it!
SAY WHAT?
Chapter 42
THIS BEACH IS FAR AWAY, BUT I HEARD IT'S SUPER AWESOME!!
Yup!
I'M NOT GOIN'.
BEST BEACH GUIDE
WELL LUCKILY...
I WON TICKETS IN A STORE GIVEAWAY. ♡
SHP
I GET IT! IT TAKES SO LONG TO GET THERE, AND WE CAN'T PLAY THAT WHOLE TIME!
BUT WE CAN JUST STAY THE NIGHT!
I'M NOT GONNA PLAY.
I DON'T HAVE ANY MONEY.
HURRAAAAY!!
WAP
Yeah, hurray!

What're You Doing Here?

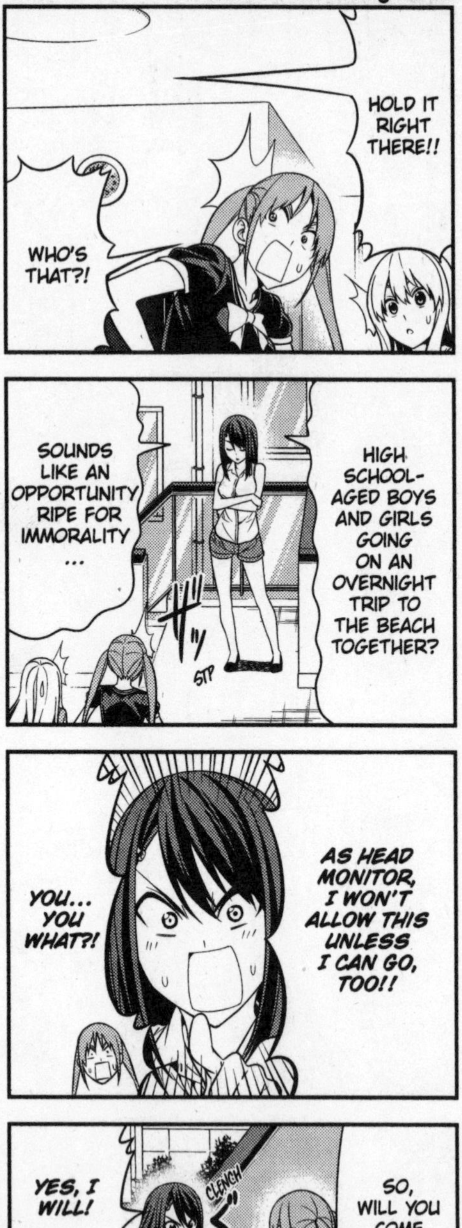
HOLD IT RIGHT THERE!!
WHO'S THAT?!
HIGH SCHOOL-AGED BOYS AND GIRLS GOING ON AN OVERNIGHT TRIP TO THE BEACH TOGETHER?
SOUNDS LIKE AN OPPORTUNITY RIPE FOR IMMORALITY...
STP
AS HEAD MONITOR, I WON'T ALLOW THIS UNLESS I CAN GO, TOO!!
YOU... YOU WHAT?!
SO, WILL YOU COME WITH US?
CLENCH
YES, I WILL!
You should come!
SERIOUSLY? YOU'RE GONNA GO...?

They Keep Coming

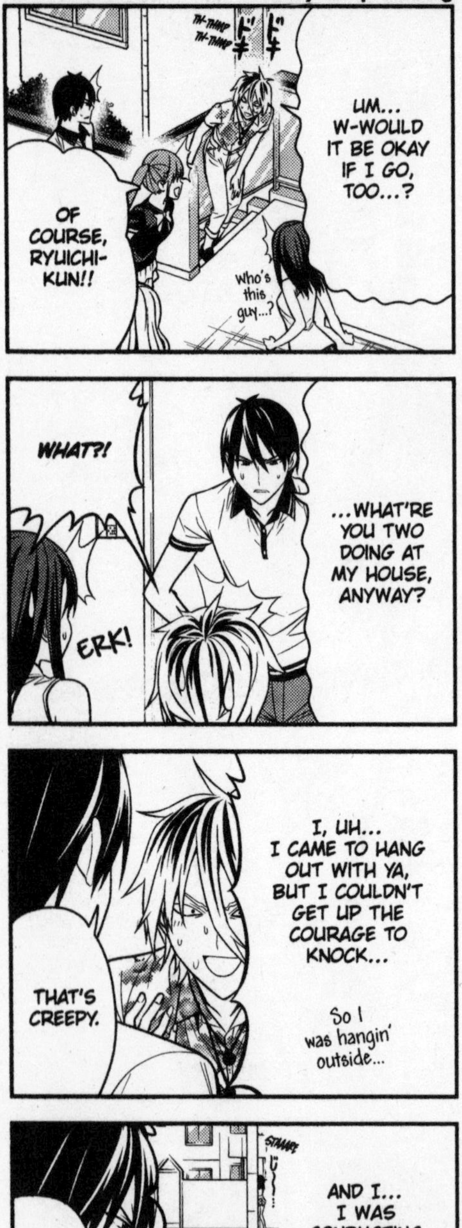
TH-THMP TH-THMP
UM... W-WOULD IT BE OKAY IF I GO, TOO...?
Who's this guy...?
OF COURSE, RYUICHI-KUN!!
...WHAT'RE YOU TWO DOING AT MY HOUSE, ANYWAY?
WHAT?!
ERK!
I, UH... I CAME TO HANG OUT WITH YA, BUT I COULDN'T GET UP THE COURAGE TO KNOCK...
So I was hangin' outside...
THAT'S CREEPY.
AND I... I WAS CONDUCTING SURVEILLANCE TO MAKE SURE THERE WAS NO INDECENCY AFOOT!!
The last three hours.
I WISH YOU'D QUIT DOIN' THAT.

Yay, Shopping!

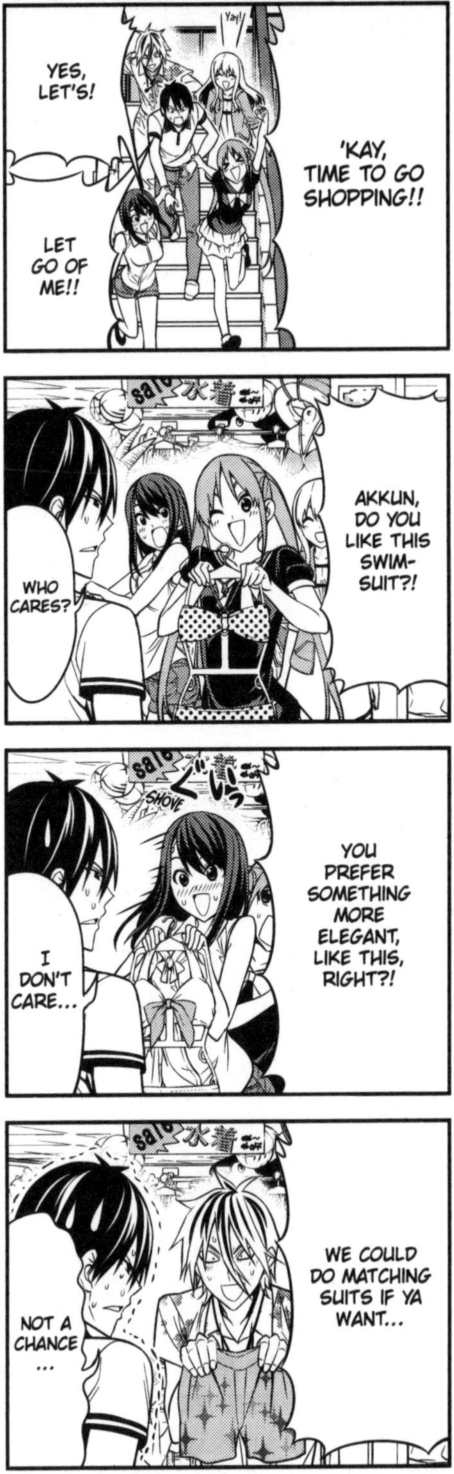
'KAY, TIME TO GO SHOPPING!!
Yay!
YES, LET'S!
LET GO OF ME!!
AKKUN, DO YOU LIKE THIS SWIM-SUIT?!
WHO CARES?
SHOVE
YOU PREFER SOMETHING MORE ELEGANT, LIKE THIS, RIGHT?!
I DON'T CARE...
WE COULD DO MATCHING SUITS IF YA WANT...
NOT A CHANCE ...

Honesty

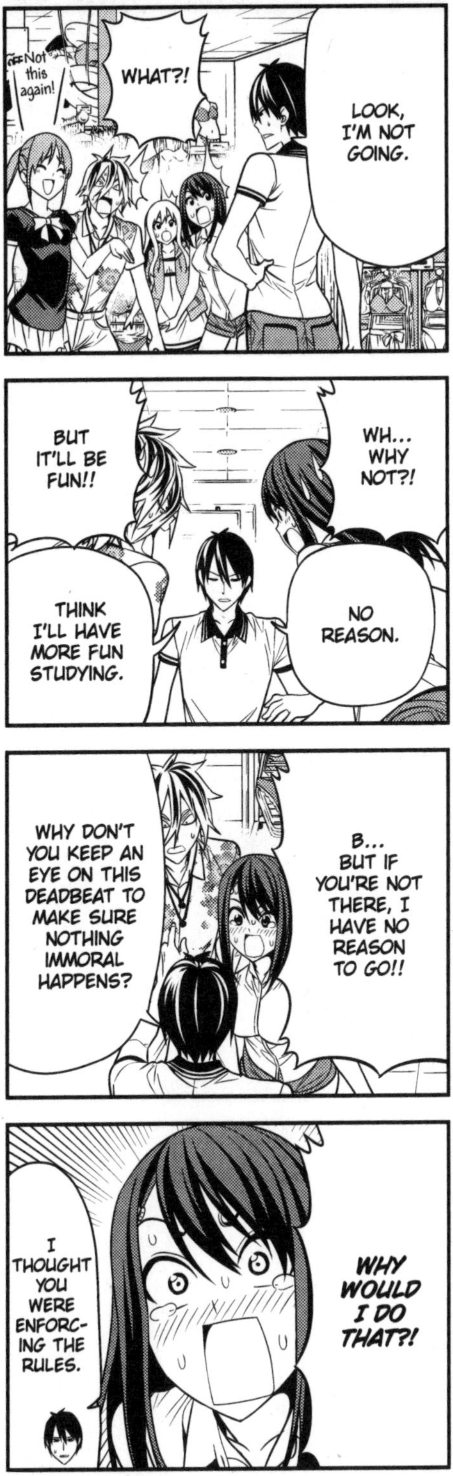
LOOK, I'M NOT GOING.
WHAT?!
Not this again!
WH... WHY NOT?!
NO REASON.
BUT IT'LL BE FUN!!
THINK I'LL HAVE MORE FUN STUDYING.
B... BUT IF YOU'RE NOT THERE, I HAVE NO REASON TO GO!!
WHY DON'T YOU KEEP AN EYE ON THIS DEADBEAT TO MAKE SURE NOTHING IMMORAL HAPPENS?
WHY WOULD I DO THAT?!
I THOUGHT YOU WERE ENFORCING THE RULES.

So Harsh!

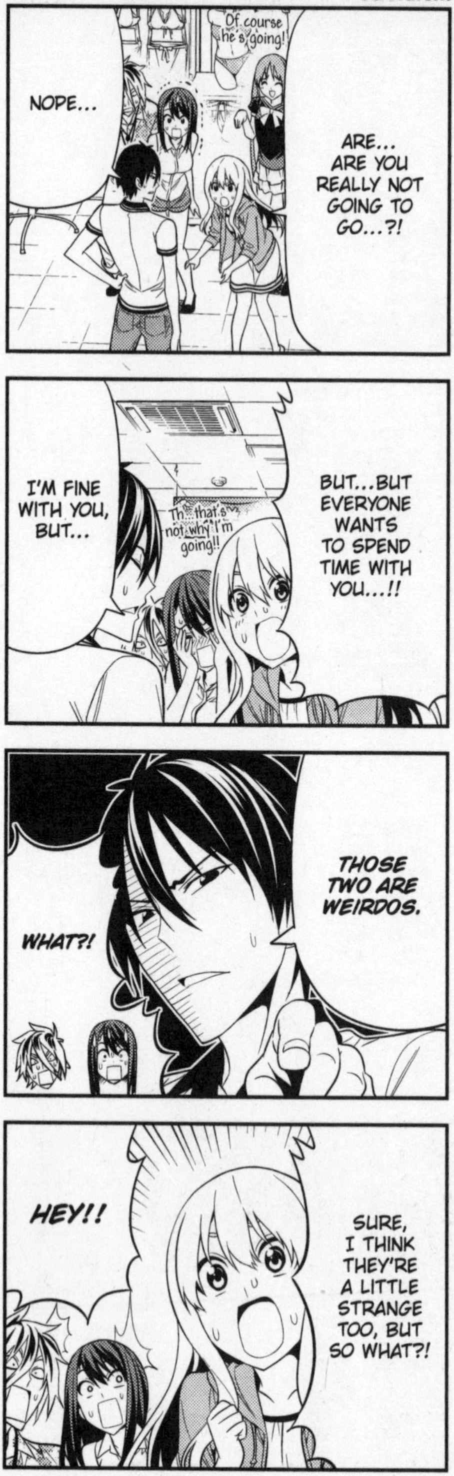
Of course he's going!
ARE... ARE YOU REALLY NOT GOING TO GO...?!
NOPE...
BUT...BUT EVERYONE WANTS TO SPEND TIME WITH YOU...!!
Th-that's not why I'm going!!
I'M FINE WITH YOU, BUT...
THOSE TWO ARE WEIRDOS.
WHAT?!
SURE, I THINK THEY'RE A LITTLE STRANGE TOO, BUT SO WHAT?!
HEY!!

Laying It Out

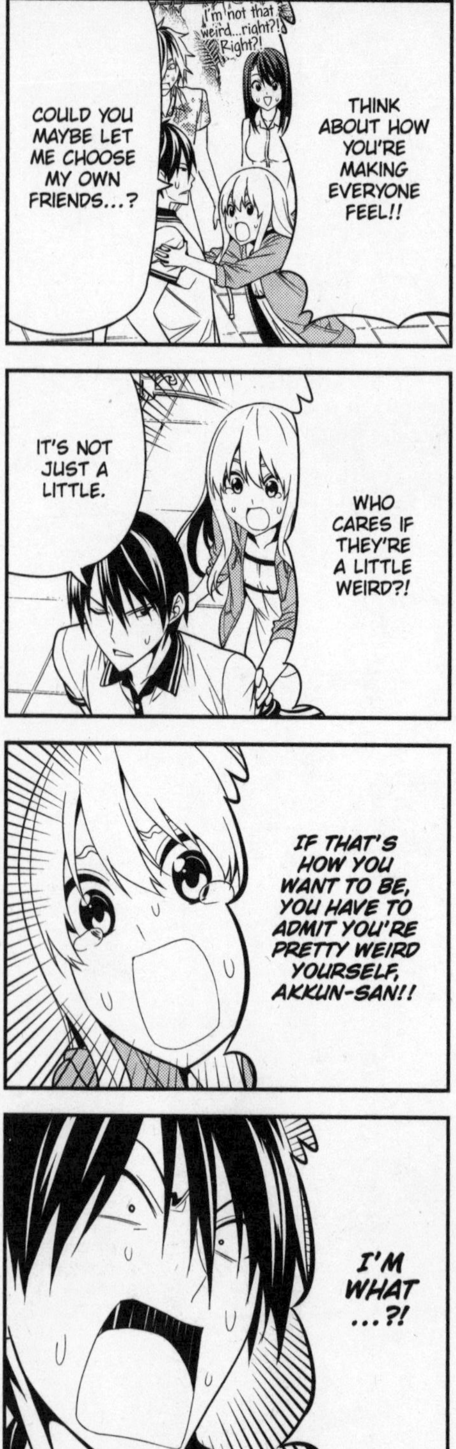
I'm not that weird...right?! Right?!
THINK ABOUT HOW YOU'RE MAKING EVERYONE FEEL!!
COULD YOU MAYBE LET ME CHOOSE MY OWN FRIENDS...?
WHO CARES IF THEY'RE A LITTLE WEIRD?!
IT'S NOT JUST A LITTLE.
IF THAT'S HOW YOU WANT TO BE, YOU HAVE TO ADMIT YOU'RE PRETTY WEIRD YOURSELF, AKKUN-SAN!!
I'M WHAT...?!

Persuasion

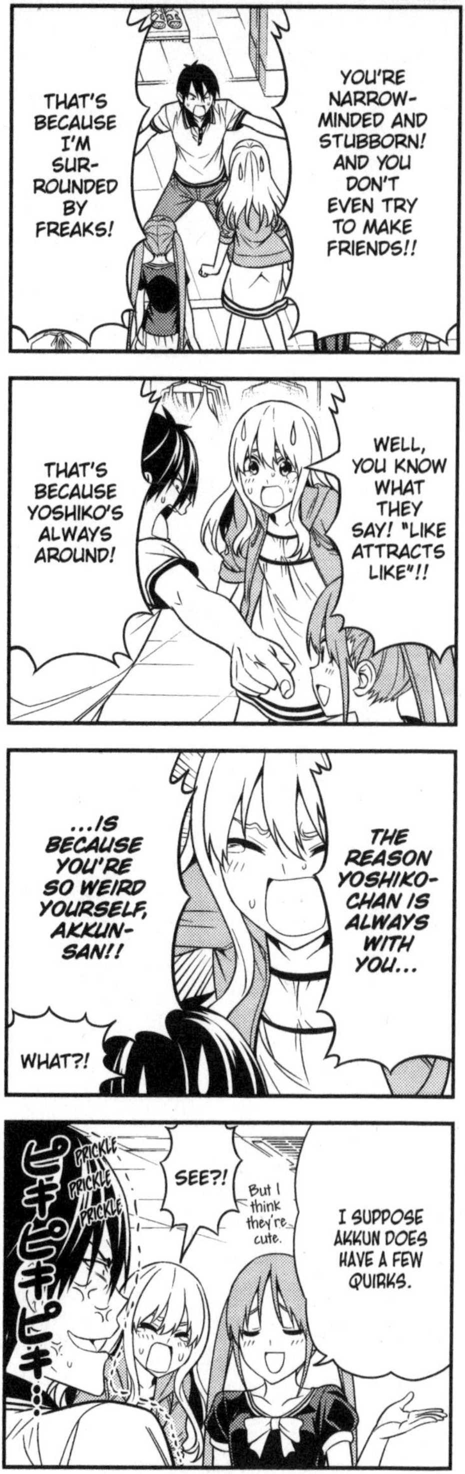
YOU'RE NARROW-MINDED AND STUBBORN! AND YOU DON'T EVEN TRY TO MAKE FRIENDS!!
THAT'S BECAUSE I'M SUR-ROUNDED BY FREAKS!
WELL, YOU KNOW WHAT THEY SAY! "LIKE ATTRACTS LIKE"!!
THAT'S BECAUSE YOSHIKO'S ALWAYS AROUND!
THE REASON YOSHIKO-CHAN IS ALWAYS WITH YOU...
...IS BECAUSE YOU'RE SO WEIRD YOURSELF, AKKUN-SAN!!
WHAT?!
I SUPPOSE AKKUN DOES HAVE A FEW QUIRKS.
But I think they're cute.
SEE?!
PRICKLE PRICKLE PRICKLE
ピキピキピキ…

Sayaka: Master Negotiator

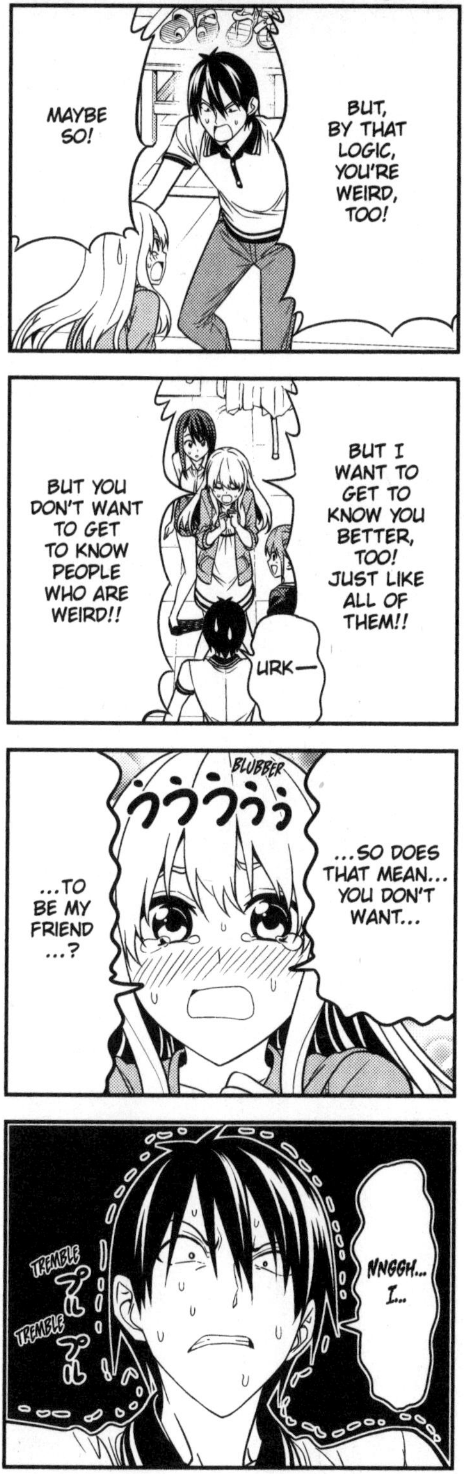
BUT, BY THAT LOGIC, YOU'RE WEIRD, TOO!
MAYBE SO!
BUT I WANT TO GET TO KNOW YOU BETTER, TOO! JUST LIKE ALL OF THEM!!
BUT YOU DON'T WANT TO GET TO KNOW PEOPLE WHO ARE WEIRD!!
URK—
BLUBBER
ううううぅ
...SO DOES THAT MEAN... YOU DON'T WANT...
...TO BE MY FRIEND ...?
NNGGH... I...
TREMBLE TREMBLE
プルプル

He's Softening up

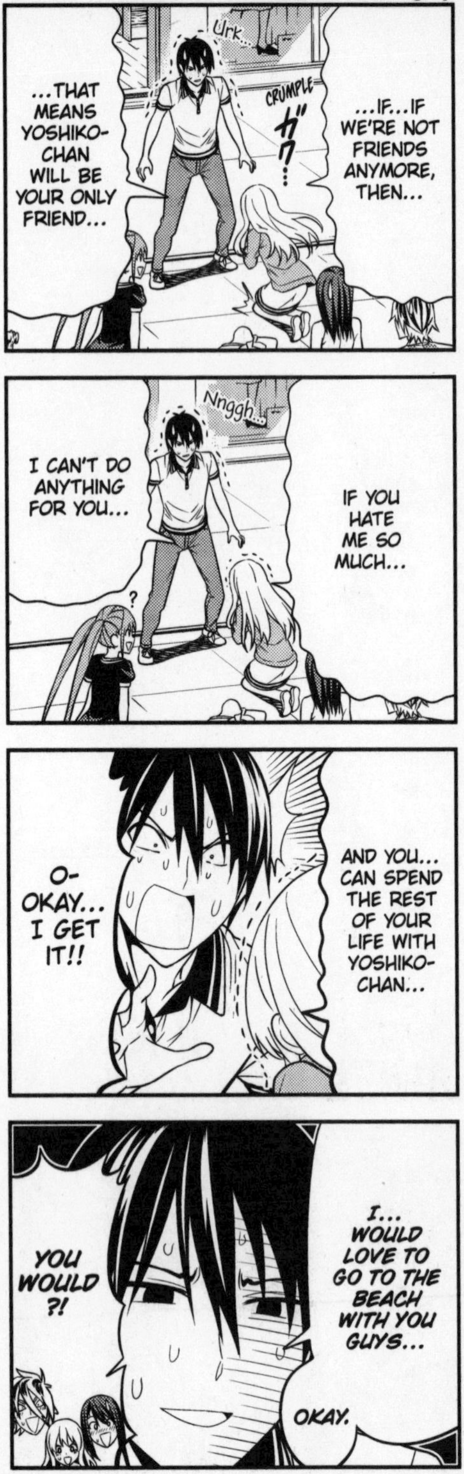
...IF...IF WE'RE NOT FRIENDS ANYMORE, THEN...
Urk...
CRUMPLE
ガク...
...THAT MEANS YOSHIKO-CHAN WILL BE YOUR ONLY FRIEND...
IF YOU HATE ME SO MUCH...
Nnggh...
I CAN'T DO ANYTHING FOR YOU...
AND YOU... CAN SPEND THE REST OF YOUR LIFE WITH YOSHIKO-CHAN...
O-OKAY... I GET IT!!
I... WOULD LOVE TO GO TO THE BEACH WITH YOU GUYS...
OKAY.
YOU WOULD ?!

Can't Let It Go

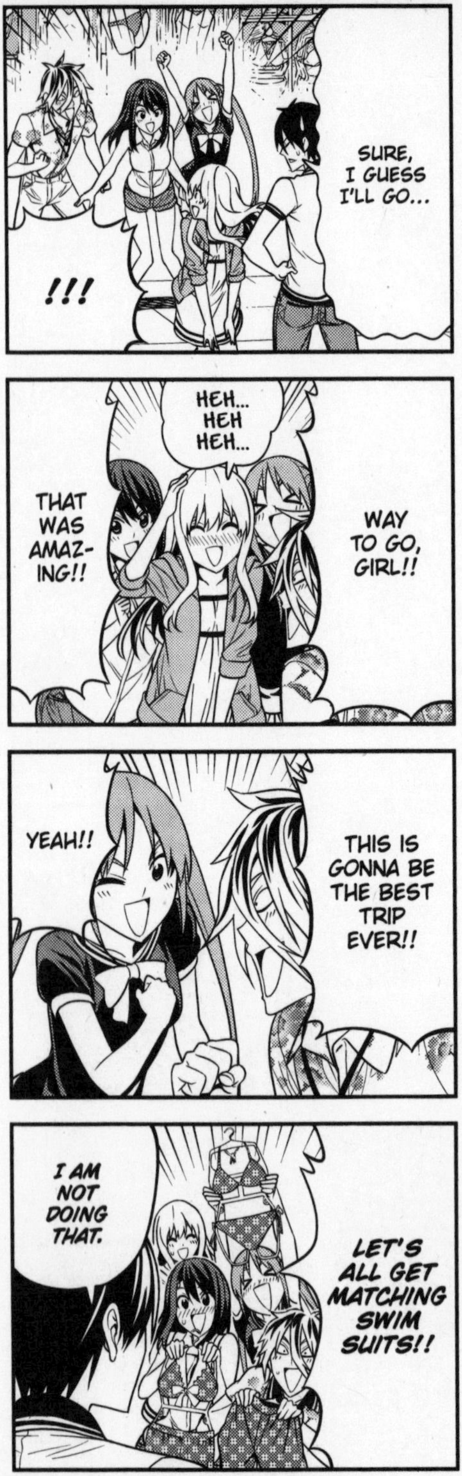
SURE, I GUESS I'LL GO...
!!!
WAY TO GO, GIRL!!
HEH... HEH HEH...
THAT WAS AMAZ-ING!!
THIS IS GONNA BE THE BEST TRIP EVER!!
YEAH!!
LET'S ALL GET MATCHING SWIM SUITS!!
I AM NOT DOING THAT.

Pavlov's Yoshiko

BEACH GEAR
HEY, YOSHIKO-CHAN! THEY HAVE A BANANA POOL FLOAT!
WOOOOAH!!
じゅるり
SLOBBER
IT'S NOT FOR EATING!!

(A hat, a swimsuit, and)

Aho-Girl

\\ˈahôˌɡərl\\ *Japanese, noun.*
A clueless girl.

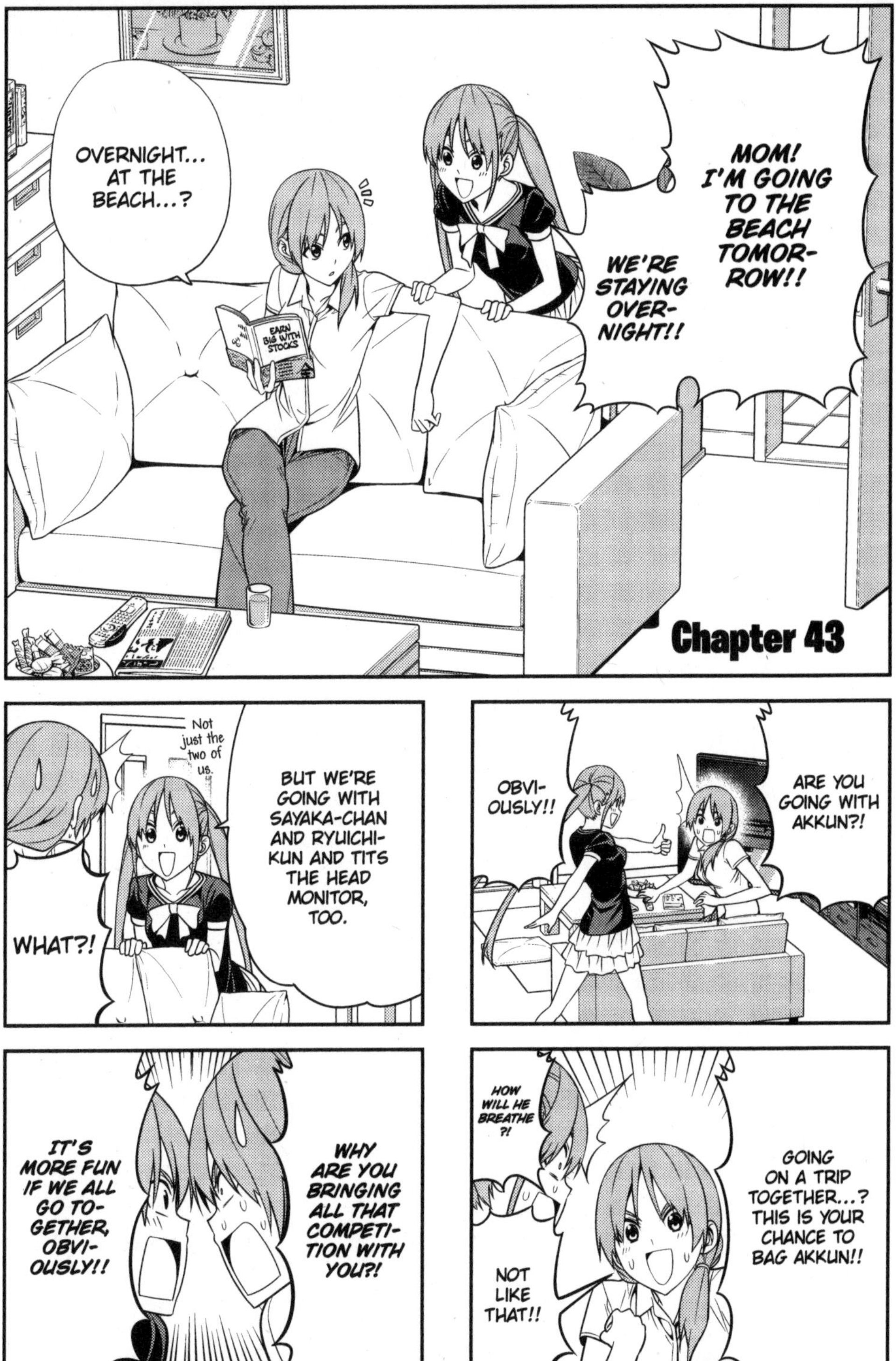
MOM! I'M GOING TO THE BEACH TOMORROW!!
WE'RE STAYING OVERNIGHT!!
EARN BIG WITH STOCKS
OVERNIGHT... AT THE BEACH...?
Chapter 43
ARE YOU GOING WITH AKKUN?!
OBVIOUSLY!!
BUT WE'RE GOING WITH SAYAKA-CHAN AND RYUICHI-KUN AND TITS THE HEAD MONITOR, TOO.
Not just the two of us.
WHAT?!
GOING ON A TRIP TOGETHER...? THIS IS YOUR CHANCE TO BAG AKKUN!!
HOW WILL HE BREATHE?!
NOT LIKE THAT!!
WHY ARE YOU BRINGING ALL THAT COMPETITION WITH YOU?!
IT'S MORE FUN IF WE ALL GO TOGETHER, OBVIOUSLY!!

We Meet Again

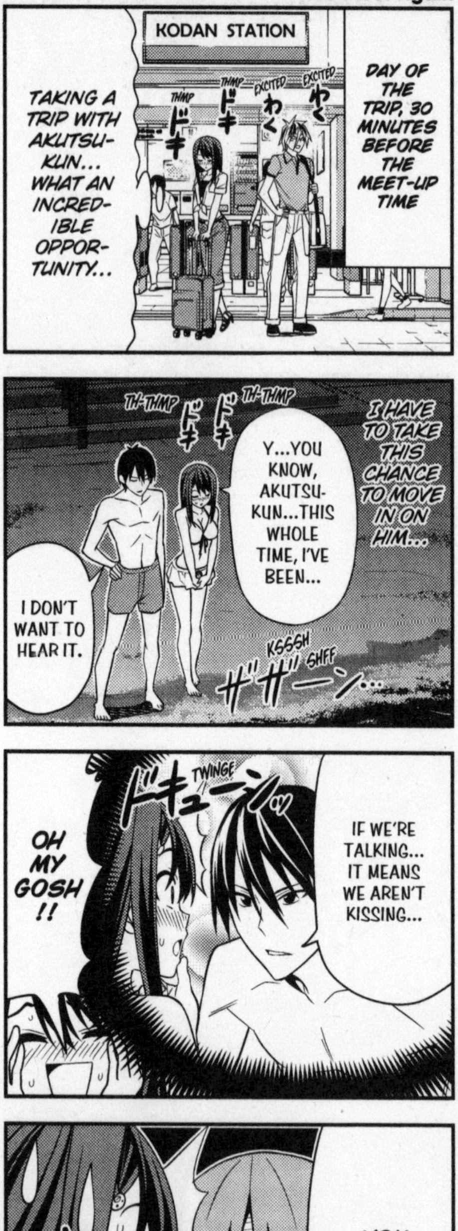
KODAN STATION
DAY OF THE TRIP, 30 MINUTES BEFORE THE MEET-UP TIME
EXCITED EXCITED
THMP THMP
TAKING A TRIP WITH AKUTSU-KUN... WHAT AN INCREDIBLE OPPORTUNITY...
I HAVE TO TAKE THIS CHANCE TO MOVE IN ON HIM...
TH-THMP TH-THMP
Y...YOU KNOW, AKUTSU-KUN...THIS WHOLE TIME, I'VE BEEN...
I DON'T WANT TO HEAR IT.
KSSSH SHFF
TWINGE
IF WE'RE TALKING... IT MEANS WE AREN'T KISSING...
OH MY GOSH!!
YOU LOOK EXCITED.
JOLT
BAP

That Word Is Just Barely Okay for a Shonen Manga

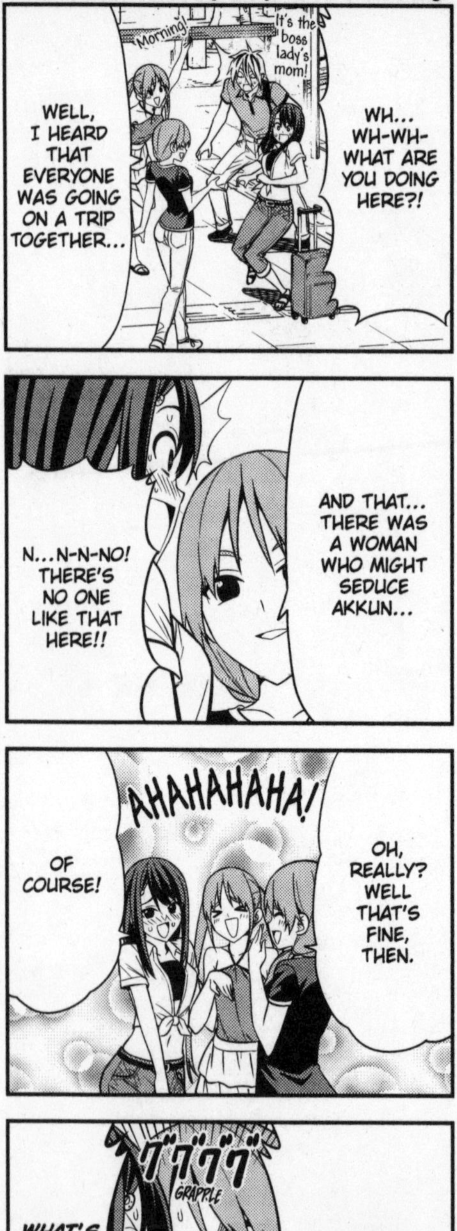
It's the boss lady's mom!
Morning!
WH... WH-WH-WHAT ARE YOU DOING HERE?!
WELL, I HEARD THAT EVERYONE WAS GOING ON A TRIP TOGETHER...
AND THAT... THERE WAS A WOMAN WHO MIGHT SEDUCE AKKUN...
N...N-N-NO! THERE'S NO ONE LIKE THAT HERE!!
AHAHAHAHA!
OH, REALLY? WELL THAT'S FINE, THEN.
OF COURSE!
GRAPPLE
YOU THINK YOU'RE FOOLING ME, YOU RUTTING SOW?!
WHAT'S THAT SUPPOSED TO MEAN?!

It's Oil-Based Ink

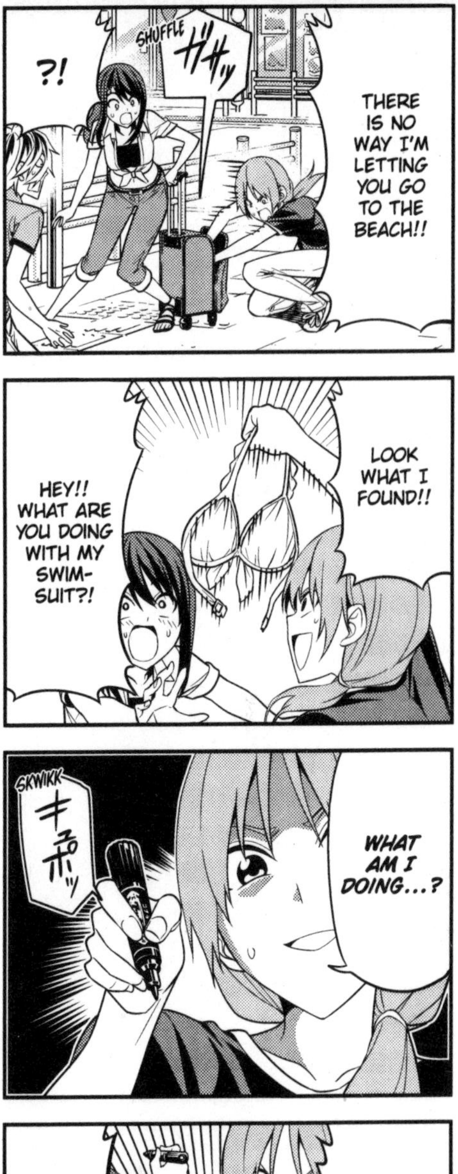
THERE IS NO WAY I'M LETTING YOU GO TO THE BEACH!!
SHUFFLE
?!
LOOK WHAT I FOUND!!
HEY!! WHAT ARE YOU DOING WITH MY SWIM-SUIT?!
WHAT AM I DOING...?
SKWIKK
I'M DRAWING ON NIPPLES!!
OH NOOOO!!
TADAAA

A Commonsense Decision

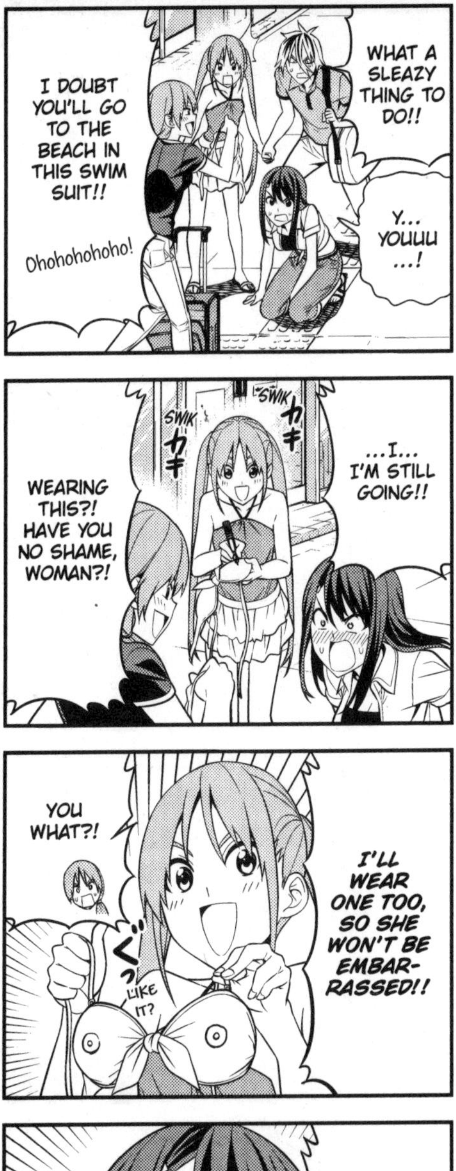
WHAT A SLEAZY THING TO DO!!
I DOUBT YOU'LL GO TO THE BEACH IN THIS SWIM SUIT!!
Y... YOUUU ...!
Ohohohohoho!
SWIK
SWIK
...I... I'M STILL GOING!!
WEARING THIS?! HAVE YOU NO SHAME, WOMAN?!
I'LL WEAR ONE TOO, SO SHE WON'T BE EMBARRASSED!!
YOU WHAT?!
LIKE IT?
I WAS JUST GOING TO WEAR A SHIRT OVER IT!!
OH! THAT MAKES SENSE!!

A Woman's Weapon

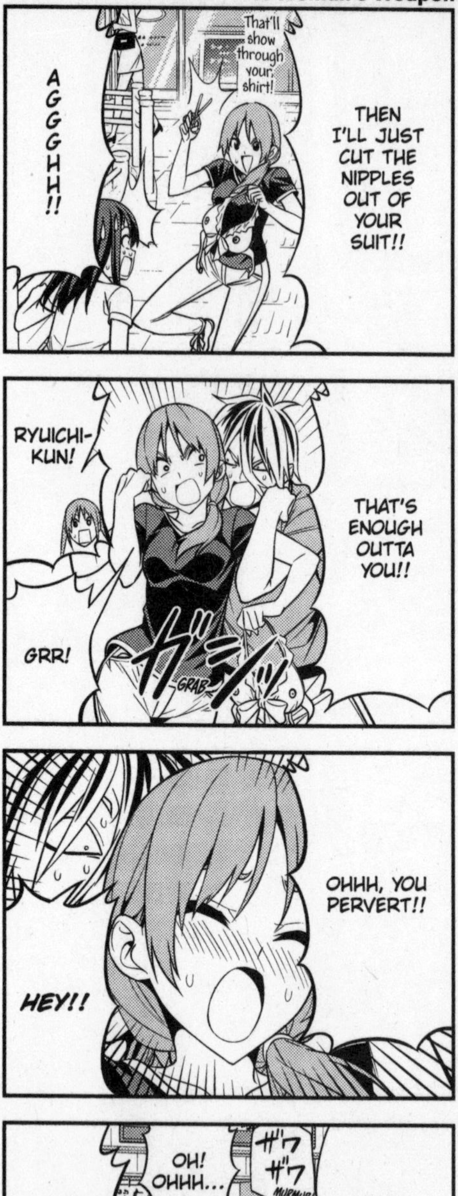
THEN I'LL JUST CUT THE NIPPLES OUT OF YOUR SUIT!!
That'll show through your shirt!
AGGGHH!!
THAT'S ENOUGH OUTTA YOU!!
RYUICHI-KUN!
GRR!
ガシッ
GRAB
OHHH, YOU PERVERT!!
HEY!!
OH, YOU LIKE OLDER WOMEN, RYUICHI-KUN?
ザワ ザワ
MURMUR MURMUR
OH! OHHH...
THAT'S NOT WHAT'S GOIN' ON HERE!!

That Pissed Her Off

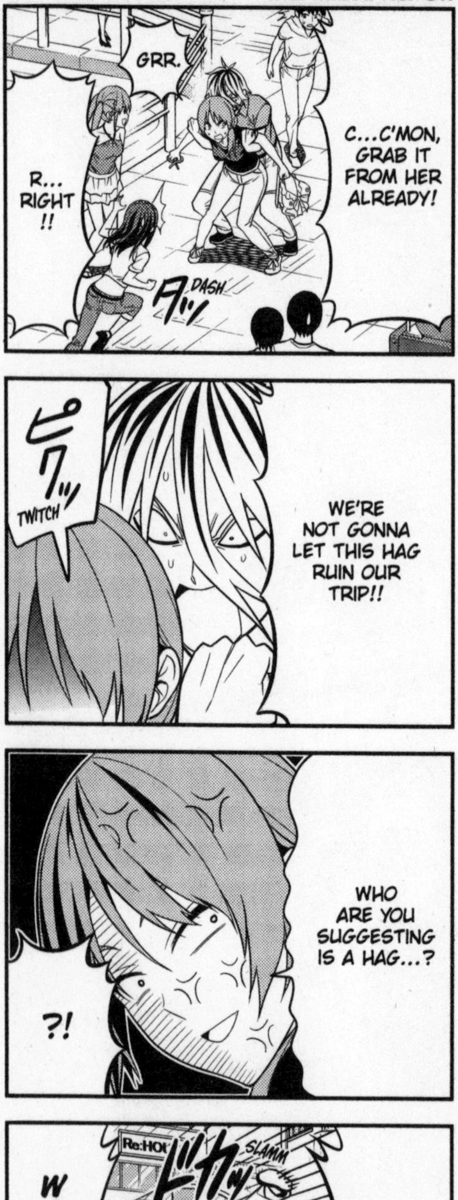
C...C'MON, GRAB IT FROM HER ALREADY!
GRR.
R... RIGHT!!
ダッ
DASH
WE'RE NOT GONNA LET THIS HAG RUIN OUR TRIP!!
ピクッ
TWITCH
WHO ARE YOU SUGGESTING IS A HAG...?
?!
I WILL END YOU!!
ドカッ
SLAMM
WAAAAUGGH!!

The End of the World

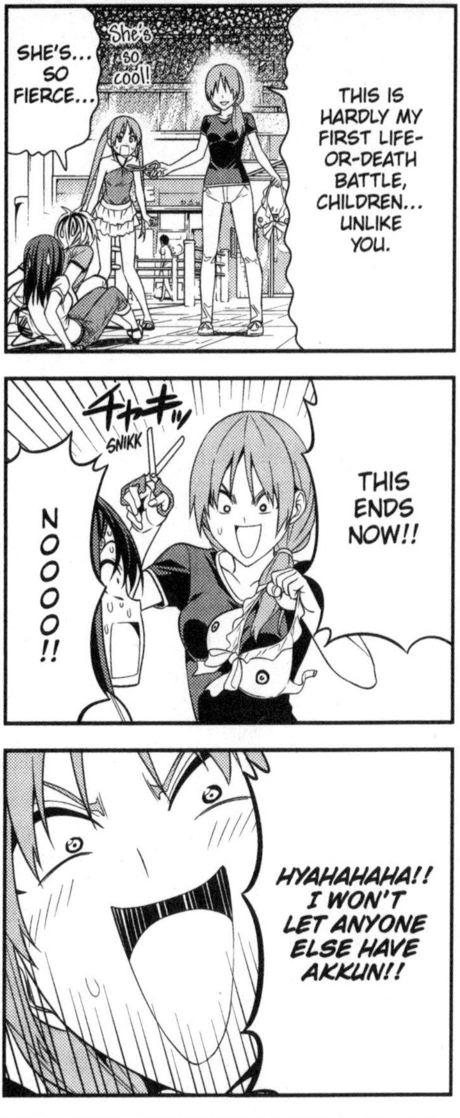
THIS IS HARDLY MY FIRST LIFE-OR-DEATH BATTLE, CHILDREN... UNLIKE YOU.
She's so cool!
SHE'S... SO FIERCE...
THIS ENDS NOW!!
チャキッ
SNIKK
NOOOOO!!
HYAHAHAHA!! I WON'T LET ANYONE ELSE HAVE AKKUN!!
WHAT ARE YOU DOING...?
IT...IT'S AKUTSU-KUN!!
NAB

Savior

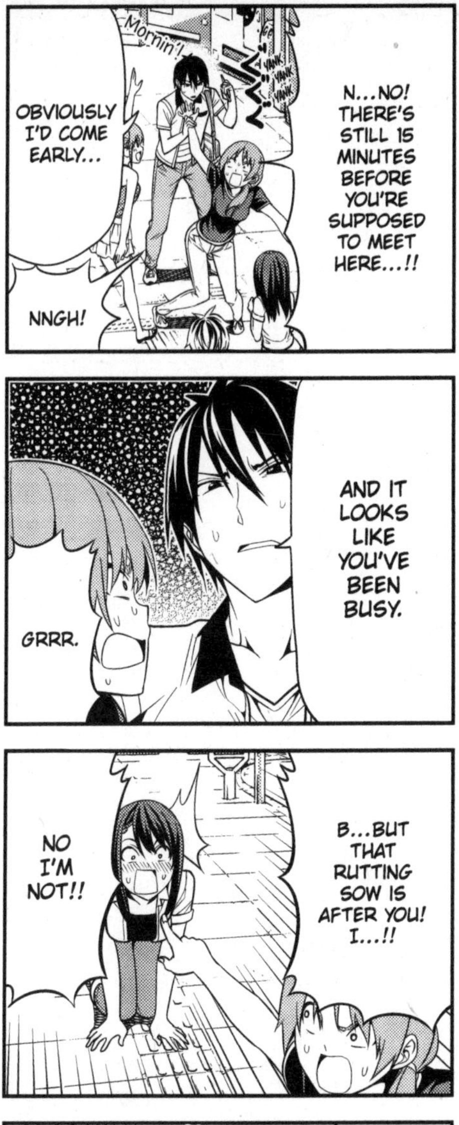
YANK YANK YANK
N...NO! THERE'S STILL 15 MINUTES BEFORE YOU'RE SUPPOSED TO MEET HERE...!!
Mornin'!
OBVIOUSLY I'D COME EARLY...
NNGH!
AND IT LOOKS LIKE YOU'VE BEEN BUSY.
GRRR.
B...BUT THAT RUTTING SOW IS AFTER YOU! I...!!
NO I'M NOT!!
LET'S ALL CALM DOWN FOR A LITTLE BIT...
To think you're almost 40...
ぐぐぐ
SPASM SPASM SPASM
WAUGGGH!

Oblivious to Public Opinion

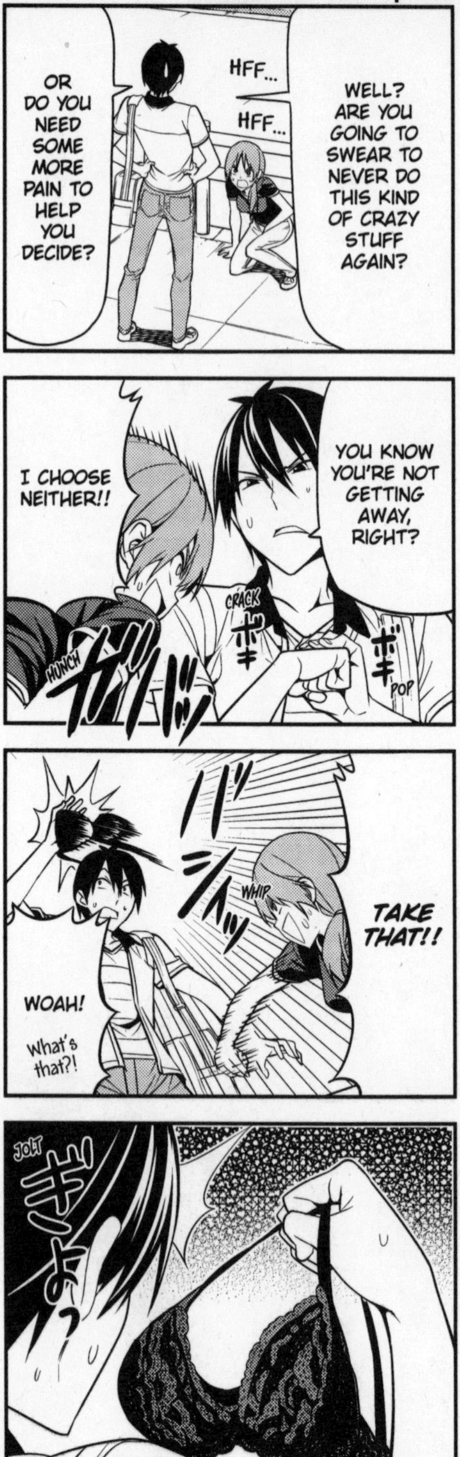
WELL? ARE YOU GOING TO SWEAR TO NEVER DO THIS KIND OF CRAZY STUFF AGAIN?
HFF...
HFF...
OR DO YOU NEED SOME MORE PAIN TO HELP YOU DECIDE?
YOU KNOW YOU'RE NOT GETTING AWAY, RIGHT?
I CHOOSE NEITHER!!
CRACK
POP
HUNCH
TAKE THAT!!
WHIP
WOAH!
What's that?!
JOLT

Arch Villain

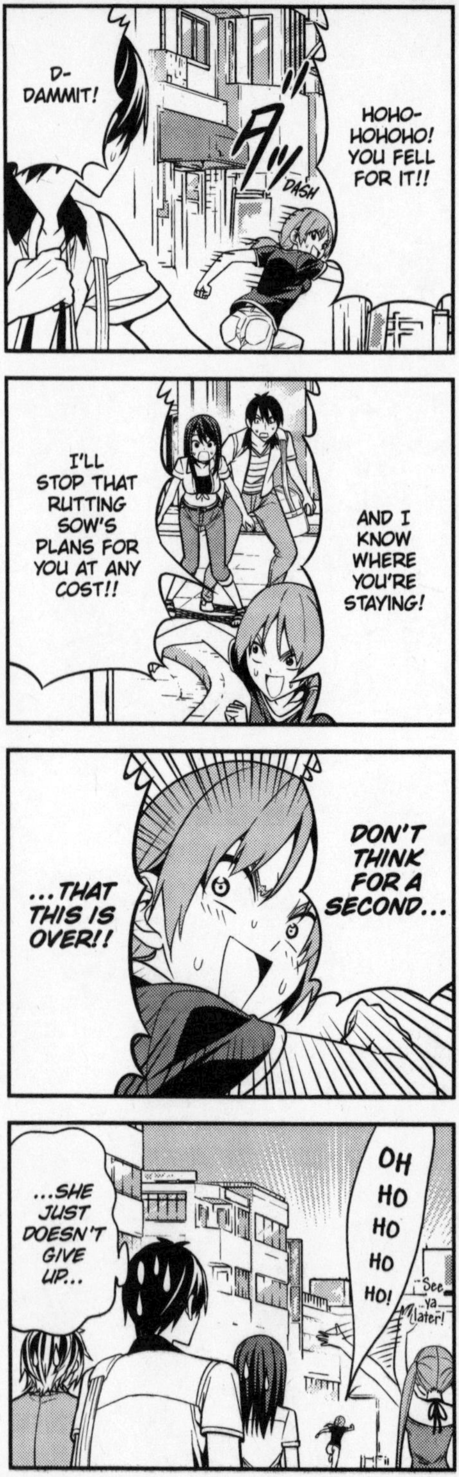
HOHO-HOHOHO! YOU FELL FOR IT!!
DASH
D-DAMMIT!
AND I KNOW WHERE YOU'RE STAYING!
I'LL STOP THAT RUTTING SOW'S PLANS FOR YOU AT ANY COST!!
DON'T THINK FOR A SECOND...
...THAT THIS IS OVER!!
OH HO HO HO HO!
See ya later!
...SHE JUST DOESN'T GIVE UP...

An Unfamiliar Problem

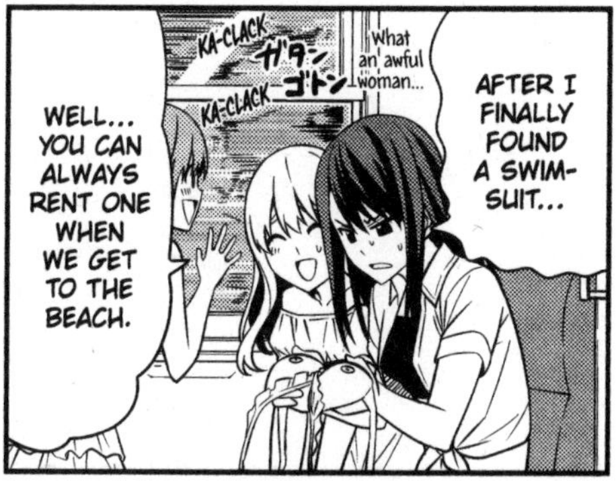
AFTER I FINALLY FOUND A SWIM-SUIT...
What an awful woman...
KA-CLACK
ガタン
ゴトン
KA-CLACK
WELL... YOU CAN ALWAYS RENT ONE WHEN WE GET TO THE BEACH.

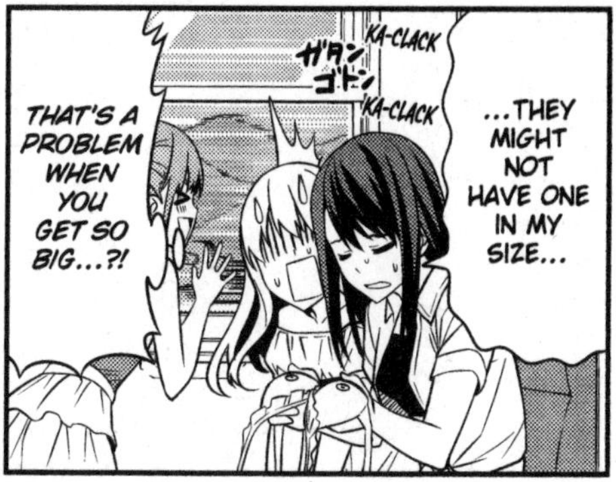
...THEY MIGHT NOT HAVE ONE IN MY SIZE...
KA-CLACK
ガタン
ゴトン
KA-CLACK
THAT'S A PROBLEM WHEN YOU GET SO BIG...?!

(You're my sun-bathed city)

Aho-Girl

\\'ahô͵gərl\\ *Japanese, noun.*
A clueless girl.

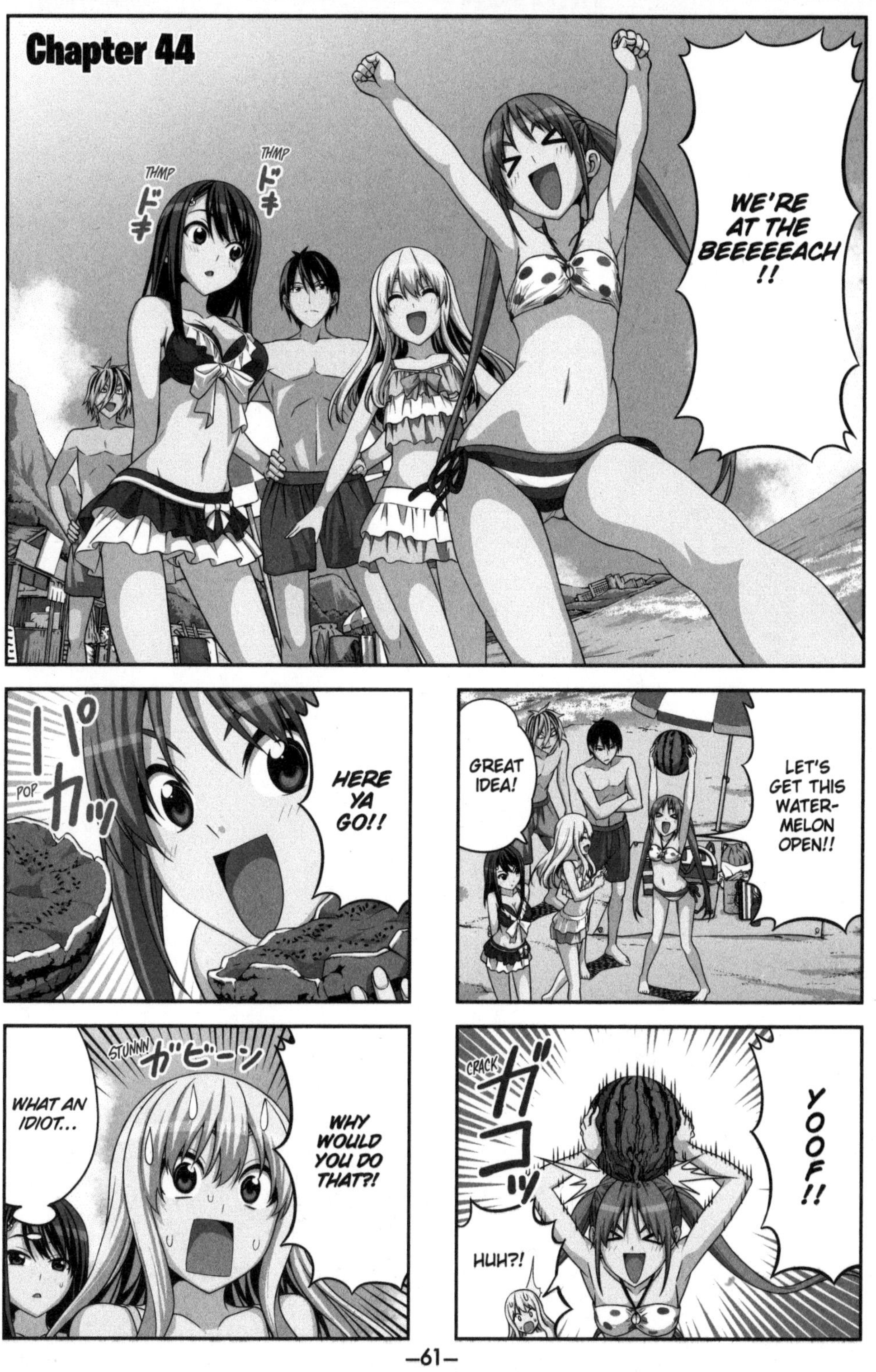
Chapter 44
WE'RE AT THE BEEEEEACH!!
THMP ドキ
THMP ドキ
LET'S GET THIS WATER-MELON OPEN!!
GREAT IDEA!
POP パカッ
HERE YA GO!!
CRACK ガコッ
YOOF!!
HUH?!
STUNNN ガビーン
WHY WOULD YOU DO THAT?!
WHAT AN IDIOT...

Allure Overdose

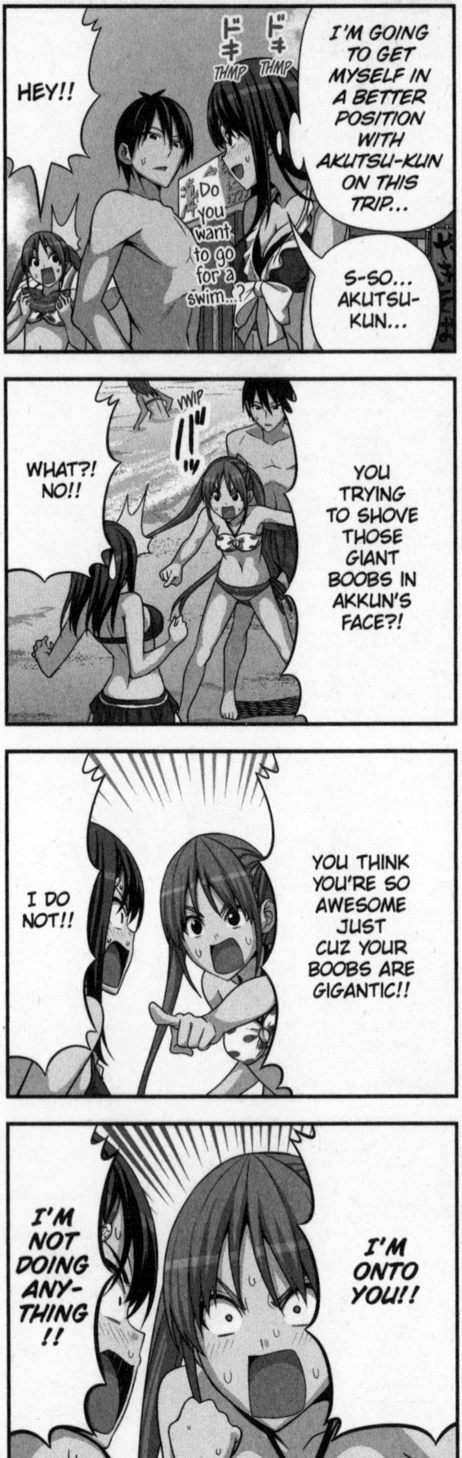
I'M GOING TO GET MYSELF IN A BETTER POSITION WITH AKUTSU-KUN ON THIS TRIP...
ドキ THMP ドキ THMP
S-SO... AKUTSU-KUN...
Do you want to go for a swim...?
HEY!!
YOU TRYING TO SHOVE THOSE GIANT BOOBS IN AKKUN'S FACE?!
VWIP バッ
WHAT?! NO!!
YOU THINK YOU'RE SO AWESOME JUST CUZ YOUR BOOBS ARE GIGANTIC!!
I DO NOT!!
I'M ONTO YOU!!
I'M NOT DOING ANY-THING!!

Just One Glance

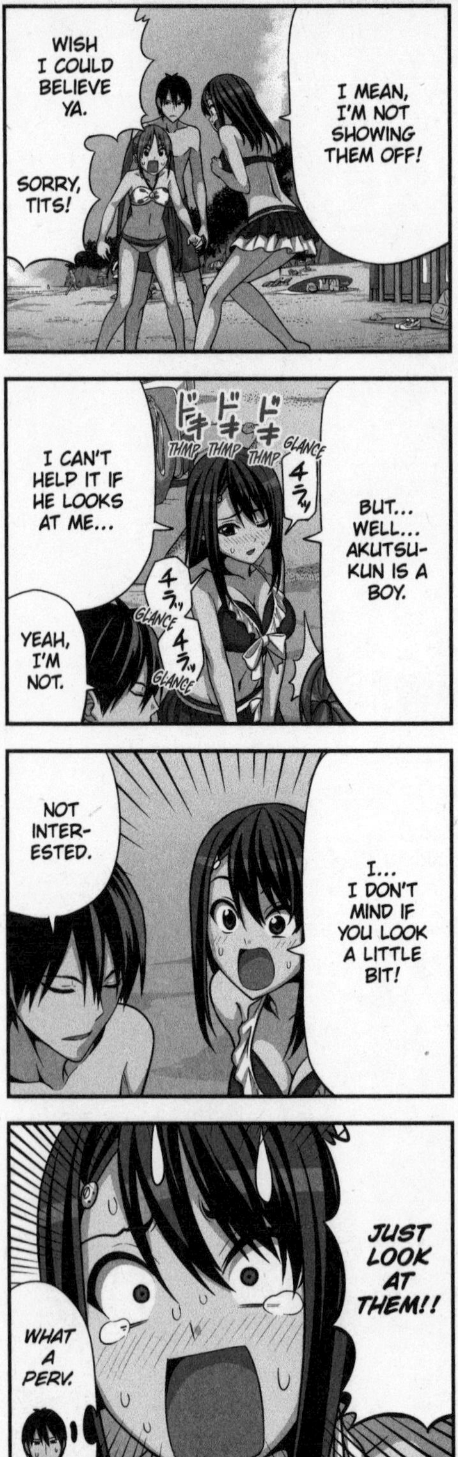
I MEAN, I'M NOT SHOWING THEM OFF!
WISH I COULD BELIEVE YA.
SORRY, TITS!
BUT... WELL... AKUTSU-KUN IS A BOY.
ドキ THMP ドキ THMP ドキ THMP
チラッ GLANCE
I CAN'T HELP IT IF HE LOOKS AT ME...
チラッ GLANCE チラッ GLANCE
YEAH, I'M NOT.
I... I DON'T MIND IF YOU LOOK A LITTLE BIT!
NOT INTERESTED.
JUST LOOK AT THEM!!
WHAT A PERV.

I'm Studying, Though

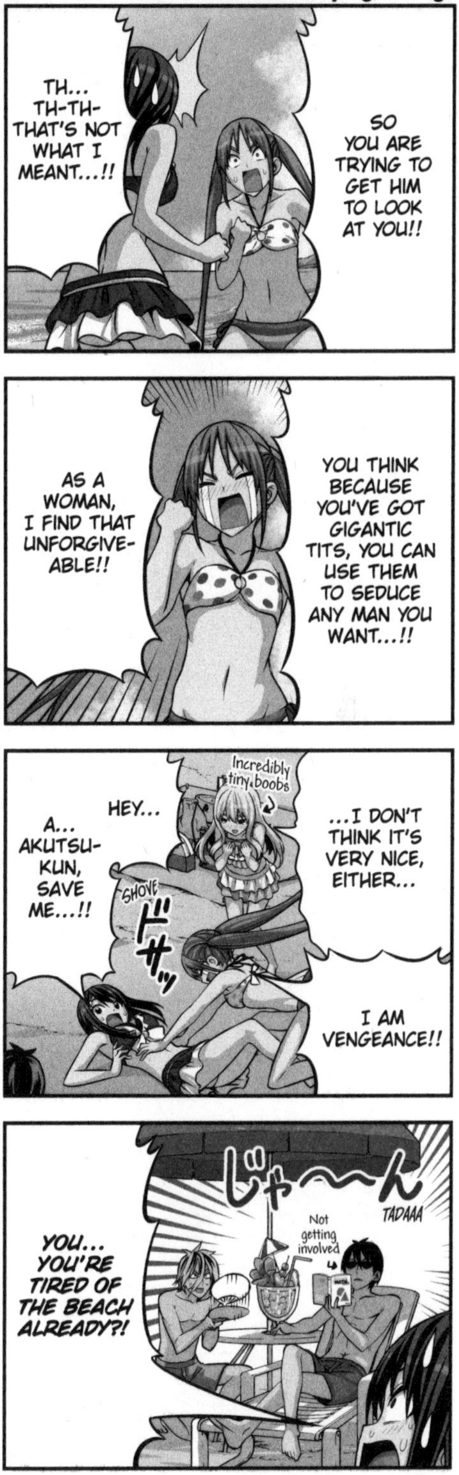
SO YOU ARE TRYING TO GET HIM TO LOOK AT YOU!!
TH... TH-TH-THAT'S NOT WHAT I MEANT...!!
YOU THINK BECAUSE YOU'VE GOT GIGANTIC TITS, YOU CAN USE THEM TO SEDUCE ANY MAN YOU WANT...!!
AS A WOMAN, I FIND THAT UNFORGIVE-ABLE!!
...I DON'T THINK IT'S VERY NICE, EITHER...
Incredibly tiny boobs
HEY...
A... AKUTSU-KUN, SAVE ME...!!
SHOVE
ドサッ
I AM VENGEANCE!!
じゃ〜ん
TADAAA
Not getting involved
YOU... YOU'RE TIRED OF THE BEACH ALREADY?!

Get the Edge

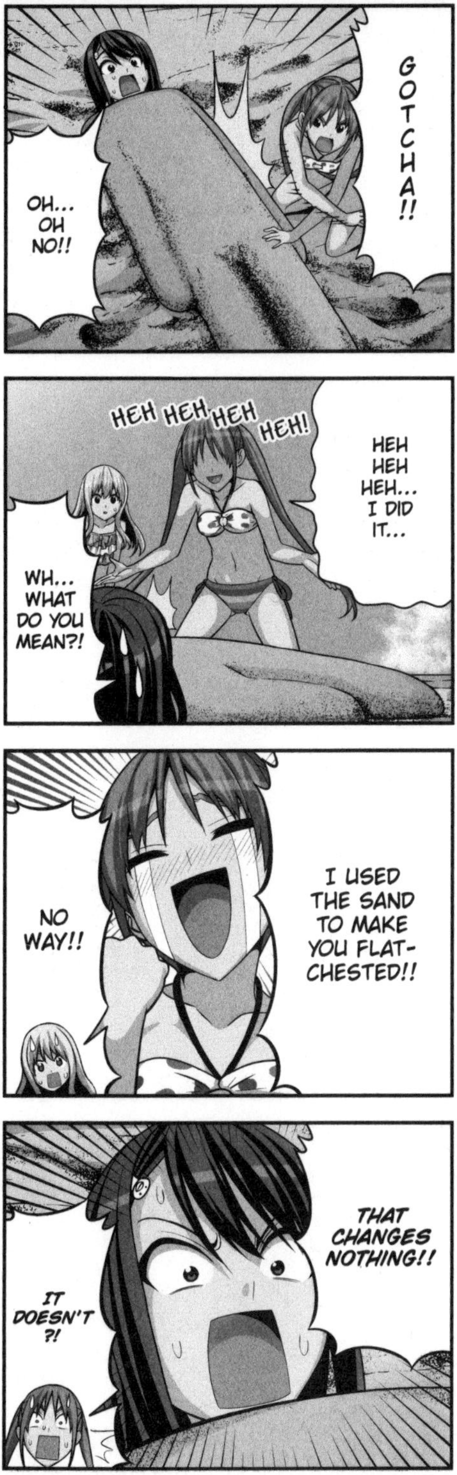
GOTCHA!!
OH... OH NO!!
HEH HEH HEH... I DID IT...
HEH HEH HEH HEH!
WH... WHAT DO YOU MEAN?!
I USED THE SAND TO MAKE YOU FLAT-CHESTED!!
NO WAY!!
THAT CHANGES NOTHING!!
IT DOESN'T?!

It's All Relative

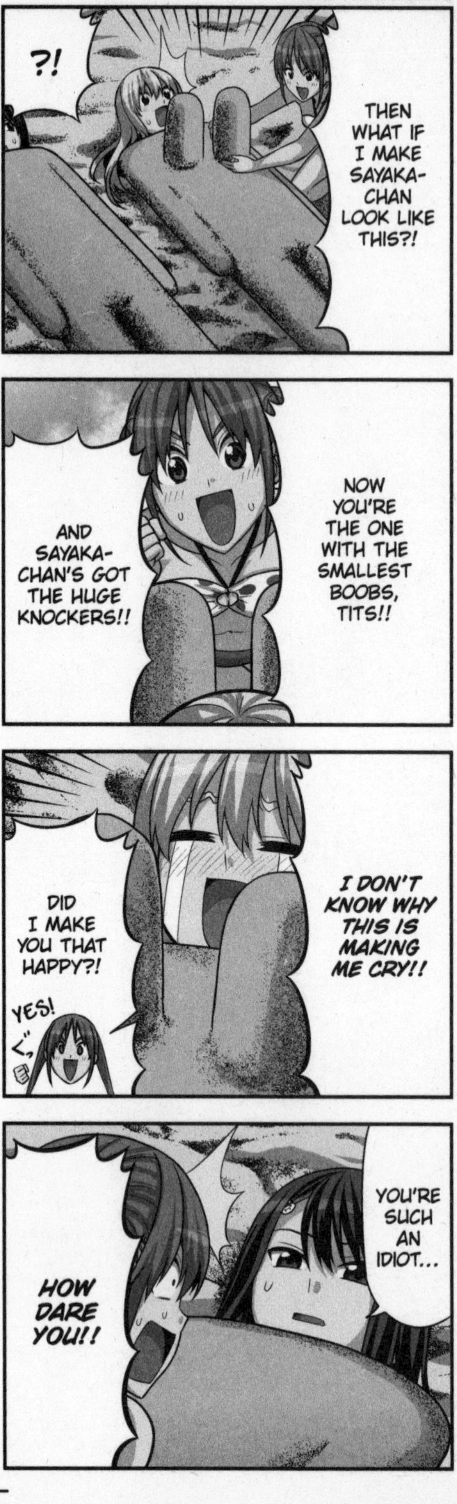
THEN WHAT IF I MAKE SAYAKA-CHAN LOOK LIKE THIS?!
?!
NOW YOU'RE THE ONE WITH THE SMALLEST BOOBS, TITS!!
AND SAYAKA-CHAN'S GOT THE HUGE KNOCKERS!!
I DON'T KNOW WHY THIS IS MAKING ME CRY!!
DID I MAKE YOU THAT HAPPY?!
YES!
ぐっ
YOU'RE SUCH AN IDIOT...
HOW DARE YOU!!

The Ace up Her Sleeve

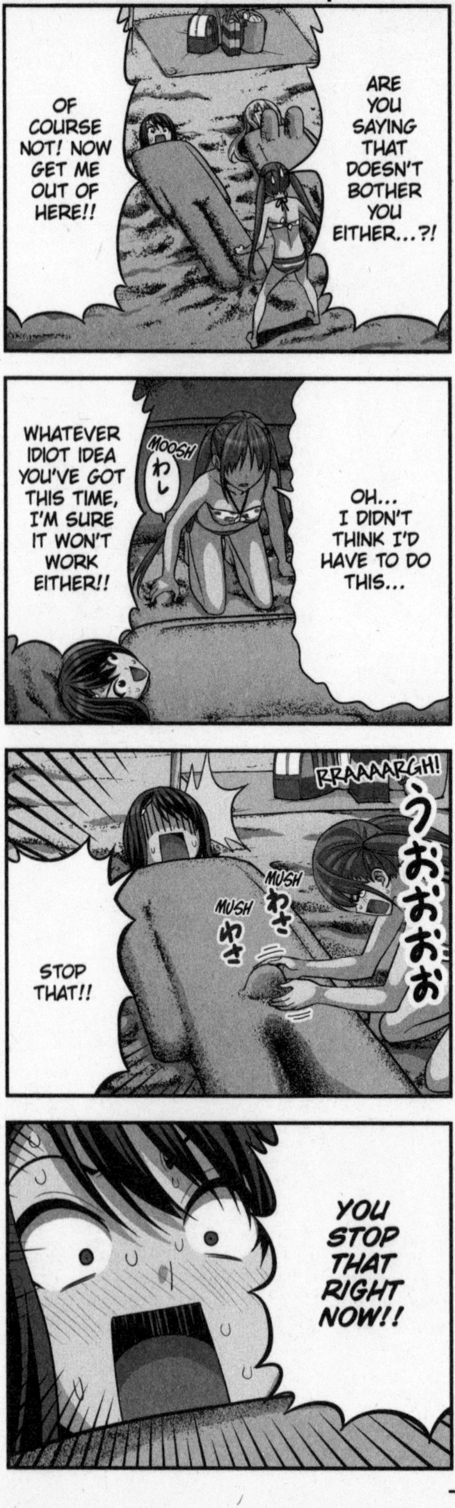
ARE YOU SAYING THAT DOESN'T BOTHER YOU EITHER...?!
OF COURSE NOT! NOW GET ME OUT OF HERE!!
OH... I DIDN'T THINK I'D HAVE TO DO THIS...
MOOSH
わし
WHATEVER IDIOT IDEA YOU'VE GOT THIS TIME, I'M SURE IT WON'T WORK EITHER!!
RRAAAARGH!
うおおおお
MUSH
わさ
MUSH
わさ
STOP THAT!!
YOU STOP THAT RIGHT NOW!!

A Runaway Idiot

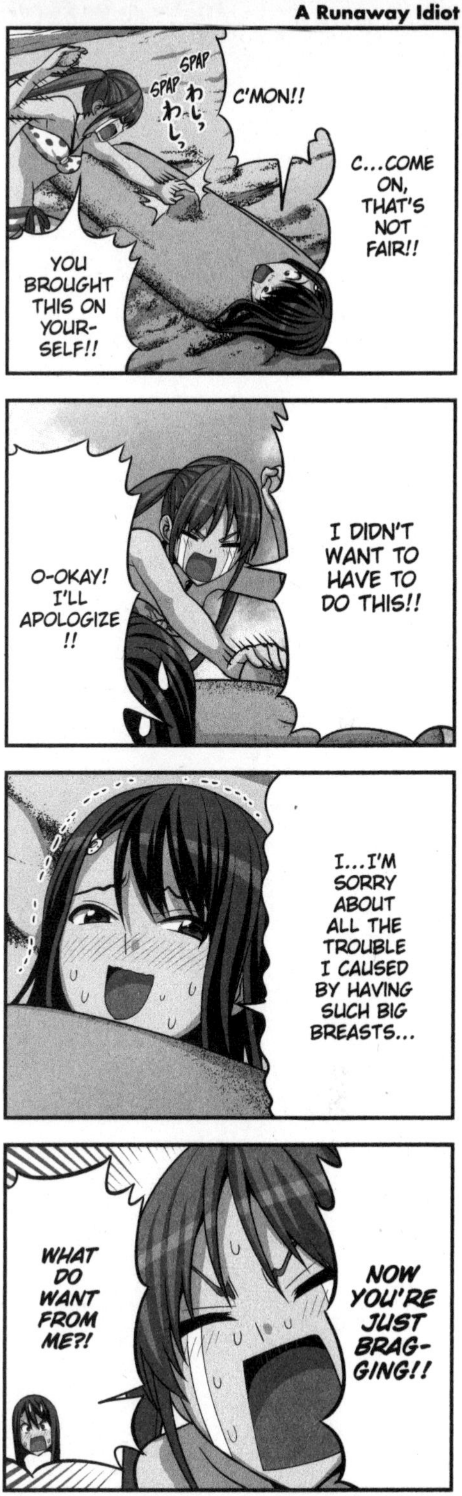
C'MON!!
SPAP SPAP わしっ わしっ
C...COME ON, THAT'S NOT FAIR!!
YOU BROUGHT THIS ON YOURSELF!!
I DIDN'T WANT TO HAVE TO DO THIS!!
O-OKAY! I'LL APOLOGIZE!!
I...I'M SORRY ABOUT ALL THE TROUBLE I CAUSED BY HAVING SUCH BIG BREASTS...
NOW YOU'RE JUST BRAGGING!!
WHAT DO WANT FROM ME?!

Sandy Winky

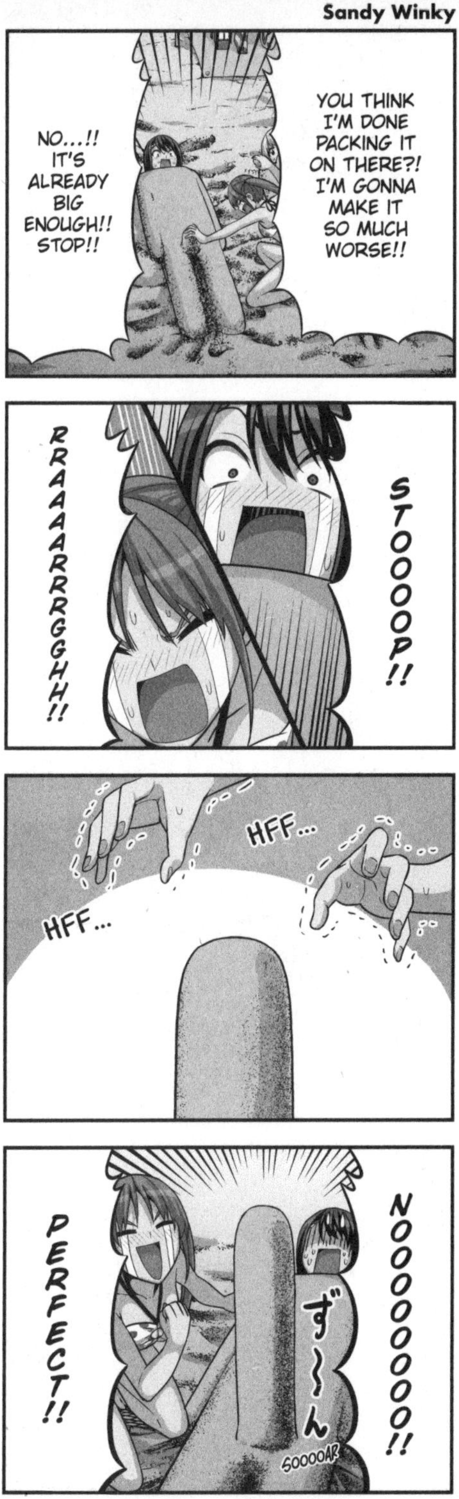
YOU THINK I'M DONE PACKING IT ON THERE?! I'M GONNA MAKE IT SO MUCH WORSE!!
NO...!! IT'S ALREADY BIG ENOUGH!! STOP!!
STOOOOOP!!
RRAAAARRRGGHH!!
HFF...
HFF...
NOOOOOOOOO!!
ず〜ん
SOOOOAR
PERFECT!!

Shame

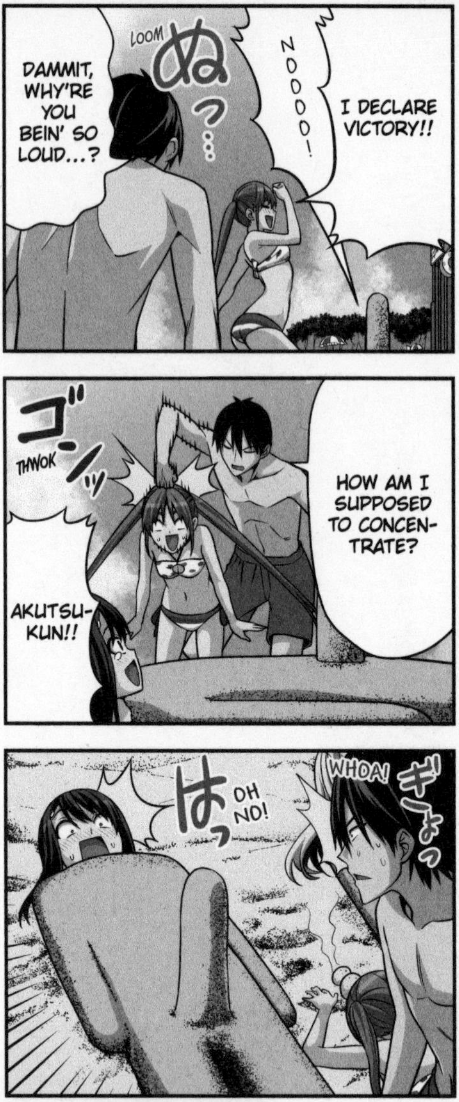
I DECLARE VICTORY!!
NOOOOO!
ぬっ…
LOOM
DAMMIT, WHY'RE YOU BEIN' SO LOUD…?
HOW AM I SUPPOSED TO CONCENTRATE?
ゴンッ
THWOK
AKUTSU-KUN!!
ぎょっ
WHOA!
はっ
OH NO!
DON'T LOOK AT ME!! NOT LIKE THIS!!

The Only Technique He Knows

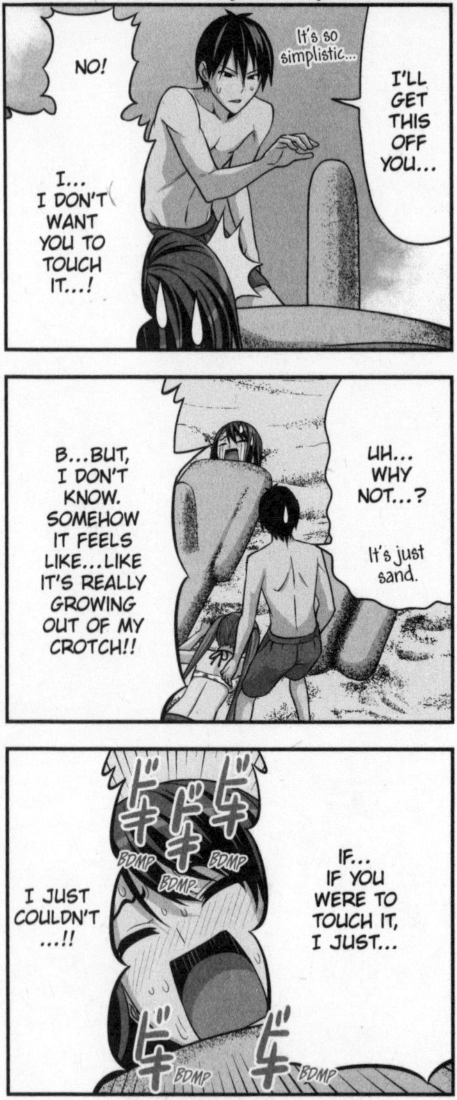
I'LL GET THIS OFF YOU…
It's so simplistic…
NO!
I… I DON'T WANT YOU TO TOUCH IT…!
UH… WHY NOT…?
It's just sand.
B…BUT, I DON'T KNOW. SOMEHOW IT FEELS LIKE…LIKE IT'S REALLY GROWING OUT OF MY CROTCH!!
ドキドキドキ
BDMP BDMP BDMP
IF… IF YOU WERE TO TOUCH IT, I JUST…
I JUST COULDN'T …!!
ドキ BDMP
ドキ BDMP
FINE.
ドカッ
THWAK
AAAAAAAAAAAGGH!!

Final Battle: Sleepy Seaside Village

…I COULD'VE SWORN THEY WERE STAYING AT AN INN AROUND HERE…
スタスタ
TMP TMP
ザッ
SHF
HOLD IT RIGHT THERE, LADY!!
I'M GONNA SAVE EVERY-ONE'S VACATION!!
ばーん
BLAZE
LITTLE UP-START…

To be continued

(Romance makes you put it on, love makes you)

Aho-Girl

\\'ahô͵gərl\\ *Japanese, noun.*
A clueless girl.

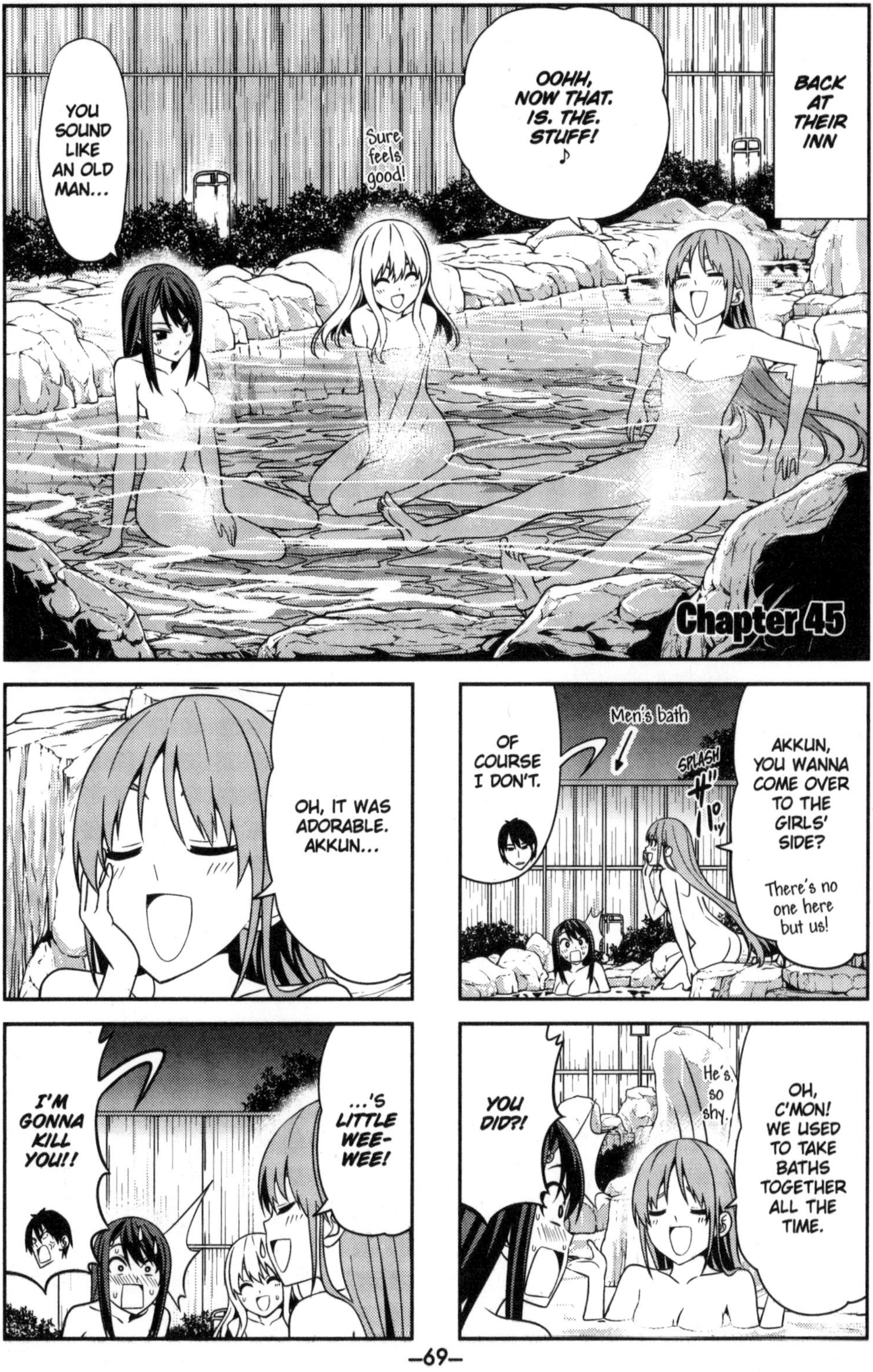
BACK AT THEIR INN
OOHH, NOW THAT. IS. THE. STUFF! ♪
Sure feels good!
YOU SOUND LIKE AN OLD MAN...
Chapter 45
AKKUN, YOU WANNA COME OVER TO THE GIRLS' SIDE?
There's no one here but us!
SPLASH
Men's bath
OF COURSE I DON'T.
OH, IT WAS ADORABLE. AKKUN...
OH, C'MON! WE USED TO TAKE BATHS TOGETHER ALL THE TIME.
He's so shy.
YOU DID?!
...'S LITTLE WEE-WEE!
I'M GONNA KILL YOU!!

It Could Happen

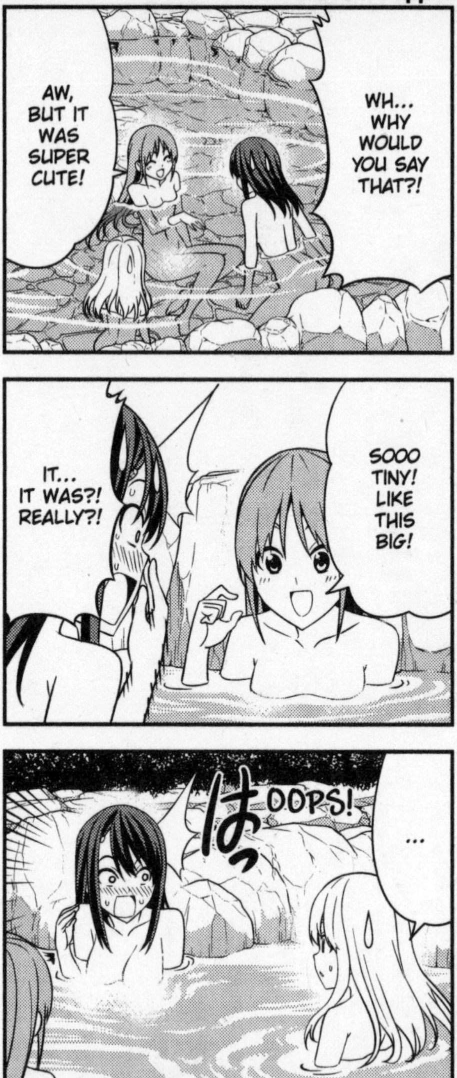
WH... WHY WOULD YOU SAY THAT?!
AW, BUT IT WAS SUPER CUTE!
SOOO TINY! LIKE THIS BIG!
IT... IT WAS?! REALLY?!
...
はっ OOPS!
N... NOT THAT I WANT TO HEAR THAT STUFF, OF COURSE!!
WHY WOULD I?!

Could It Be? They're the Ones Peeping?!

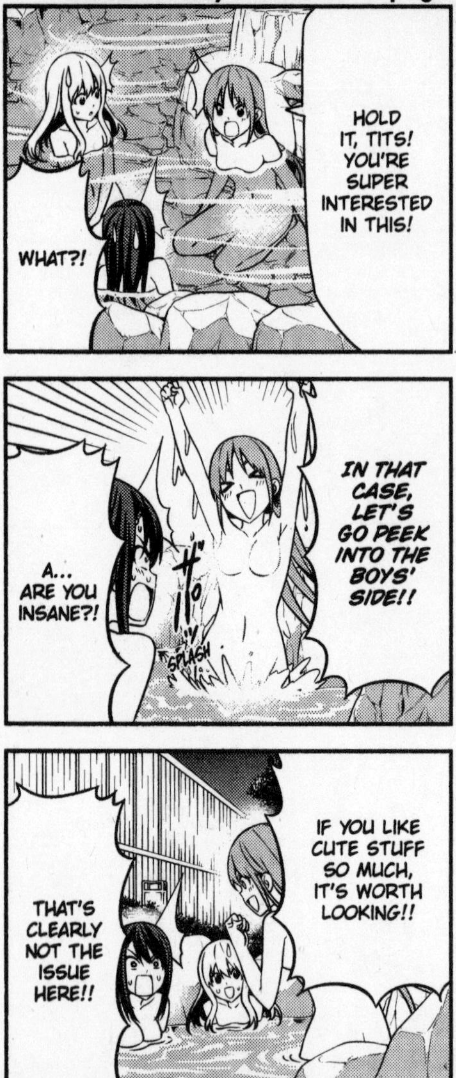
HOLD IT, TITS! YOU'RE SUPER INTERESTED IN THIS!
WHAT?!
IN THAT CASE, LET'S GO PEEK INTO THE BOYS' SIDE!!
A... ARE YOU INSANE?!
SPLASH
IF YOU LIKE CUTE STUFF SO MUCH, IT'S WORTH LOOKING!!
THAT'S CLEARLY NOT THE ISSUE HERE!!
BESIDES, I DOUBT IT'S VERY CUTE ANYMORE!!
HOW DARE YOU!!

The Conversation of Naked Women

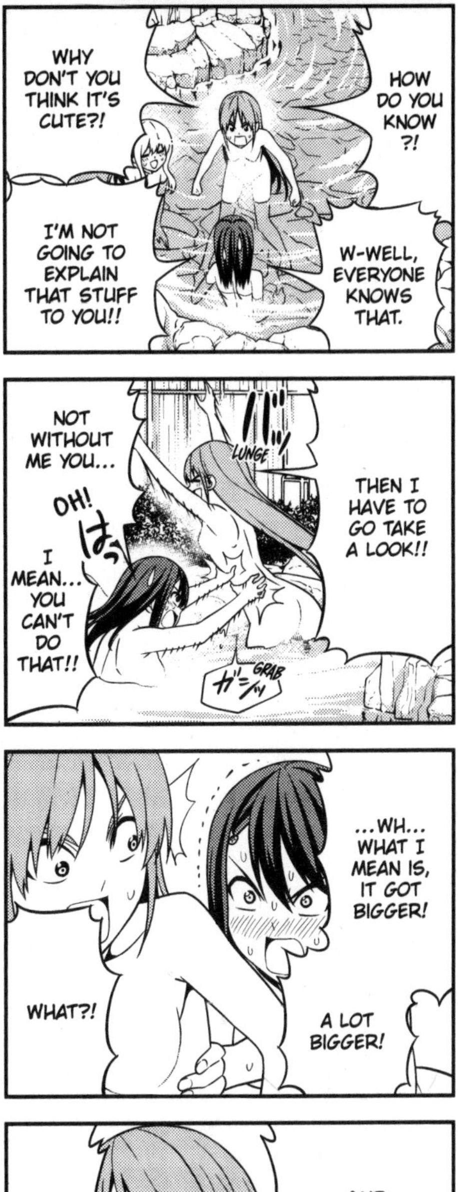
HOW DO YOU KNOW?!
WHY DON'T YOU THINK IT'S CUTE?!
W-WELL, EVERYONE KNOWS THAT.
I'M NOT GOING TO EXPLAIN THAT STUFF TO YOU!!
THEN I HAVE TO GO TAKE A LOOK!!
バッ LUNGE
NOT WITHOUT ME YOU...
はっ OH!
I MEAN... YOU CAN'T DO THAT!!
ガシッ GRAB
...WH... WHAT I MEAN IS, IT GOT BIGGER!
WHAT?!
A LOT BIGGER!
AND AS THEY DEVELOP, THE SHAPE OF THE TIP CHANGES, TOO!!
THAT SOUNDS AWE-SOME!!

Hopeless on Her Own

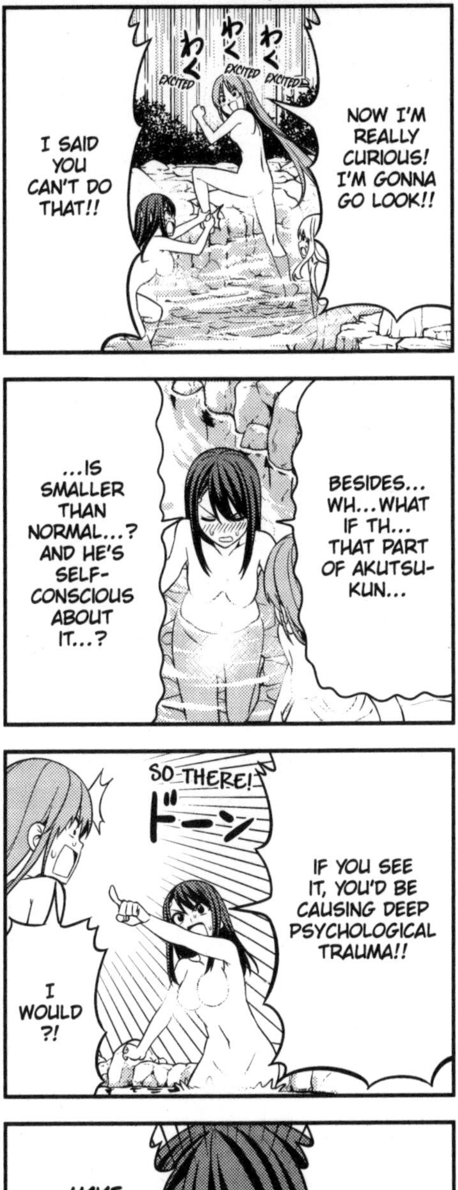
わくわく EXCITED EXCITED EXCITED
NOW I'M REALLY CURIOUS! I'M GONNA GO LOOK!!
I SAID YOU CAN'T DO THAT!!
BESIDES... WH...WHAT IF TH... THAT PART OF AKUTSU-KUN...
...IS SMALLER THAN NORMAL...? AND HE'S SELF-CONSCIOUS ABOUT IT...?
ドーン SO THERE!
IF YOU SEE IT, YOU'D BE CAUSING DEEP PSYCHOLOGICAL TRAUMA!!
I WOULD?!
I'VE HEARD THAT MEN AS PERFECT AS AKUTSU-KUN...
...HAVE INTENSE COMPLEXES ABOUT THAT KIND OF THING!!
WOAH, YOU'RE SO SMART!!

Fill His Heart with Love

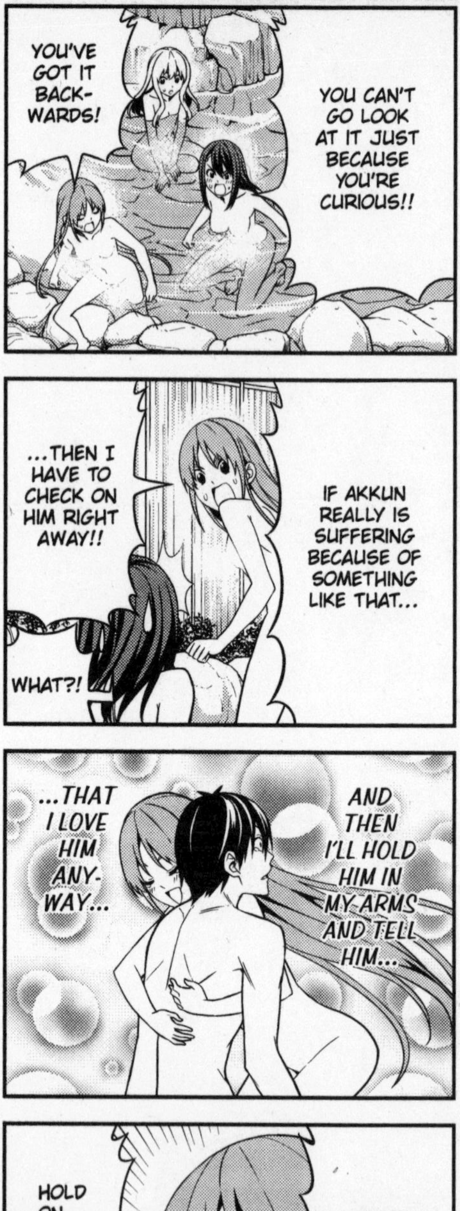
YOU CAN'T GO LOOK AT IT JUST BECAUSE YOU'RE CURIOUS!!
YOU'VE GOT IT BACKWARDS!
IF AKKUN REALLY IS SUFFERING BECAUSE OF SOMETHING LIKE THAT...
...THEN I HAVE TO CHECK ON HIM RIGHT AWAY!!
WHAT?!
AND THEN I'LL HOLD HIM IN MY ARMS AND TELL HIM...
...THAT I LOVE HIM ANYWAY...
AND OUR LOVE WILL BECOME EVEN STRONGER!!
HOLD ON...

Sacrifice

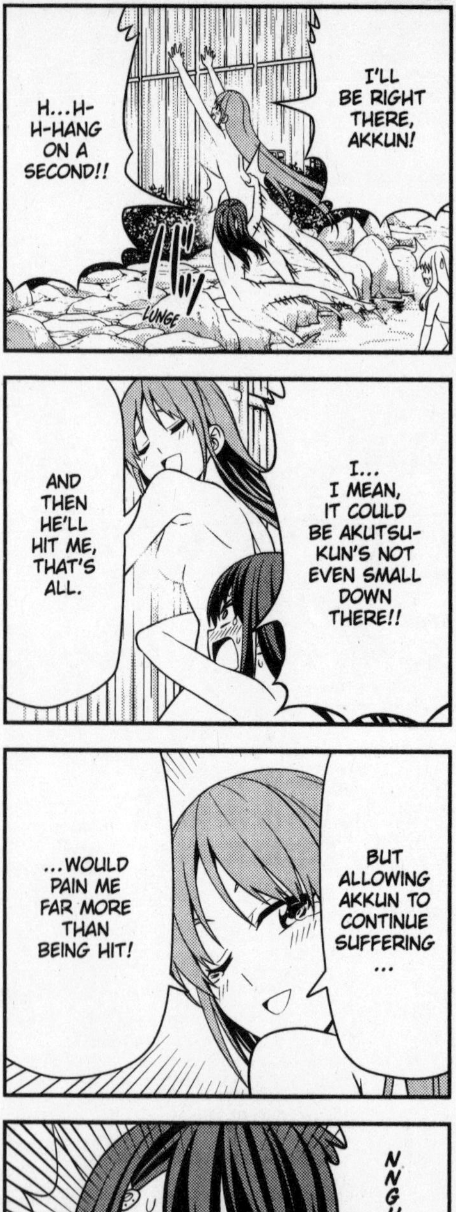
I'LL BE RIGHT THERE, AKKUN!
H...H-H-HANG ON A SECOND!!
LUNGE
I... I MEAN, IT COULD BE AKUTSU-KUN'S NOT EVEN SMALL DOWN THERE!!
AND THEN HE'LL HIT ME, THAT'S ALL.
BUT ALLOWING AKKUN TO CONTINUE SUFFERING...
...WOULD PAIN ME FAR MORE THAN BEING HIT!
NNGH...GHRRRGGHH!!

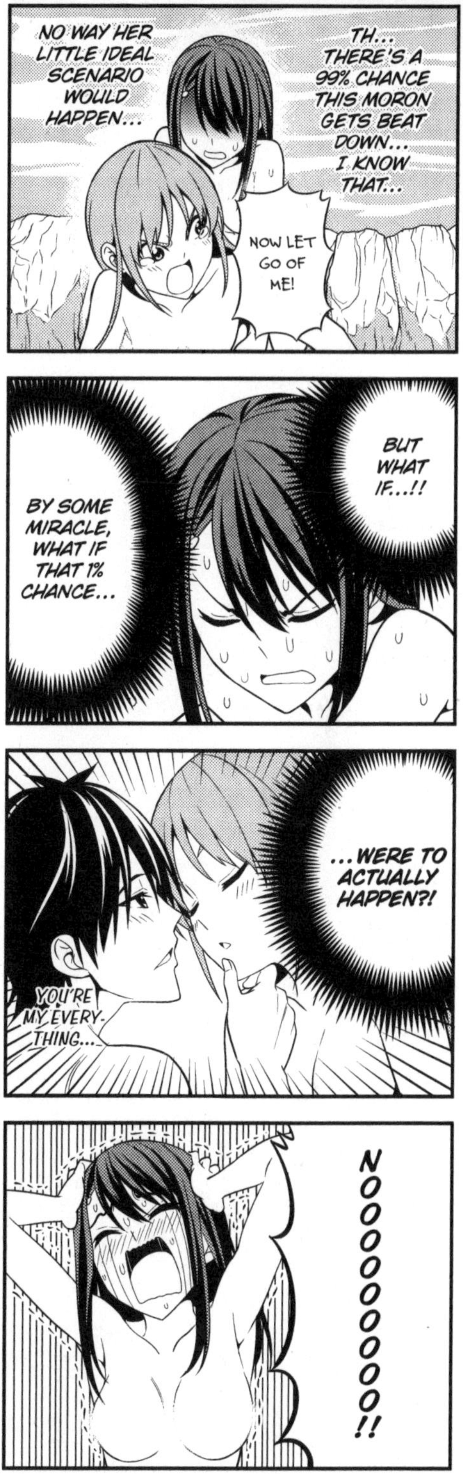
TH... THERE'S A 99% CHANCE THIS MORON GETS BEAT DOWN... I KNOW THAT...
NO WAY HER LITTLE IDEAL SCENARIO WOULD HAPPEN...
NOW LET GO OF ME!
BUT WHAT IF...!!
BY SOME MIRACLE, WHAT IF THAT 1% CHANCE...
...WERE TO ACTUALLY HAPPEN?!
YOU'RE MY EVERYTHING...
NOOOOOOOOO!!

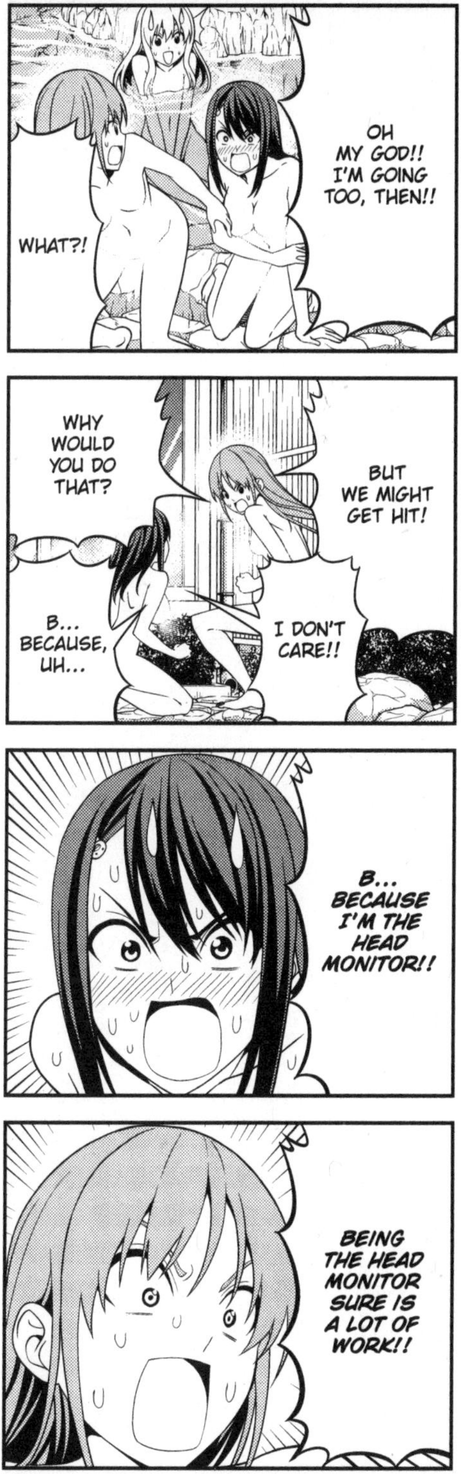
OH MY GOD!! I'M GOING TOO, THEN!!
WHAT?!
BUT WE MIGHT GET HIT!
I DON'T CARE!!
WHY WOULD YOU DO THAT?
B... BECAUSE, UH...
B... BECAUSE I'M THE HEAD MONITOR!!
BEING THE HEAD MONITOR SURE IS A LOT OF WORK!!

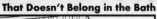

That Doesn't Belong in the Bath

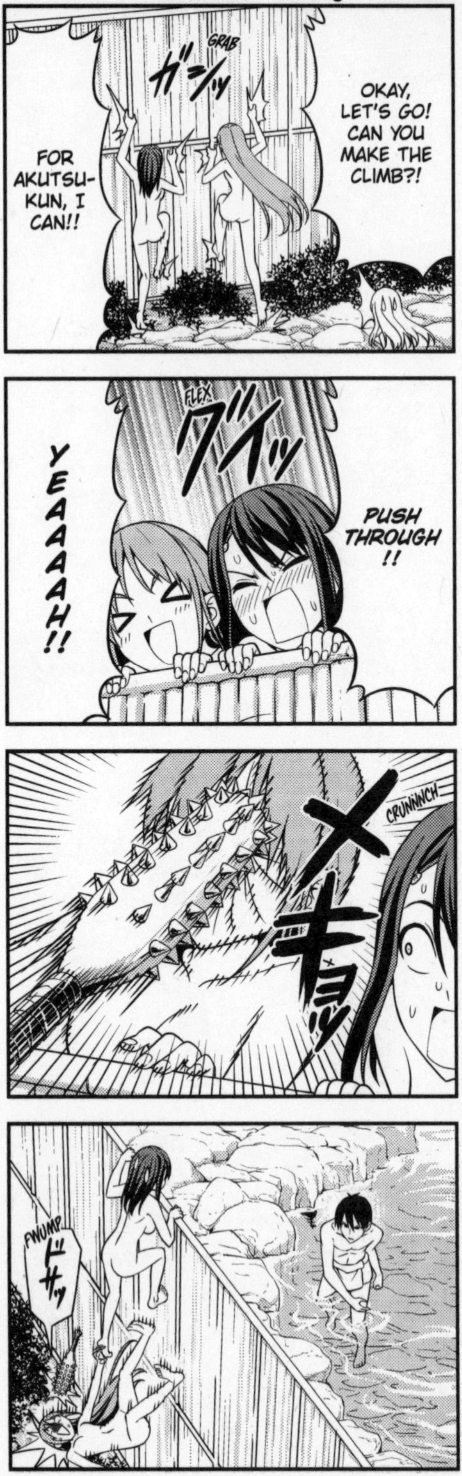
GRAB
OKAY, LET'S GO! CAN YOU MAKE THE CLIMB?!
FOR AKUTSU-KUN, I CAN!!
FLEX
PUSH THROUGH!!
YEAAAAAH!!
CRUNNNCH
FWUMP

Happy Ending

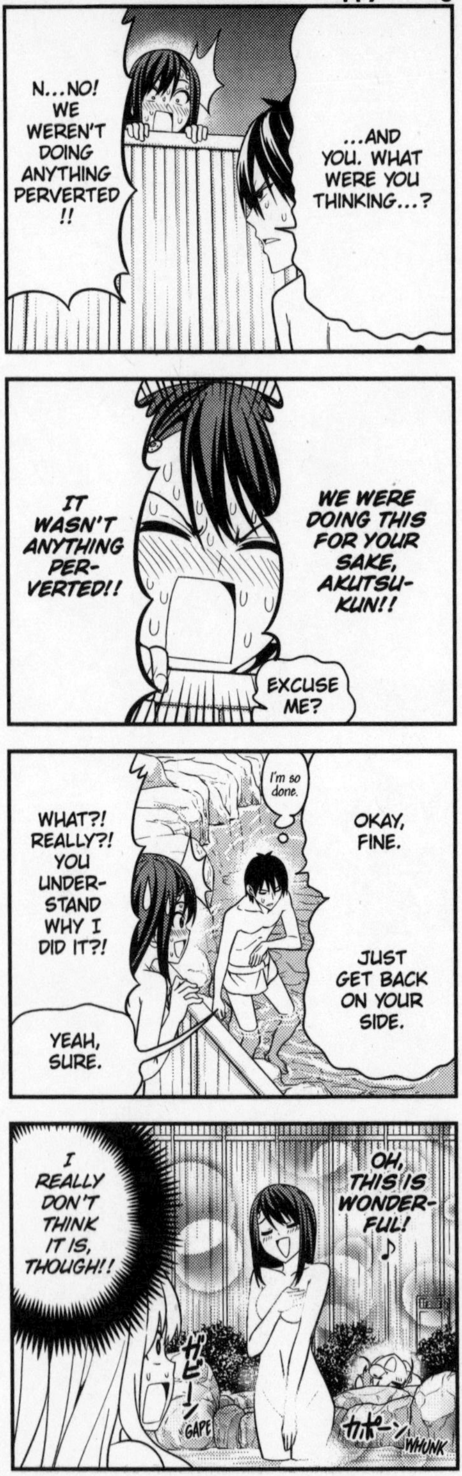
...AND YOU. WHAT WERE YOU THINKING...?
N...NO! WE WEREN'T DOING ANYTHING PERVERTED!!
WE WERE DOING THIS FOR YOUR SAKE, AKUTSU-KUN!!
IT WASN'T ANYTHING PER-VERTED!!
EXCUSE ME?
I'm so done.
OKAY, FINE.
JUST GET BACK ON YOUR SIDE.
WHAT?! REALLY?! YOU UNDERSTAND WHY I DID IT?!
YEAH, SURE.
OH, THIS IS WONDER-FUL! ♪
WHUNK
GAPE
I REALLY DON'T THINK IT IS, THOUGH!!

Part Two

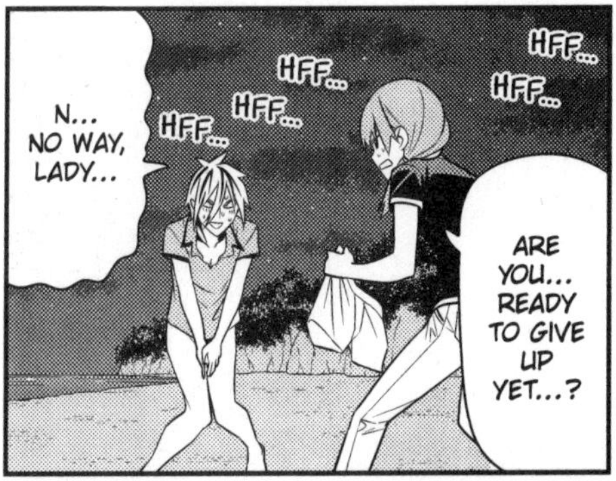
ARE YOU... READY TO GIVE UP YET...?
HFF...
HFF...
HFF...
HFF...
HFF...
HFF...
N... NO WAY, LADY...

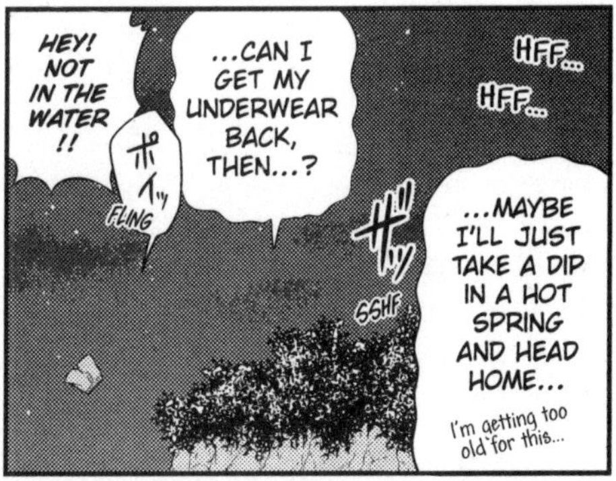
HFF...
HFF...
...MAYBE I'LL JUST TAKE A DIP IN A HOT SPRING AND HEAD HOME...
I'm getting too old for this...
ザッ
SSHF
...CAN I GET MY UNDERWEAR BACK, THEN...?
ポイッ
FLING
HEY! NOT IN THE WATER!!

(Standing in opposition to the mysterious white light, I am)

Aho-Girl

\\'ahô͵gərl\ *Japanese, noun.*
A clueless girl.

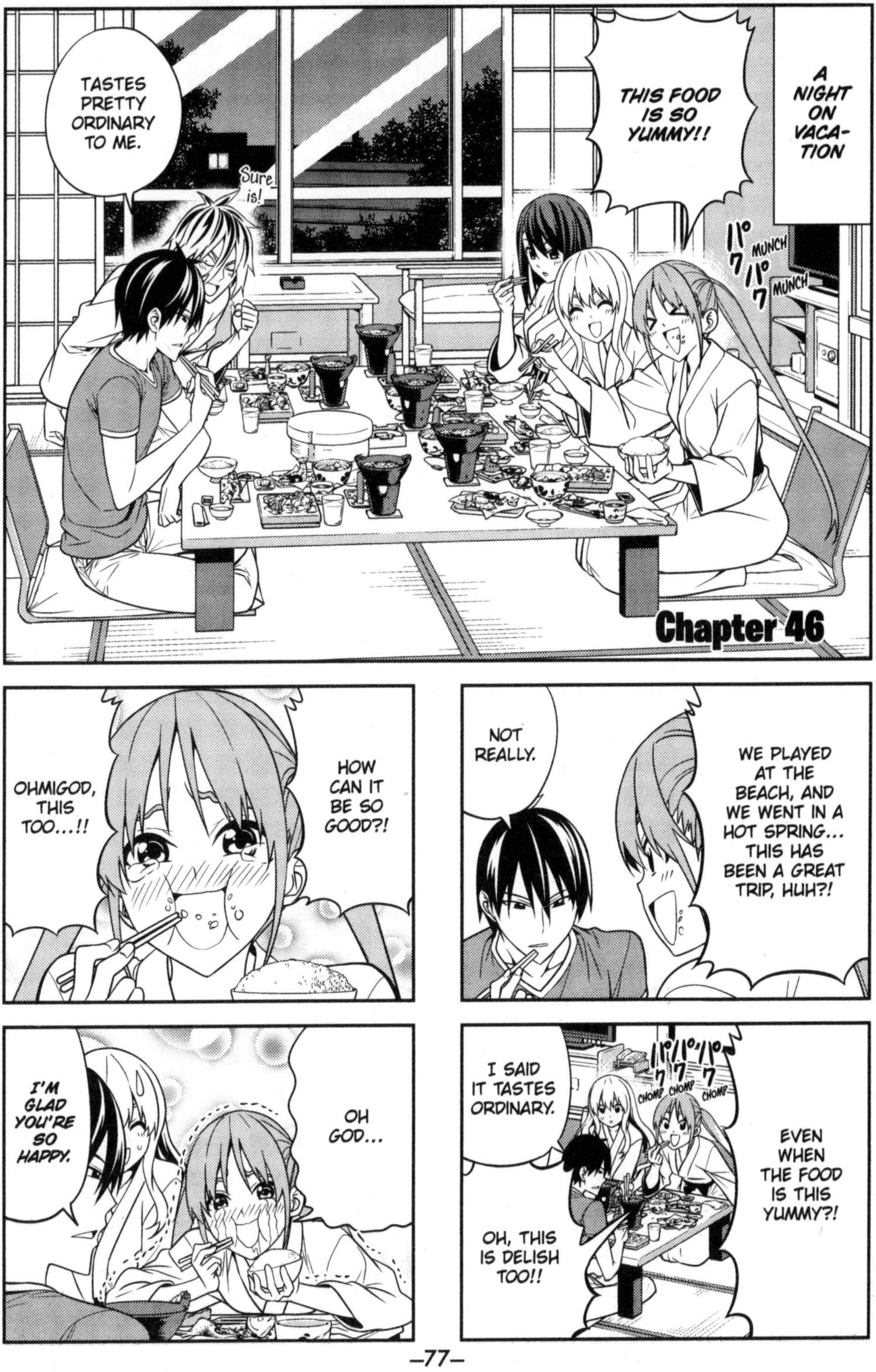

A NIGHT ON VACATION
パク MUNCH
パク MUNCH
THIS FOOD IS SO YUMMY!!
Sure is!
TASTES PRETTY ORDINARY TO ME.
Chapter 46
WE PLAYED AT THE BEACH, AND WE WENT IN A HOT SPRING... THIS HAS BEEN A GREAT TRIP, HUH?!
NOT REALLY.
HOW CAN IT BE SO GOOD?!
OHMIGOD, THIS TOO...!!
EVEN WHEN THE FOOD IS THIS YUMMY?!
パク CHOMP
パク CHOMP
パク CHOMP
I SAID IT TASTES ORDINARY.
OH, THIS IS DELISH TOO!!
OH GOD...
I'M GLAD YOU'RE SO HAPPY.

On Different Wavelengths

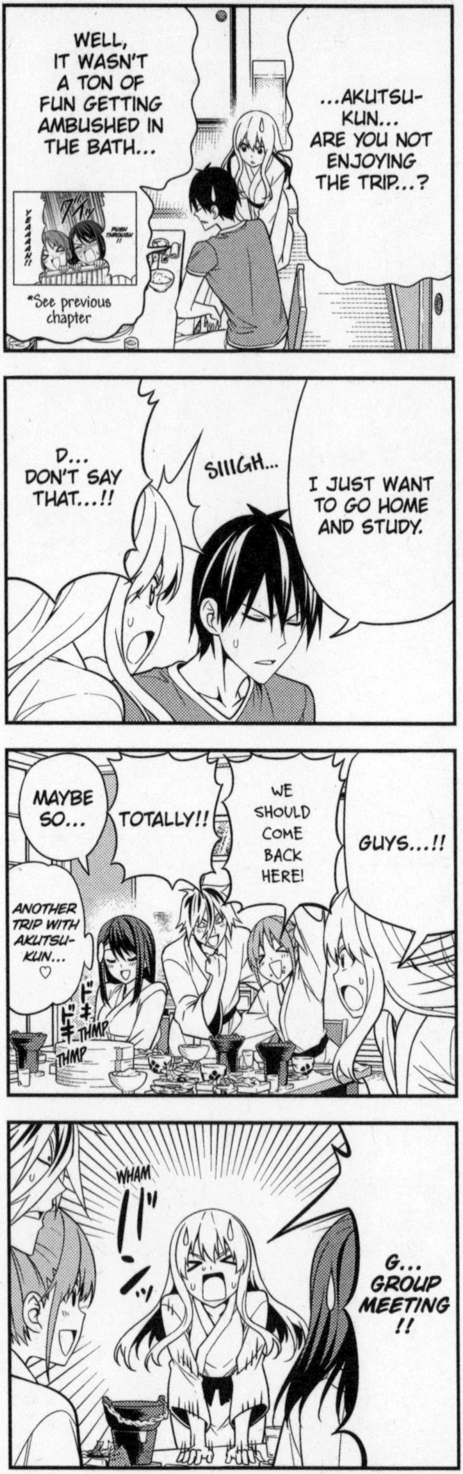
...AKUTSU-KUN... ARE YOU NOT ENJOYING THE TRIP...?
WELL, IT WASN'T A TON OF FUN GETTING AMBUSHED IN THE BATH...
PUSH THROUGH!!
YEAAAAH!!
*See previous chapter
I JUST WANT TO GO HOME AND STUDY.
SIIIGH...
D... DON'T SAY THAT...!!
GUYS...!!
WE SHOULD COME BACK HERE!
TOTALLY!!
MAYBE SO...
ANOTHER TRIP WITH AKUTSU-KUN... ♡
THMP
THMP
WHAM
G... GROUP MEETING!!

Sex Appeal Isn't Going to Work

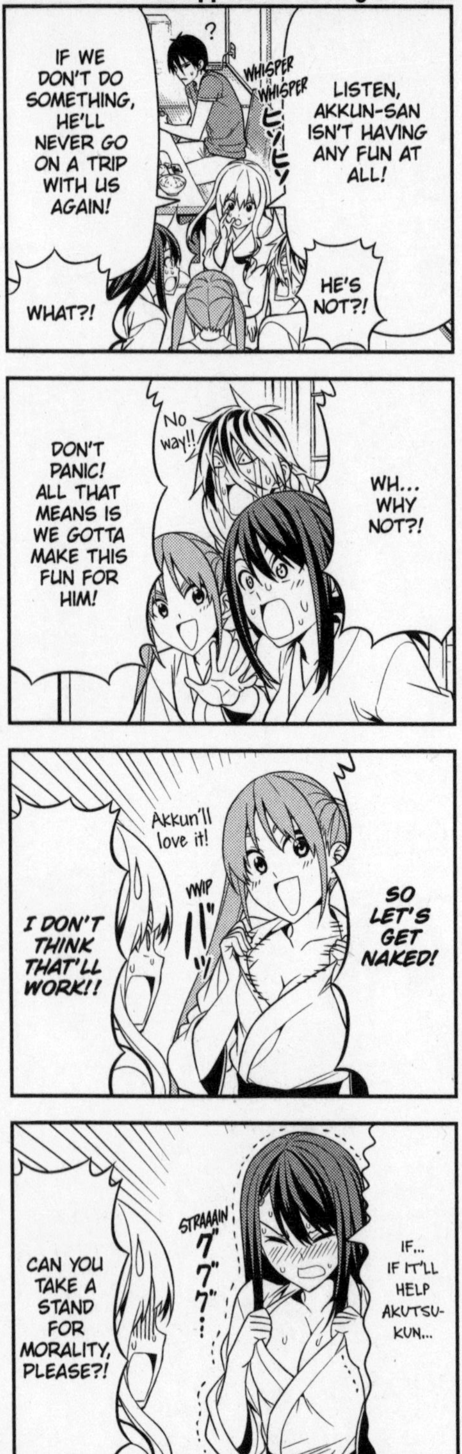
LISTEN, AKKUN-SAN ISN'T HAVING ANY FUN AT ALL!
WHISPER
WHISPER
?
IF WE DON'T DO SOMETHING, HE'LL NEVER GO ON A TRIP WITH US AGAIN!
HE'S NOT?!
WHAT?!
WH... WHY NOT?!
No way!!
DON'T PANIC! ALL THAT MEANS IS WE GOTTA MAKE THIS FUN FOR HIM!
SO LET'S GET NAKED!
Akkun'll love it!
VWIP
I DON'T THINK THAT'LL WORK!!
IF... IF IT'LL HELP AKUTSU-KUN...
STRAAAIN
CAN YOU TAKE A STAND FOR MORALITY, PLEASE?!

Where Did You Learn to Do That, Ryuichi?

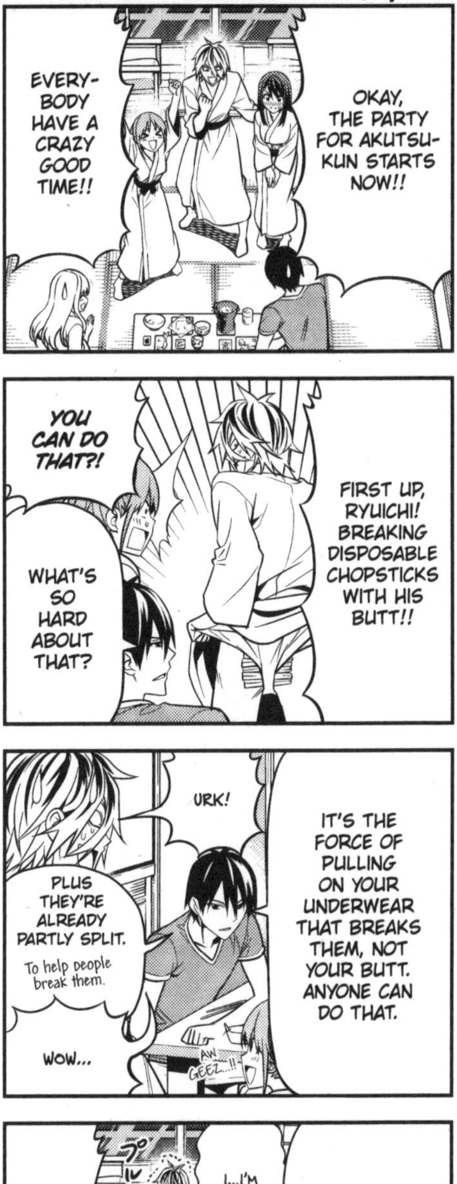
OKAY, THE PARTY FOR AKUTSU-KUN STARTS NOW!!
EVERYBODY HAVE A CRAZY GOOD TIME!!
FIRST UP, RYUICHI! BREAKING DISPOSABLE CHOPSTICKS WITH HIS BUTT!!
YOU CAN DO THAT?!
WHAT'S SO HARD ABOUT THAT?
IT'S THE FORCE OF PULLING ON YOUR UNDERWEAR THAT BREAKS THEM, NOT YOUR BUTT. ANYONE CAN DO THAT.
URK!
PLUS THEY'RE ALREADY PARTLY SPLIT.
To help people break them.
WOW...
AW GEEZ...!!
DID YOU REALLY THINK SUCH A PATHETIC EFFORT WOULD ENTERTAIN ME?
I...I'M SORRY.
プル TREMBLE
N... NEXT! LET'S GO!!
プル TREMBLE

She's Even Got the Smug Look

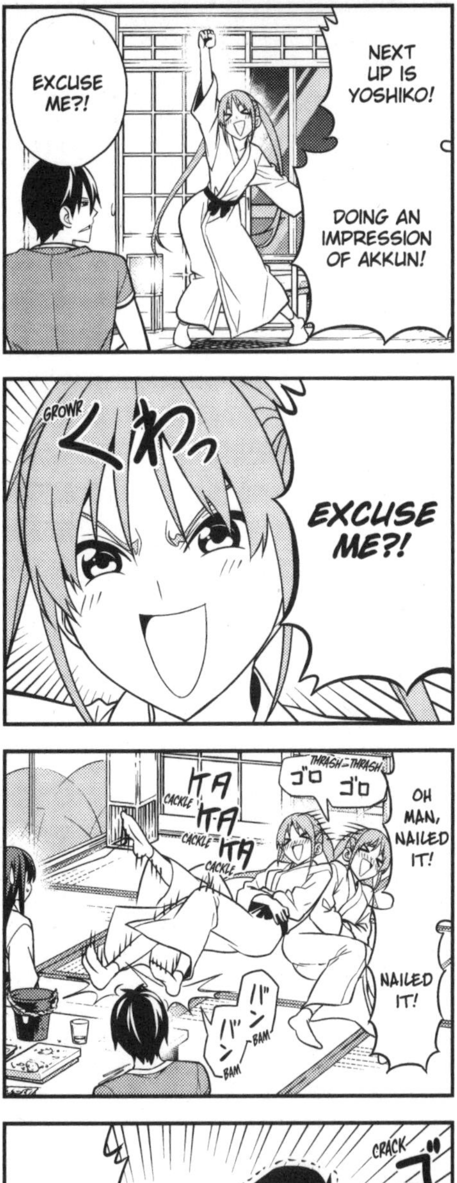
NEXT UP IS YOSHIKO!
DOING AN IMPRESSION OF AKKUN!
EXCUSE ME?!
EXCUSE ME?!
くわっ GROWR
OH MAN, NAILED IT!
ゴロ ゴロ THRASH-THRASH
KA KA KA CACKLE CACKLE CACKLE
NAILED IT!
バン バン BAM BAM
ゴキゴキゴキッ CRACK CRACK CRACK
GWAAAGH!!

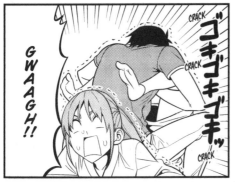

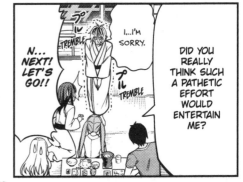

She's Got a Bathing Suit on

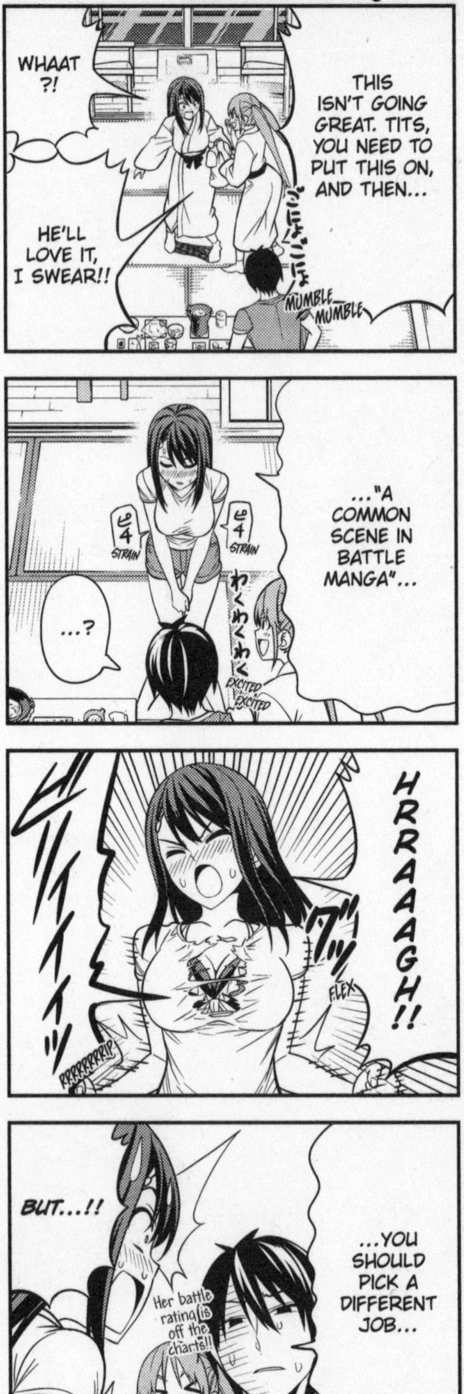
THIS ISN'T GOING GREAT. TITS, YOU NEED TO PUT THIS ON, AND THEN...
WHAAT ?!
HE'LL LOVE IT, I SWEAR!!
MUMBLE MUMBLE
..."A COMMON SCENE IN BATTLE MANGA"...
ピク STRAIN
ピク STRAIN
わくわくわくわく EXCITED EXCITED
...?
HRRAAAGH!!
FLEX
RRRRRRRIP
...YOU SHOULD PICK A DIFFERENT JOB...
BUT...!!
Her battle rating is off the charts!!

Brick Wall

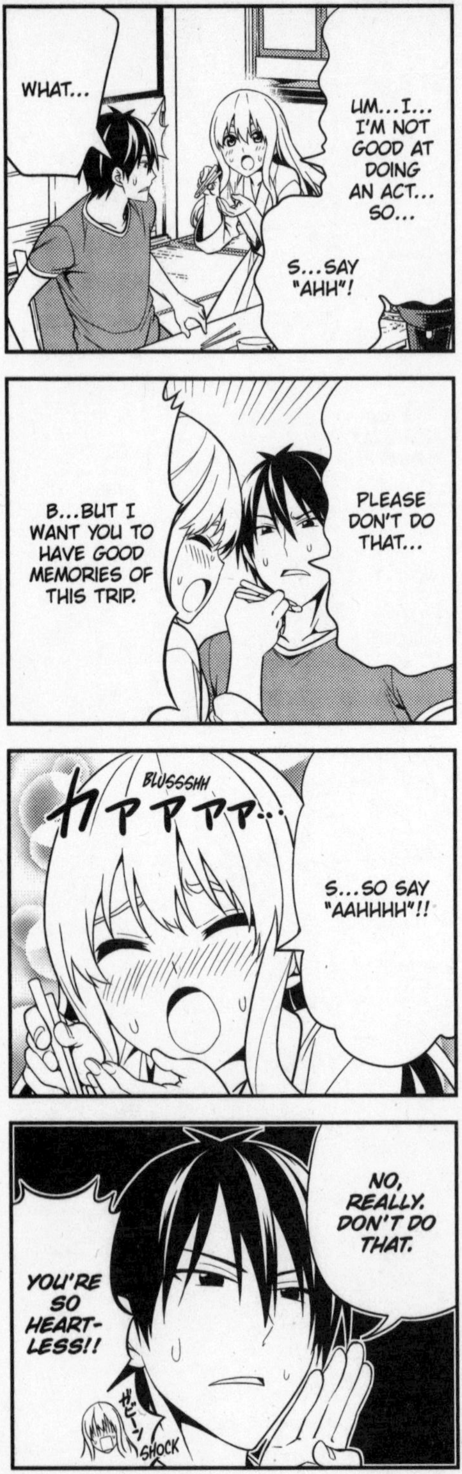
UM...I... I'M NOT GOOD AT DOING AN ACT... SO...
S...SAY "AHH"!
WHAT...
PLEASE DON'T DO THAT...
B...BUT I WANT YOU TO HAVE GOOD MEMORIES OF THIS TRIP.
S...SO SAY "AAHHHH"!!
BLUSSSHH
カァァァァ...
NO, REALLY. DON'T DO THAT.
YOU'RE SO HEARTLESS!!
SHOCK

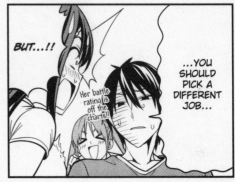

Sayaka Never Gives up

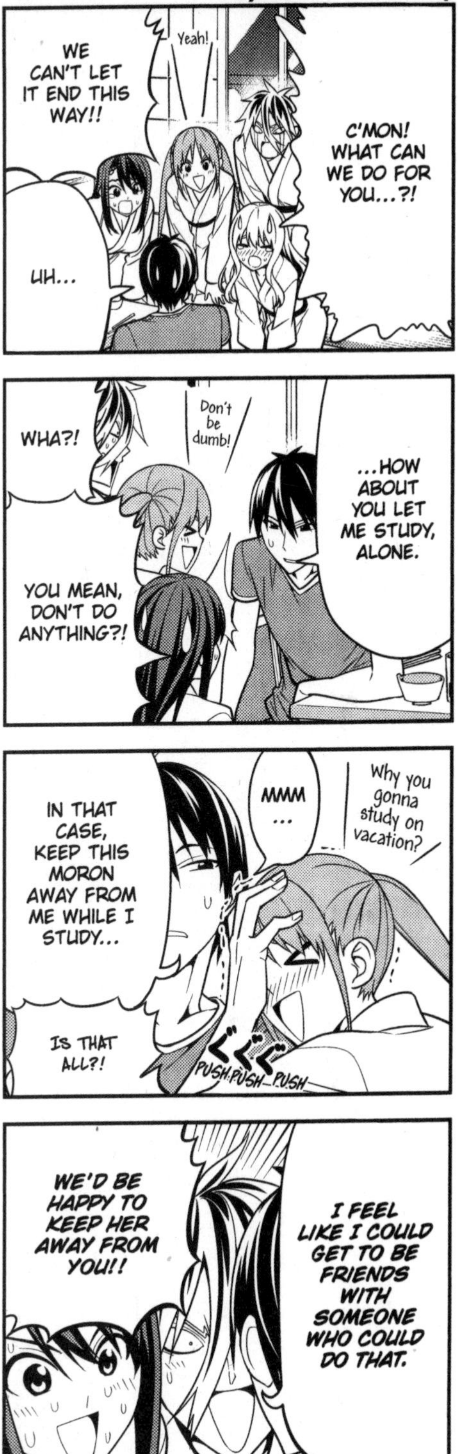
WE CAN'T LET IT END THIS WAY!!
Yeah!
C'MON! WHAT CAN WE DO FOR YOU...?!
UH...
...HOW ABOUT YOU LET ME STUDY, ALONE.
WHA?!
Don't be dumb!
YOU MEAN, DON'T DO ANYTHING?!
Why you gonna study on vacation?
MMM ...
IN THAT CASE, KEEP THIS MORON AWAY FROM ME WHILE I STUDY...
IS THAT ALL?!
ぐぐぐ
PUSH PUSH PUSH
I FEEL LIKE I COULD GET TO BE FRIENDS WITH SOMEONE WHO COULD DO THAT.
WE'D BE HAPPY TO KEEP HER AWAY FROM YOU!!

Death

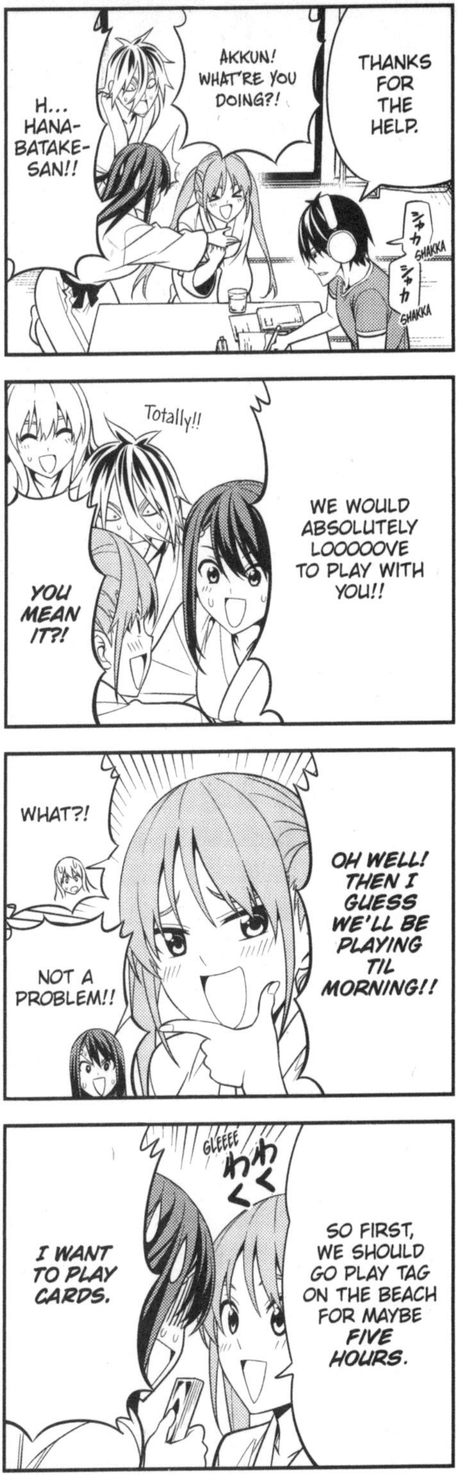
THANKS FOR THE HELP.
AKKUN! WHAT'RE YOU DOING?!
H... HANA-BATAKE-SAN!!
シャカ SHAKKA
シャカ SHAKKA
WE WOULD ABSOLUTELY LOOOOOVE TO PLAY WITH YOU!!
Totally!!
YOU MEAN IT?!
OH WELL! THEN I GUESS WE'LL BE PLAYING TIL MORNING!!
WHAT?!
NOT A PROBLEM!!
GLEEEE
わくわく
SO FIRST, WE SHOULD GO PLAY TAG ON THE BEACH FOR MAYBE FIVE HOURS.
I WANT TO PLAY CARDS.

How'd Your Night Go?

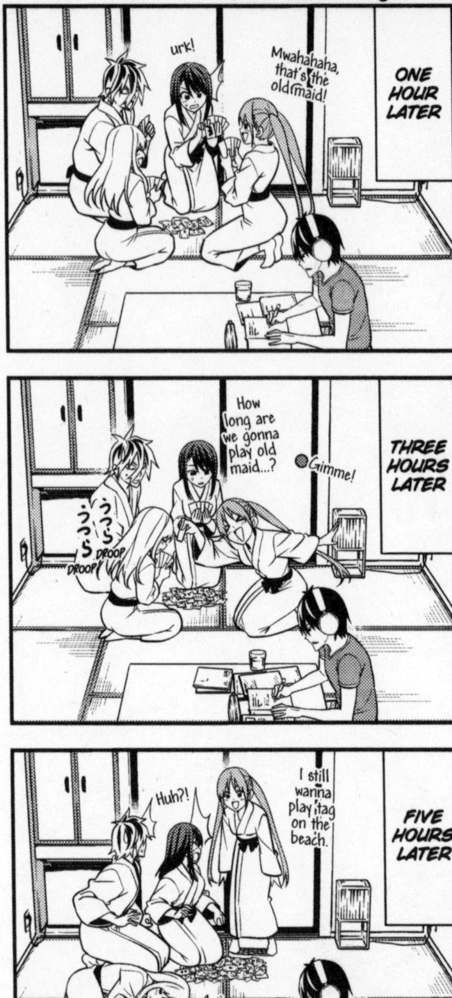
ONE HOUR LATER
Mwahahaha, that's the old maid!
urk!
THREE HOURS LATER
Gimme!
How long are we gonna play old maid...?
うつら うつら
DROOP DROOP
FIVE HOURS LATER
I still wanna play tag on the beach.
Huh?!
zzz
EIGHT HOURS LATER
That was so much fun...!
G... gonna die...
Is that the time...?
Mmm...
zzz

Farewell, Inn. I Return to My Faraway Home.

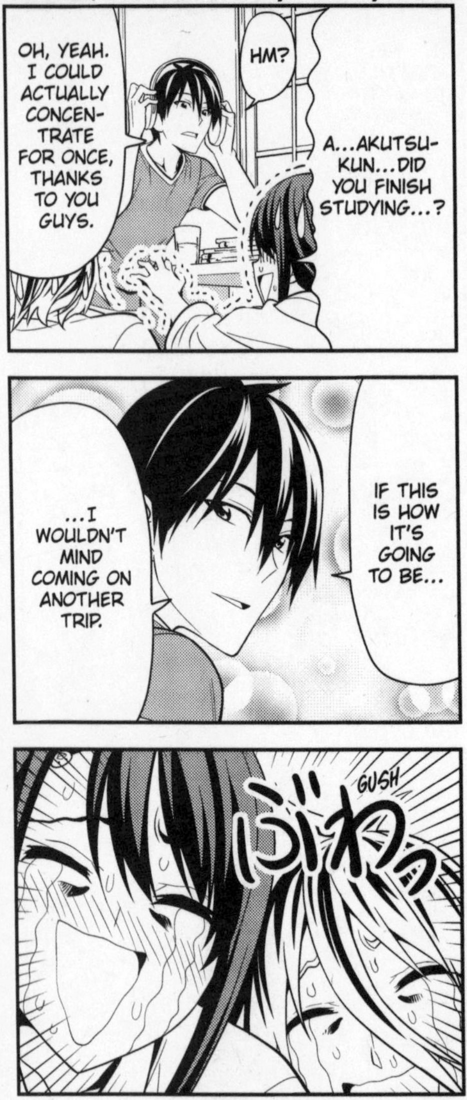
HM?
A...AKUTSU-KUN...DID YOU FINISH STUDYING...?
OH, YEAH. I COULD ACTUALLY CONCENTRATE FOR ONCE, THANKS TO YOU GUYS.
IF THIS IS HOW IT'S GOING TO BE...
...I WOULDN'T MIND COMING ON ANOTHER TRIP.
ぶわっ
GUSH
SO NEXT YEAR, WE CAN DO A TWELVE-HOUR ENDURANCE SESSION OF TAG!!
HOLD ON!!
DON'T PUSH IT.
ゴスッ
WHAK
WAUGH!

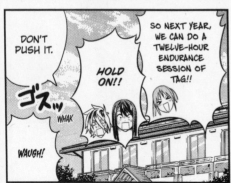

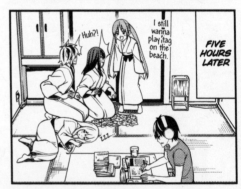

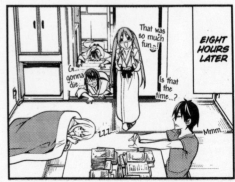

She Never Misses It

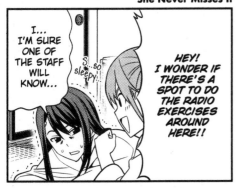

HEY! I WONDER IF THERE'S A SPOT TO DO THE RADIO EXERCISES AROUND HERE!!
S...so sleepy...
I... I'M SURE ONE OF THE STAFF WILL KNOW...
ARM AND LEG EXERCISES, LET'S GO!
YAAAY!!
...Whozzat?
THERE'S GOTTA BE A LIMIT, EVEN ON HER ENERGY.

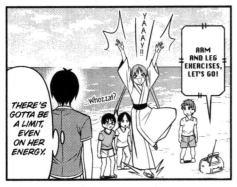

Aho-Girl

\\'ahô͵gərl\\ *Japanese, noun.*
A clueless girl.

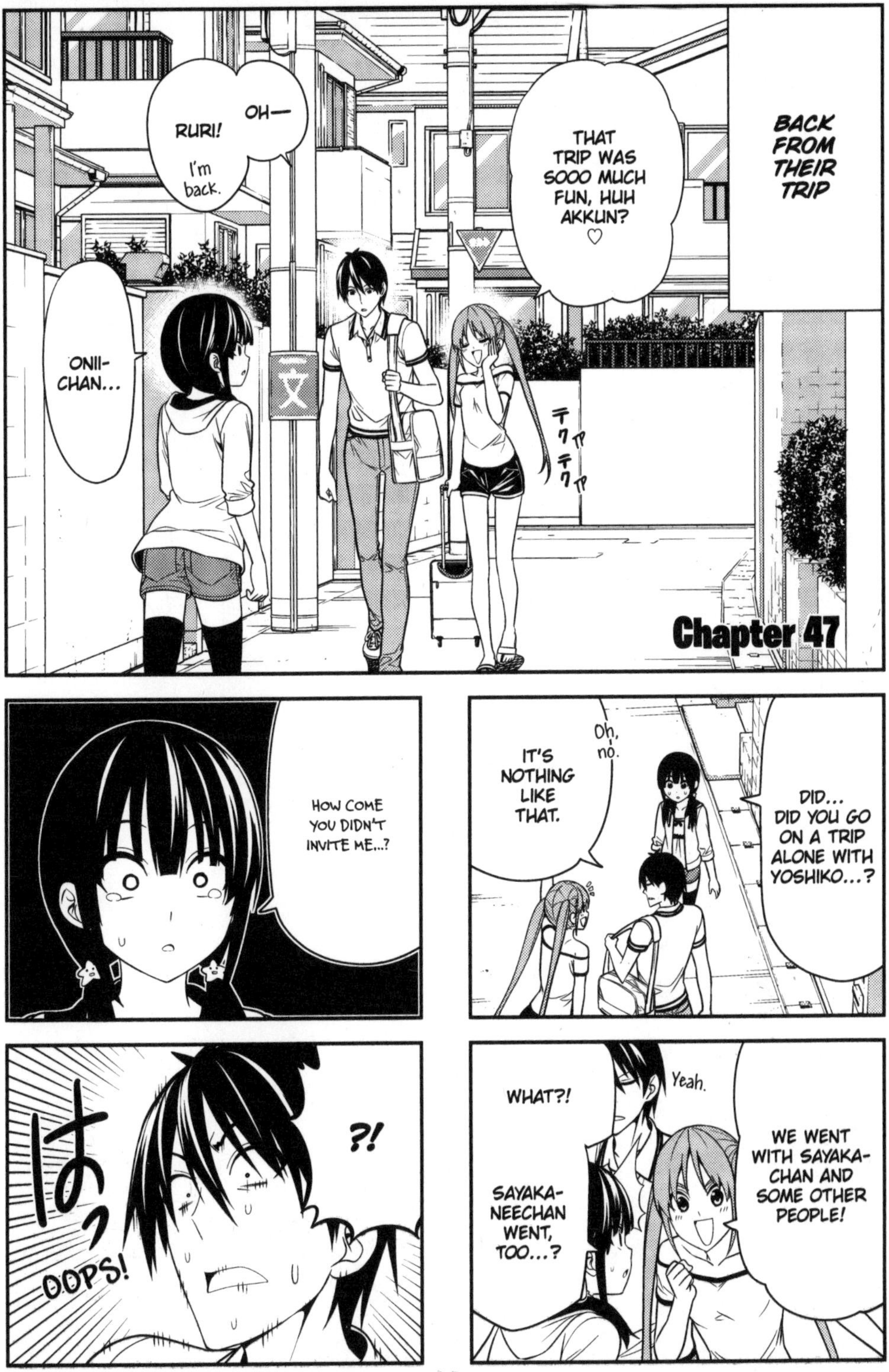

BACK FROM THEIR TRIP
THAT TRIP WAS SOOO MUCH FUN, HUH AKKUN? ♡
テクテク TP TP
OH— RURI! I'm back.
ONII-CHAN…
Chapter 47
DID… DID YOU GO ON A TRIP ALONE WITH YOSHIKO…?
Oh, no. IT'S NOTHING LIKE THAT.
HOW COME YOU DIDN'T INVITE ME…?
WE WENT WITH SAYAKA-CHAN AND SOME OTHER PEOPLE!
Yeah.
WHAT?!
SAYAKA-NEECHAN WENT, TOO…?
?!
はっ OOPS!

My Summer Vacation

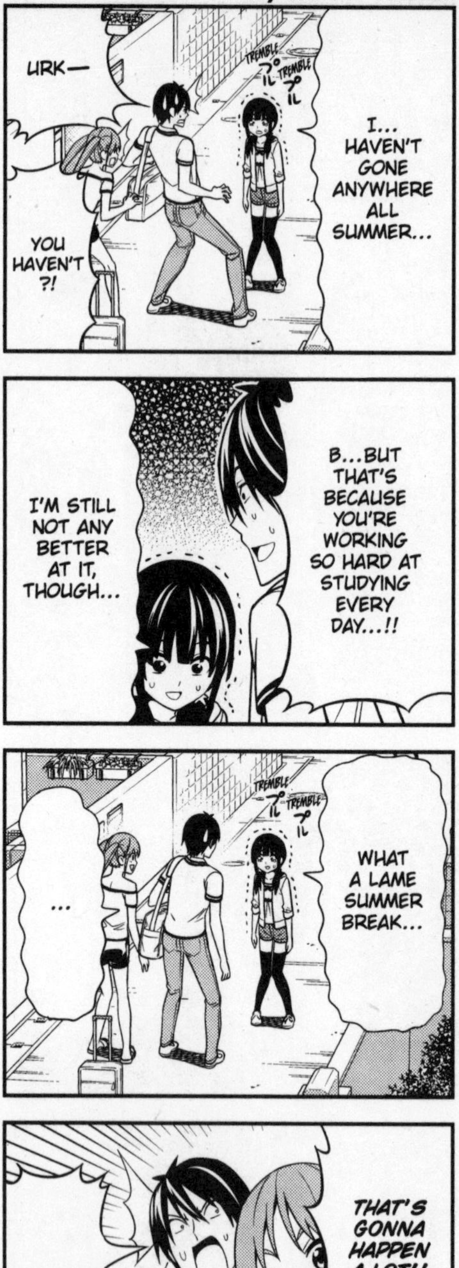
TREMBLE
TREMBLE
I... HAVEN'T GONE ANYWHERE ALL SUMMER...
URK—
YOU HAVEN'T ?!
B...BUT THAT'S BECAUSE YOU'RE WORKING SO HARD AT STUDYING EVERY DAY...!!
I'M STILL NOT ANY BETTER AT IT, THOUGH...
TREMBLE
TREMBLE
WHAT A LAME SUMMER BREAK...
...
THAT'S GONNA HAPPEN A LOT!!
THAT'S NOT TRUE!!

That Happens a Lot

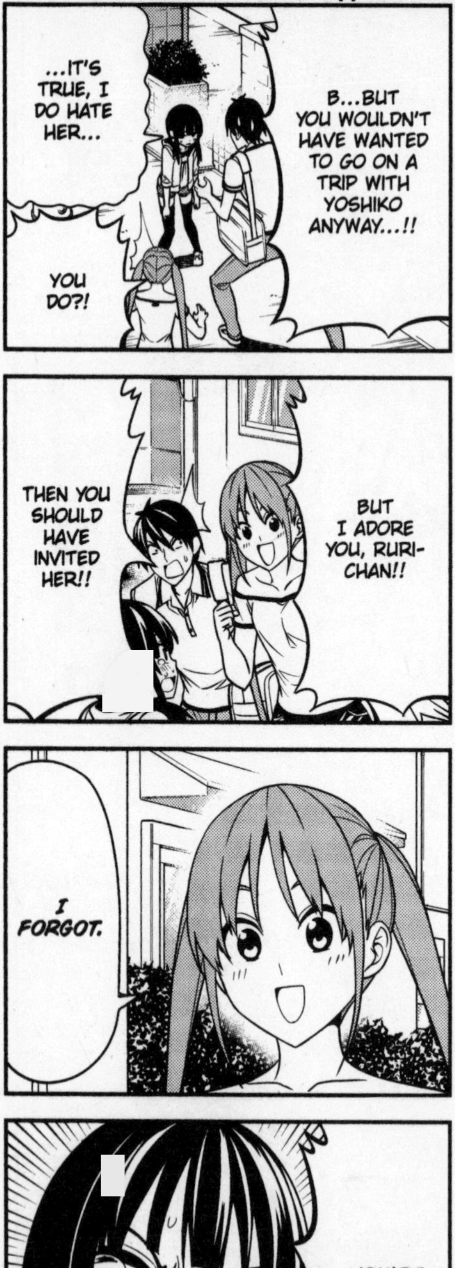
B...BUT YOU WOULDN'T HAVE WANTED TO GO ON A TRIP WITH YOSHIKO ANYWAY...!!
...IT'S TRUE, I DO HATE HER...
YOU DO?!
BUT I ADORE YOU, RURI-CHAN!!
THEN YOU SHOULD HAVE INVITED HER!!
I FORGOT.
YOU'RE SUCH AN AIRHEAD!!

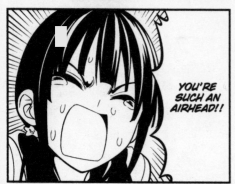

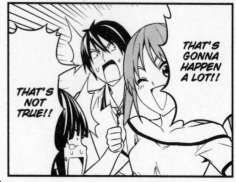

I Cannot Tell a Lie

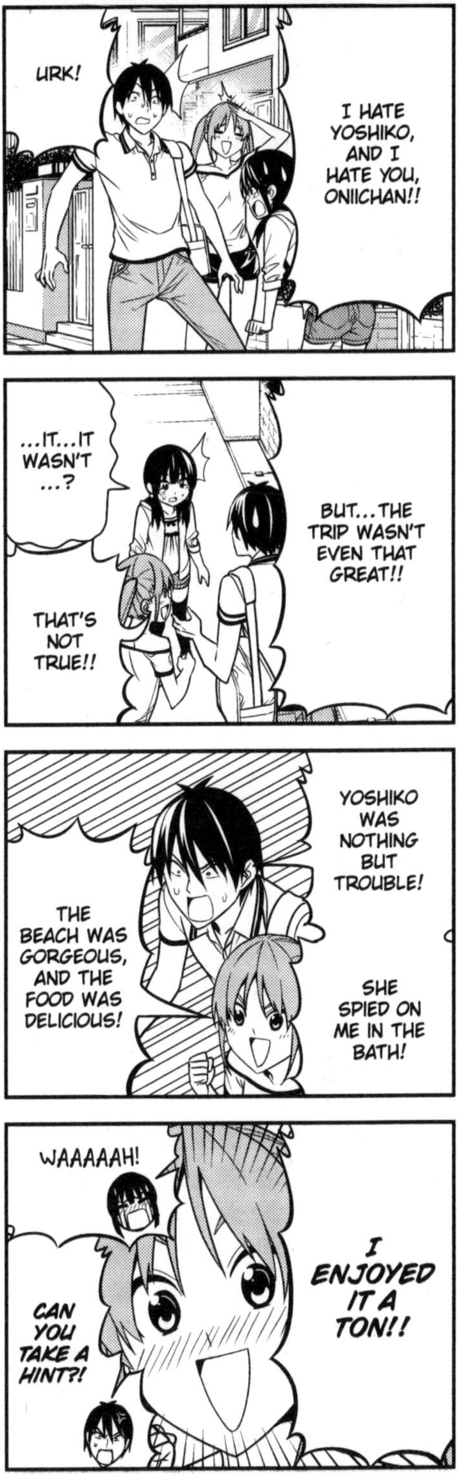
I HATE YOSHIKO, AND I HATE YOU, ONIICHAN!!
URK!
BUT... THE TRIP WASN'T EVEN THAT GREAT!!
...IT...IT WASN'T ...?
THAT'S NOT TRUE!!
YOSHIKO WAS NOTHING BUT TROUBLE!
THE BEACH WAS GORGEOUS, AND THE FOOD WAS DELICIOUS!
SHE SPIED ON ME IN THE BATH!
I ENJOYED IT A TON!!
WAAAAAH!
CAN YOU TAKE A HINT?!

Nothing We Can Do

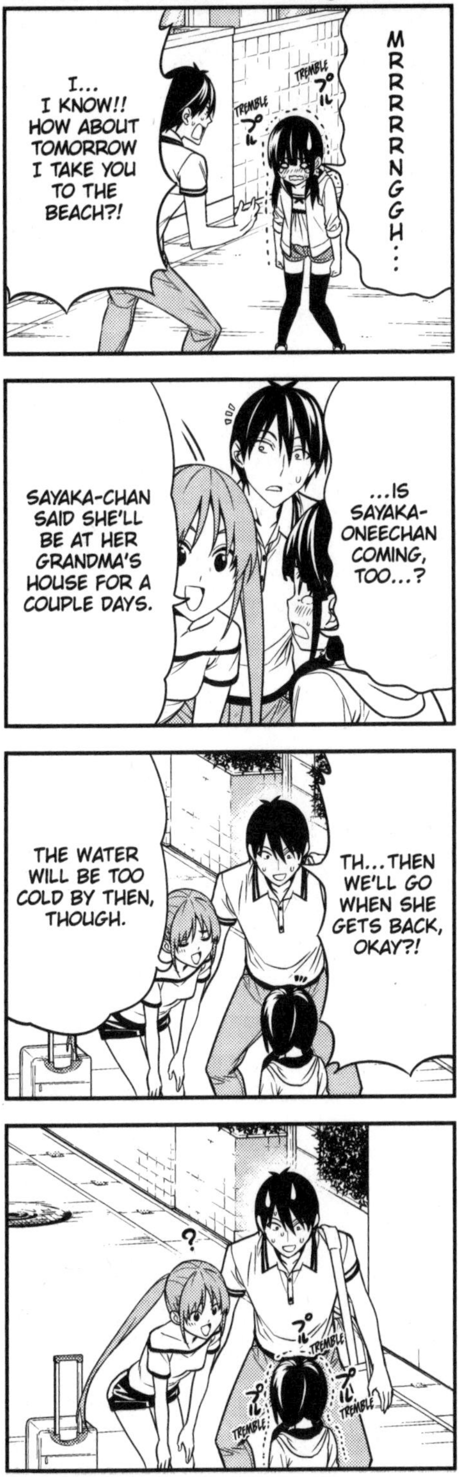
MRRRRNGGH...
TREMBLE
TREMBLE
I... I KNOW!! HOW ABOUT TOMORROW I TAKE YOU TO THE BEACH?!
...IS SAYAKA-ONEECHAN COMING, TOO...?
SAYAKA-CHAN SAID SHE'LL BE AT HER GRANDMA'S HOUSE FOR A COUPLE DAYS.
TH...THEN WE'LL GO WHEN SHE GETS BACK, OKAY?!
THE WATER WILL BE TOO COLD BY THEN, THOUGH.
TREMBLE
TREMBLE
TREMBLE
TREMBLE
?

I've Received a Sign

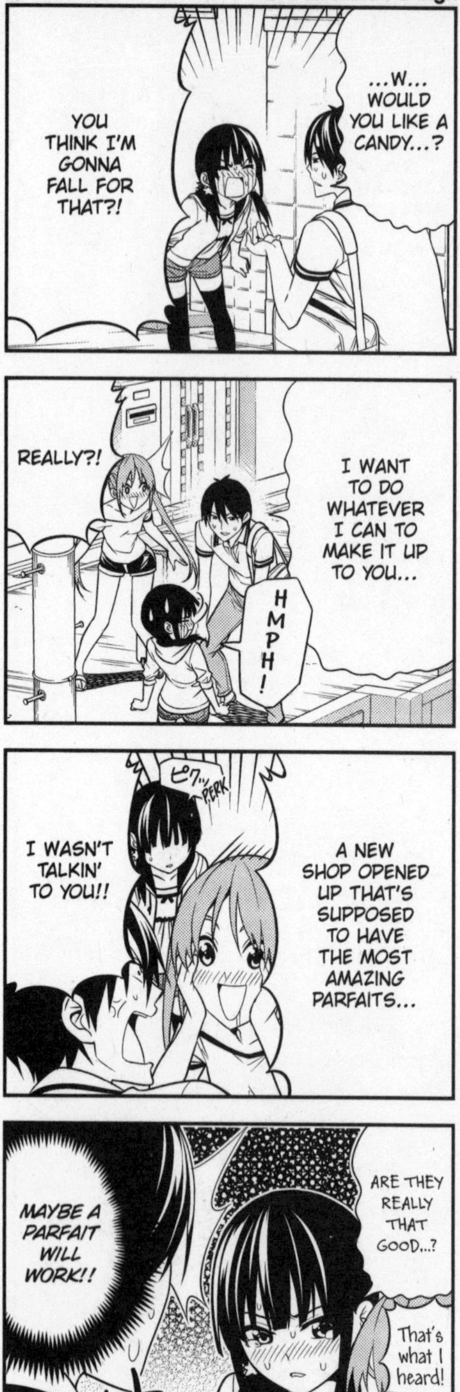
...W... WOULD YOU LIKE A CANDY...?
YOU THINK I'M GONNA FALL FOR THAT?!
I WANT TO DO WHATEVER I CAN TO MAKE IT UP TO YOU...
HMPH!
REALLY?!
A NEW SHOP OPENED UP THAT'S SUPPOSED TO HAVE THE MOST AMAZING PARFAITS...
ピクッ PERK
I WASN'T TALKIN' TO YOU!!
ARE THEY REALLY THAT GOOD...?
That's what I heard!
MAYBE A PARFAIT WILL WORK!!
はっ -OH!

Someone's Excited!

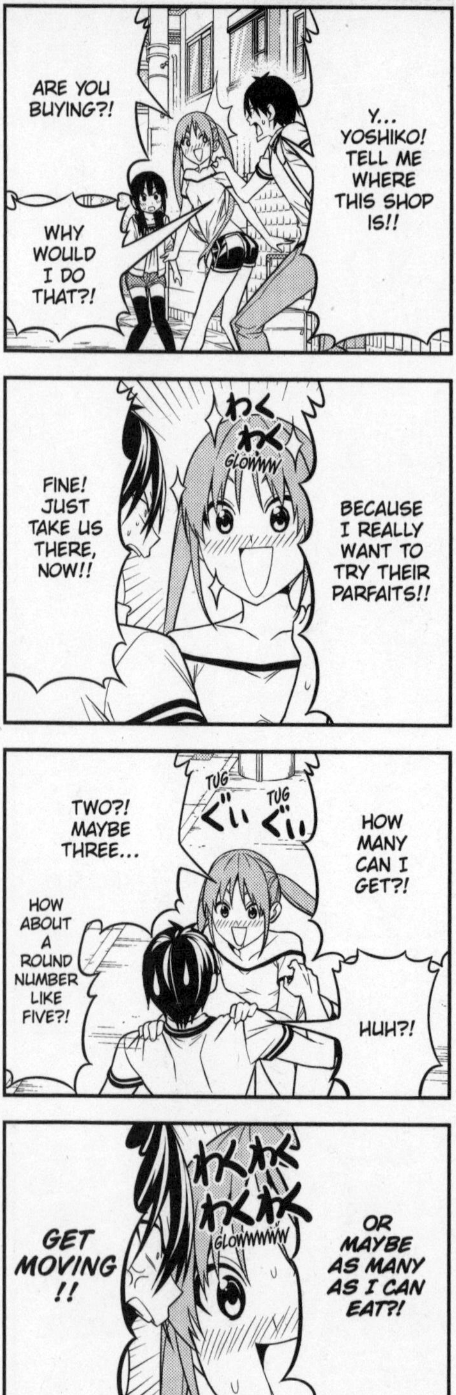
Y... YOSHIKO! TELL ME WHERE THIS SHOP IS!!
ARE YOU BUYING?!
WHY WOULD I DO THAT?!
BECAUSE I REALLY WANT TO TRY THEIR PARFAITS!!
わく わく GLOWWW
FINE! JUST TAKE US THERE, NOW!!
HOW MANY CAN I GET?!
ぐい ぐい TUG TUG
TWO?! MAYBE THREE...
HUH?!
HOW ABOUT A ROUND NUMBER LIKE FIVE?!
OR MAYBE AS MANY AS I CAN EAT?!
わくわく わくわく GLOWWWW
GET MOVING!!

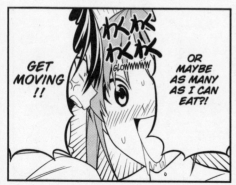

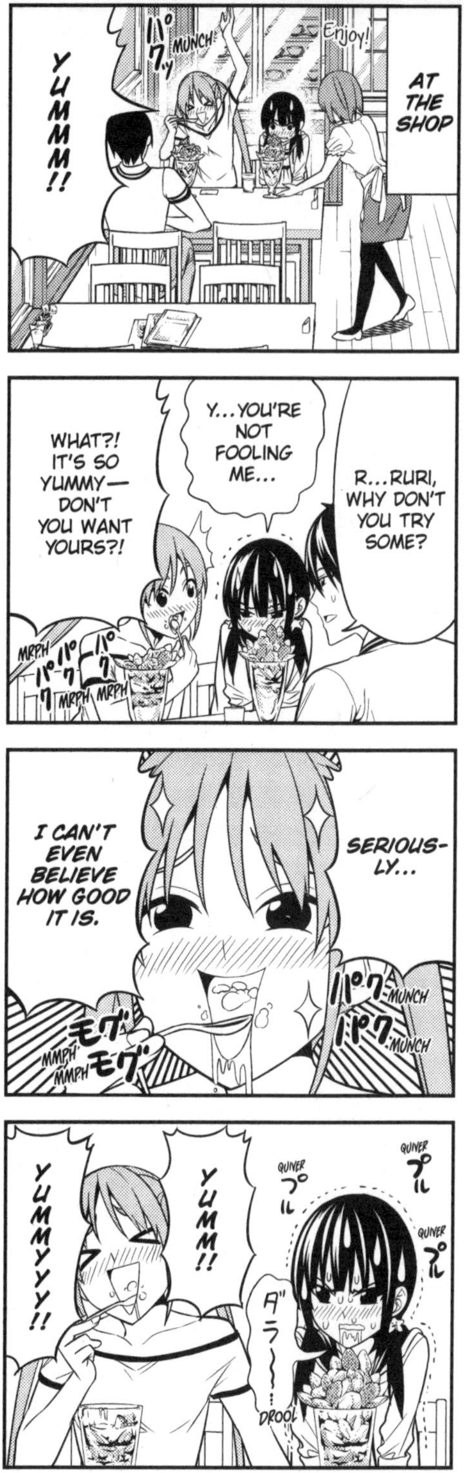
AT THE SHOP
Enjoy!
パクッ MUNCH
YUMMMM!!
R...RURI, WHY DON'T YOU TRY SOME?
Y...YOU'RE NOT FOOLING ME...
WHAT?! IT'S SO YUMMY—DON'T YOU WANT YOURS?!
パクパク MRPH MRPH
パクパク MRPH MRPH
SERIOUSLY...
I CAN'T EVEN BELIEVE HOW GOOD IT IS.
パク MUNCH
パク MUNCH
モグ MMPH
モグ MMPH
QUIVER プル
QUIVER プル
YUMM!!
YUMMYYY!!
QUIVER プル
ダラ〜… DROOL

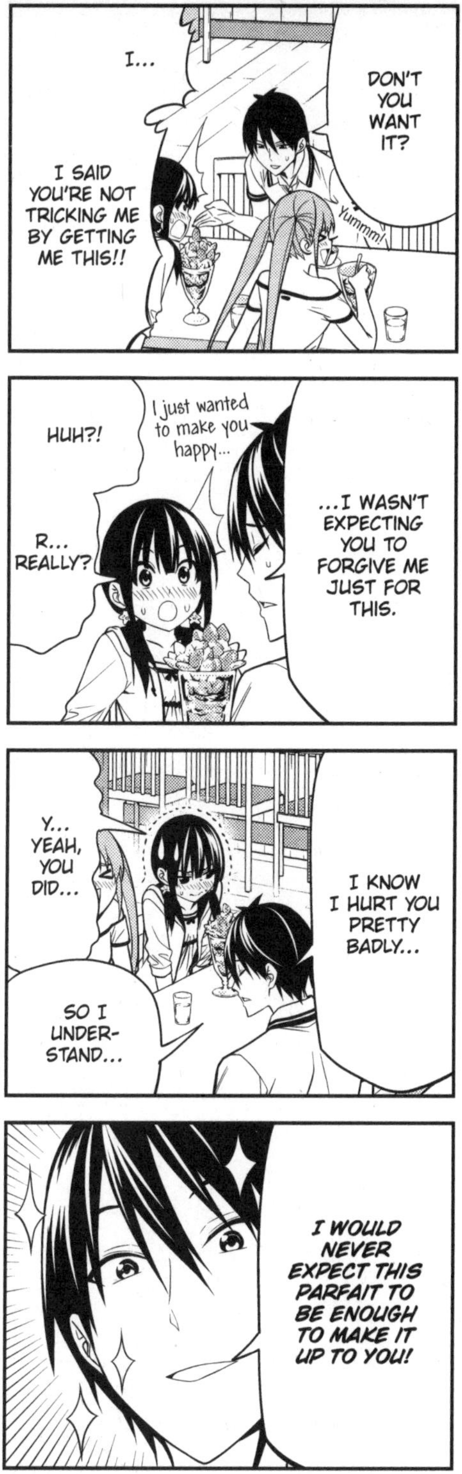
DON'T YOU WANT IT?
I...
I SAID YOU'RE NOT TRICKING ME BY GETTING ME THIS!!
Yummm!
...I WASN'T EXPECTING YOU TO FORGIVE ME JUST FOR THIS.
I just wanted to make you happy...
HUH?!
R... REALLY?
I KNOW I HURT YOU PRETTY BADLY...
Y... YEAH, YOU DID...
SO I UNDERSTAND...
I WOULD NEVER EXPECT THIS PARFAIT TO BE ENOUGH TO MAKE IT UP TO YOU!

Beaming

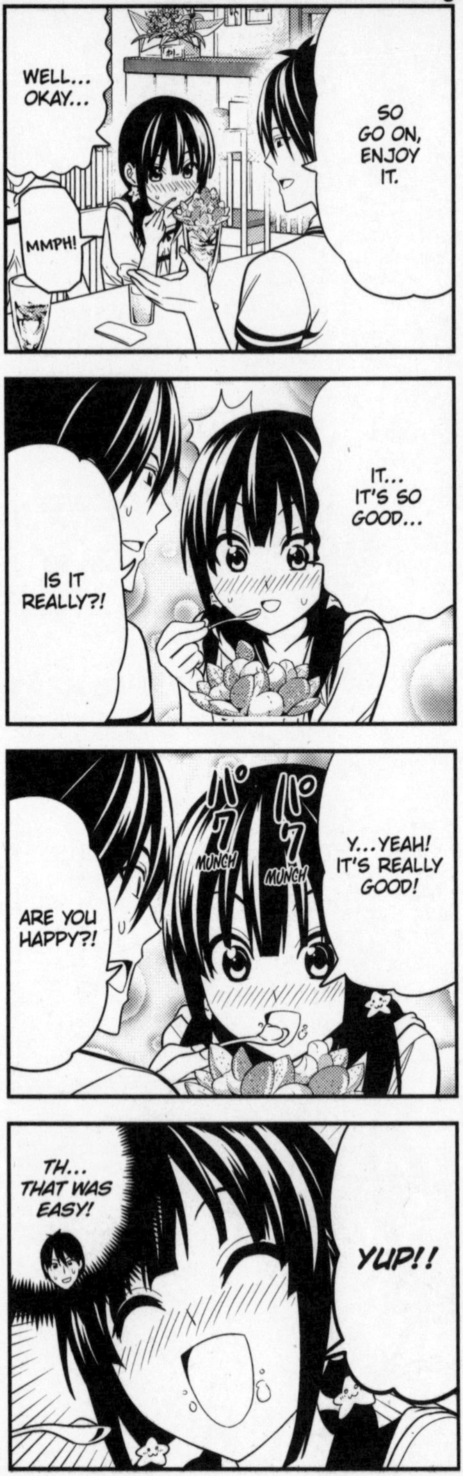
SO GO ON, ENJOY IT.
WELL... OKAY...
MMPH!
IT... IT'S SO GOOD...
IS IT REALLY?!
パク MUNCH
パク MUNCH
Y...YEAH! IT'S REALLY GOOD!
ARE YOU HAPPY?!
YUP!!
TH... THAT WAS EASY!

All for Nothing

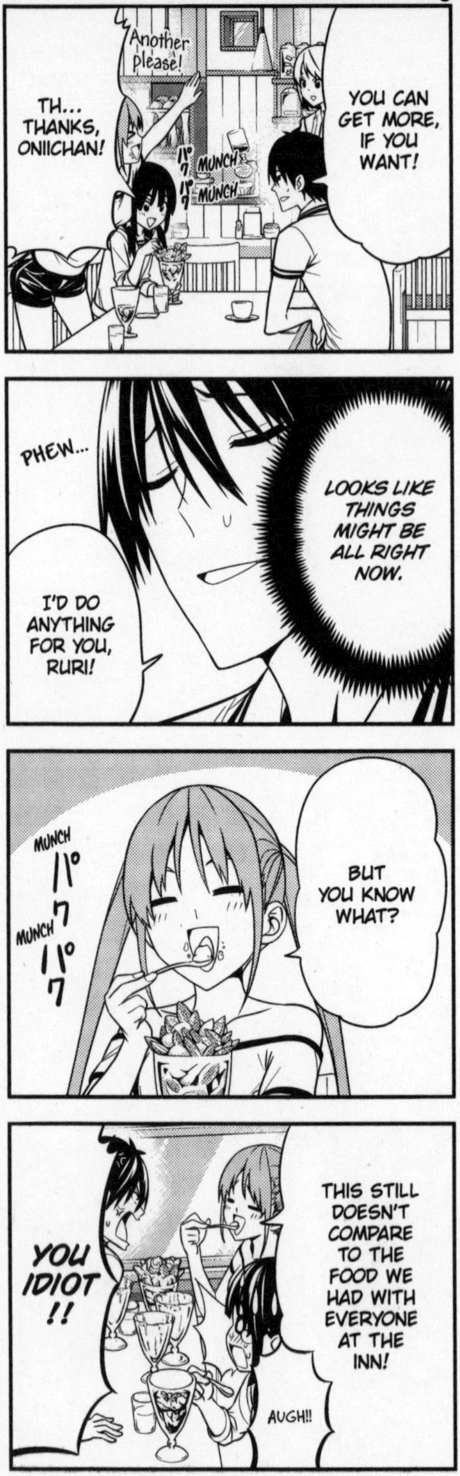
YOU CAN GET MORE, IF YOU WANT!
パク MUNCH
パク MUNCH
Another please!
TH... THANKS, ONIICHAN!
LOOKS LIKE THINGS MIGHT BE ALL RIGHT NOW.
PHEW...
I'D DO ANYTHING FOR YOU, RURI!
BUT YOU KNOW WHAT?
MUNCH パク
MUNCH パク
THIS STILL DOESN'T COMPARE TO THE FOOD WE HAD WITH EVERYONE AT THE INN!
AUGH!!
YOU IDIOT!!

Lots of Expenses This Summer

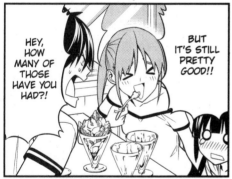

BUT IT'S STILL PRETTY GOOD!!
HEY, HOW MANY OF THOSE HAVE YOU HAD?!
DING
¥8.600
URGGH ...

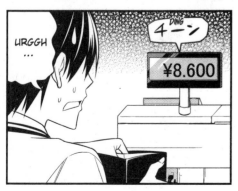

Aho-Girl

\ˈahô͵gərl\ *Japanese, noun.*
A clueless girl.

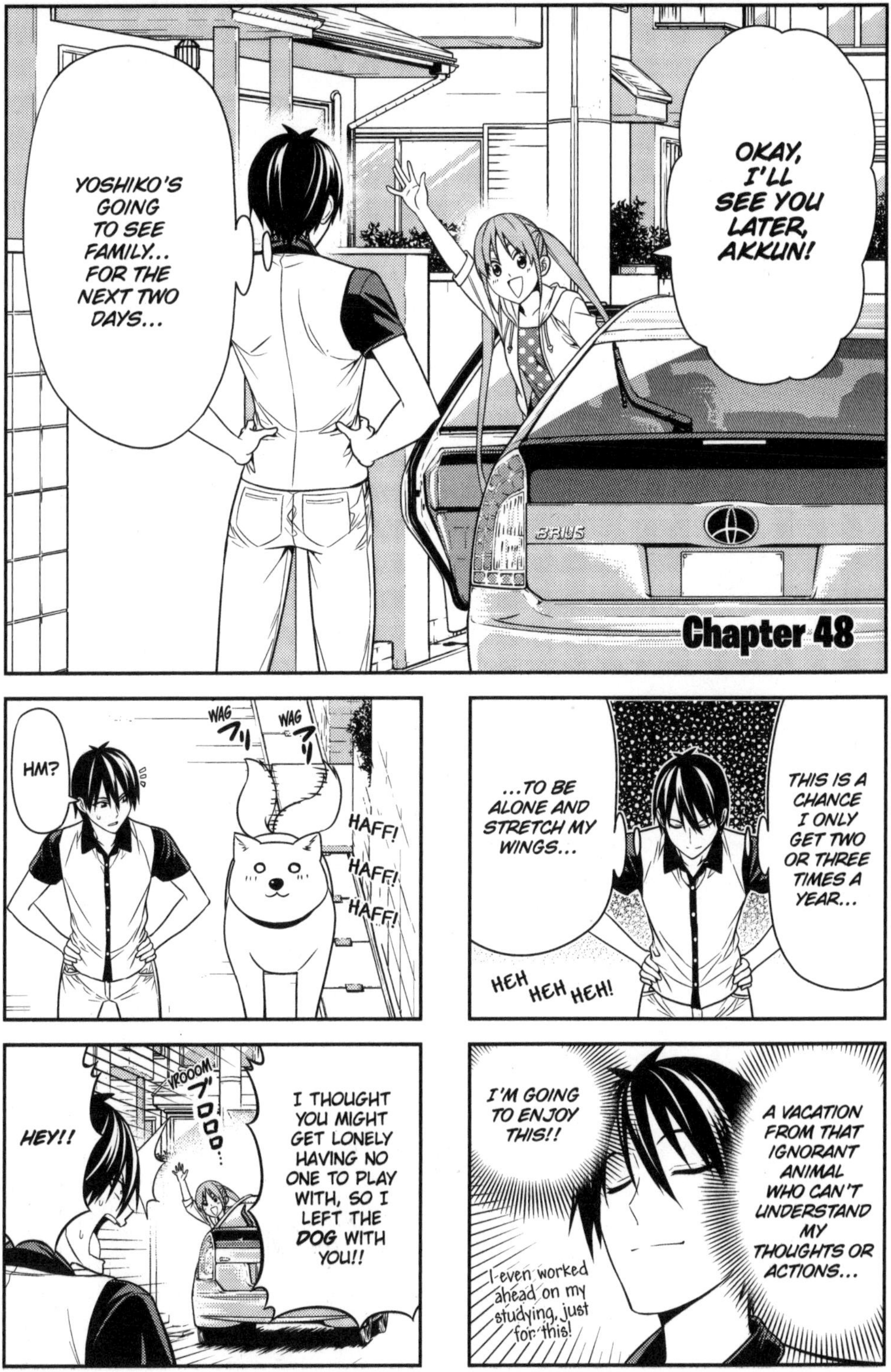
OKAY, I'LL SEE YOU LATER, AKKUN!
YOSHIKO'S GOING TO SEE FAMILY... FOR THE NEXT TWO DAYS...
Chapter 48
THIS IS A CHANCE I ONLY GET TWO OR THREE TIMES A YEAR...
...TO BE ALONE AND STRETCH MY WINGS...
HEH HEH HEH!
WAG
WAG
HAFF! HAFF! HAFF!
HM?
A VACATION FROM THAT IGNORANT ANIMAL WHO CAN'T UNDERSTAND MY THOUGHTS OR ACTIONS...
I'M GOING TO ENJOY THIS!!
I even worked ahead on my studying, just for this!
I THOUGHT YOU MIGHT GET LONELY HAVING NO ONE TO PLAY WITH, SO I LEFT THE DOG WITH YOU!!
VROOOM
HEY!!

There's Something Wrong with That One

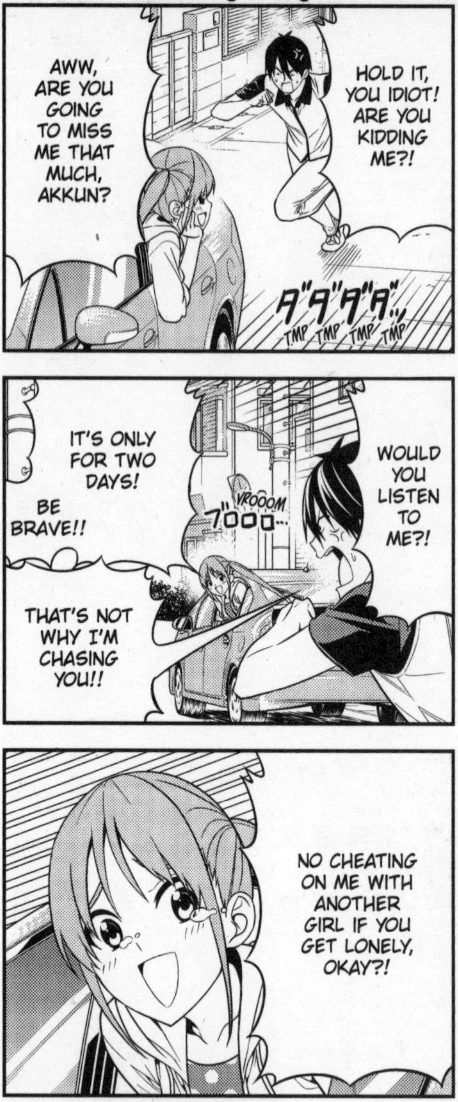
HOLD IT, YOU IDIOT! ARE YOU KIDDING ME?!
AWW, ARE YOU GOING TO MISS ME THAT MUCH, AKKUN?
TMP TMP TMP TMP
WOULD YOU LISTEN TO ME?!
VROOOM
IT'S ONLY FOR TWO DAYS!
BE BRAVE!!
THAT'S NOT WHY I'M CHASING YOU!!
NO CHEATING ON ME WITH ANOTHER GIRL IF YOU GET LONELY, OKAY?!
LEAVE ALREADY!!

Instant Bond

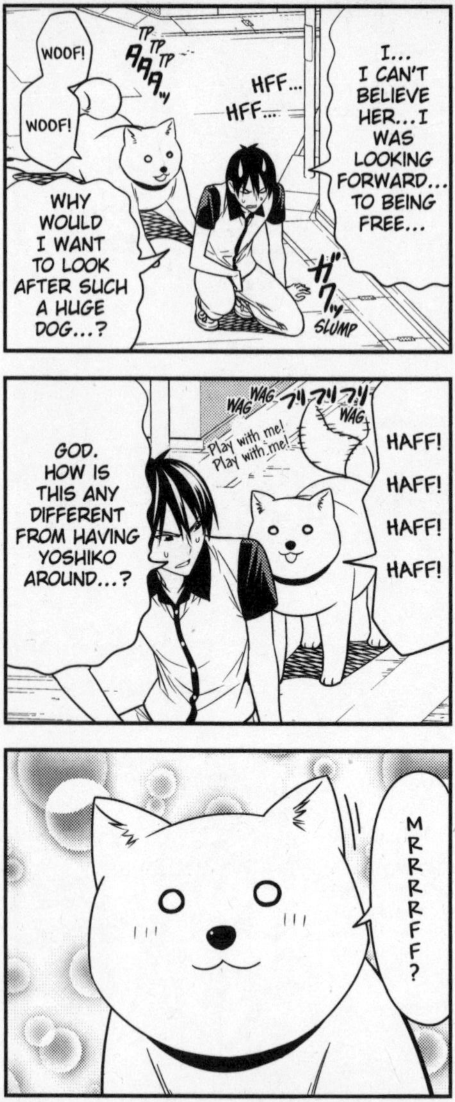
I... I CAN'T BELIEVE HER...I WAS LOOKING FORWARD... TO BEING FREE...
HFF... HFF...
TP TP TP
WOOF!
WOOF!
WHY WOULD I WANT TO LOOK AFTER SUCH A HUGE DOG...?
SLUMP
HAFF! HAFF! HAFF! HAFF!
WAG WAG WAG
Play with me! Play with me!
GOD. HOW IS THIS ANY DIFFERENT FROM HAVING YOSHIKO AROUND...?
MRRRRFF?
SIIIGH...
SLURP SLURP
AND ITS BREATH STINKS.

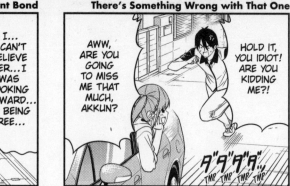

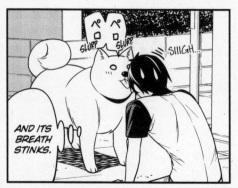

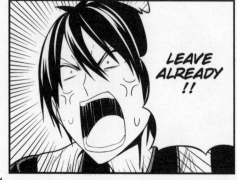

A Woman Bested by a Dog

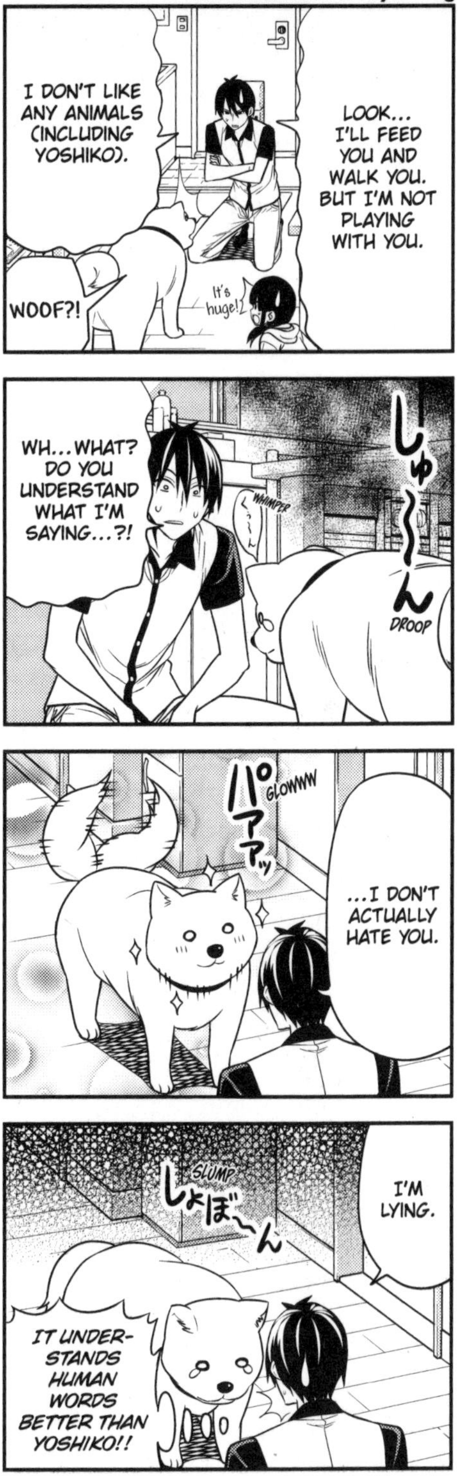
LOOK... I'LL FEED YOU AND WALK YOU. BUT I'M NOT PLAYING WITH YOU.
I DON'T LIKE ANY ANIMALS (INCLUDING YOSHIKO).
It's huge!
WOOF?!
しゅ〜〜ん DROOP
くぅ〜ん WHIMPER
WH...WHAT? DO YOU UNDERSTAND WHAT I'M SAYING...?!
パアアッ GLOWWW
...I DON'T ACTUALLY HATE YOU.
I'M LYING.
しょぼ〜ん SLUMP
IT UNDER-STANDS HUMAN WORDS BETTER THAN YOSHIKO!!

The Eyes Are Windows

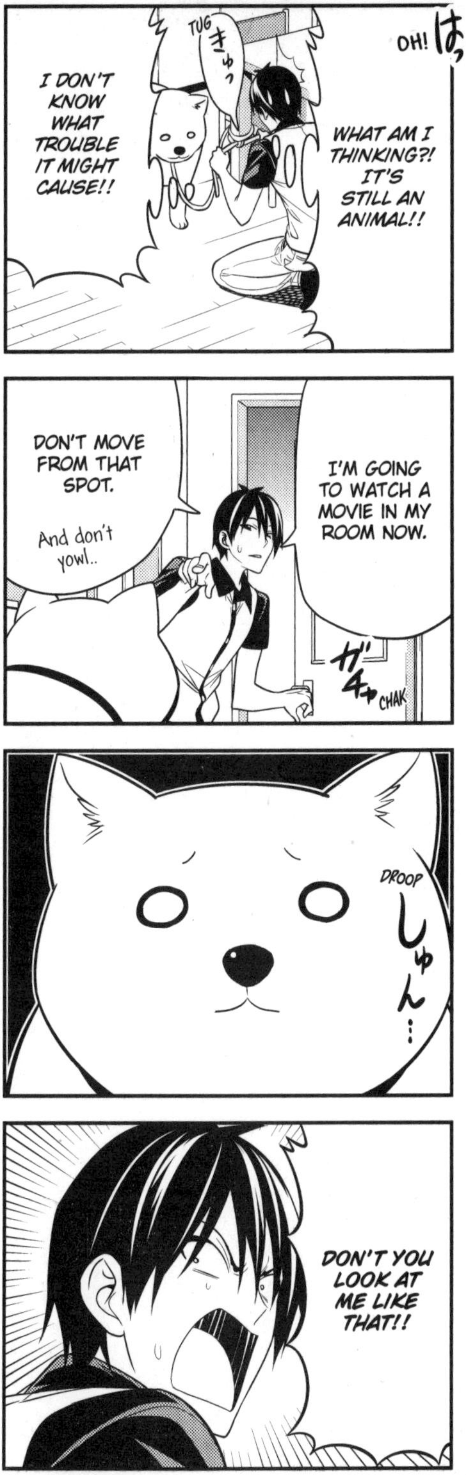
はっ OH!
WHAT AM I THINKING?! IT'S STILL AN ANIMAL!!
きゅっ TUG
I DON'T KNOW WHAT TROUBLE IT MIGHT CAUSE!!
I'M GOING TO WATCH A MOVIE IN MY ROOM NOW.
ガチャ CHAK
DON'T MOVE FROM THAT SPOT.
And don't yowl..
しゅん… DROOP
DON'T YOU LOOK AT ME LIKE THAT!!

Masterpiece

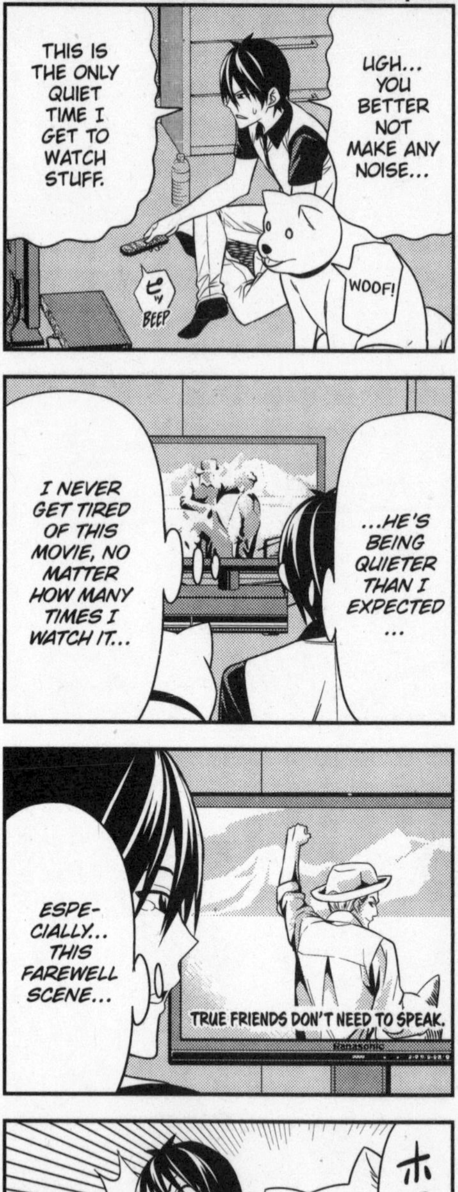
UGH... YOU BETTER NOT MAKE ANY NOISE...
THIS IS THE ONLY QUIET TIME I GET TO WATCH STUFF.
ピッ BEEP
WOOF!
...HE'S BEING QUIETER THAN I EXPECTED...
I NEVER GET TIRED OF THIS MOVIE, NO MATTER HOW MANY TIMES I WATCH IT...
ESPE-CIALLY... THIS FAREWELL SCENE...
TRUE FRIENDS DON'T NEED TO SPEAK.
ホロリ… TEAR
WHA?!

Sharing an Emotion

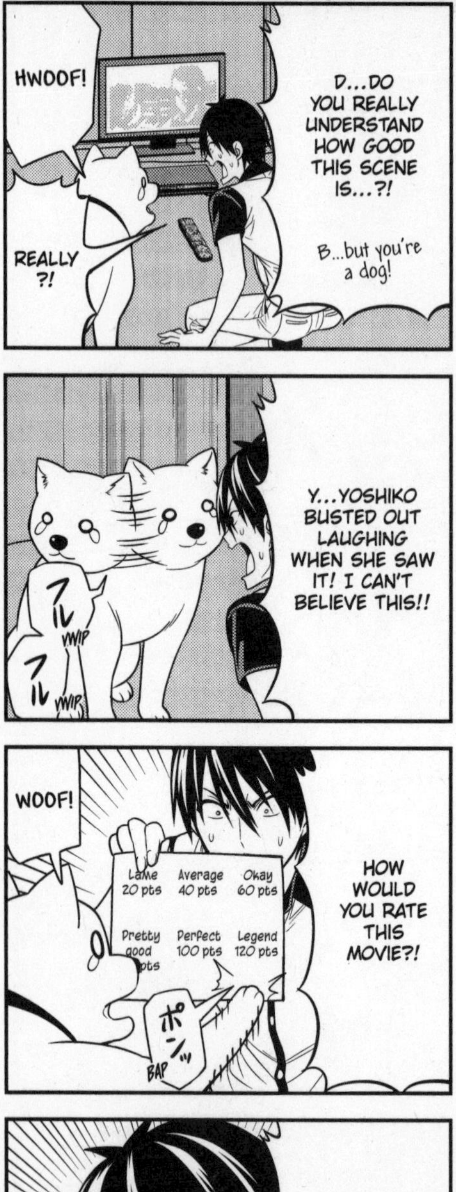
D...DO YOU REALLY UNDERSTAND HOW GOOD THIS SCENE IS...?!
HWOOF!
B...but you're a dog!
REALLY ?!
Y...YOSHIKO BUSTED OUT LAUGHING WHEN SHE SAW IT! I CAN'T BELIEVE THIS!!
フル VWIP
フル VWIP
HOW WOULD YOU RATE THIS MOVIE?!
WOOF!
Lame 20 pts
Average 40 pts
Okay 60 pts
Pretty good
Perfect 100 pts
Legend 120 pts
ポンッ BAP
YOU'RE AMAZING!!

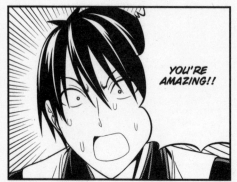

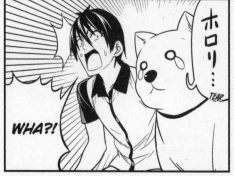

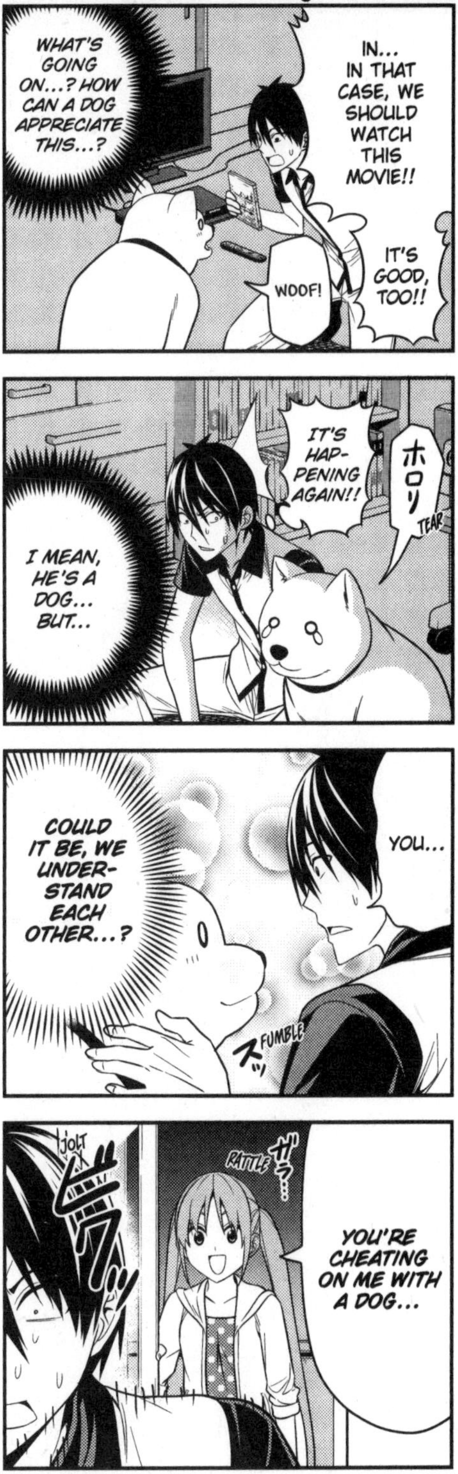
IN... IN THAT CASE, WE SHOULD WATCH THIS MOVIE!!
WHAT'S GOING ON...? HOW CAN A DOG APPRECIATE THIS...?
IT'S GOOD, TOO!!
WOOF!
ホロリ
TEAR
IT'S HAPPENING AGAIN!!
I MEAN, HE'S A DOG... BUT...
YOU...
COULD IT BE, WE UNDERSTAND EACH OTHER...?
FUMBLE
ガラ...
RATTLE
JOLT
YOU'RE CHEATING ON ME WITH A DOG...

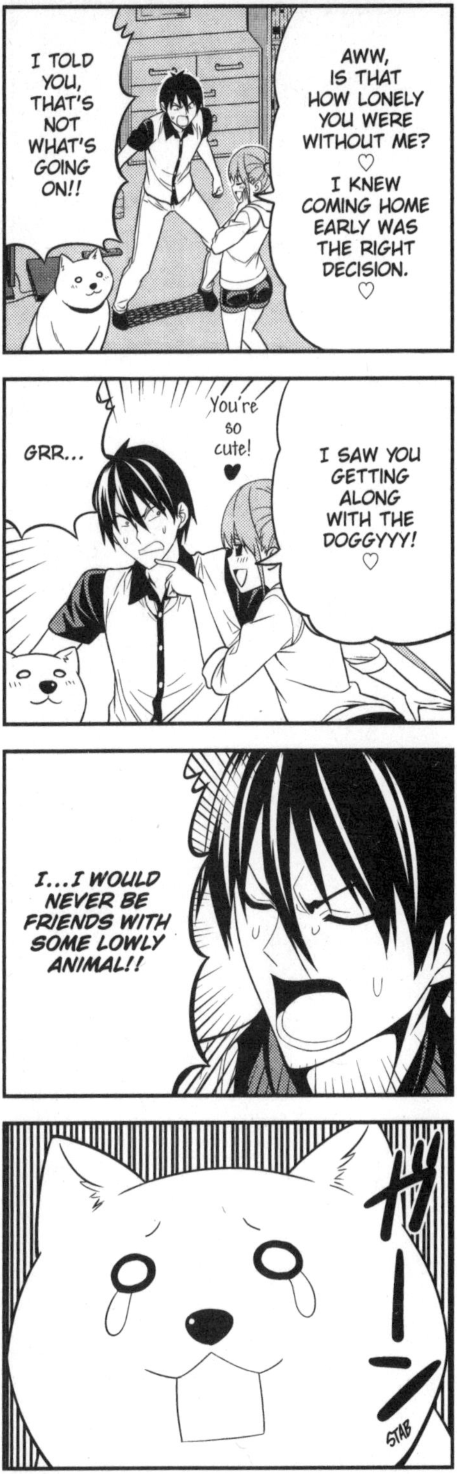
AWW, IS THAT HOW LONELY YOU WERE WITHOUT ME? ♡ I KNEW COMING HOME EARLY WAS THE RIGHT DECISION. ♡
I TOLD YOU, THAT'S NOT WHAT'S GOING ON!!
I SAW YOU GETTING ALONG WITH THE DOGGYYY! ♡
You're so cute! ♥
GRR...
I...I WOULD NEVER BE FRIENDS WITH SOME LOWLY ANIMAL!!
STAB

It's a Misunderstanding

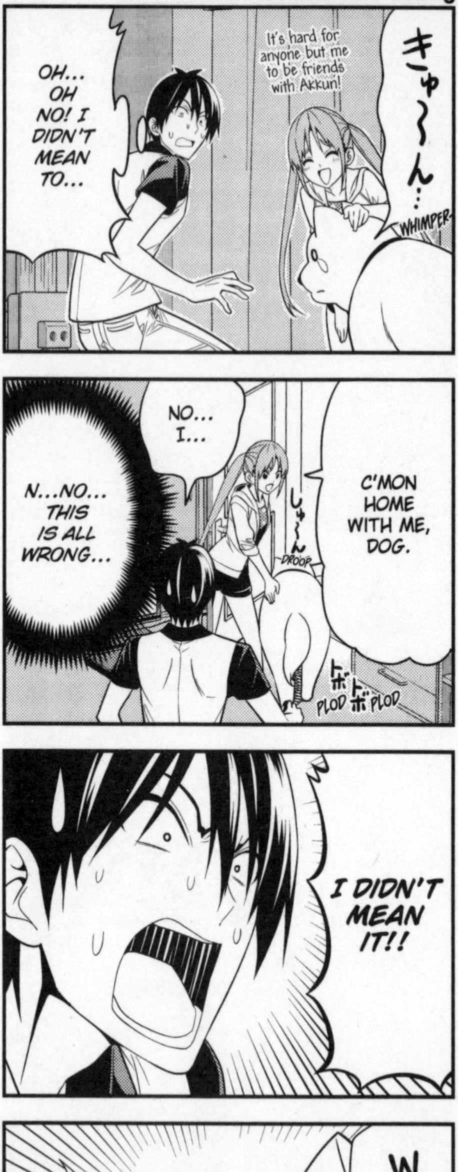
きゅ~ん…
WHIMPER
It's hard for anyone but me to be friends with Akkun!
OH... OH NO! I DIDN'T MEAN TO...
C'MON HOME WITH ME, DOG.
NO... I...
しゅ~ん
DROOP
N...NO... THIS IS ALL WRONG...
トボトボ
PLOD PLOD
I DIDN'T MEAN IT!!
WOOF?!

I...Understand...

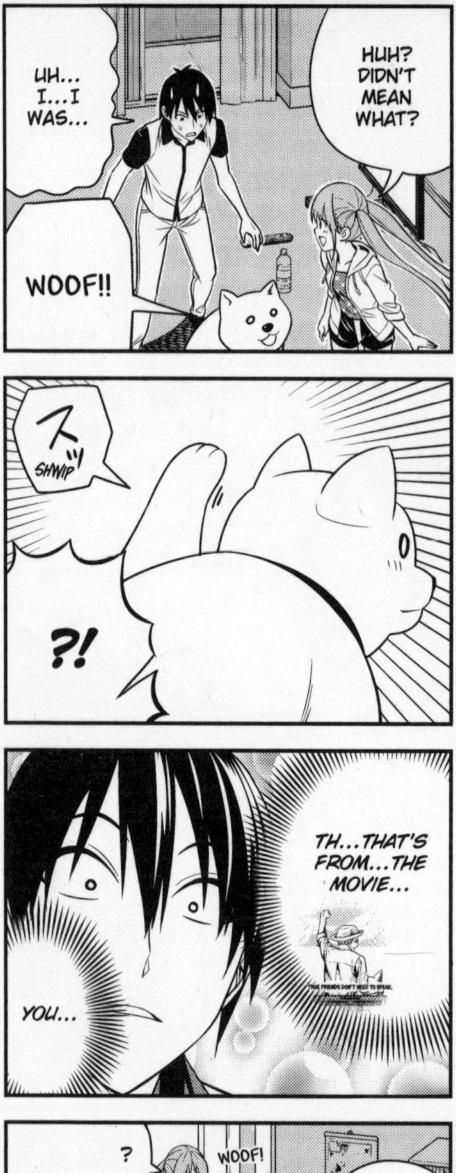
HUH? DIDN'T MEAN WHAT?
UH... I...I WAS...
WOOF!!
スッ
SHWIP
?!
TH...THAT'S FROM...THE MOVIE...
TRUE FRIENDS DON'T NEED TO SPEAK.
YOU...
WE'LL HANG OUT AGAIN...
HEH.
WOOF!
?
ARE YOU TIRED, AKKUN?
A SUMMER FRIENDSHIP

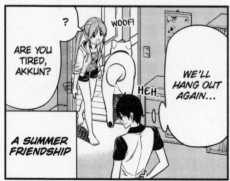

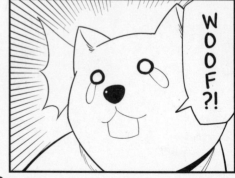

They're Friends

LATER ON
YOU WANT THIS?
WOOF!
WAS THAT GOOD?
MNCH MNCH
WOOF!
THIS IS HOW AKKUN RELAXES

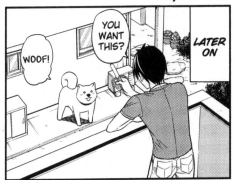

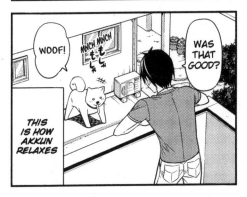

Aho-Girl

\\'ahô͵gərl\\ *Japanese, noun.*

A clueless girl.

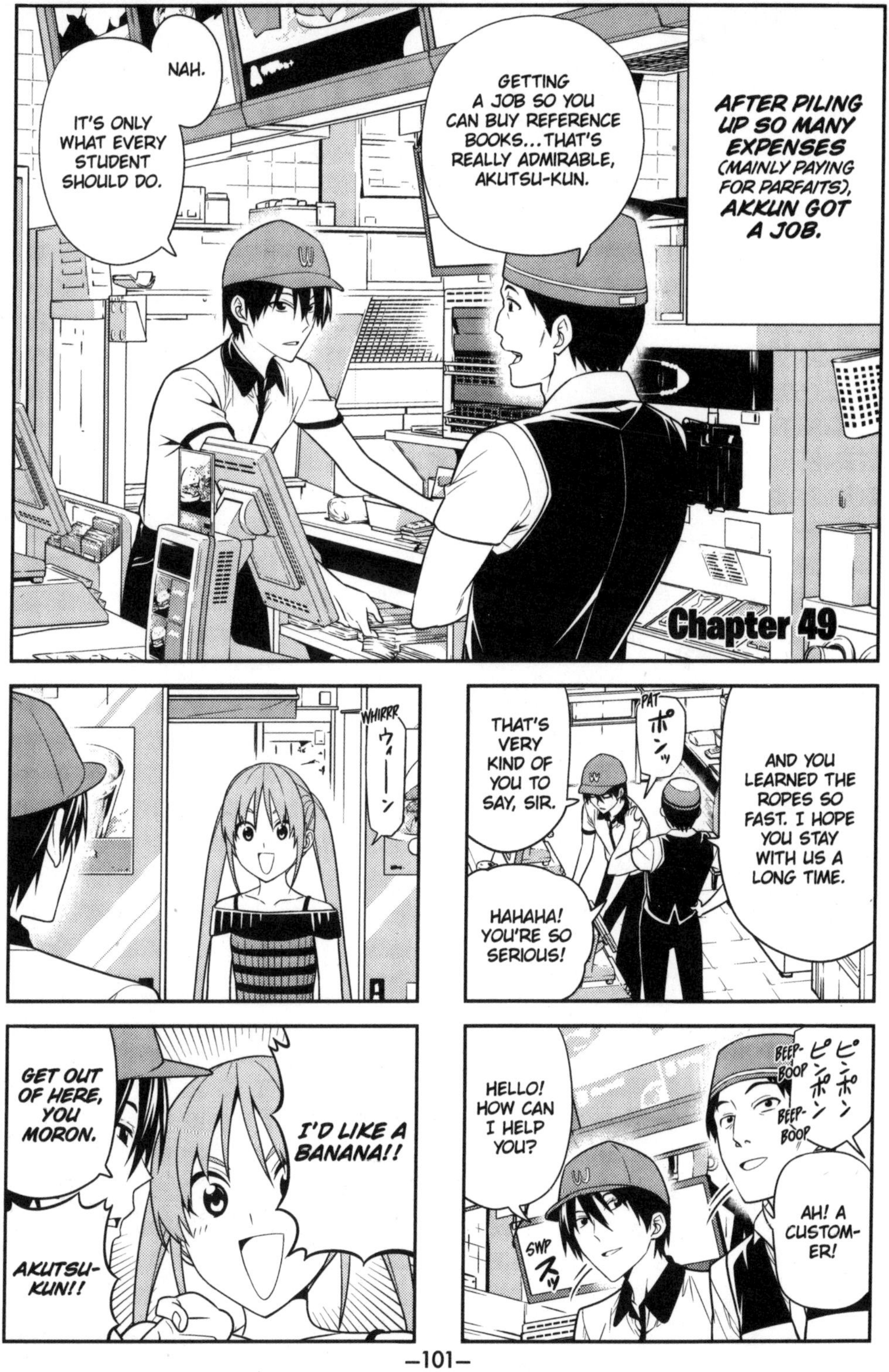
AFTER PILING UP SO MANY EXPENSES (MAINLY PAYING FOR PARFAITS), AKKUN GOT A JOB.
GETTING A JOB SO YOU CAN BUY REFERENCE BOOKS...THAT'S REALLY ADMIRABLE, AKUTSU-KUN.
NAH.
IT'S ONLY WHAT EVERY STUDENT SHOULD DO.
Chapter 49
AND YOU LEARNED THE ROPES SO FAST. I HOPE YOU STAY WITH US A LONG TIME.
PAT ポンッ
THAT'S VERY KIND OF YOU TO SAY, SIR.
HAHAHA! YOU'RE SO SERIOUS!
WHIRRR ウィーン
BEEP-BOOP ピンポン BEEP-BOOP
AH! A CUSTOMER!
HELLO! HOW CAN I HELP YOU?
SWP スッ
I'D LIKE A BANANA!!
GET OUT OF HERE, YOU MORON.
AKUTSU-KUN!!

But This Is Japan!

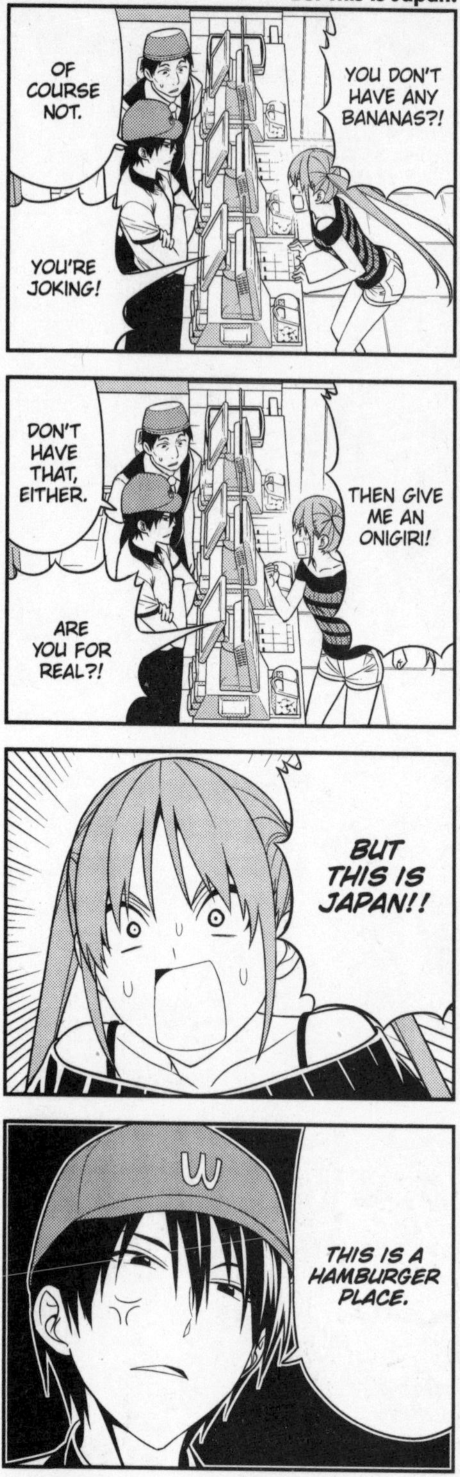
YOU DON'T HAVE ANY BANANAS?!
OF COURSE NOT.
YOU'RE JOKING!
THEN GIVE ME AN ONIGIRI!
DON'T HAVE THAT, EITHER.
ARE YOU FOR REAL?!
BUT THIS IS JAPAN!!
THIS IS A HAMBURGER PLACE.

Conflicted

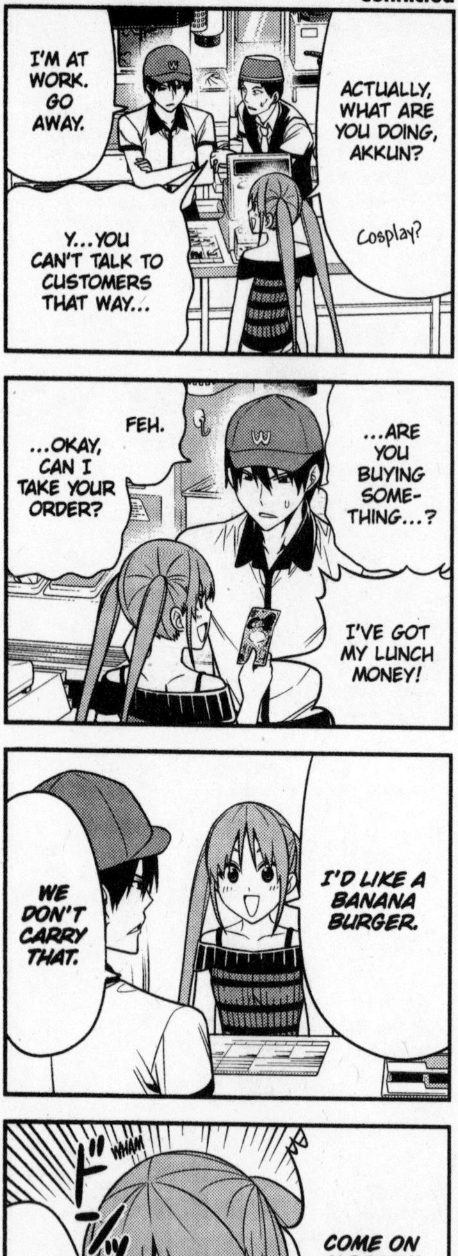
ACTUALLY, WHAT ARE YOU DOING, AKKUN?
Cosplay?
I'M AT WORK. GO AWAY.
Y...YOU CAN'T TALK TO CUSTOMERS THAT WAY...
...ARE YOU BUYING SOMETHING...?
I'VE GOT MY LUNCH MONEY!
FEH.
...OKAY, CAN I TAKE YOUR ORDER?
I'D LIKE A BANANA BURGER.
WE DON'T CARRY THAT.
COME ON ALREADY! WHAT DO YOU WANT FROM ME?!
WHAM
CAN YOU PLEASE LEAVE?

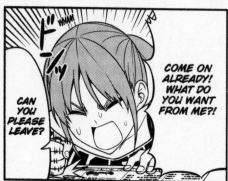

A Discovery

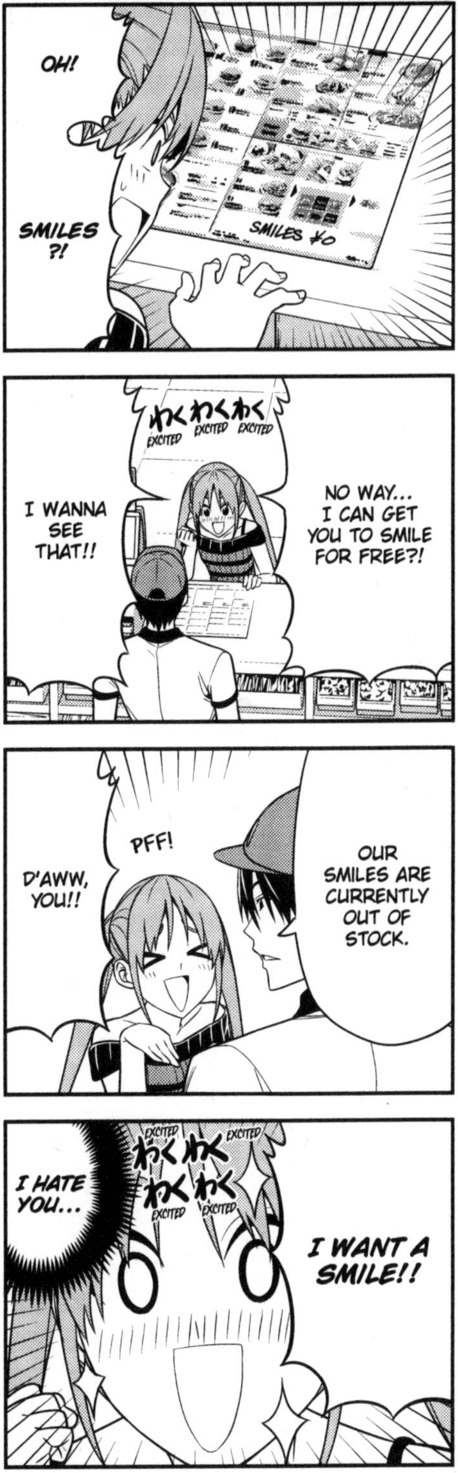

OH!
SMILES ¥0
SMILES ?!
わくわくわく
EXCITED EXCITED EXCITED
NO WAY... I CAN GET YOU TO SMILE FOR FREE?!
I WANNA SEE THAT!!
OUR SMILES ARE CURRENTLY OUT OF STOCK.
PFF!
D'AWW, YOU!!
わくわくわくわく
EXCITED EXCITED EXCITED EXCITED
I WANT A SMILE!!
I HATE YOU...

An Evil Smirk

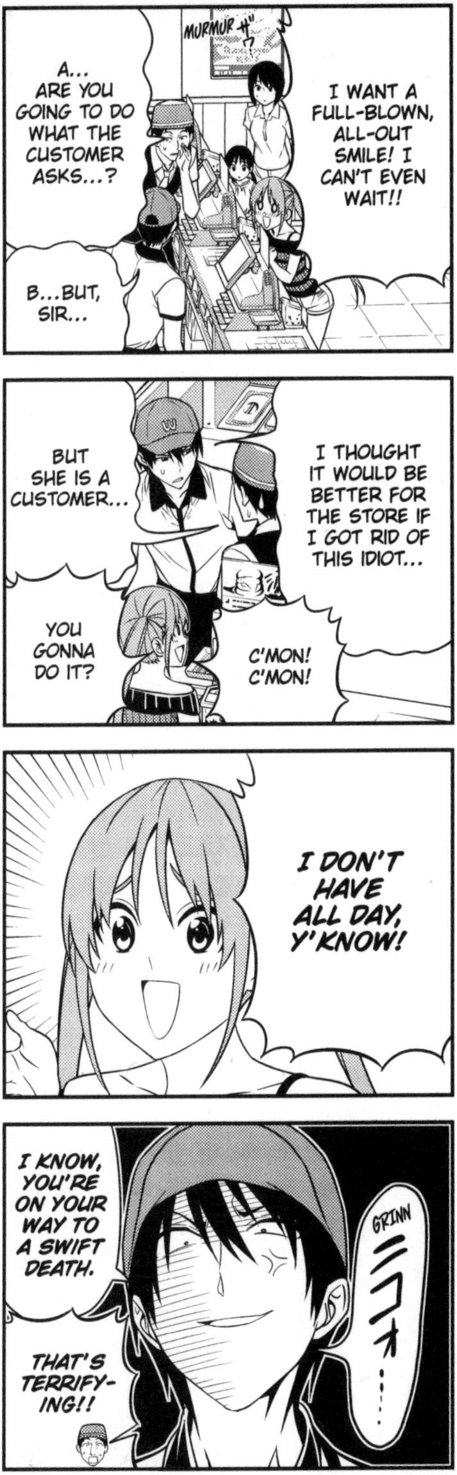

MURMUR ザワ
I WANT A FULL-BLOWN, ALL-OUT SMILE! I CAN'T EVEN WAIT!!
A... ARE YOU GOING TO DO WHAT THE CUSTOMER ASKS...?
B...BUT, SIR...
I THOUGHT IT WOULD BE BETTER FOR THE STORE IF I GOT RID OF THIS IDIOT...
BUT SHE IS A CUSTOMER...
C'MON! C'MON!
YOU GONNA DO IT?
I DON'T HAVE ALL DAY, Y'KNOW!
GRINN
ニコォ…
I KNOW, YOU'RE ON YOUR WAY TO A SWIFT DEATH.
THAT'S TERRIFYING!!

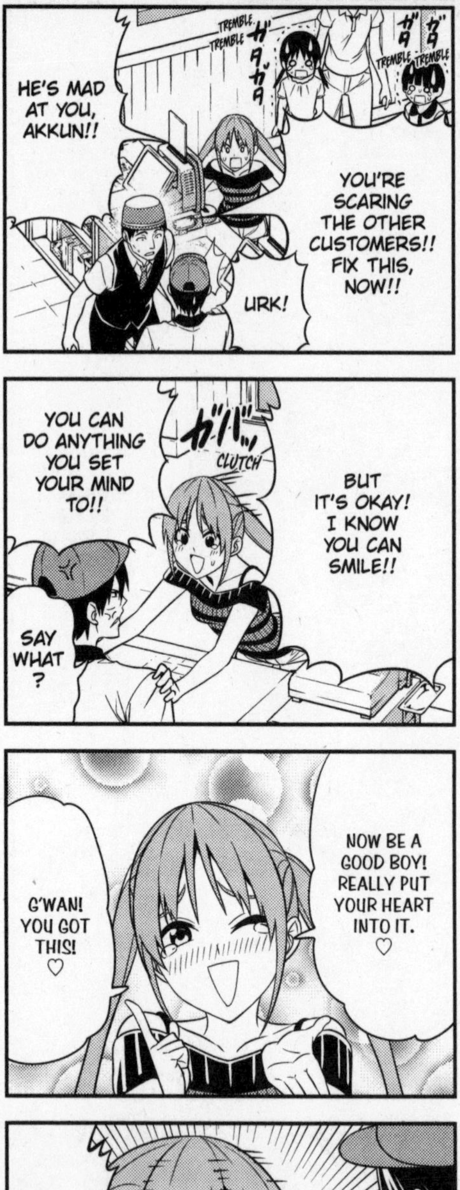
ガタ ガタ
TREMBLE TREMBLE
TREMBLE TREMBLE
ガタガタ
HE'S MAD AT YOU, AKKUN!!
YOU'RE SCARING THE OTHER CUSTOMERS!! FIX THIS, NOW!!
URK!
BUT IT'S OKAY! I KNOW YOU CAN SMILE!!
ガバッ
CLUTCH
YOU CAN DO ANYTHING YOU SET YOUR MIND TO!!
SAY WHAT?
NOW BE A GOOD BOY! REALLY PUT YOUR HEART INTO IT. ♡
G'WAN! YOU GOT THIS! ♡
AKU-TSU-KUN, NO!!
ズボッ
SHWAKK

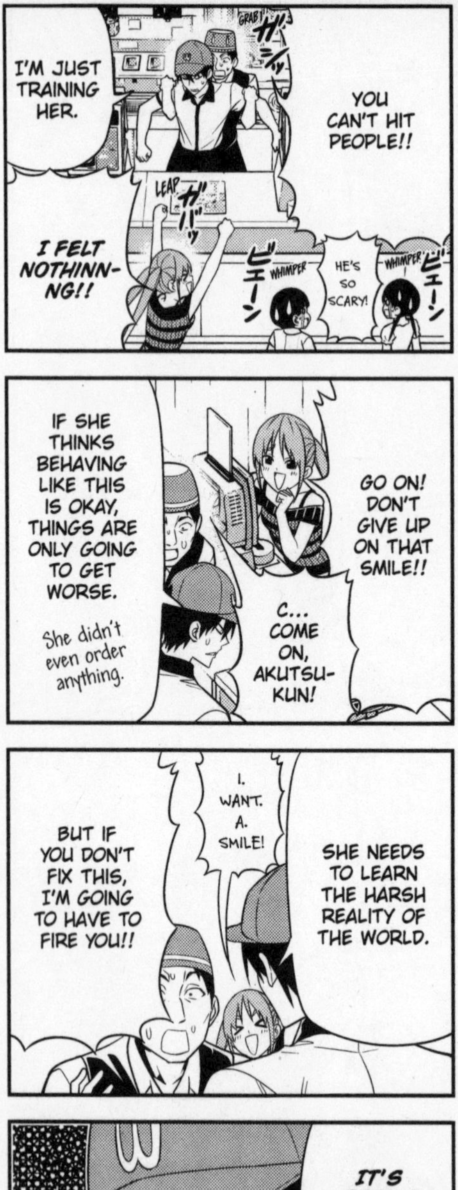
GRAB!
ガシッ
YOU CAN'T HIT PEOPLE!!
I'M JUST TRAINING HER.
LEAP
ガバッ
I FELT NOTHINN-NG!!
WHIMPER
ビェーン
HE'S SO SCARY!
WHIMPER
ビェーン
GO ON! DON'T GIVE UP ON THAT SMILE!!
C... COME ON, AKUTSU-KUN!
IF SHE THINKS BEHAVING LIKE THIS IS OKAY, THINGS ARE ONLY GOING TO GET WORSE.
She didn't even order anything.
SHE NEEDS TO LEARN THE HARSH REALITY OF THE WORLD.
I. WANT. A. SMILE!
BUT IF YOU DON'T FIX THIS, I'M GOING TO HAVE TO FIRE YOU!!
IT'S BEEN A PLEASURE, SIR.
YOU DIDN'T EVEN HESI-TATE!!

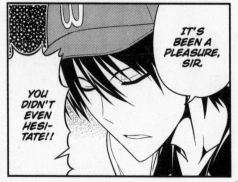

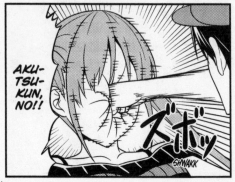

In All Honesty

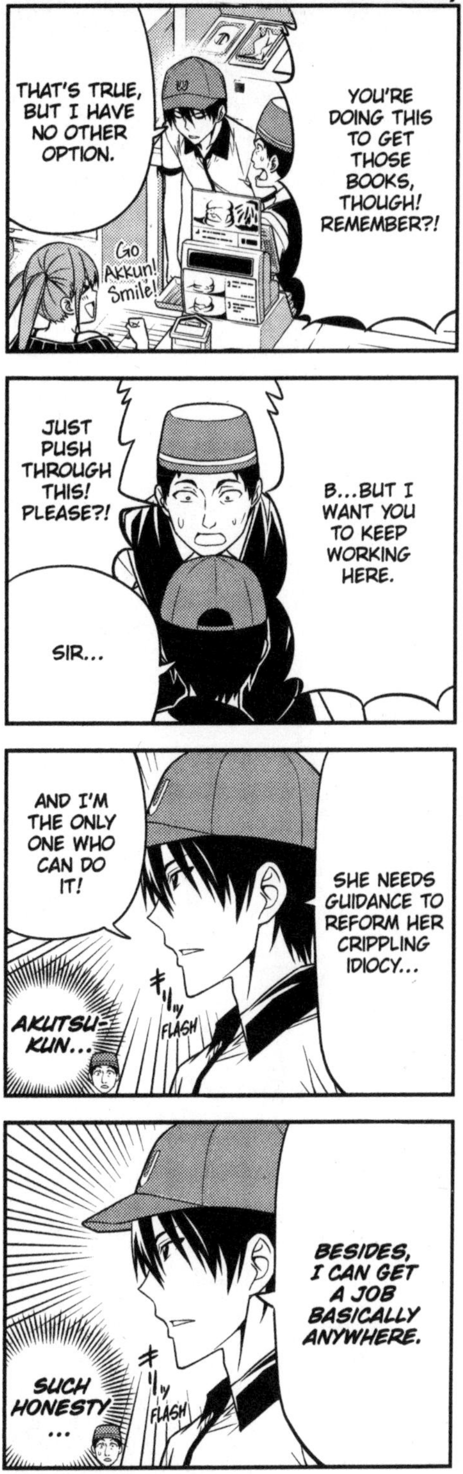
YOU'RE DOING THIS TO GET THOSE BOOKS, THOUGH! REMEMBER?!
THAT'S TRUE, BUT I HAVE NO OTHER OPTION.
Go Akkun! Smile!
B...BUT I WANT YOU TO KEEP WORKING HERE.
JUST PUSH THROUGH THIS! PLEASE?!
SIR...
SHE NEEDS GUIDANCE TO REFORM HER CRIPPLING IDIOCY...
AND I'M THE ONLY ONE WHO CAN DO IT!
FLASH
AKUTSU-KUN...
BESIDES, I CAN GET A JOB BASICALLY ANYWHERE.
FLASH
SUCH HONESTY...

It Makes Sense, Really

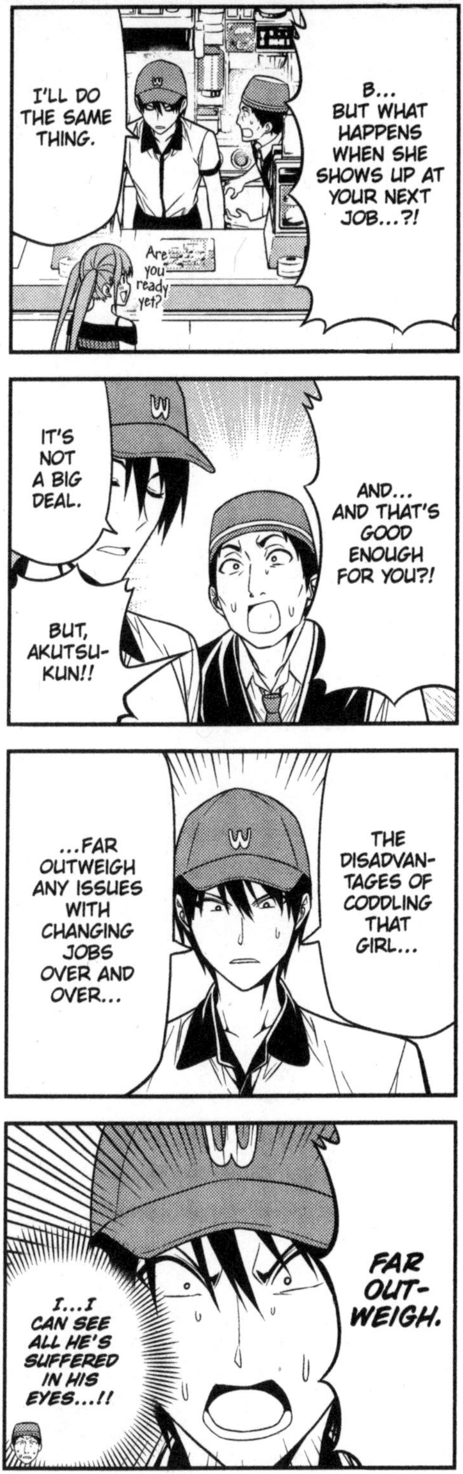
B... BUT WHAT HAPPENS WHEN SHE SHOWS UP AT YOUR NEXT JOB...?!
I'LL DO THE SAME THING.
Are you ready yet?
AND... AND THAT'S GOOD ENOUGH FOR YOU?!
IT'S NOT A BIG DEAL.
BUT, AKUTSU-KUN!!
THE DISADVANTAGES OF CODDLING THAT GIRL...
...FAR OUTWEIGH ANY ISSUES WITH CHANGING JOBS OVER AND OVER...
FAR OUTWEIGH.
I...I CAN SEE ALL HE'S SUFFERED IN HIS EYES...!!

Goodbye, Sir

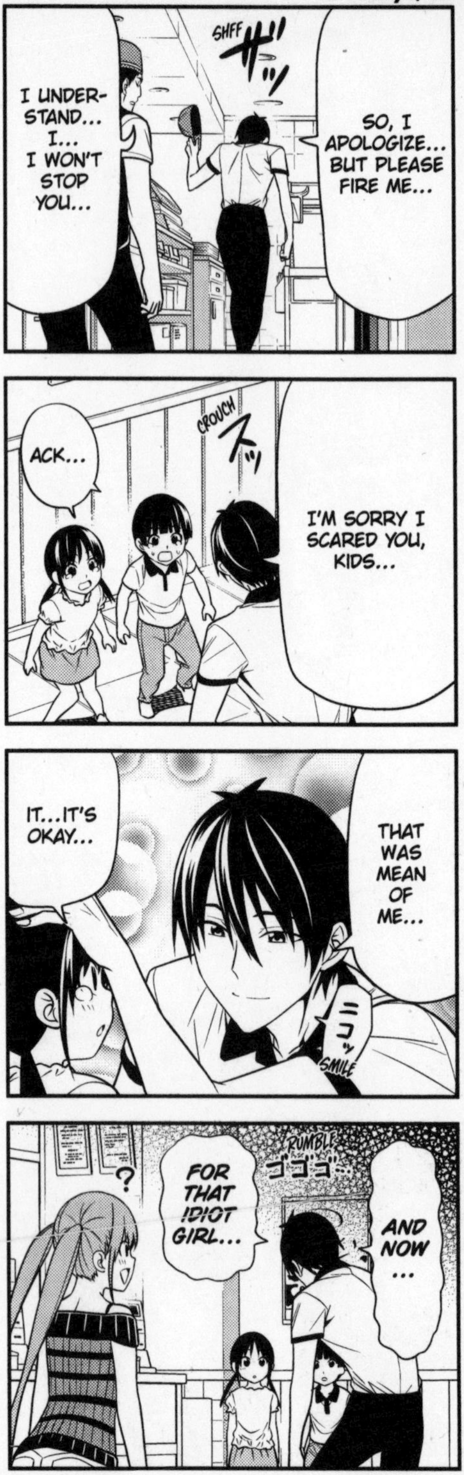
SO, I APOLOGIZE... BUT PLEASE FIRE ME...
SHFF
I UNDER-STAND... I... I WON'T STOP YOU...
I'M SORRY I SCARED YOU, KIDS...
CROUCH
ACK...
THAT WAS MEAN OF ME...
SMILE
IT...IT'S OKAY...
AND NOW...
RUMBLE
FOR THAT IDIOT GIRL...
?

Once More unto the Breach

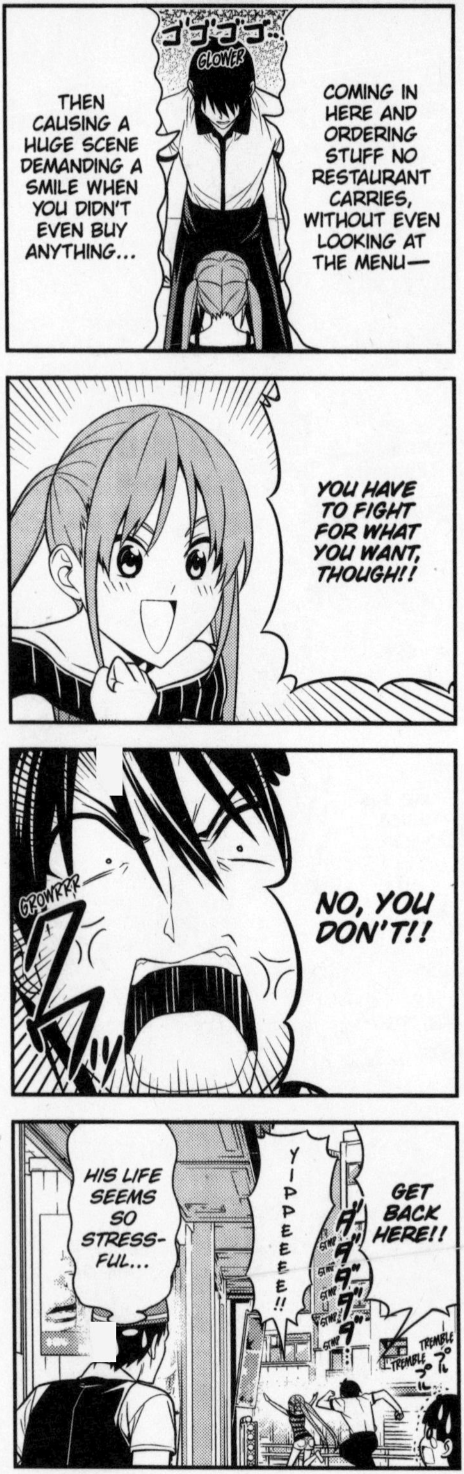
COMING IN HERE AND ORDERING STUFF NO RESTAURANT CARRIES, WITHOUT EVEN LOOKING AT THE MENU—
GLOWER
THEN CAUSING A HUGE SCENE DEMANDING A SMILE WHEN YOU DIDN'T EVEN BUY ANYTHING...
YOU HAVE TO FIGHT FOR WHAT YOU WANT, THOUGH!!
NO, YOU DON'T!!
GROWRRR
GET BACK HERE!!
TREMBLE TREMBLE
STMP STMP STMP STMP STMP
YIPPEEEE!!
HIS LIFE SEEMS SO STRESS-FUL...

Jobs without End

AKKUN'S FIRST DAY AT WORK IN A CONVENIENCE STORE.
YOU'RE A GREAT EMPLOYEE, AKUTSU-KUN!
THANKS.
PUSH
PUSH
ピンポンピンポン
BEEP-BOOP BEEP-BOOP
ウィーン
WHIRRRR
COMMENCE LOOP.

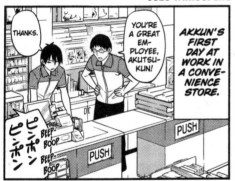

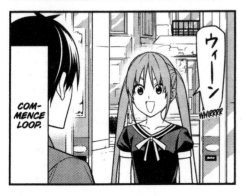

Aho-Girl

\ˈahô͵gərl \ *Japanese, noun.*
A clueless girl.

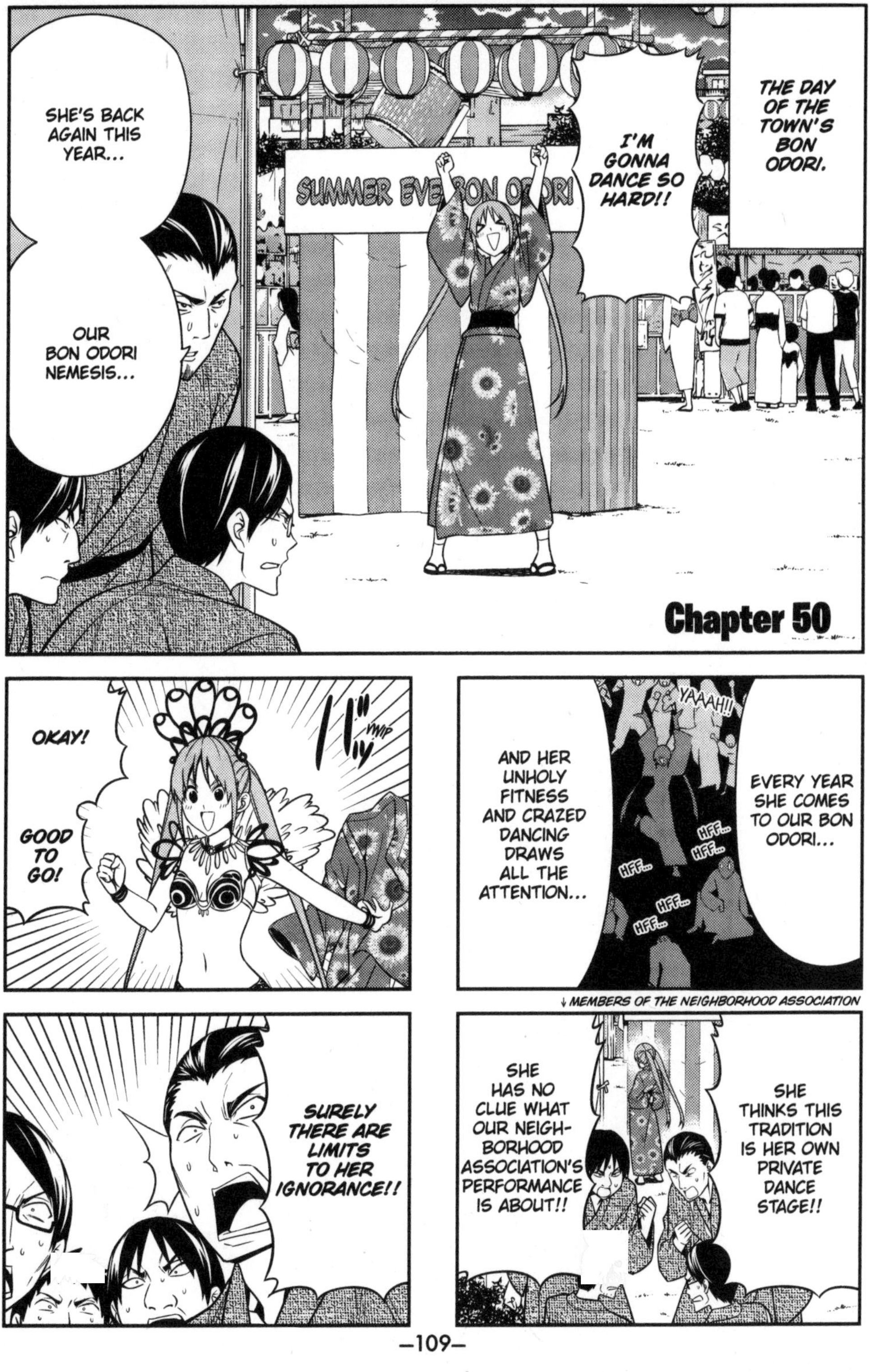
THE DAY OF THE TOWN'S BON ODORI.
I'M GONNA DANCE SO HARD!!
SHE'S BACK AGAIN THIS YEAR...
OUR BON ODORI NEMESIS...
Chapter 50
EVERY YEAR SHE COMES TO OUR BON ODORI...
YAAAH!!
HFF... HFF...
HFF... HFF...
AND HER UNHOLY FITNESS AND CRAZED DANCING DRAWS ALL THE ATTENTION...
OKAY!
GOOD TO GO!
↓ MEMBERS OF THE NEIGHBORHOOD ASSOCIATION
SHE THINKS THIS TRADITION IS HER OWN PRIVATE DANCE STAGE!!
SHE HAS NO CLUE WHAT OUR NEIGHBORHOOD ASSOCIATION'S PERFORMANCE IS ABOUT!!
SURELY THERE ARE LIMITS TO HER IGNORANCE!!

Real Sorry about It

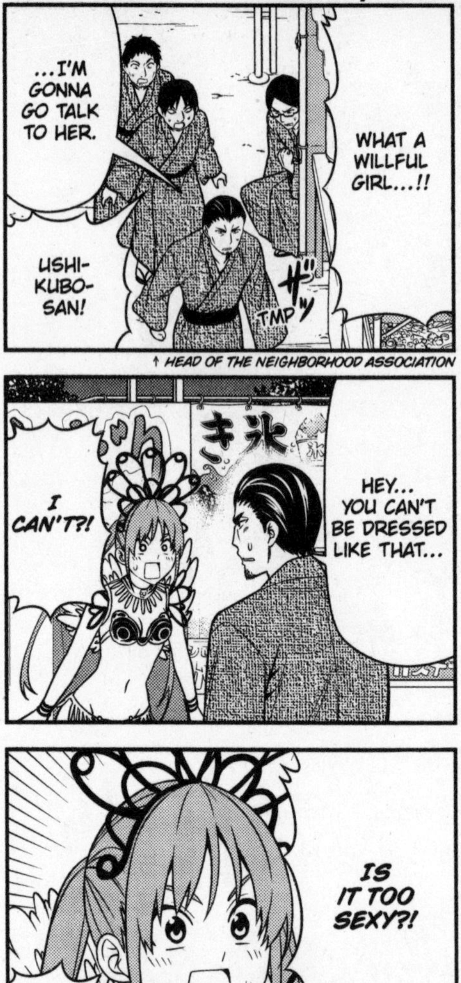
WHAT A WILLFUL GIRL...!!
...I'M GONNA GO TALK TO HER.
TMP
USHI-KUBO-SAN!
↑ HEAD OF THE NEIGHBORHOOD ASSOCIATION
HEY... YOU CAN'T BE DRESSED LIKE THAT...
I CAN'T?!
IS IT TOO SEXY?!
WHAT?!
UH...Y... YEAH, IT IS.
FLUSTER FLUSTER
WELL, NO ARGUING WITH THAT, I GUESS.
SLP
HE'S EMBARRASSED!!
SHE ACTUALLY LISTENED!

I'm in Charge Here

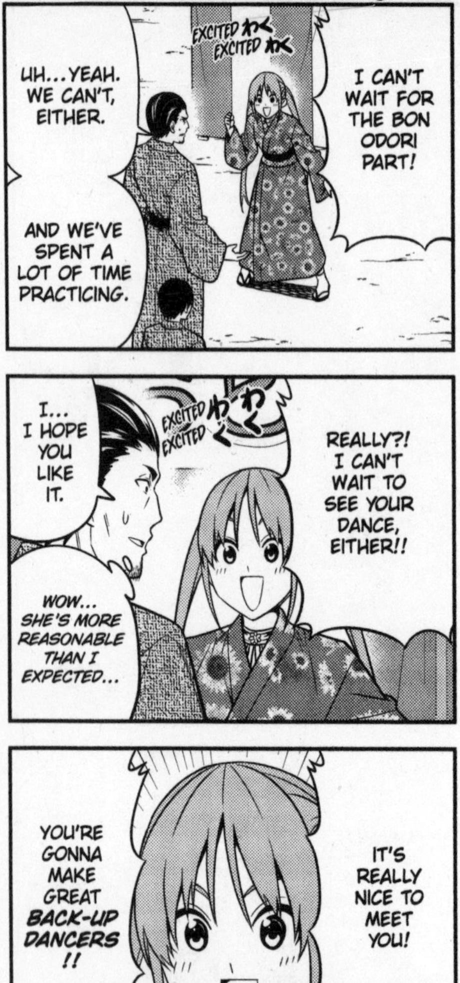
I CAN'T WAIT FOR THE BON ODORI PART!
EXCITED EXCITED
UH...YEAH. WE CAN'T, EITHER.
AND WE'VE SPENT A LOT OF TIME PRACTICING.
REALLY?! I CAN'T WAIT TO SEE YOUR DANCE, EITHER!!
EXCITED EXCITED
I... I HOPE YOU LIKE IT.
WOW... SHE'S MORE REASONABLE THAN I EXPECTED...
IT'S REALLY NICE TO MEET YOU!
YOU'RE GONNA MAKE GREAT BACK-UP DANCERS!!
Y... YOU LITTLE...!!

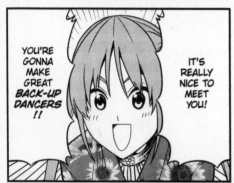

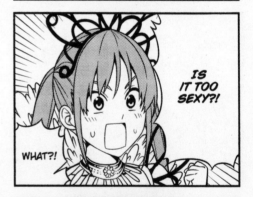

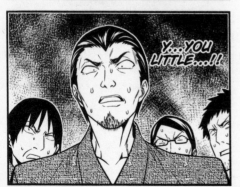

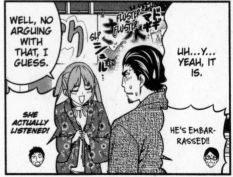

She Really Appreciates It

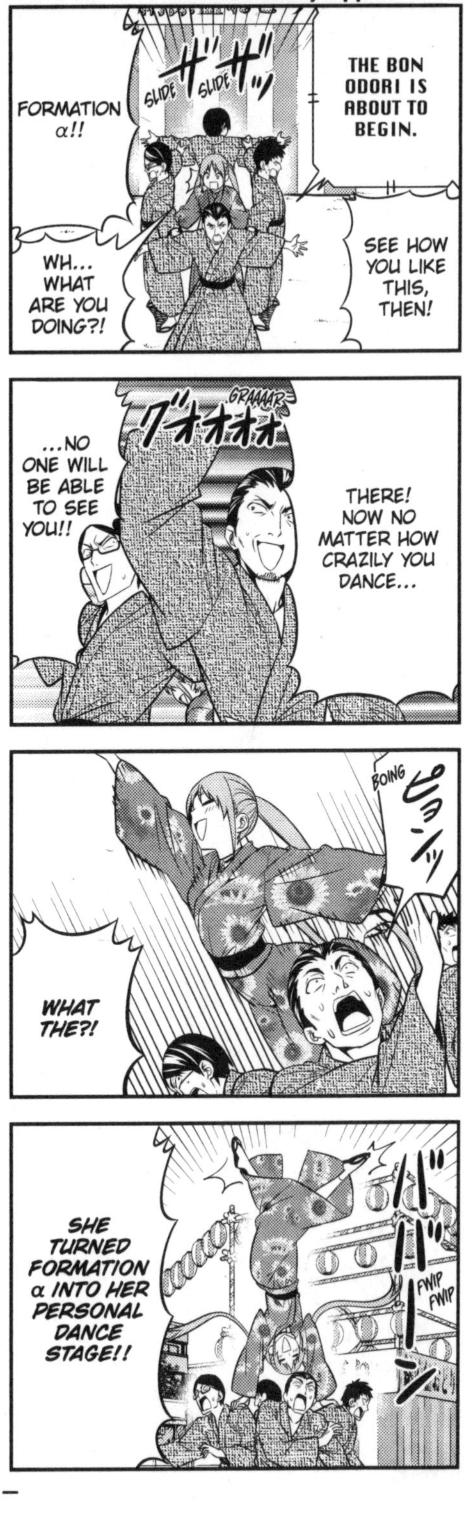
THE BON ODORI IS ABOUT TO BEGIN.
SLIDE
SLIDE
FORMATION α!!
SEE HOW YOU LIKE THIS, THEN!
WH... WHAT ARE YOU DOING?!
GRAAAAR
THERE! NOW NO MATTER HOW CRAZILY YOU DANCE...
...NO ONE WILL BE ABLE TO SEE YOU!!
BOING
WHAT THE?!
FWIP FWIP
SHE TURNED FORMATION α INTO HER PERSONAL DANCE STAGE!!

Born to Be a Star

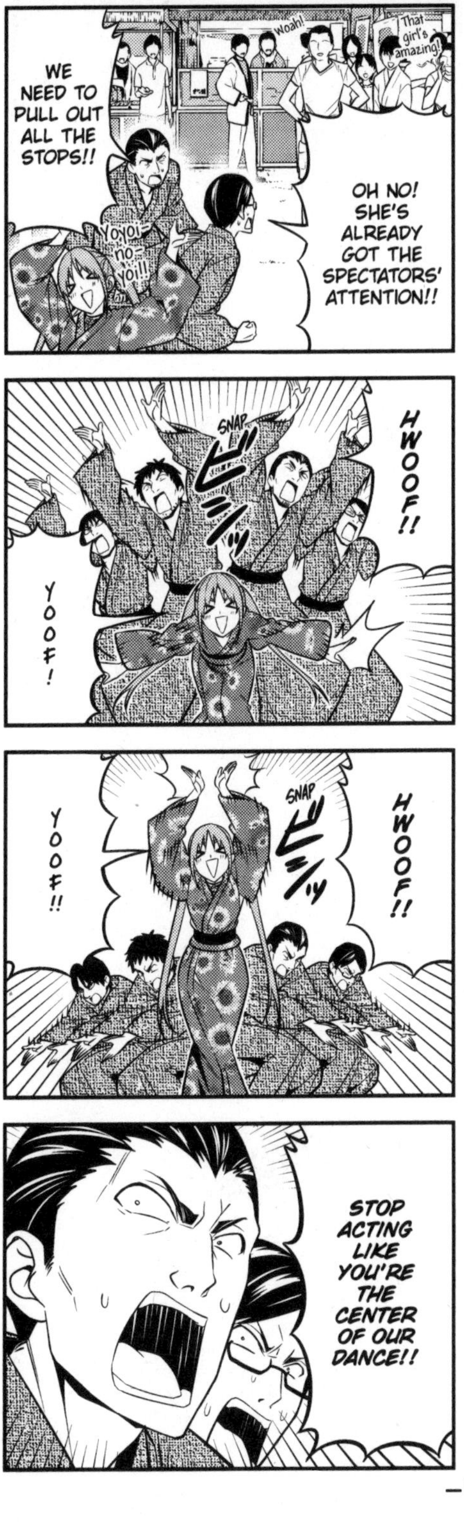
That girl's amazing!
Woah!
OH NO! SHE'S ALREADY GOT THE SPECTATORS' ATTENTION!!
WE NEED TO PULL OUT ALL THE STOPS!!
Yoyoi-no-yoi!!
HWOOOF!!
SNAP
YOOOF!
HWOOOF!!
SNAP
YOOOF!!
STOP ACTING LIKE YOU'RE THE CENTER OF OUR DANCE!!

The Girl Is Terrifying

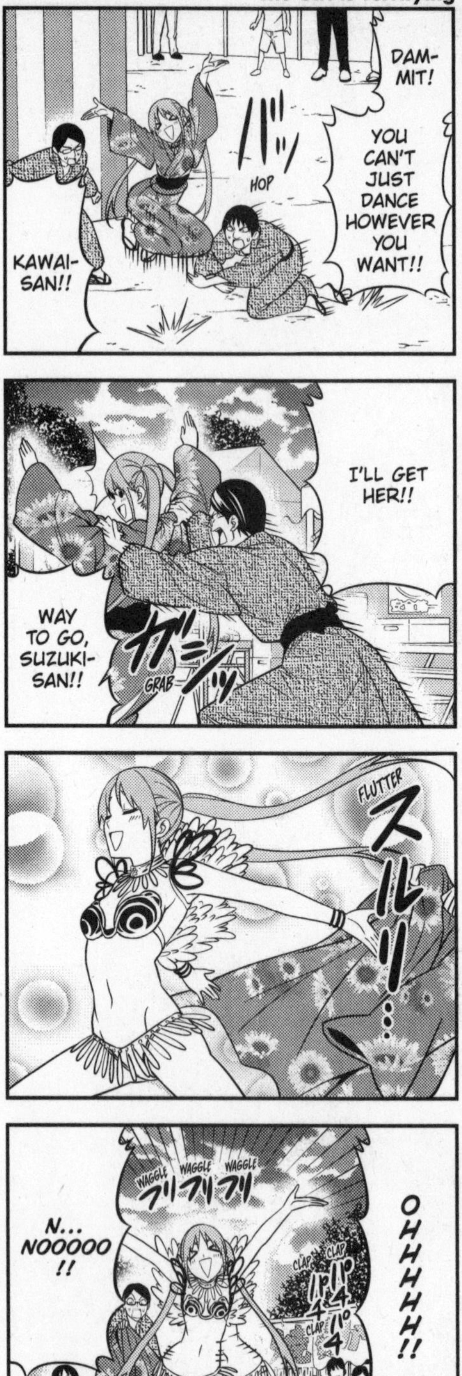
DAM-MIT!
YOU CAN'T JUST DANCE HOWEVER YOU WANT!!
バッ
HOP
KAWAI-SAN!!
I'LL GET HER!!
WAY TO GO, SUZUKI-SAN!!
ガシッ
GRAB
FLUTTER
スルリ…
OHHHHH!!
WAGGLE WAGGLE WAGGLE
フリフリフリ
CLAP CLAP CLAP
パチパチパチ
N... NOOOOO!!

We've Been Training for This

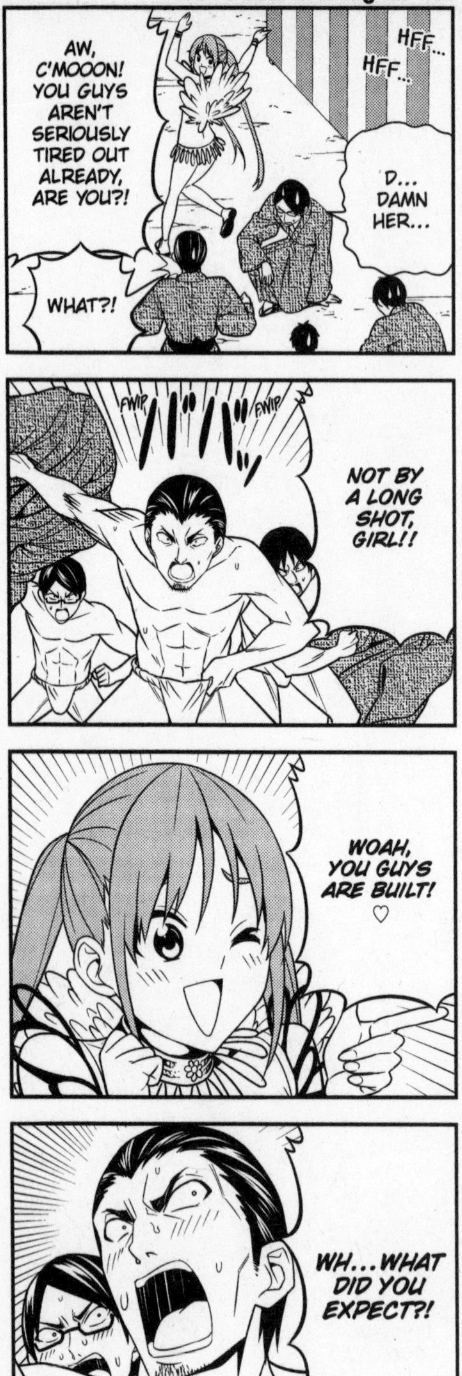
HFF...
HFF...
D... DAMN HER...
AW, C'MOOON! YOU GUYS AREN'T SERIOUSLY TIRED OUT ALREADY, ARE YOU?!
WHAT?!
FWIP
バババッ
FWIP
NOT BY A LONG SHOT, GIRL!!
WOAH, YOU GUYS ARE BUILT! ♡
WH...WHAT DID YOU EXPECT?!

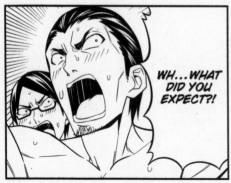

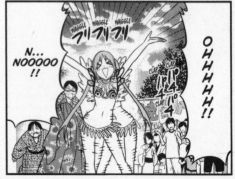

So High Energy

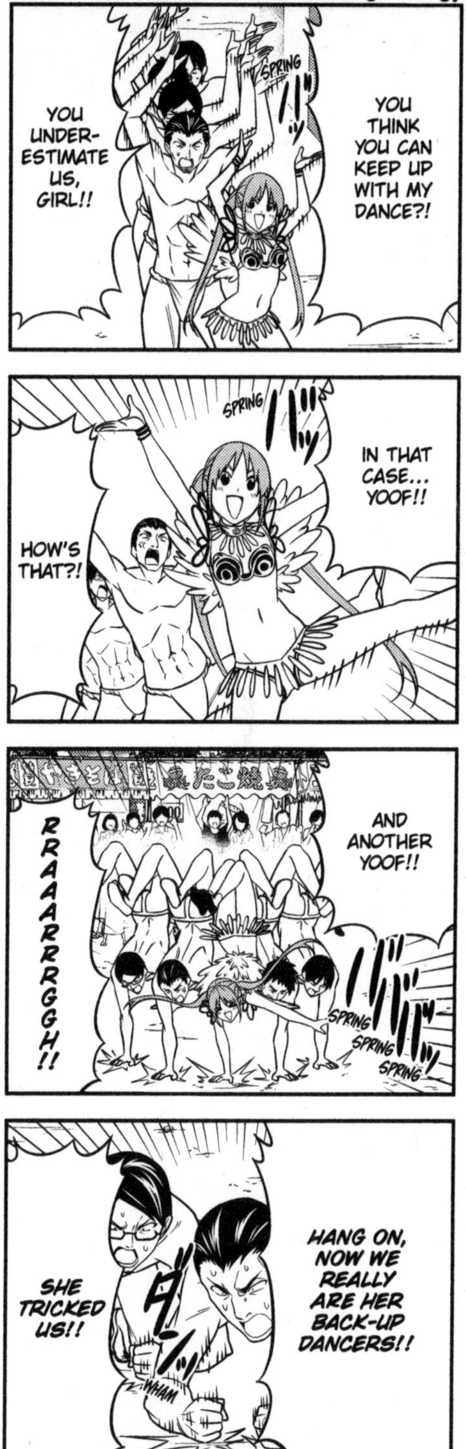
YOU THINK YOU CAN KEEP UP WITH MY DANCE?!
SPRING
YOU UNDER-ESTIMATE US, GIRL!!
SPRING
IN THAT CASE... YOOF!!
HOW'S THAT?!
AND ANOTHER YOOF!!
SPRING
SPRING
SPRING
RRAAAARRRGGH!!
HANG ON, NOW WE REALLY ARE HER BACK-UP DANCERS!!
WHAM
SHE TRICKED US!!

All to Wow the Audience

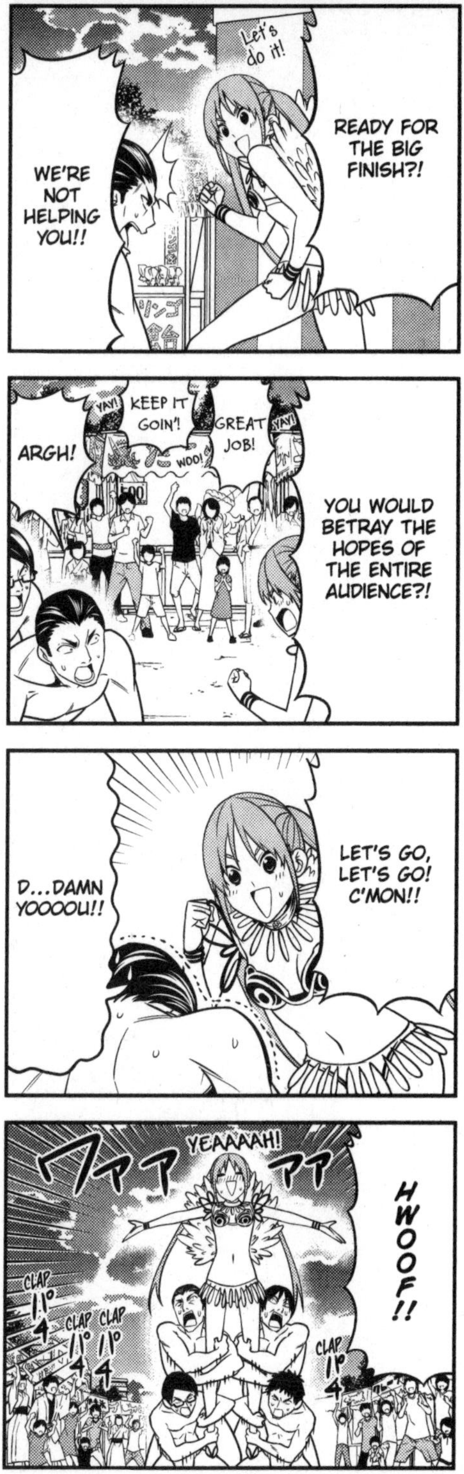
Let's do it!
READY FOR THE BIG FINISH?!
WE'RE NOT HELPING YOU!!
YOU WOULD BETRAY THE HOPES OF THE ENTIRE AUDIENCE?!
YAY!
GREAT JOB!
WOO!
KEEP IT GOIN'!
YAY!
ARGH!
LET'S GO, LET'S GO! C'MON!!
D...DAMN YOOOOU!!
HWOOOF!!
ワァ ア アア
YEAAAAH!
CLAP
CLAP
CLAP
CLAP

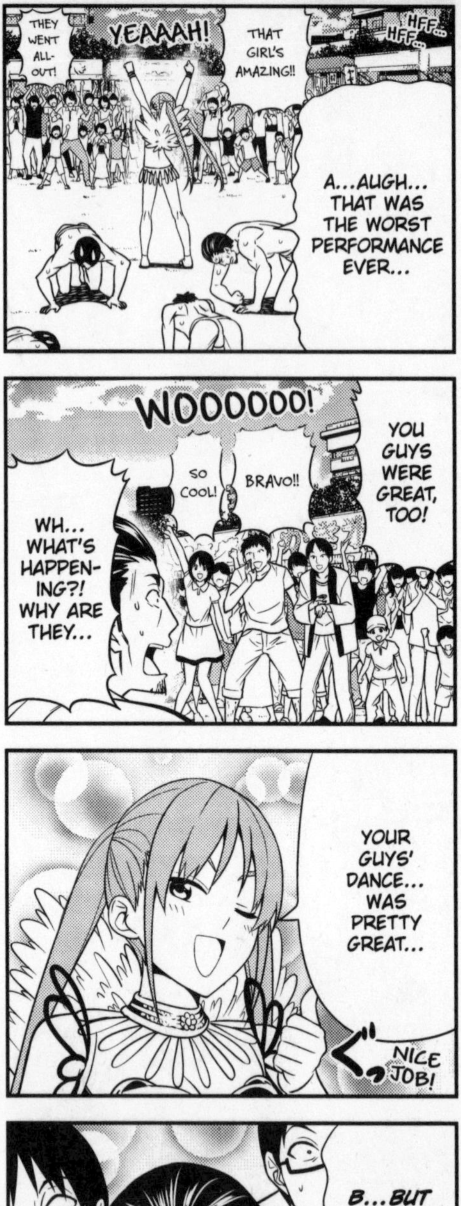
HFF... HFF...
A...AUGH... THAT WAS THE WORST PERFORMANCE EVER...
THAT GIRL'S AMAZING!!
YEAAAH!
THEY WENT ALL-OUT!
YOU GUYS WERE GREAT, TOO!
WOOOOOO!
BRAVO!!
SO COOL!
WH... WHAT'S HAPPEN-ING?! WHY ARE THEY...
YOUR GUYS' DANCE... WAS PRETTY GREAT...
NICE JOB!
B...BUT YOU'RE OUR NEMESIS ...

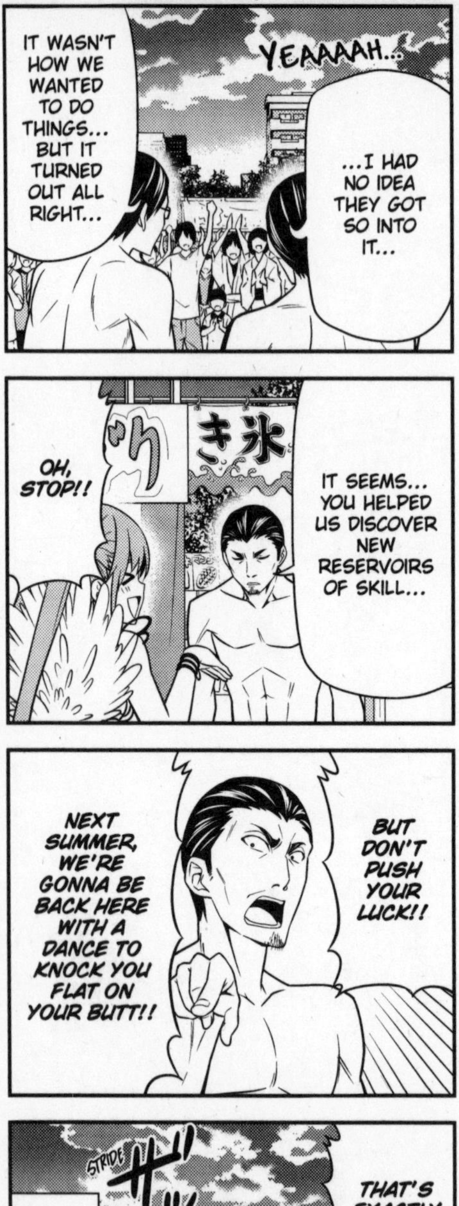
...I HAD NO IDEA THEY GOT SO INTO IT...
YEAAAAH...
IT WASN'T HOW WE WANTED TO DO THINGS... BUT IT TURNED OUT ALL RIGHT...
IT SEEMS... YOU HELPED US DISCOVER NEW RESERVOIRS OF SKILL...
OH, STOP!!
BUT DON'T PUSH YOUR LUCK!!
NEXT SUMMER, WE'RE GONNA BE BACK HERE WITH A DANCE TO KNOCK YOU FLAT ON YOUR BUTT!!
THAT'S EXACTLY WHAT I WANT!!
STRIDE
AND SO A RIVALRY IS BORN.

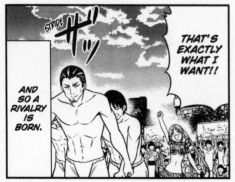

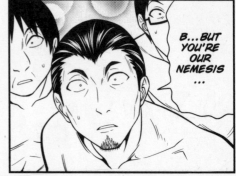

She Would Dress Her Dog Up

THE NEXT DAY
じゃーーん
TADAAA
HE MAKES IT WORK!!
WOOF!
He kinda does...

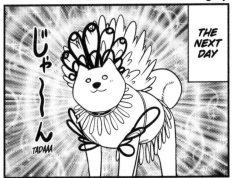

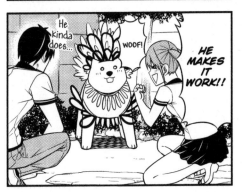

Aho-Girl

(EZ Do)

\\'ahô͵gərl\\ *Japanese, noun.*
A clueless girl.

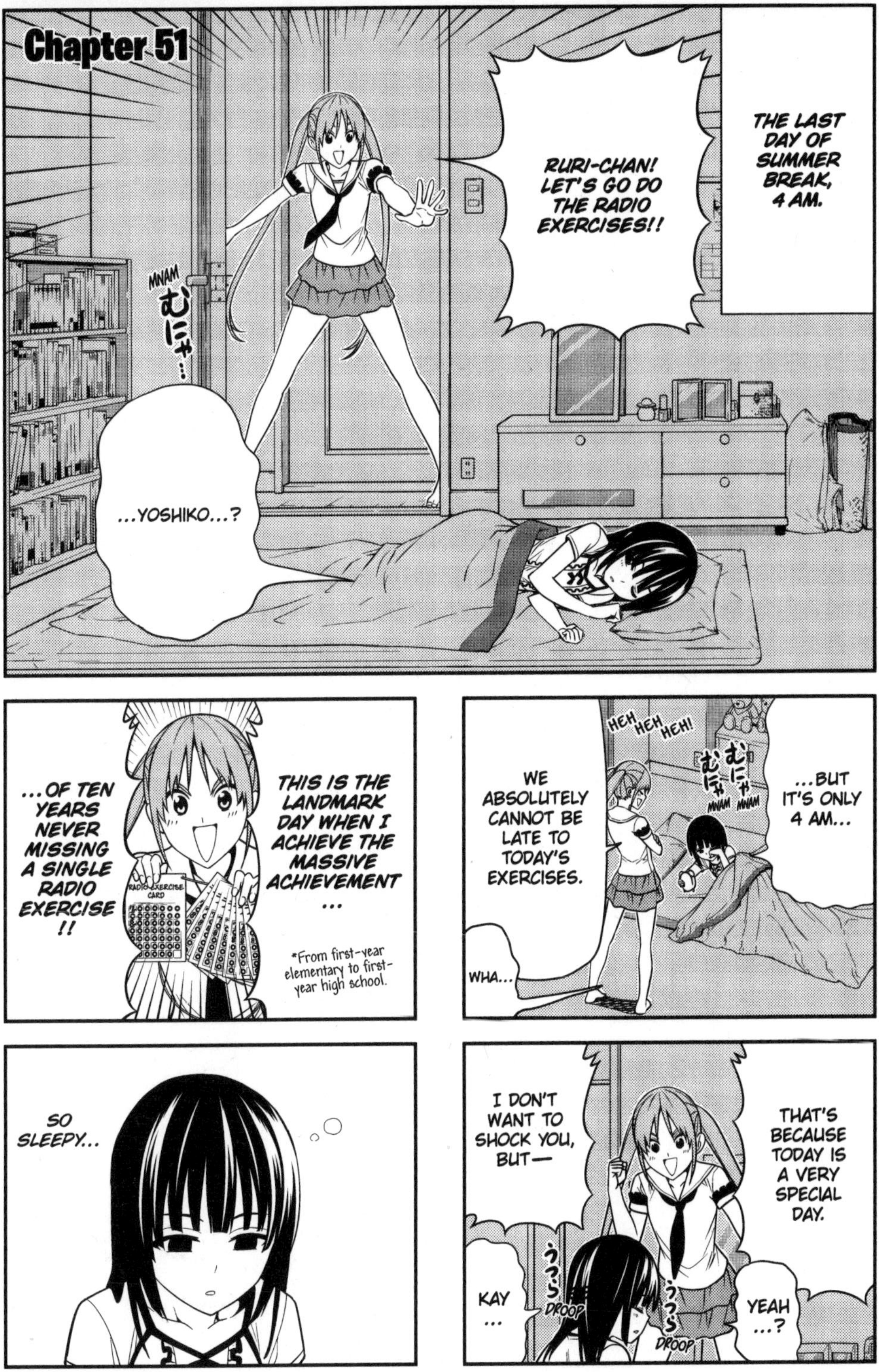
Chapter 51
THE LAST DAY OF SUMMER BREAK, 4 AM.
RURI-CHAN! LET'S GO DO THE RADIO EXERCISES!!
MNAM むにゃ…
...YOSHIKO...?
HEH HEH HEH!
...BUT IT'S ONLY 4 AM...
むにゃむにゃ MNAM MNAM
WE ABSOLUTELY CANNOT BE LATE TO TODAY'S EXERCISES.
WHA...
THIS IS THE LANDMARK DAY WHEN I ACHIEVE THE MASSIVE ACHIEVEMENT ...
...OF TEN YEARS NEVER MISSING A SINGLE RADIO EXERCISE!!
RADIO EXERCISE CARD
*From first-year elementary to first-year high school.
THAT'S BECAUSE TODAY IS A VERY SPECIAL DAY.
I DON'T WANT TO SHOCK YOU, BUT—
YEAH ...?
うつら DROOP
うつら DROOP
KAY ...
SO SLEEPY...

Something Happened

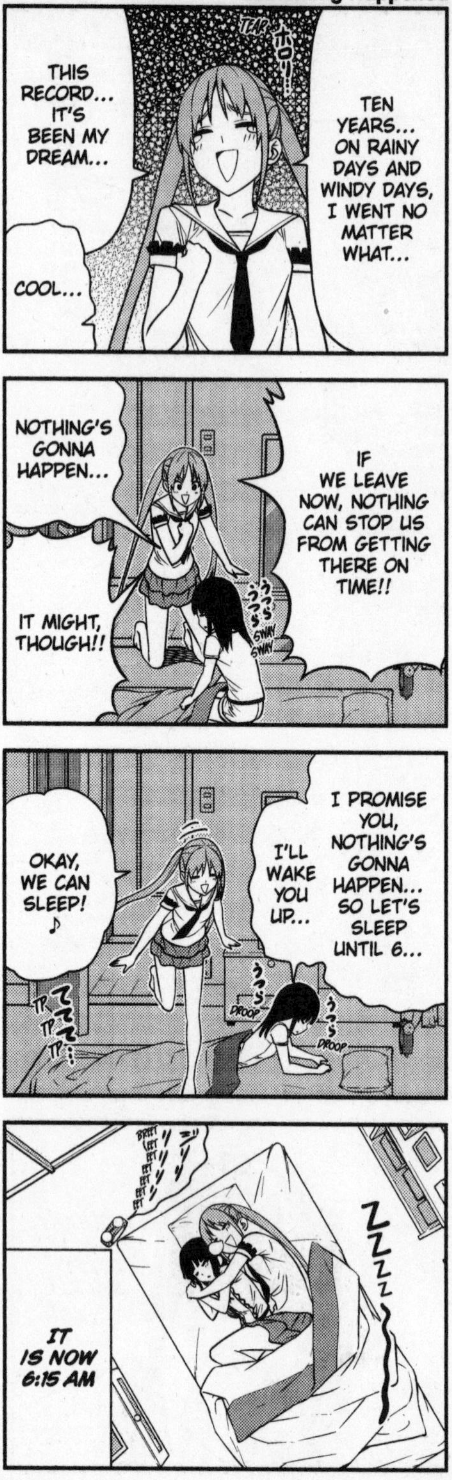
TEAR ホロリ…
TEN YEARS... ON RAINY DAYS AND WINDY DAYS, I WENT NO MATTER WHAT...
THIS RECORD... IT'S BEEN MY DREAM...
COOL...
IF WE LEAVE NOW, NOTHING CAN STOP US FROM GETTING THERE ON TIME!!
うつらうつら SWAY SWAY
NOTHING'S GONNA HAPPEN...
IT MIGHT, THOUGH!!
I PROMISE YOU, NOTHING'S GONNA HAPPEN... SO LET'S SLEEP UNTIL 6...
I'LL WAKE YOU UP...
OKAY, WE CAN SLEEP! ♪
うつら DROOP
うつら DROOP
TP TP TP TP
BREET EET EET EET EET EET
ZZZZ~
IT IS NOW 6:15 AM

Panic

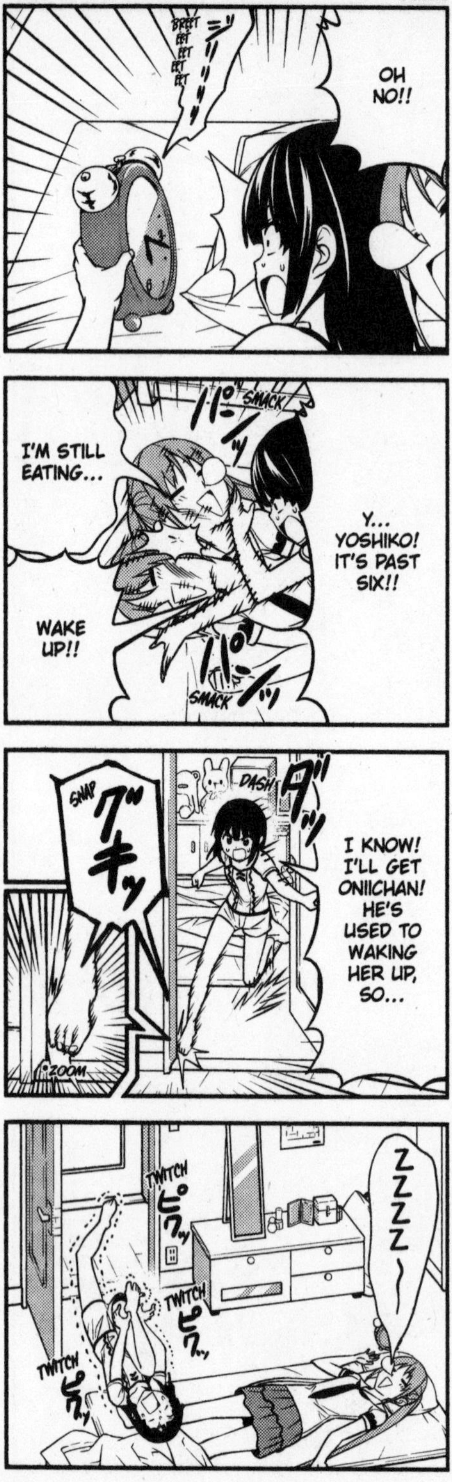
BREET EET EET EET EET
OH NO!!
Y... YOSHIKO! IT'S PAST SIX!!
SMACK
I'M STILL EATING...
WAKE UP!!
SMACK
I KNOW! I'LL GET ONIICHAN! HE'S USED TO WAKING HER UP, SO...
DASH
SNAP
ZOOM
ZZZZ~
TWITCH
TWITCH
TWITCH

She's Still in Pain

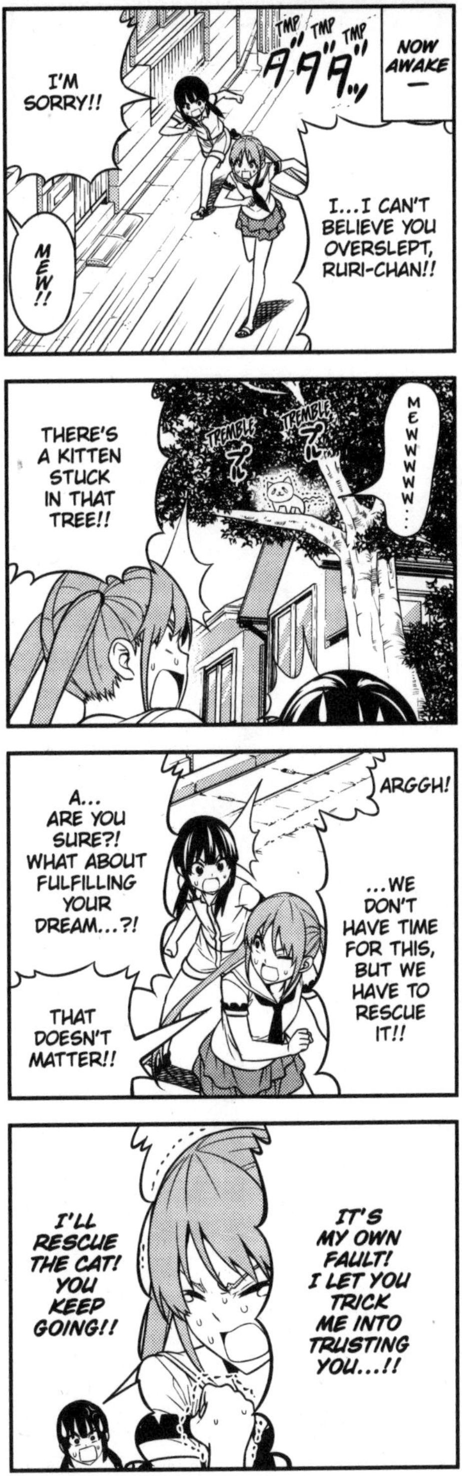
NOW AWAKE —
TMP TMP TMP
I...I CAN'T BELIEVE YOU OVERSLEPT, RURI-CHAN!!
I'M SORRY!!
MEW!!
MEWWWWWW...
TREMBLE
TREMBLE
THERE'S A KITTEN STUCK IN THAT TREE!!
ARGGH!
...WE DON'T HAVE TIME FOR THIS, BUT WE HAVE TO RESCUE IT!!
A... ARE YOU SURE?! WHAT ABOUT FULFILLING YOUR DREAM...?!
THAT DOESN'T MATTER!!
IT'S MY OWN FAULT! I LET YOU TRICK ME INTO TRUSTING YOU...!!
I'LL RESCUE THE CAT! YOU KEEP GOING!!

That Won't Help

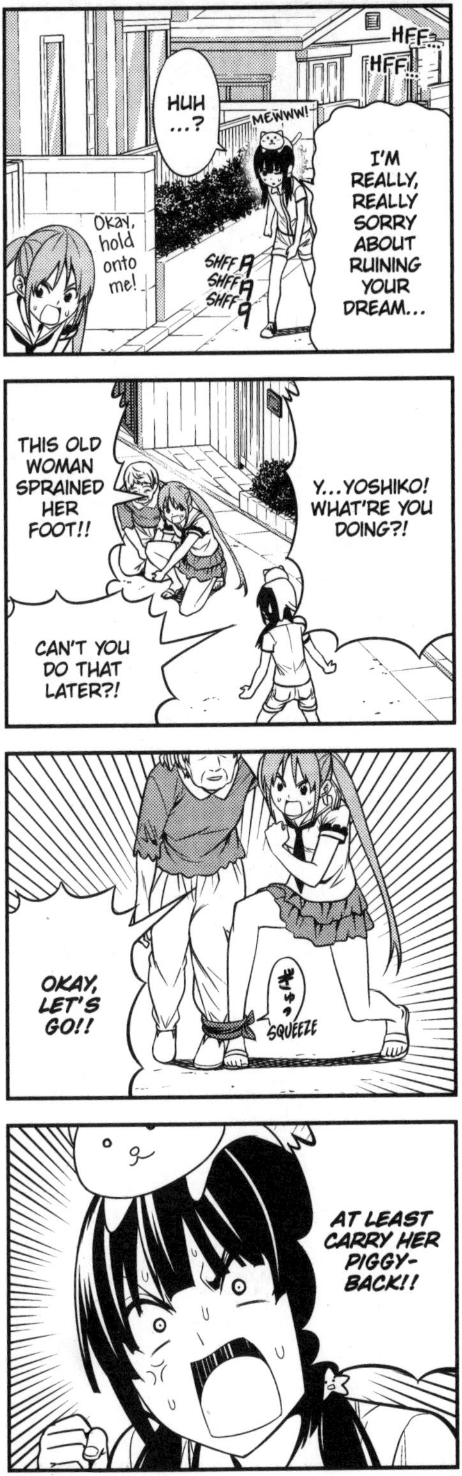
HFF...
HFF...
MEWWW!
I'M REALLY, REALLY SORRY ABOUT RUINING YOUR DREAM...
HUH ...?
SHFF SHFF SHFF
Okay, hold onto me!
Y...YOSHIKO! WHAT'RE YOU DOING?!
THIS OLD WOMAN SPRAINED HER FOOT!!
CAN'T YOU DO THAT LATER?!
ぎゅっ
SQUEEZE
OKAY, LET'S GO!!
AT LEAST CARRY HER PIGGY-BACK!!

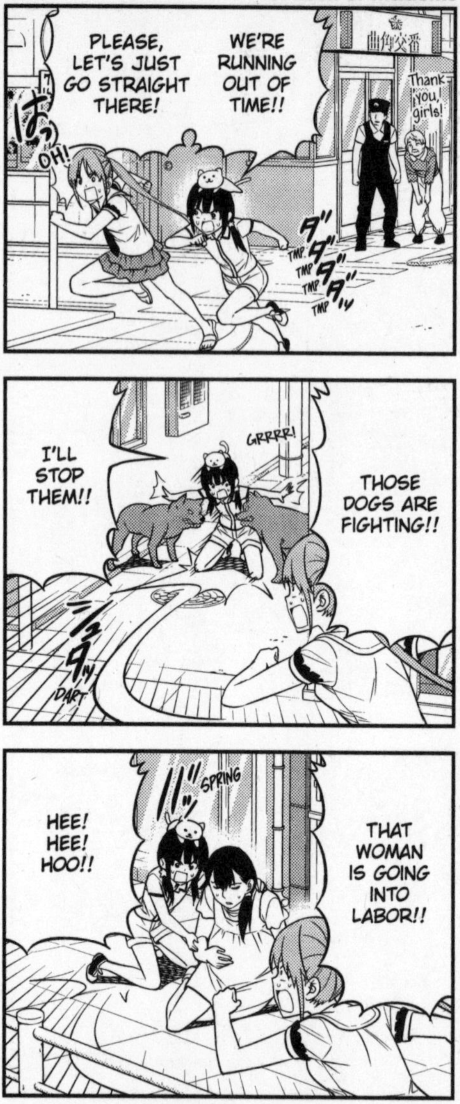
曲角交番
Thank you, girls!
WE'RE RUNNING OUT OF TIME!!
PLEASE, LET'S JUST GO STRAIGHT THERE!
OH!
TMP TMP TMP TMP
THOSE DOGS ARE FIGHTING!!
GRRRR!
I'LL STOP THEM!!
DART
SPRING
THAT WOMAN IS GOING INTO LABOR!!
HEE! HEE! HOO!!
THOSE TWO ARE ABOUT TO RUN INTO EACH OTHER!!
LET IT GO! THEY'RE FATED TO MEET!!

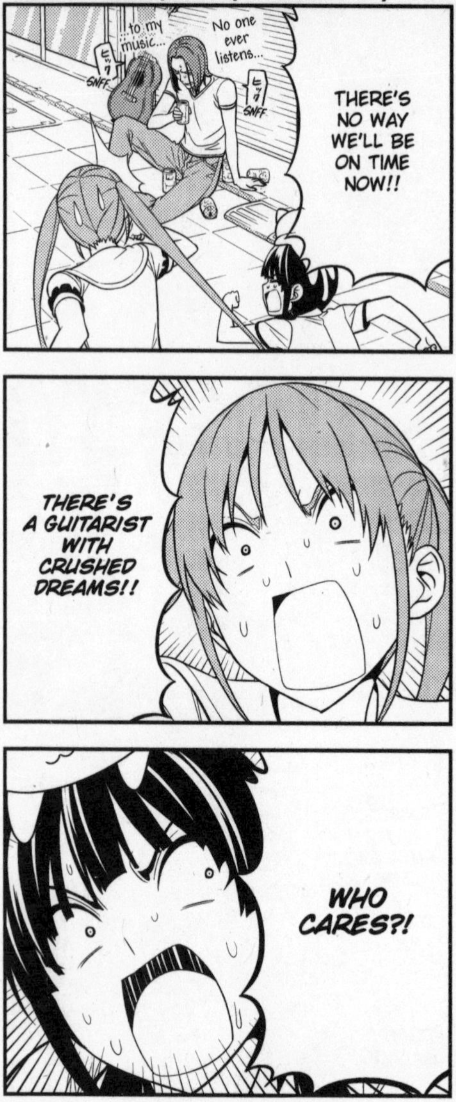
THERE'S NO WAY WE'LL BE ON TIME NOW!!
No one ever listens...
...to my music...
SNFF
SNFF
THERE'S A GUITARIST WITH CRUSHED DREAMS!!
WHO CARES?!
WHAT KIND OF MON-STER ARE YOU...?
Nrigh... I'm so worthless...
TREMBLE
HOW AM I THE BAD ONE HERE?!
TREMBLE

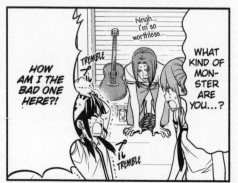

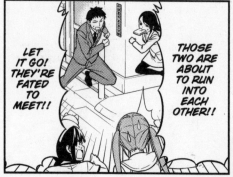

It's Obvious Why

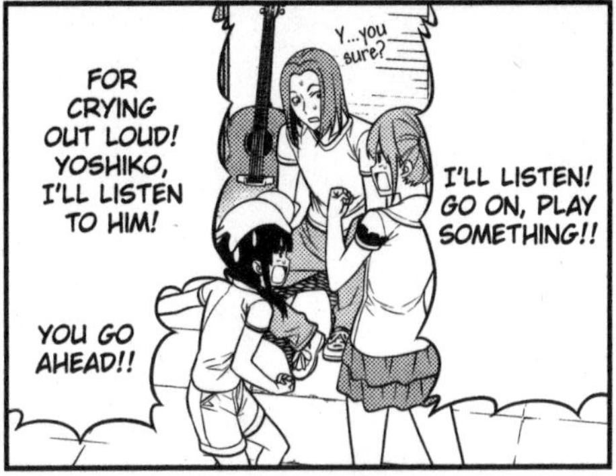
Y...you sure?
I'LL LISTEN! GO ON, PLAY SOMETHING!!
FOR CRYING OUT LOUD! YOSHIKO, I'LL LISTEN TO HIM!
YOU GO AHEAD!!

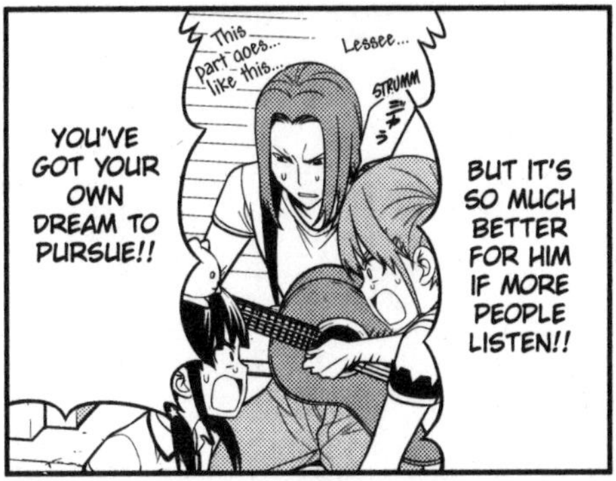
Lessee...
STRUMM
This part goes... like this...
BUT IT'S SO MUCH BETTER FOR HIM IF MORE PEOPLE LISTEN!!
YOU'VE GOT YOUR OWN DREAM TO PURSUE!!

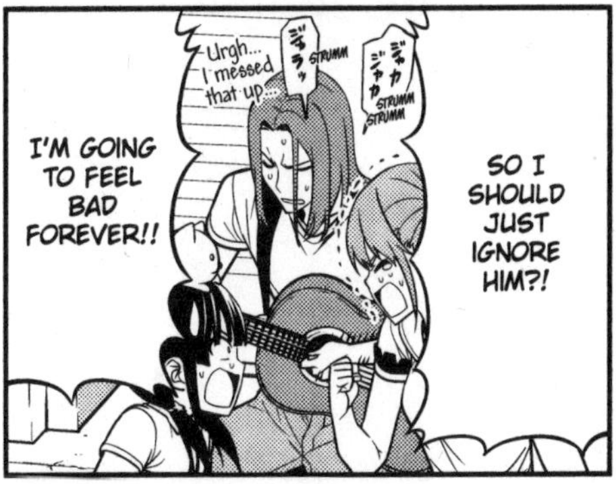
STRUMM STRUMM
STRUMM
Urgh... I messed that up...
SO I SHOULD JUST IGNORE HIM?!
I'M GOING TO FEEL BAD FOREVER!!

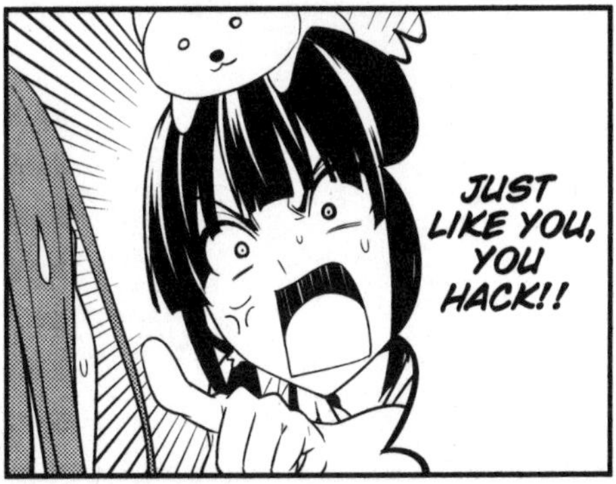
JUST LIKE YOU, YOU HACK!!

You're Not Wrong

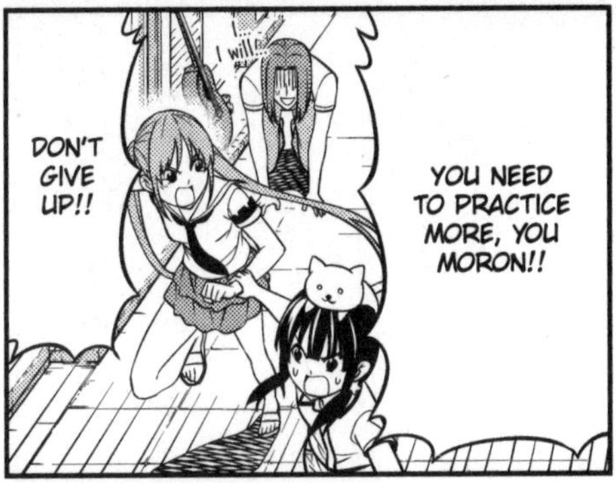
YOU NEED TO PRACTICE MORE, YOU MORON!!
I... I will...
DON'T GIVE UP!!

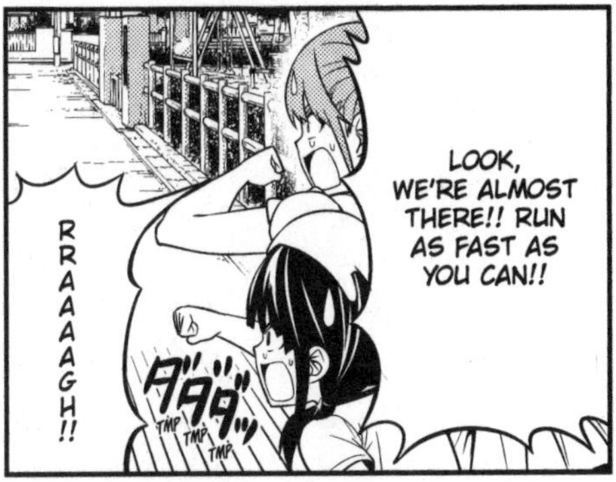
LOOK, WE'RE ALMOST THERE!! RUN AS FAST AS YOU CAN!!
RRAAAAAGH!!
ダダダッ
TMP TMP TMP

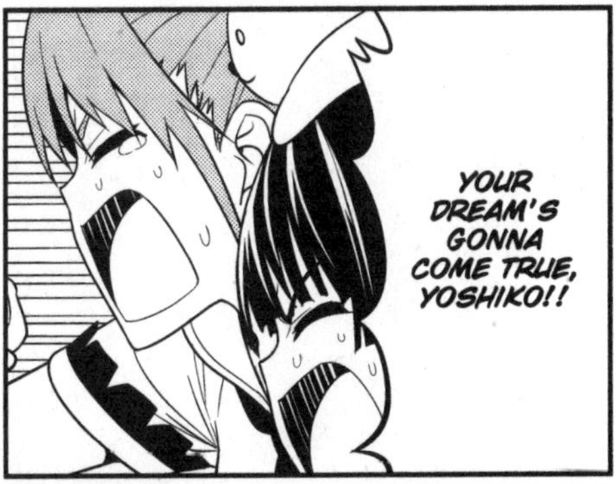
YOUR DREAM'S GONNA COME TRUE, YOSHIKO!!

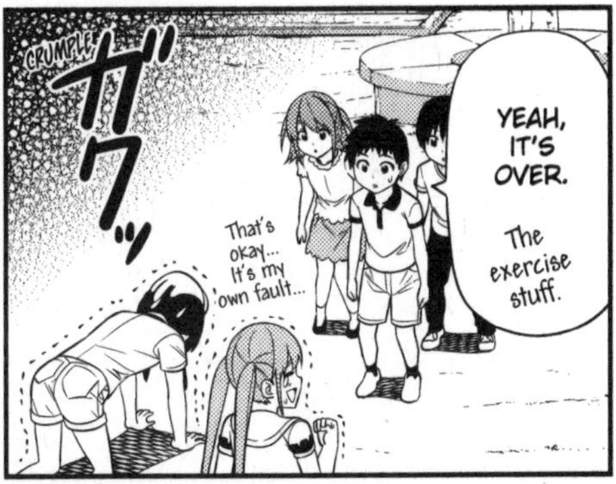
YEAH, IT'S OVER.
The exercise stuff.
That's okay... It's my own fault...
CRUMPLE
ガクッ

The Gleam of a Miracle

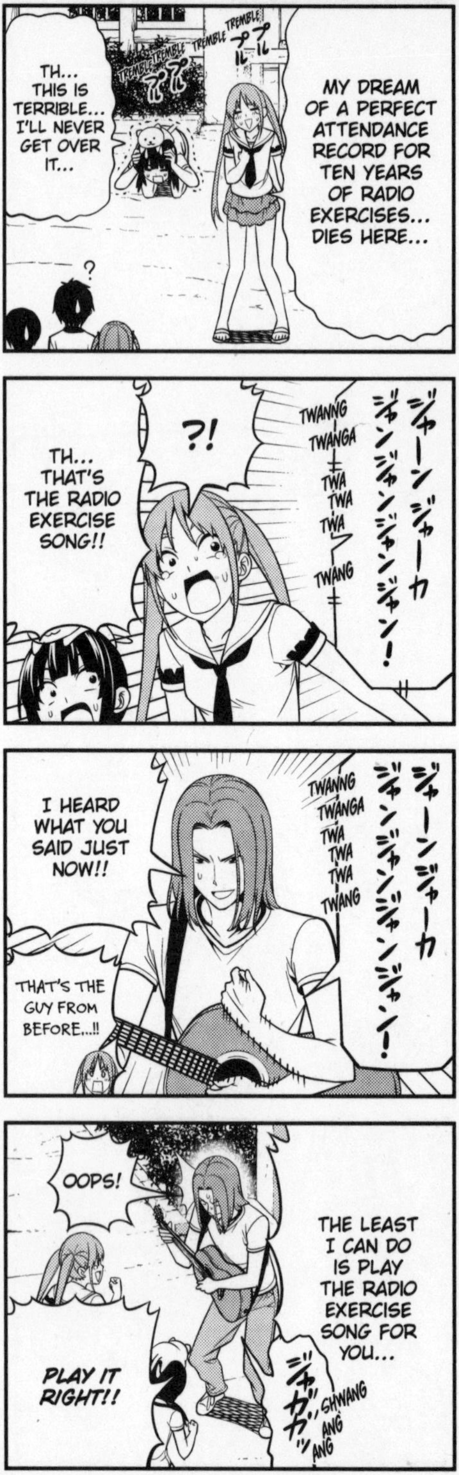

TREMBLE プル
TREMBLE プ
TREMBLE プ
MY DREAM OF A PERFECT ATTENDANCE RECORD FOR TEN YEARS OF RADIO EXERCISES... DIES HERE...
TH... THIS IS TERRIBLE... I'LL NEVER GET OVER IT...
?
ジャーン ジャーカ ジャンジャンジャンジャン!
TWANNG TWANGA TWA TWA TWA TWANG
?!
TH... THAT'S THE RADIO EXERCISE SONG!!
ジャーンジャーカ ジャンジャンジャンジャン!
TWANNG TWANGA TWA TWA TWA TWANG
I HEARD WHAT YOU SAID JUST NOW!!
THAT'S THE GUY FROM BEFORE...!!
THE LEAST I CAN DO IS PLAY THE RADIO EXERCISE SONG FOR YOU...
OOPS!
ジャガガッ
SHWANG ANG ANG
PLAY IT RIGHT!!

Congratulations!

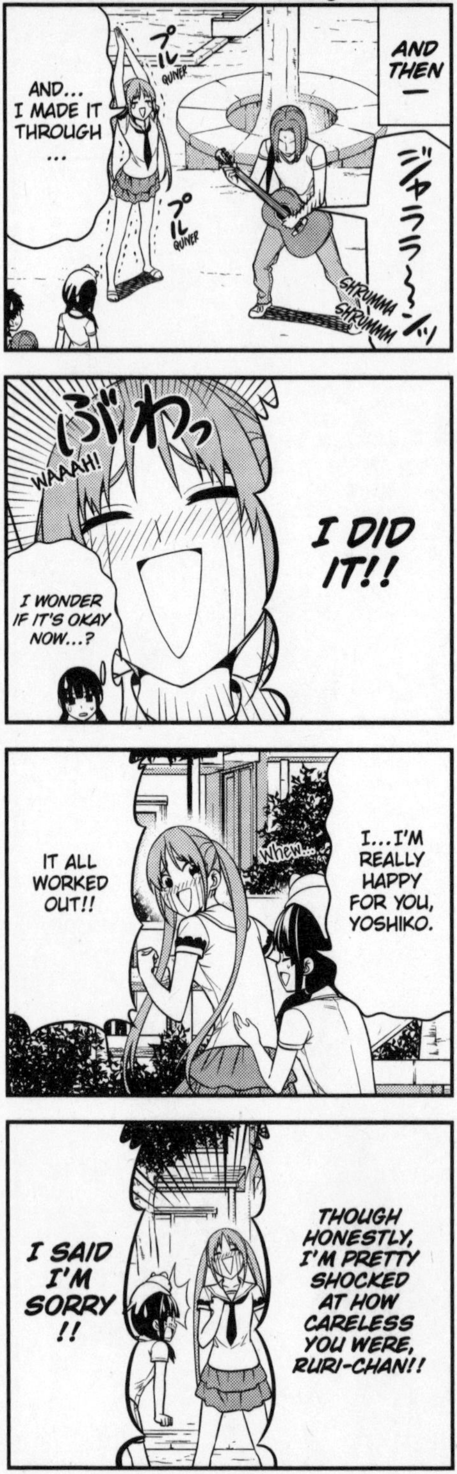

AND THEN—
ジャララ〜〜ンッ
SHRUMMA SHRUMMM
プル QUIVER
AND... I MADE IT THROUGH...
プル QUIVER
I DID IT!!
ぶわっ
WAAAH!
I WONDER IF IT'S OKAY NOW...?
I...I'M REALLY HAPPY FOR YOU, YOSHIKO.
Whew...
IT ALL WORKED OUT!!
THOUGH HONESTLY, I'M PRETTY SHOCKED AT HOW CARELESS YOU WERE, RURI-CHAN!!
I SAID I'M SORRY!!

I'll Look You up When I Hit the Big Time

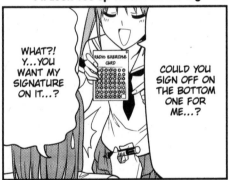

COULD YOU SIGN OFF ON THE BOTTOM ONE FOR ME...?
RADIO EXERCISE CARD
WHAT?! Y...YOU WANT MY SIGNATURE ON IT...?
OF COURSE... SOMEDAY, I'LL HAVE THE AUTOGRAPH OF THE BEST GUITARIST IN JAPAN...
Y... YOU GOT IT!!

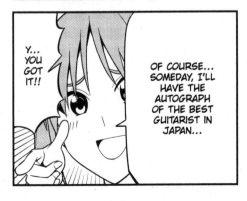

(Run, Lola)

Aho-Girl

\\ˈahôˌgərl\\ *Japanese, noun.*
A clueless girl.

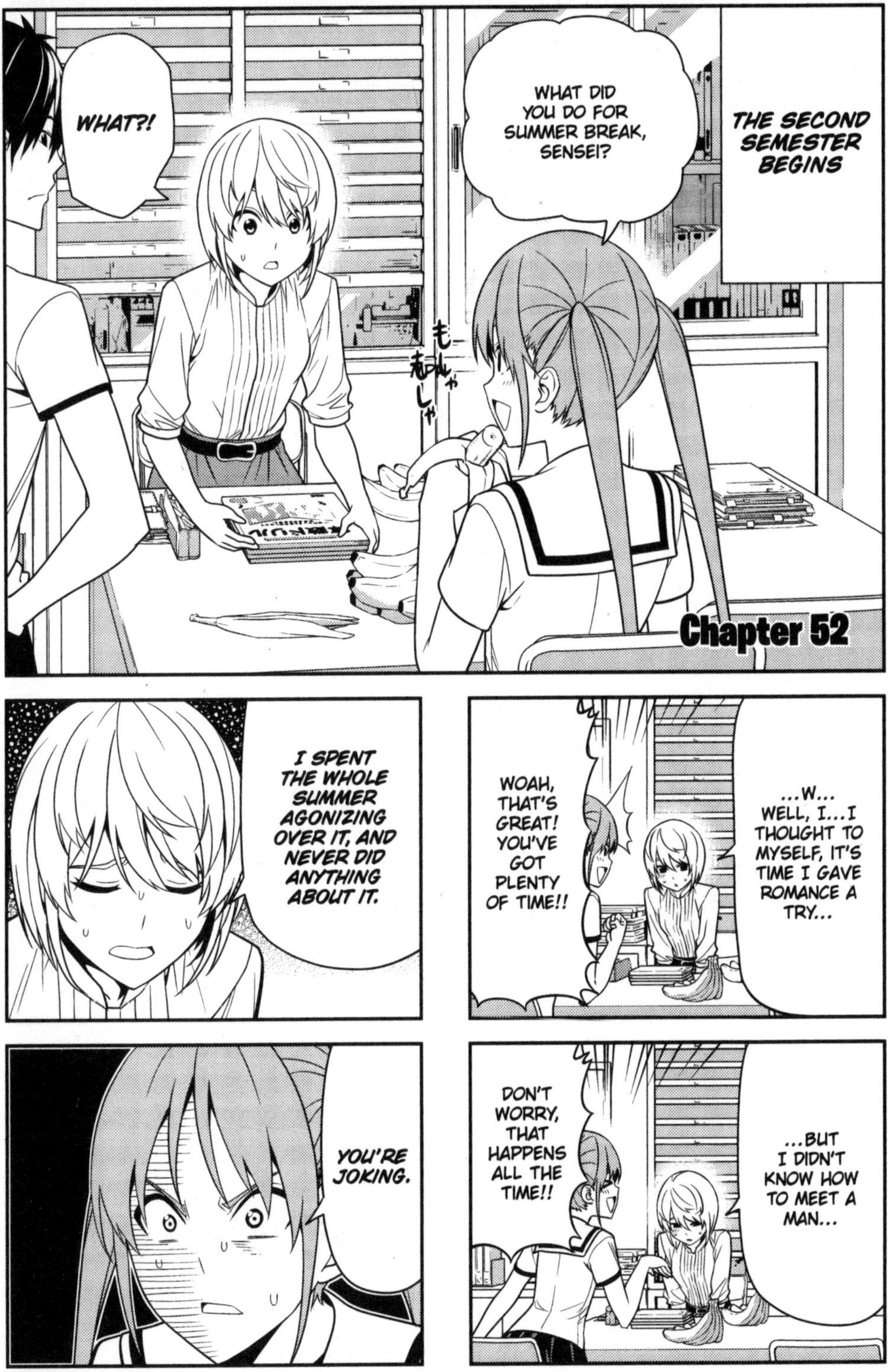
THE SECOND SEMESTER BEGINS
WHAT DID YOU DO FOR SUMMER BREAK, SENSEI?
WHAT?!
Chapter 52
...W... WELL, I...I THOUGHT TO MYSELF, IT'S TIME I GAVE ROMANCE A TRY...
WOAH, THAT'S GREAT! YOU'VE GOT PLENTY OF TIME!!
I SPENT THE WHOLE SUMMER AGONIZING OVER IT, AND NEVER DID ANYTHING ABOUT IT.
...BUT I DIDN'T KNOW HOW TO MEET A MAN...
DON'T WORRY, THAT HAPPENS ALL THE TIME!!
YOU'RE JOKING.

Don't Hold Back

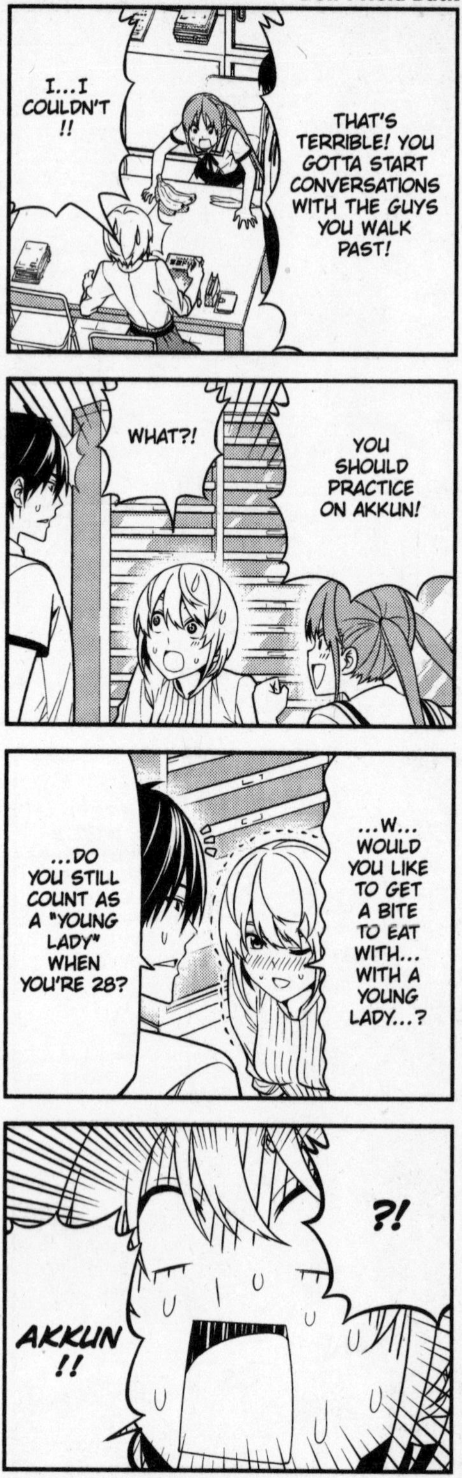
THAT'S TERRIBLE! YOU GOTTA START CONVERSATIONS WITH THE GUYS YOU WALK PAST!
I...I COULDN'T !!
YOU SHOULD PRACTICE ON AKKUN!
WHAT?!
...W... WOULD YOU LIKE TO GET A BITE TO EAT WITH... WITH A YOUNG LADY...?
...DO YOU STILL COUNT AS A "YOUNG LADY" WHEN YOU'RE 28?
?!
AKKUN !!

With a Straight Face

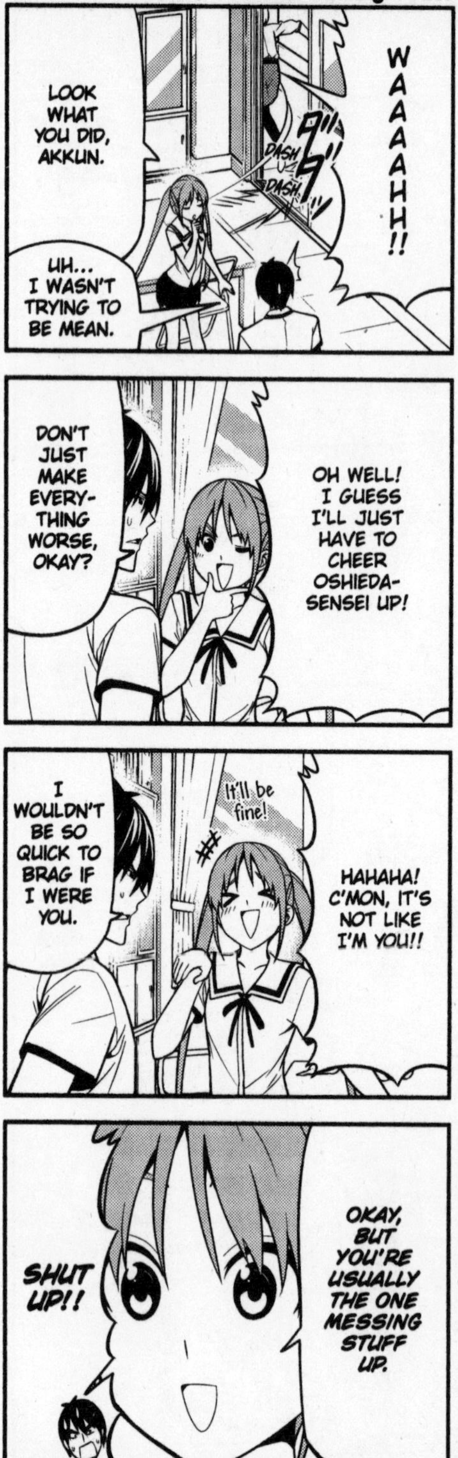
WAAAAAHH!!
DASH
DASH
LOOK WHAT YOU DID, AKKUN.
UH... I WASN'T TRYING TO BE MEAN.
OH WELL! I GUESS I'LL JUST HAVE TO CHEER OSHIEDA-SENSEI UP!
DON'T JUST MAKE EVERY-THING WORSE, OKAY?
It'll be fine!
HAHAHA! C'MON, IT'S NOT LIKE I'M YOU!!
I WOULDN'T BE SO QUICK TO BRAG IF I WERE YOU.
OKAY, BUT YOU'RE USUALLY THE ONE MESSING STUFF UP.
SHUT UP!!

Zero Resistance to Men

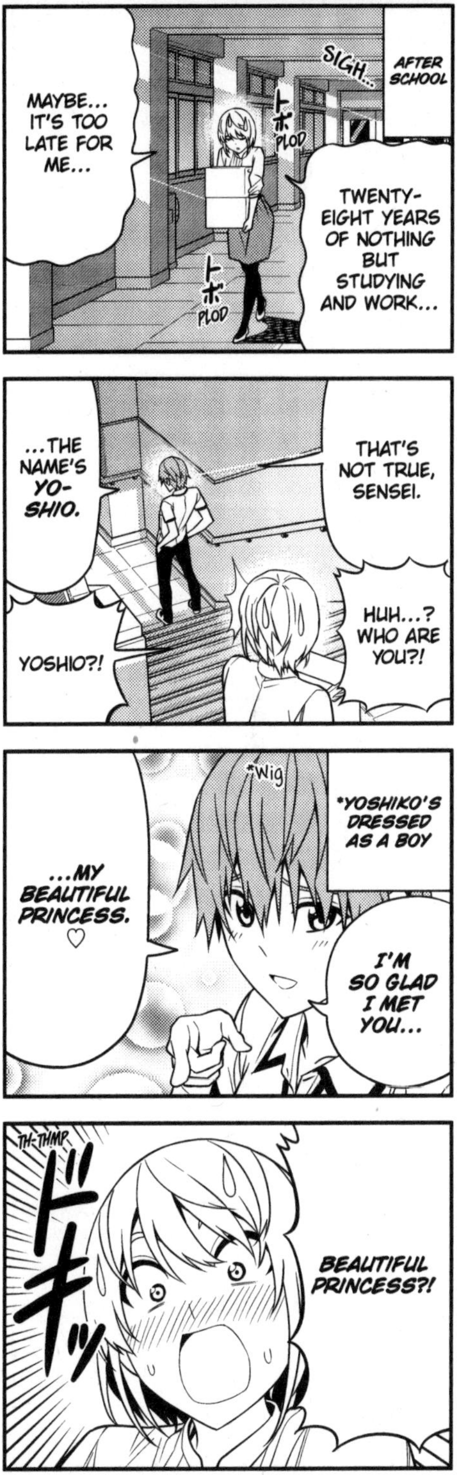
AFTER SCHOOL
SIGH...
トボ
PLOD
TWENTY-EIGHT YEARS OF NOTHING BUT STUDYING AND WORK...
MAYBE... IT'S TOO LATE FOR ME...
トボ
PLOD
THAT'S NOT TRUE, SENSEI.
...THE NAME'S YO-SHIO.
HUH...? WHO ARE YOU?!
YOSHIO?!
*YOSHIKO'S DRESSED AS A BOY
*Wig
I'M SO GLAD I MET YOU...
...MY BEAUTIFUL PRINCESS. ♡
TH-THMP
ドキッ
BEAUTIFUL PRINCESS?!

Falling Headlong

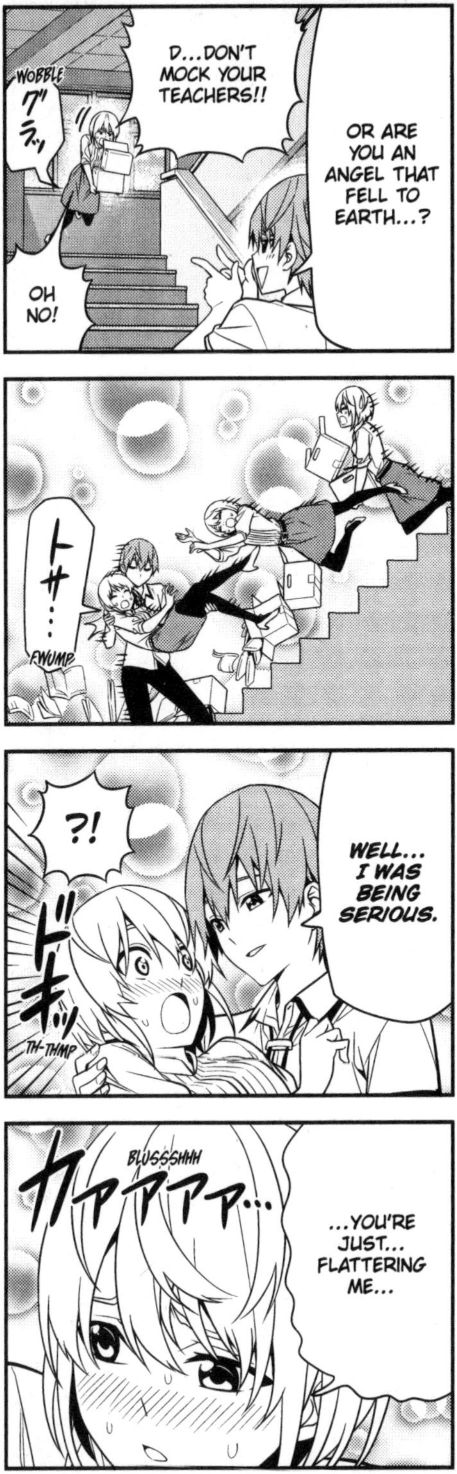
OR ARE YOU AN ANGEL THAT FELL TO EARTH...?
D...DON'T MOCK YOUR TEACHERS!!
WOBBLE
グラッ
OH NO!
トサ...
FWUMP
WELL... I WAS BEING SERIOUS.
?!
ドキッ
TH-THMP
...YOU'RE JUST... FLATTERING ME...
カァァァァ...
BLUSSSHHH

That's Just Your Impression

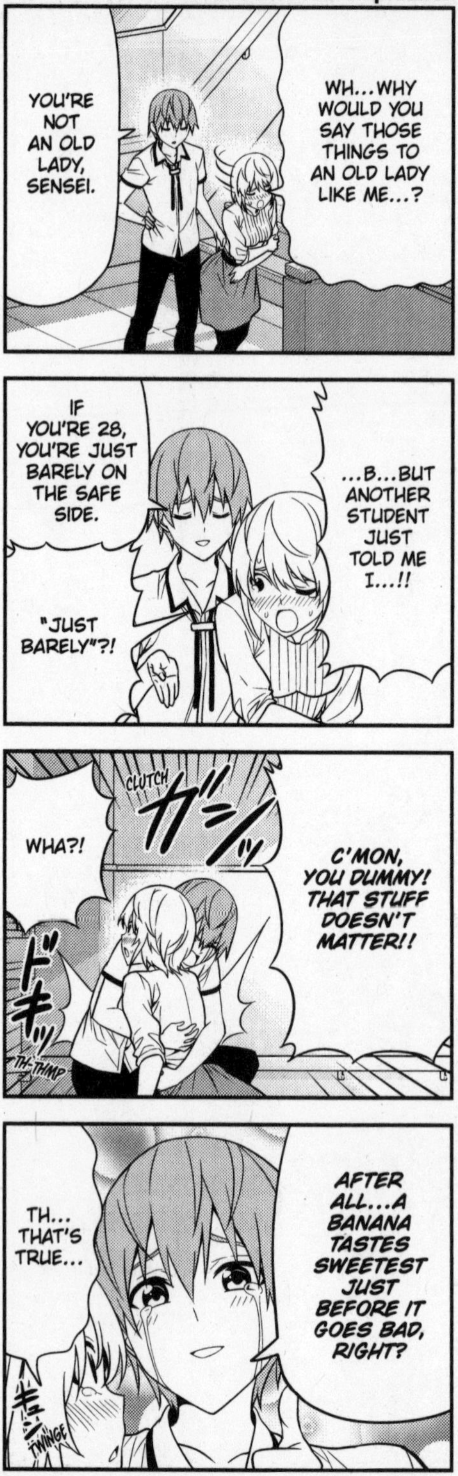
WH...WHY WOULD YOU SAY THOSE THINGS TO AN OLD LADY LIKE ME...?
YOU'RE NOT AN OLD LADY, SENSEI.
...B...BUT ANOTHER STUDENT JUST TOLD ME I...!!
IF YOU'RE 28, YOU'RE JUST BARELY ON THE SAFE SIDE.
"JUST BARELY"?!
CLUTCH!
C'MON, YOU DUMMY! THAT STUFF DOESN'T MATTER!!
WHA?!
TH-THMP
AFTER ALL...A BANANA TASTES SWEETEST JUST BEFORE IT GOES BAD, RIGHT?
TH... THAT'S TRUE...
TWINGE

You Got It Bad, Sensei

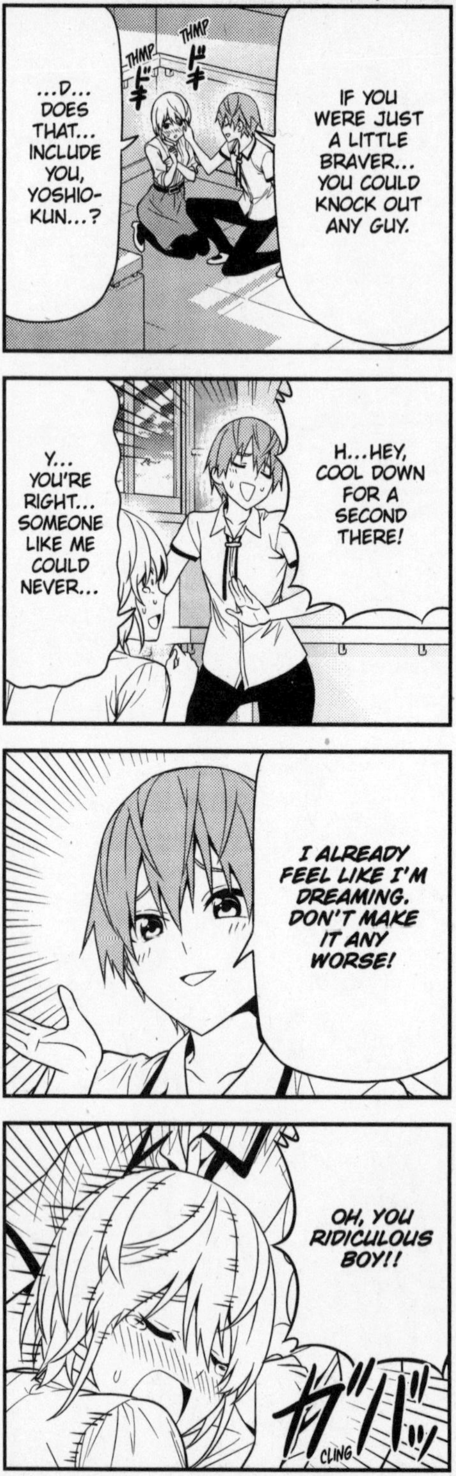
IF YOU WERE JUST A LITTLE BRAVER... YOU COULD KNOCK OUT ANY GUY.
THMP
THMP
...D... DOES THAT... INCLUDE YOU, YOSHIO-KUN...?
H...HEY, COOL DOWN FOR A SECOND THERE!
Y... YOU'RE RIGHT... SOMEONE LIKE ME COULD NEVER...
I ALREADY FEEL LIKE I'M DREAMING. DON'T MAKE IT ANY WORSE!
OH, YOU RIDICULOUS BOY!!
CLING

Fanning the Flames

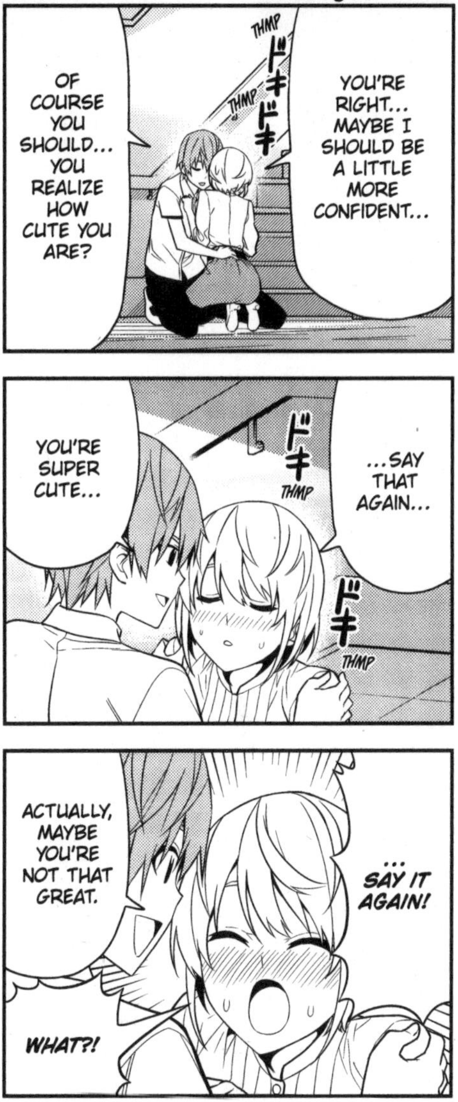
YOU'RE RIGHT... MAYBE I SHOULD BE A LITTLE MORE CONFIDENT...
THMP ドキ
THMP ドキ
OF COURSE YOU SHOULD... YOU REALIZE HOW CUTE YOU ARE?
...SAY THAT AGAIN...
ドキ THMP
YOU'RE SUPER CUTE...
ドキ THMP
... SAY IT AGAIN!
ACTUALLY, MAYBE YOU'RE NOT THAT GREAT.
WHAT?!
I'M. KIDDING. ♡
...OH YOU! ♡
THROB キュ～ン…ッ

Love Potion No. 9thmp

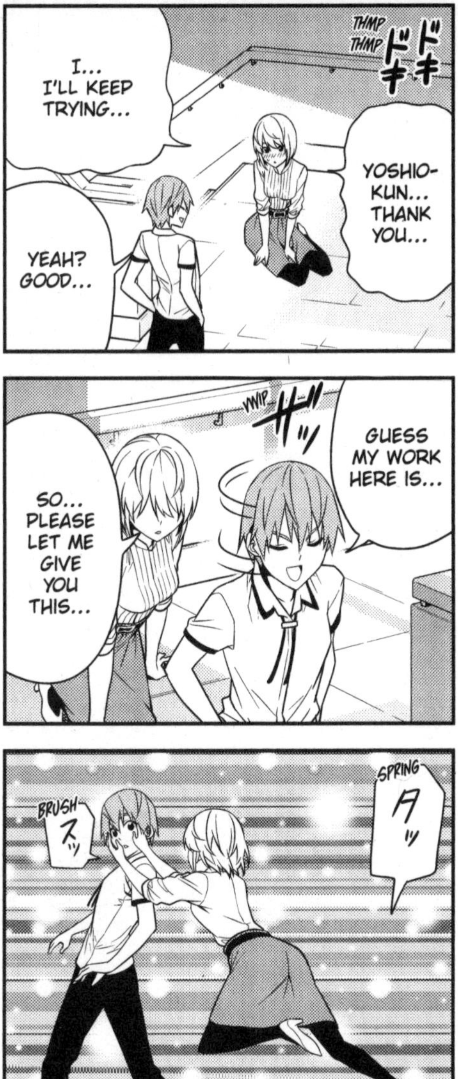
THMP THMP ドキドキ
YOSHIO-KUN... THANK YOU...
I... I'LL KEEP TRYING...
YEAH? GOOD...
GUESS MY WORK HERE IS...
VWIP ザッ
SO... PLEASE LET ME GIVE YOU THIS...
SPRING タッ
BRUSH スッ
THE FULL MEASURE OF MY COURAGE...

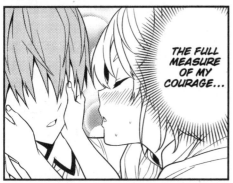

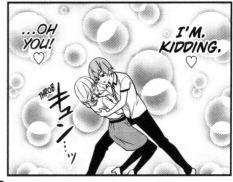

Devastated

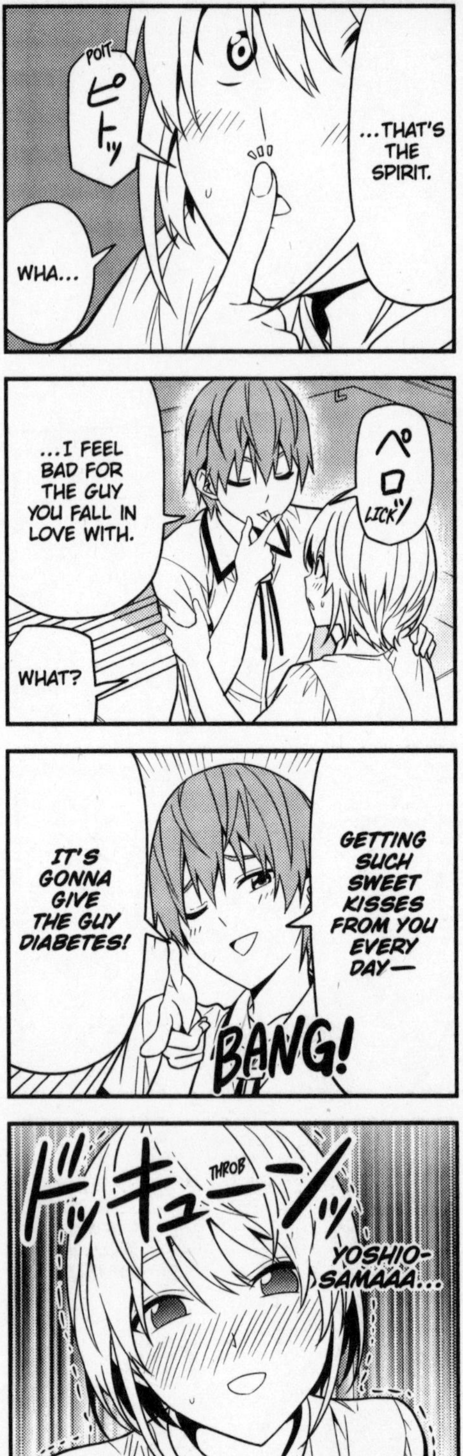
...THAT'S THE SPIRIT.
POIT
ピトッ
WHA...
ペロッ
LICK
...I FEEL BAD FOR THE GUY YOU FALL IN LOVE WITH.
WHAT?
GETTING SUCH SWEET KISSES FROM YOU EVERY DAY—
IT'S GONNA GIVE THE GUY DIABETES!
BANG!
ドッキューンッ
THROB
YOSHIO-SAMAAA...

The Secret Paths of Love

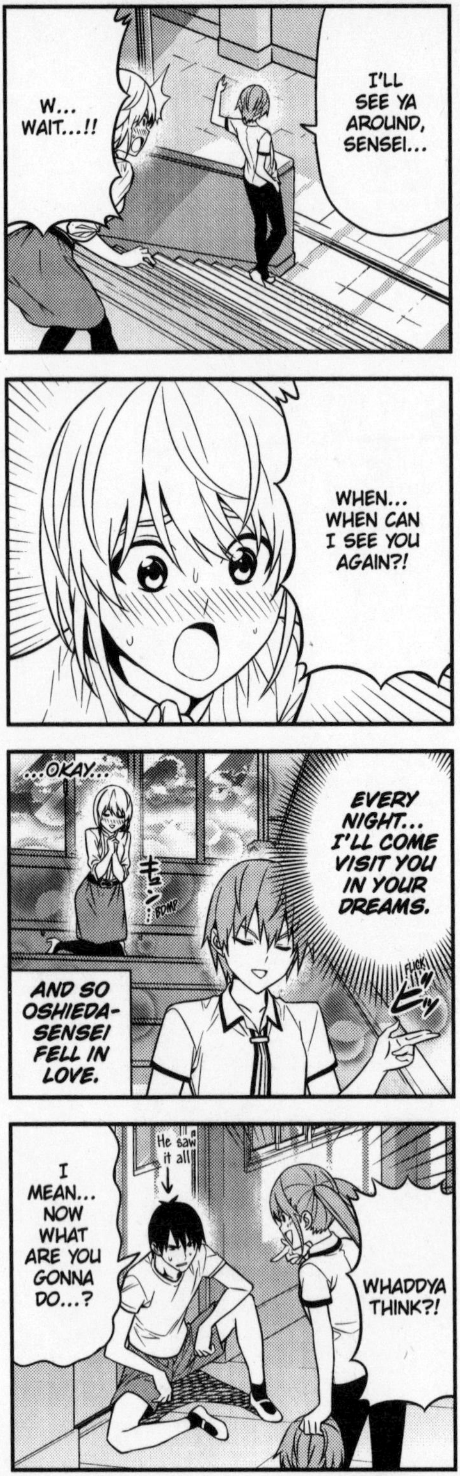
I'LL SEE YA AROUND, SENSEI...
W... WAIT...!!
WHEN... WHEN CAN I SEE YOU AGAIN?!
EVERY NIGHT... I'LL COME VISIT YOU IN YOUR DREAMS.
FLICK
ピッ
キュン
BOMP
...OKAY...
AND SO OSHIEDA-SENSEI FELL IN LOVE.
WHADDYA THINK?!
He saw it all
I MEAN... NOW WHAT ARE YOU GONNA DO...?

With Fevered Sigh

SIIIGHHHH...
O... OSHIEDA-SENSEI SEEMS SO...SEXY LATELY...
Quiz Time: 15 Minutes
SIIIGH...
...

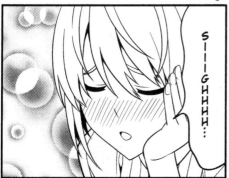

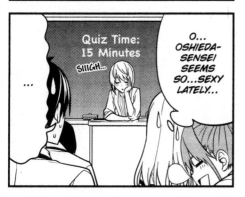

(Jaka jaka jan ☆ Jaka jaka jan ☆ Jaka jaka jaka jaka jan ken)

Aho-Girl

\\\'ahô͵gərl\\ *Japanese, noun.*
A clueless girl.

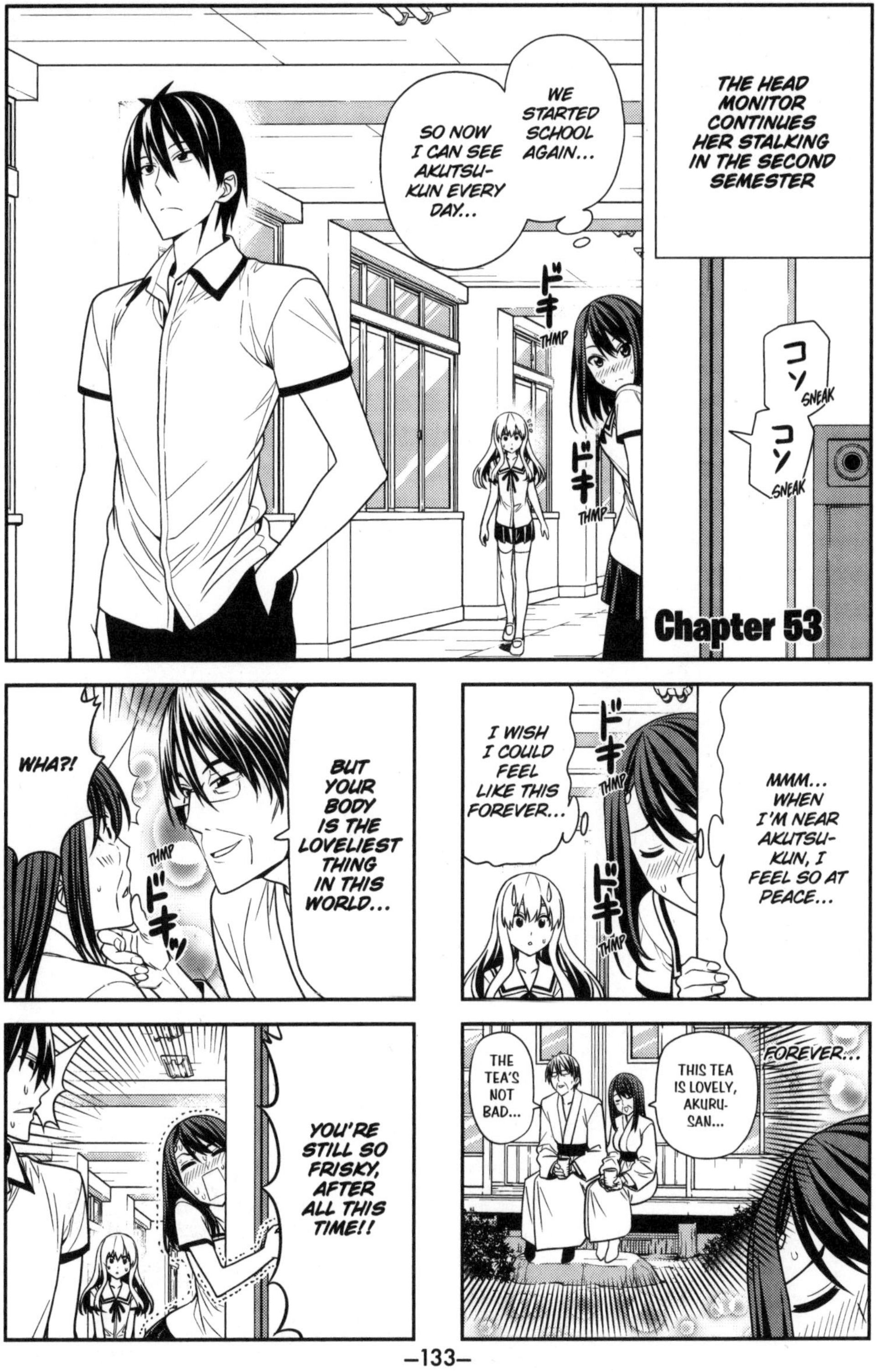
THE HEAD MONITOR CONTINUES HER STALKING IN THE SECOND SEMESTER
コソ SNEAK
コソ SNEAK
WE STARTED SCHOOL AGAIN...
SO NOW I CAN SEE AKUTSU-KUN EVERY DAY...
ドキ THMP
ドキ THMP
Chapter 53
MMM... WHEN I'M NEAR AKUTSU-KUN, I FEEL SO AT PEACE...
I WISH I COULD FEEL LIKE THIS FOREVER...
ドキ THMP
ドキ THMP
BUT YOUR BODY IS THE LOVELIEST THING IN THIS WORLD...
ドキッ THMP
WHA?!
FOREVER...
THIS TEA IS LOVELY, AKURU-SAN...
THE TEA'S NOT BAD...
YOU'RE STILL SO FRISKY, AFTER ALL THIS TIME!!

That's What It Looks Like

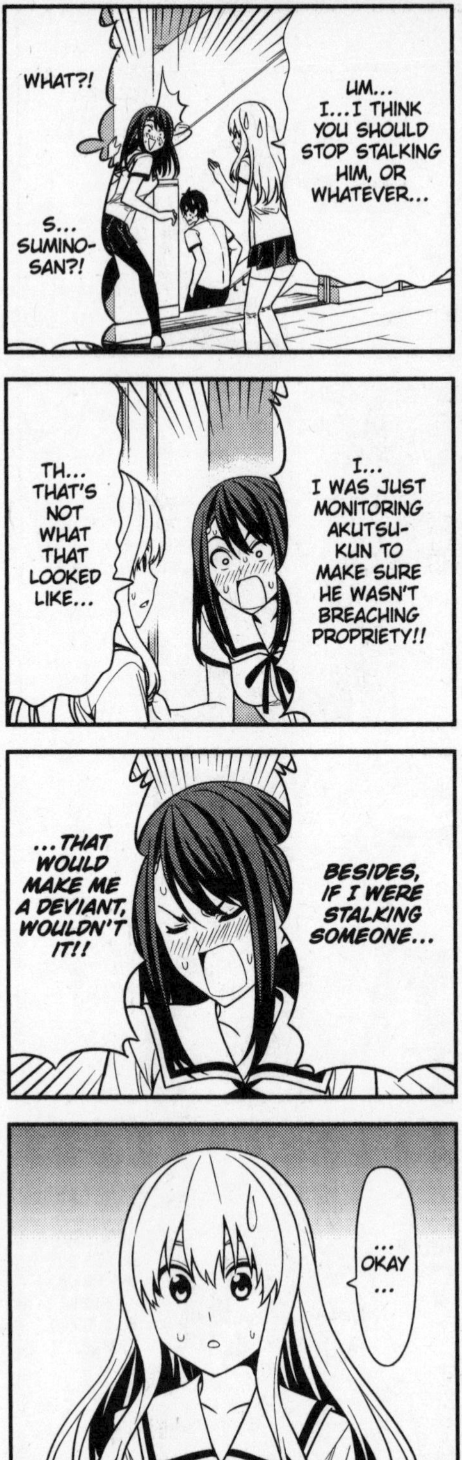
UM... I...I THINK YOU SHOULD STOP STALKING HIM, OR WHATEVER...
WHAT?!
S... SUMINO-SAN?!
I... I WAS JUST MONITORING AKUTSU-KUN TO MAKE SURE HE WASN'T BREACHING PROPRIETY!!
TH... THAT'S NOT WHAT THAT LOOKED LIKE...
BESIDES, IF I WERE STALKING SOMEONE...
...THAT WOULD MAKE ME A DEVIANT, WOULDN'T IT!!
... OKAY ...

But She Never Told Anyone That

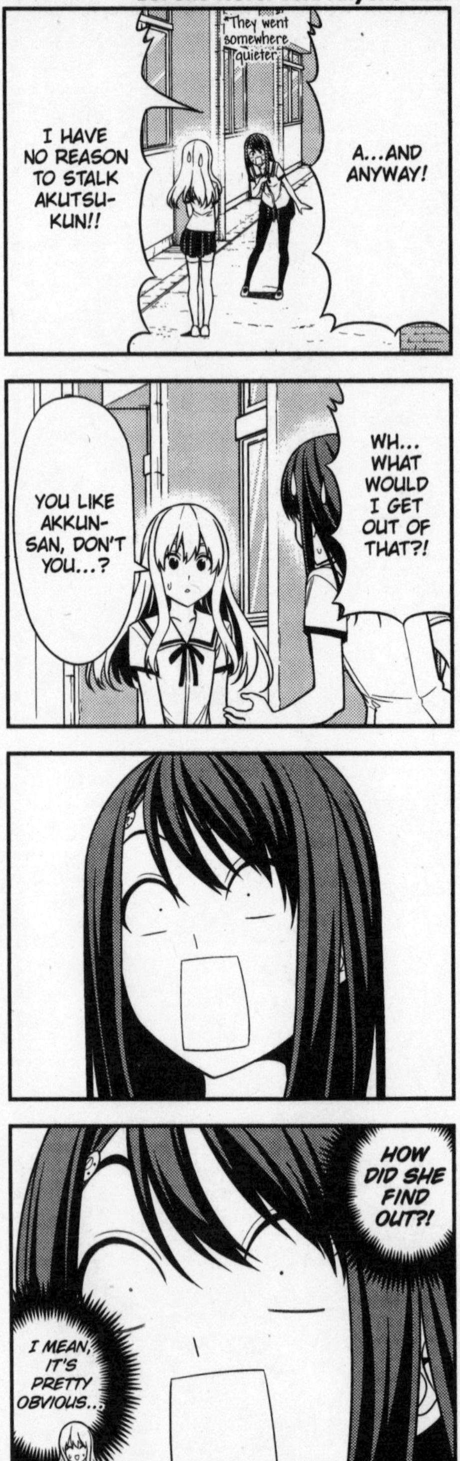
A...AND ANYWAY!
*They went somewhere quieter
I HAVE NO REASON TO STALK AKUTSU-KUN!!
WH... WHAT WOULD I GET OUT OF THAT?!
YOU LIKE AKKUN-SAN, DON'T YOU...?
HOW DID SHE FIND OUT?!
I MEAN, IT'S PRETTY OBVIOUS...

Leading Questions

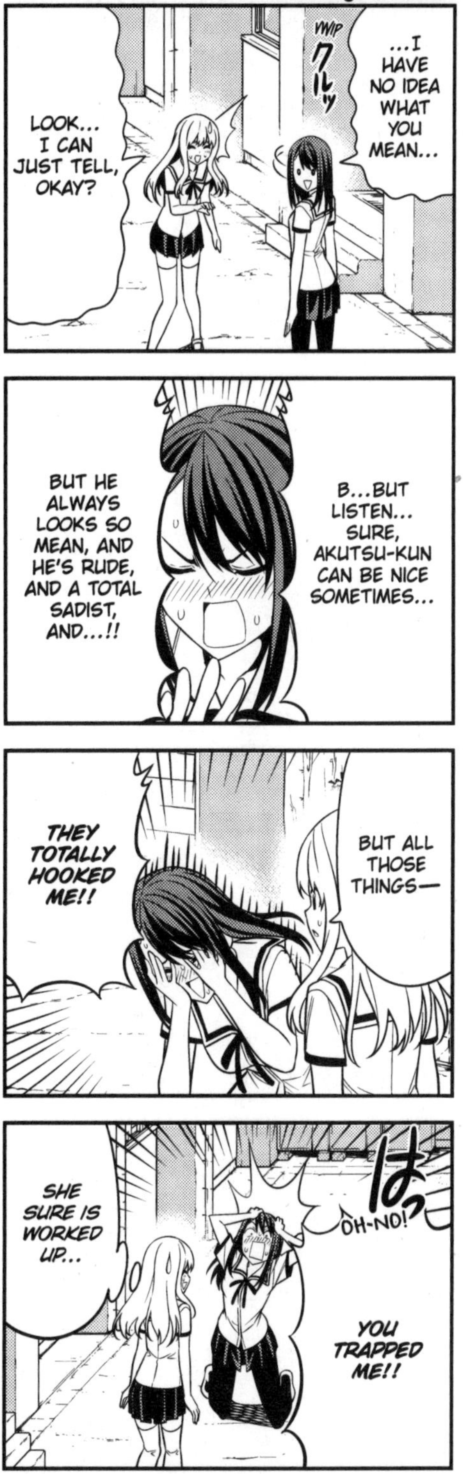
...I HAVE NO IDEA WHAT YOU MEAN...
VWIP
クルッ
LOOK... I CAN JUST TELL, OKAY?
B...BUT LISTEN... SURE, AKUTSU-KUN CAN BE NICE SOMETIMES...
BUT HE ALWAYS LOOKS SO MEAN, AND HE'S RUDE, AND A TOTAL SADIST, AND...!!
BUT ALL THOSE THINGS—
THEY TOTALLY HOOKED ME!!
はっ
OH-NO!
SHE SURE IS WORKED UP...
YOU TRAPPED ME!!

She's Positive

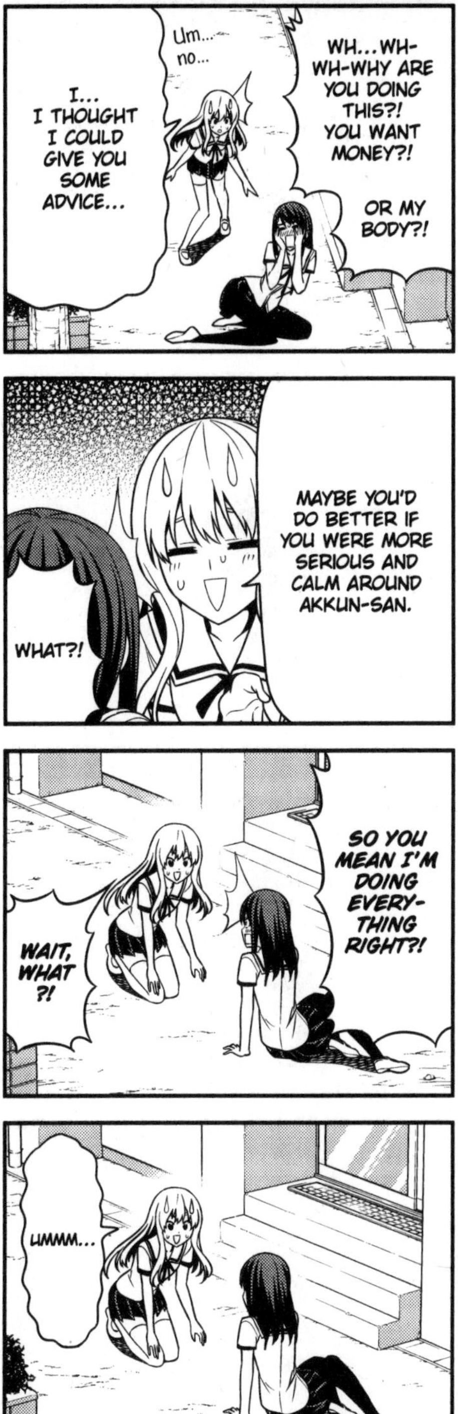
WH...WH-WH-WHY ARE YOU DOING THIS?! YOU WANT MONEY?!
OR MY BODY?!
Um... no...
I... I THOUGHT I COULD GIVE YOU SOME ADVICE...
MAYBE YOU'D DO BETTER IF YOU WERE MORE SERIOUS AND CALM AROUND AKKUN-SAN.
WHAT?!
SO YOU MEAN I'M DOING EVERY-THING RIGHT?!
WAIT, WHAT?!
UMMM...

I Noticed...

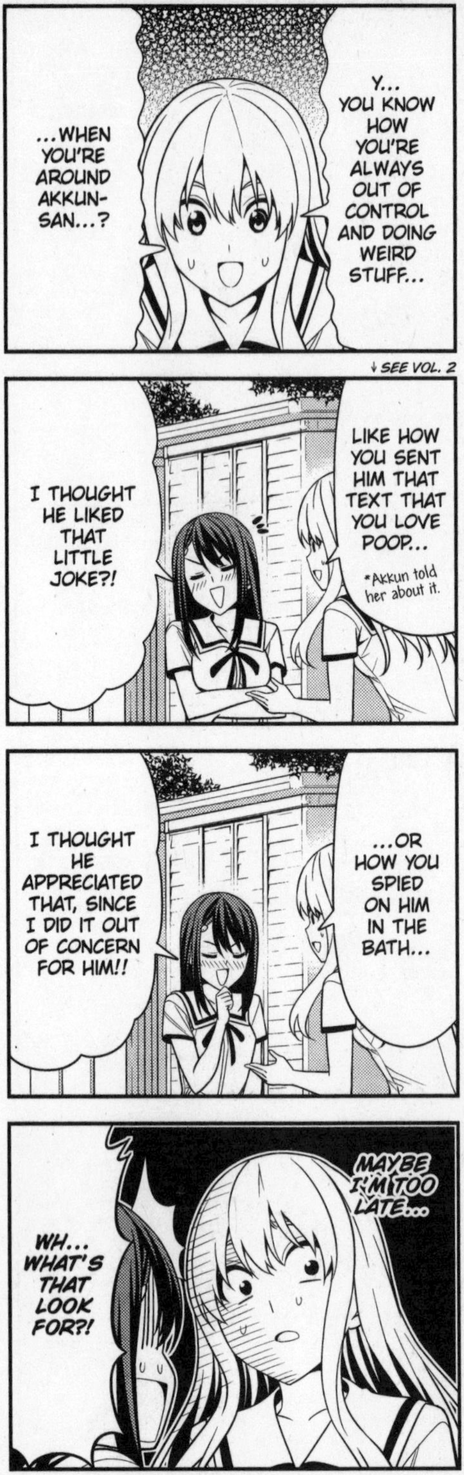

Y... YOU KNOW HOW YOU'RE ALWAYS OUT OF CONTROL AND DOING WEIRD STUFF...
...WHEN YOU'RE AROUND AKKUN-SAN...?
↓ SEE VOL. 2
LIKE HOW YOU SENT HIM THAT TEXT THAT YOU LOVE POOP...
*Akkun told her about it.
I THOUGHT HE LIKED THAT LITTLE JOKE?!
...OR HOW YOU SPIED ON HIM IN THE BATH...
I THOUGHT HE APPRECIATED THAT, SINCE I DID IT OUT OF CONCERN FOR HIM!!
MAYBE I'M TOO LATE...
WH... WHAT'S THAT LOOK FOR?!

Positive

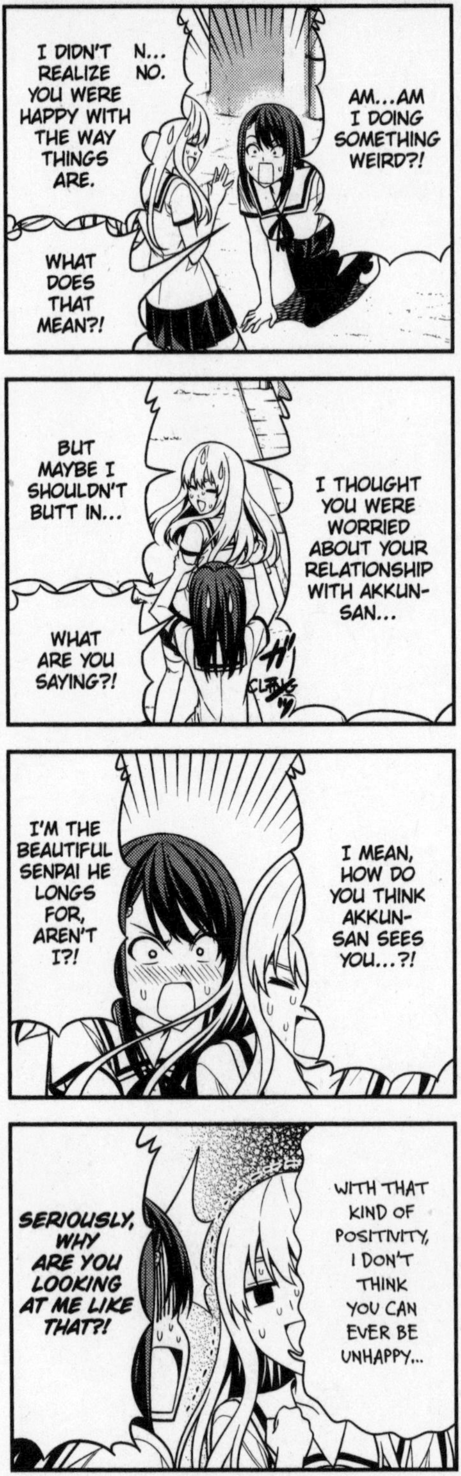

AM...AM I DOING SOMETHING WEIRD?!
N... NO.
I DIDN'T REALIZE YOU WERE HAPPY WITH THE WAY THINGS ARE.
WHAT DOES THAT MEAN?!
I THOUGHT YOU WERE WORRIED ABOUT YOUR RELATIONSHIP WITH AKKUN-SAN...
BUT MAYBE I SHOULDN'T BUTT IN...
WHAT ARE YOU SAYING?!
CLING
I MEAN, HOW DO YOU THINK AKKUN-SAN SEES YOU...?!
I'M THE BEAUTIFUL SENPAI HE LONGS FOR, AREN'T I?!
WITH THAT KIND OF POSITIVITY, I DON'T THINK YOU CAN EVER BE UNHAPPY...
SERIOUSLY, WHY ARE YOU LOOKING AT ME LIKE THAT?!

Extremely Positive

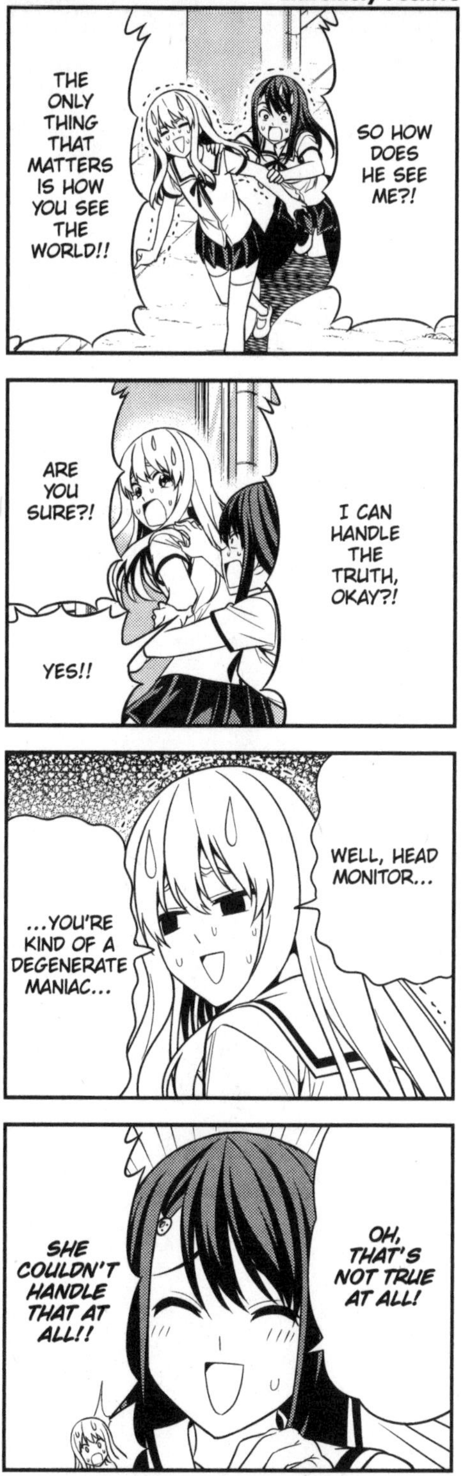
SO HOW DOES HE SEE ME?!
THE ONLY THING THAT MATTERS IS HOW YOU SEE THE WORLD!!
I CAN HANDLE THE TRUTH, OKAY?!
ARE YOU SURE?!
YES!!
WELL, HEAD MONITOR...
...YOU'RE KIND OF A DEGENERATE MANIAC...
OH, THAT'S NOT TRUE AT ALL!
SHE COULDN'T HANDLE THAT AT ALL!!

Constant Coddling

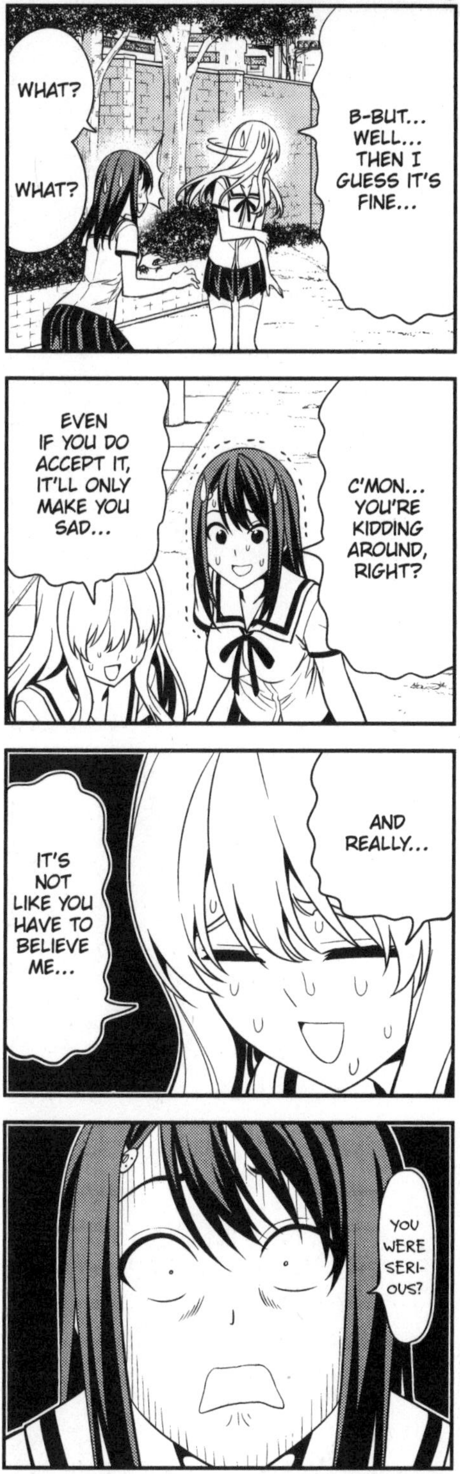
B-BUT... WELL... THEN I GUESS IT'S FINE...
WHAT?
WHAT?
C'MON... YOU'RE KIDDING AROUND, RIGHT?
EVEN IF YOU DO ACCEPT IT, IT'LL ONLY MAKE YOU SAD...
AND REALLY...
IT'S NOT LIKE YOU HAVE TO BELIEVE ME...
YOU WERE SERIOUS?

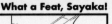

Sayaka, What Do I Do?

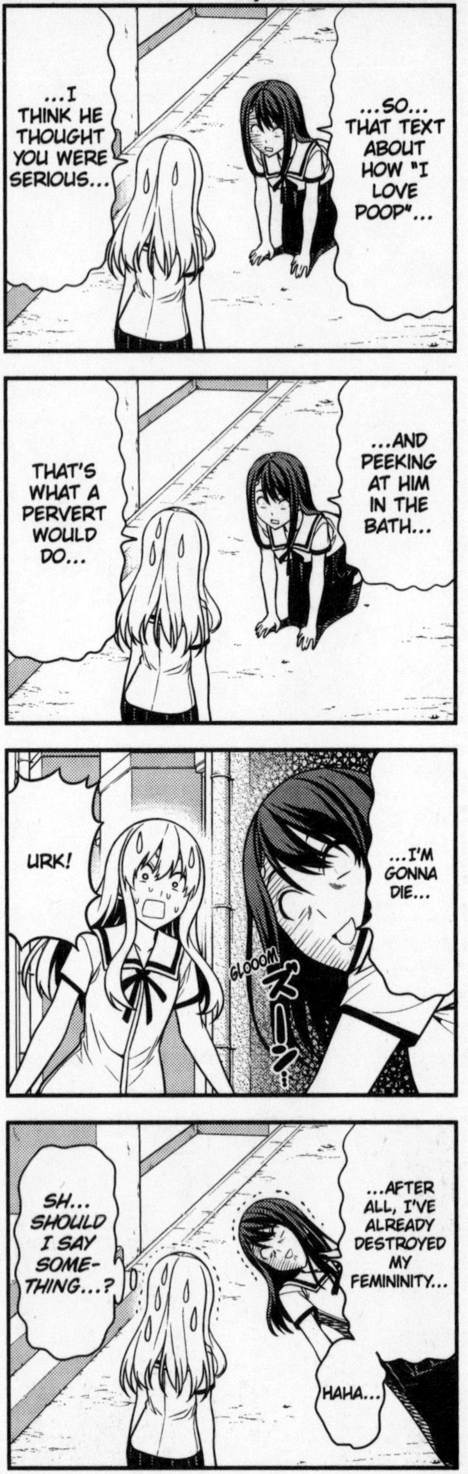
...SO... THAT TEXT ABOUT HOW "I LOVE POOP"...
...I THINK HE THOUGHT YOU WERE SERIOUS...
...AND PEEKING AT HIM IN THE BATH...
THAT'S WHAT A PERVERT WOULD DO...
...I'M GONNA DIE...
GLOOOM
URK!
...AFTER ALL, I'VE ALREADY DESTROYED MY FEMININITY...
HAHA...
SH... SHOULD I SAY SOME-THING...?

What a Feat, Sayaka!

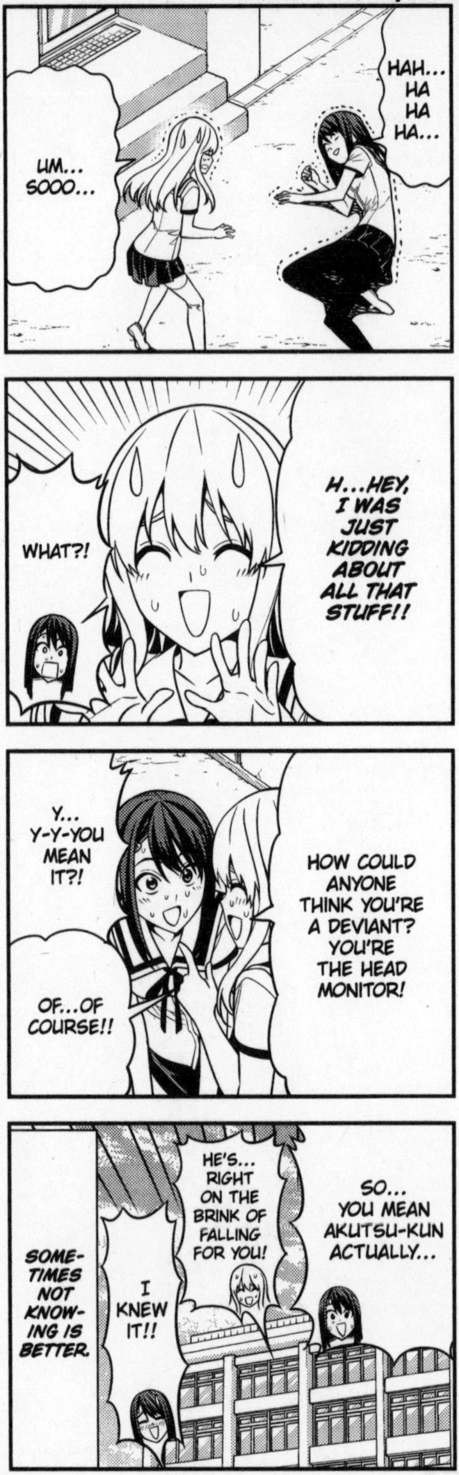
HAH... HA HA HA...
UM... SOOO...
H...HEY, I WAS JUST KIDDING ABOUT ALL THAT STUFF!!
WHAT?!
HOW COULD ANYONE THINK YOU'RE A DEVIANT? YOU'RE THE HEAD MONITOR!
Y... Y-Y-YOU MEAN IT?!
OF...OF COURSE!!
SO... YOU MEAN AKUTSU-KUN ACTUALLY...
HE'S... RIGHT ON THE BRINK OF FALLING FOR YOU!
I KNEW IT!!
SOME-TIMES NOT KNOW-ING IS BETTER.

No, It's No Use, Sayaka

HUH?!

SO WILL YOU SUPPORT ME BEING FRIENDS WITH AKUTSU-KUN?!

I...DON'T REALLY FEEL LIKE I'LL BE MUCH HELP.

S... SUUURE...

Aho-Girl

\ˈahô͵gərl\ *Japanese, noun*.
A clueless girl.

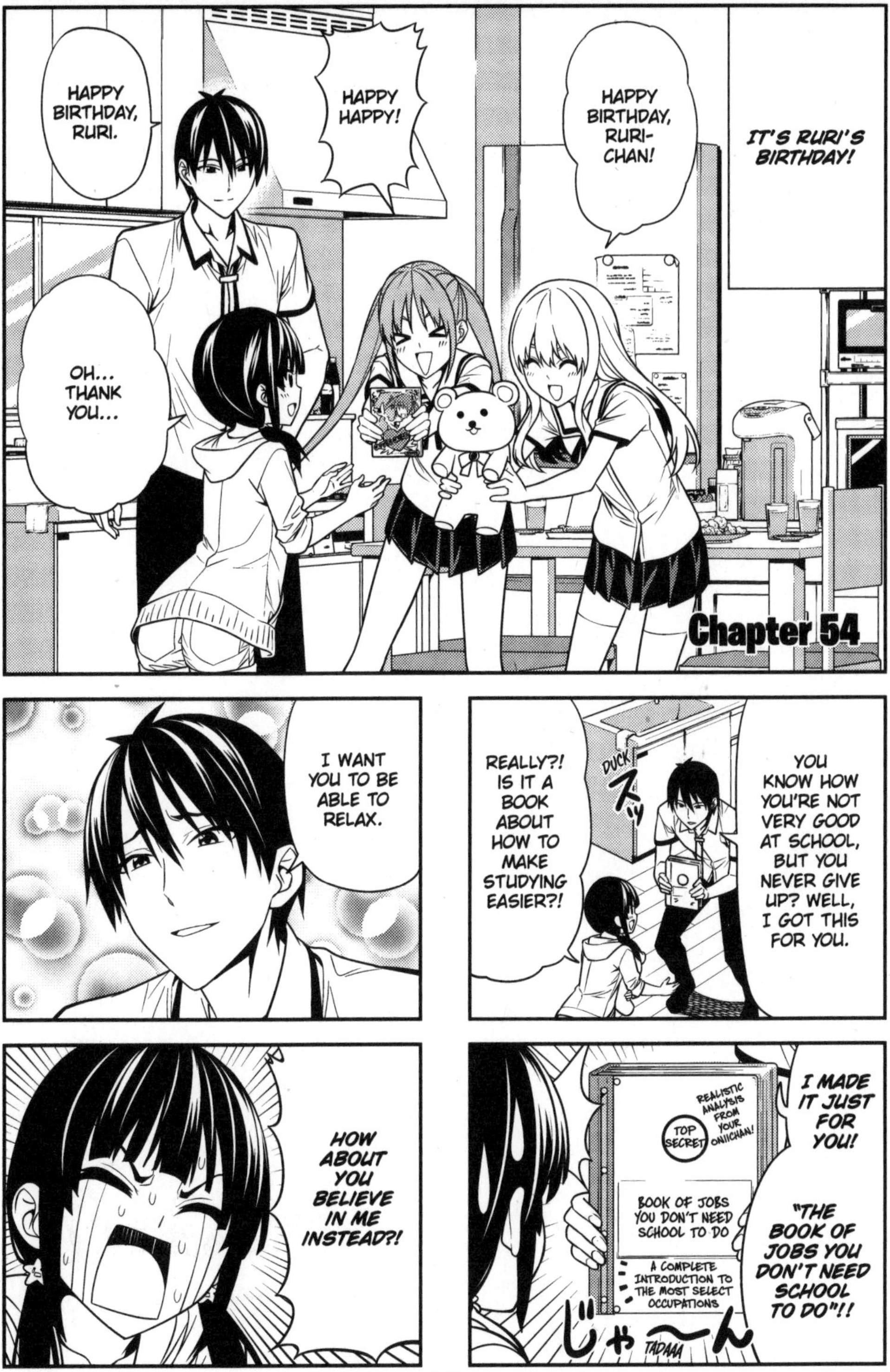
IT'S RURI'S BIRTHDAY!
HAPPY BIRTHDAY, RURI-CHAN!
HAPPY HAPPY!
HAPPY BIRTHDAY, RURI.
OH... THANK YOU...
Chapter 54
YOU KNOW HOW YOU'RE NOT VERY GOOD AT SCHOOL, BUT YOU NEVER GIVE UP? WELL, I GOT THIS FOR YOU.
スッ
DUCK
REALLY?! IS IT A BOOK ABOUT HOW TO MAKE STUDYING EASIER?!
I WANT YOU TO BE ABLE TO RELAX.
I MADE IT JUST FOR YOU!
"THE BOOK OF JOBS YOU DON'T NEED SCHOOL TO DO"!!
REALISTIC ANALYSIS FROM YOUR ONIICHAN!
TOP SECRET
BOOK OF JOBS YOU DON'T NEED SCHOOL TO DO
A COMPLETE INTRODUCTION TO THE MOST SELECT OCCUPATIONS
じゃ〜ん
TADAAA
HOW ABOUT YOU BELIEVE IN ME INSTEAD?!

That's a Funny Joke

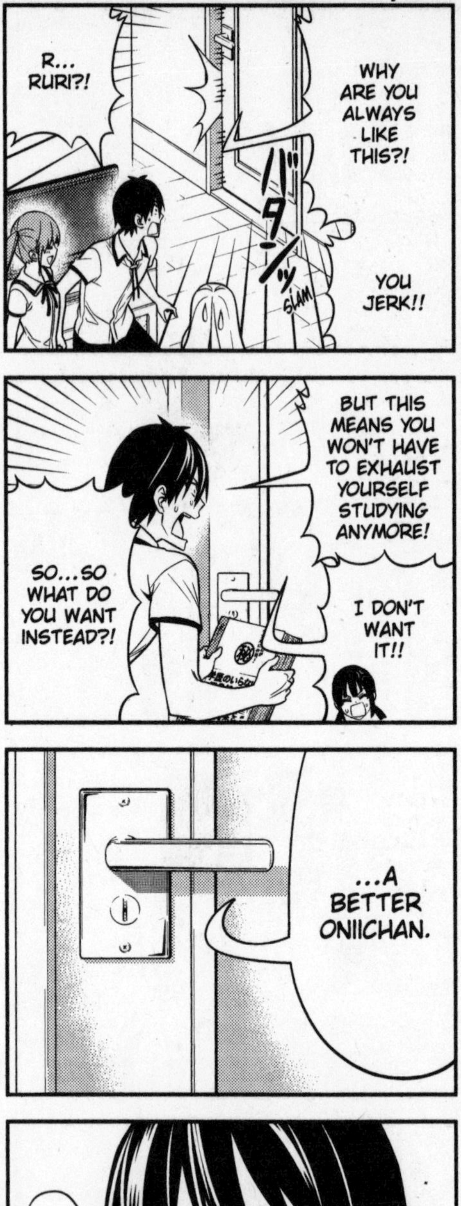
WHY ARE YOU ALWAYS LIKE THIS?!
R... RURI?!
バタン
SLAM
YOU JERK!!
BUT THIS MEANS YOU WON'T HAVE TO EXHAUST YOURSELF STUDYING ANYMORE!
I DON'T WANT IT!!
SO...SO WHAT DO YOU WANT INSTEAD?!
...A BETTER ONIICHAN.
OUCH...

Sayaka-chan Said It

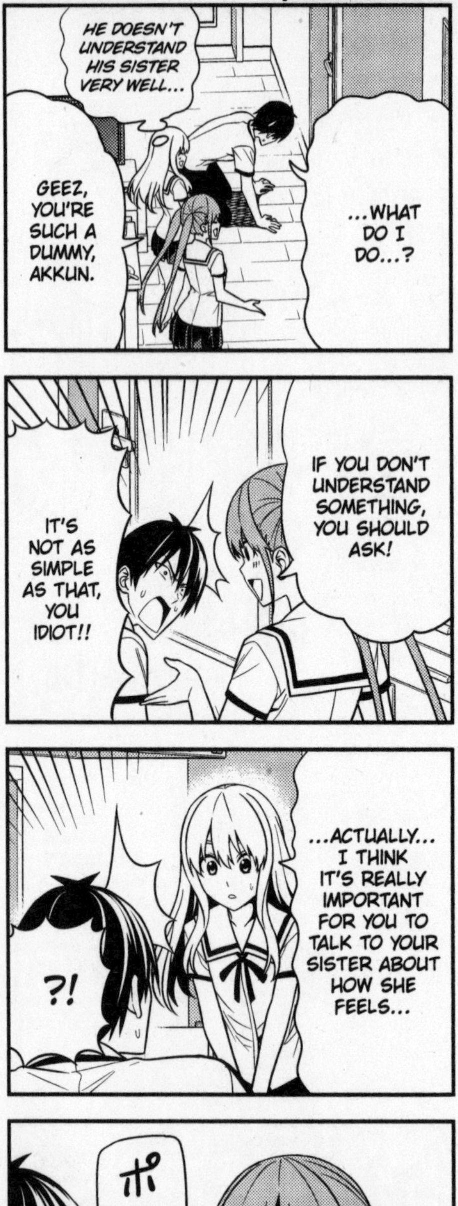
HE DOESN'T UNDERSTAND HIS SISTER VERY WELL...
...WHAT DO I DO...?
GEEZ, YOU'RE SUCH A DUMMY, AKKUN.
IF YOU DON'T UNDERSTAND SOMETHING, YOU SHOULD ASK!
IT'S NOT AS SIMPLE AS THAT, YOU IDIOT!!
...ACTUALLY... I THINK IT'S REALLY IMPORTANT FOR YOU TO TALK TO YOUR SISTER ABOUT HOW SHE FEELS...
?!
ポンッ
BAP

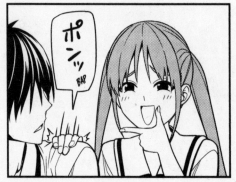

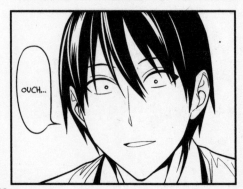

A Crushing Blow

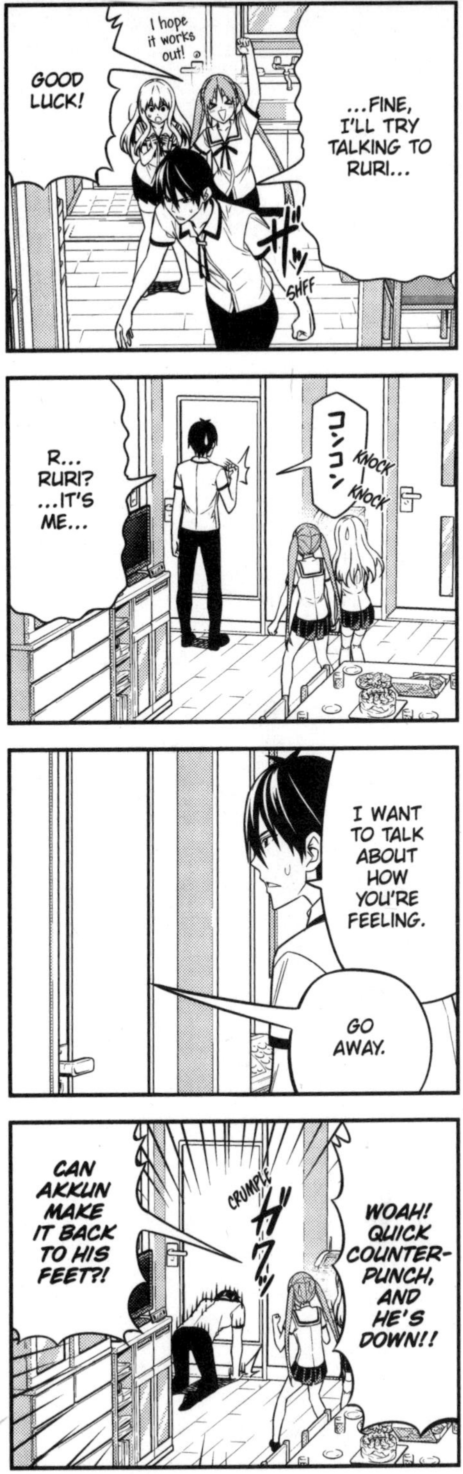
...FINE, I'LL TRY TALKING TO RURI...
I hope it works out!
GOOD LUCK!
ザッ
SHFF
コンコン
KNOCK KNOCK
R... RURI? ...IT'S ME...
I WANT TO TALK ABOUT HOW YOU'RE FEELING.
GO AWAY.
WOAH! QUICK COUNTER-PUNCH, AND HE'S DOWN!!
ガクッ
CRUMPLE
CAN AKKUN MAKE IT BACK TO HIS FEET?!

An Impossible Conundrum

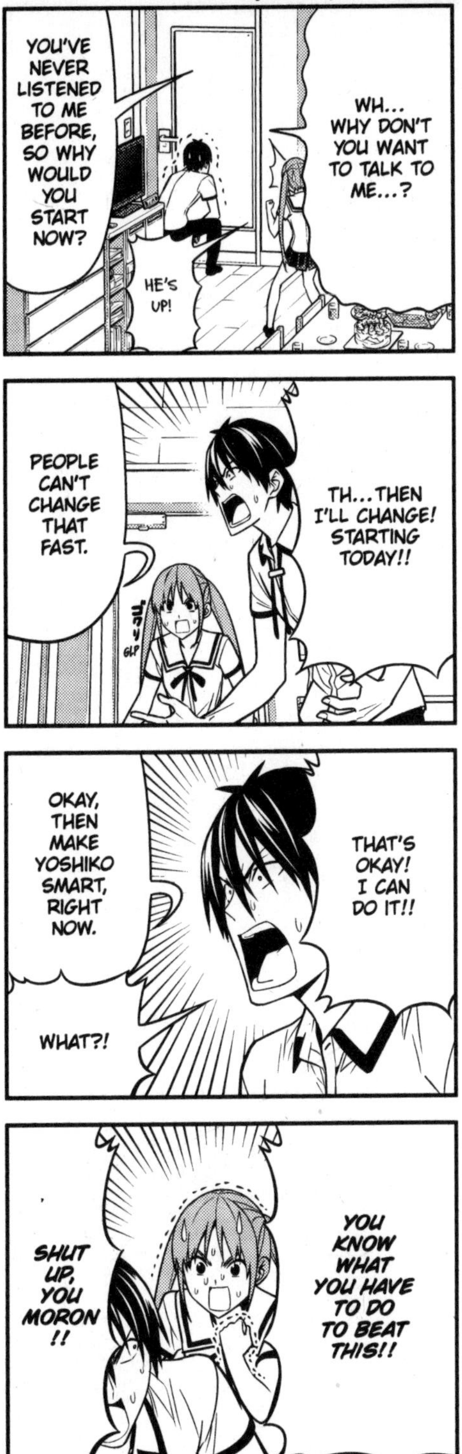
WH... WHY DON'T YOU WANT TO TALK TO ME...?
YOU'VE NEVER LISTENED TO ME BEFORE, SO WHY WOULD YOU START NOW?
HE'S UP!
TH...THEN I'LL CHANGE! STARTING TODAY!!
PEOPLE CAN'T CHANGE THAT FAST.
ゴクリ
GLP
THAT'S OKAY! I CAN DO IT!!
OKAY, THEN MAKE YOSHIKO SMART, RIGHT NOW.
WHAT?!
YOU KNOW WHAT YOU HAVE TO DO TO BEAT THIS!!
SHUT UP, YOU MORON!!

Ruri's Pushing Hard

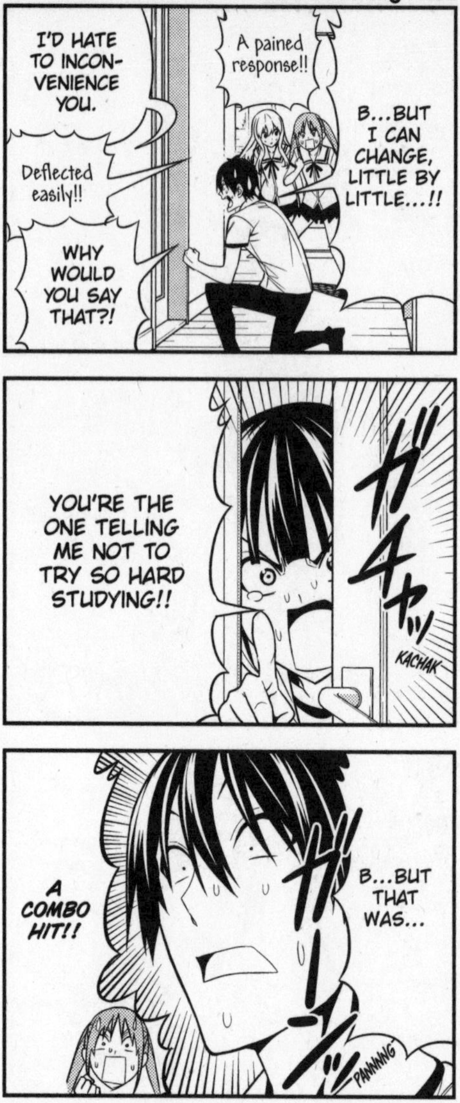

B...BUT I CAN CHANGE, LITTLE BY LITTLE...!!
A pained response!!
I'D HATE TO INCONVENIENCE YOU.
Deflected easily!!
WHY WOULD YOU SAY THAT?!
ガチャッ
KACHAK
YOU'RE THE ONE TELLING ME NOT TO TRY SO HARD STUDYING!!
B...BUT THAT WAS...
A COMBO HIT!!
PANNNNG
AKKUN IS UNABLE TO LEVERAGE HIS NORMAL FORCE AGAINST THIS UNFAMILIAR FOE!!
I was...
バタンッ
SLAM
HE SINKS TO THE MAT, UNABLE TO MUSTER EVEN A HARSH COMMENT FOR ME!!

Get up, Akkun

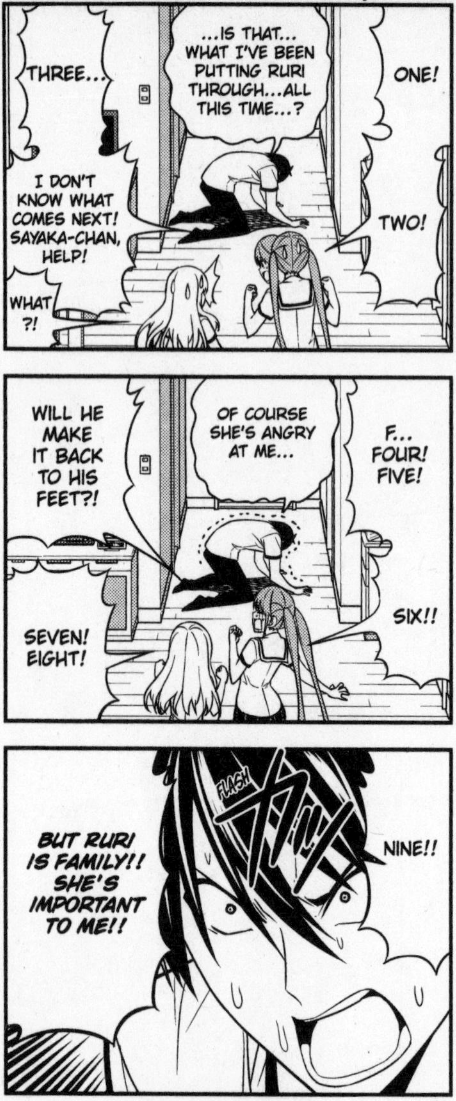

ONE!
...IS THAT... WHAT I'VE BEEN PUTTING RURI THROUGH...ALL THIS TIME...?
TWO!
THREE...
I DON'T KNOW WHAT COMES NEXT! SAYAKA-CHAN, HELP!
WHAT?!
F... FOUR! FIVE!
OF COURSE SHE'S ANGRY AT ME...
WILL HE MAKE IT BACK TO HIS FEET?!
SIX!!
SEVEN! EIGHT!
NINE!!
FLASH
BUT RURI IS FAMILY!! SHE'S IMPORTANT TO ME!!
I'M NEVER GIVING UP ON YOU!!
CRASH
HE...HE BURSTS INTO HIS OPPONENT'S STRONGHOLD!!

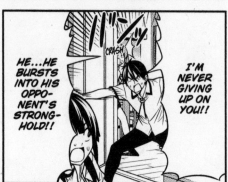

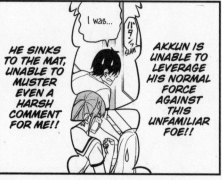

Strained Negotiations

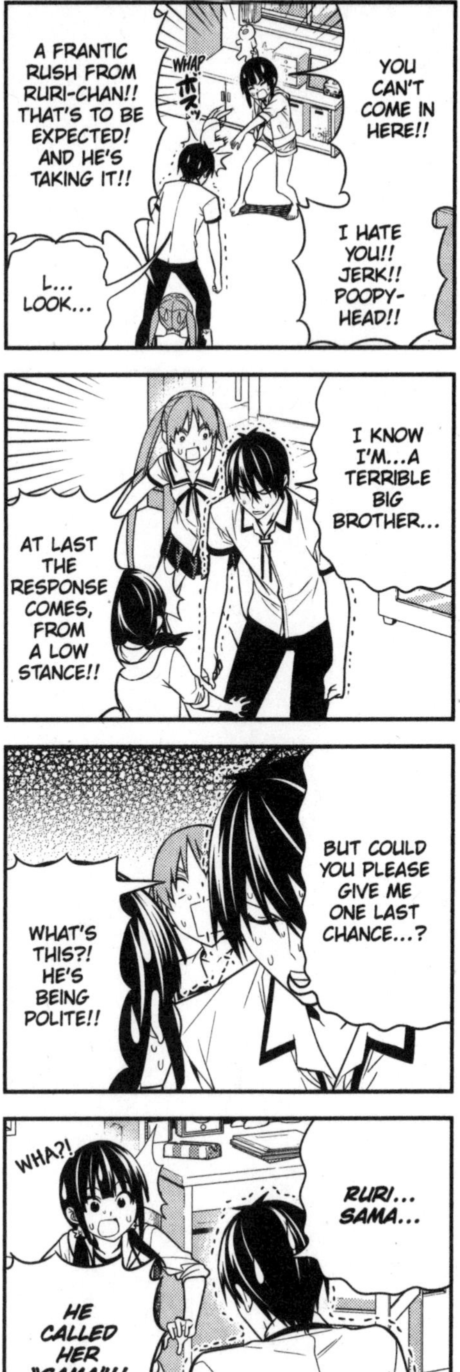
YOU CAN'T COME IN HERE!!
A FRANTIC RUSH FROM RURI-CHAN!! THAT'S TO BE EXPECTED! AND HE'S TAKING IT!!
WHAP
I HATE YOU!! JERK!! POOPY-HEAD!!
L... LOOK...
I KNOW I'M...A TERRIBLE BIG BROTHER...
AT LAST THE RESPONSE COMES, FROM A LOW STANCE!!
BUT COULD YOU PLEASE GIVE ME ONE LAST CHANCE...?
WHAT'S THIS?! HE'S BEING POLITE!!
RURI... SAMA...
WHA?!
HE CALLED HER "SAMA"!!

The Life of an Older Brother

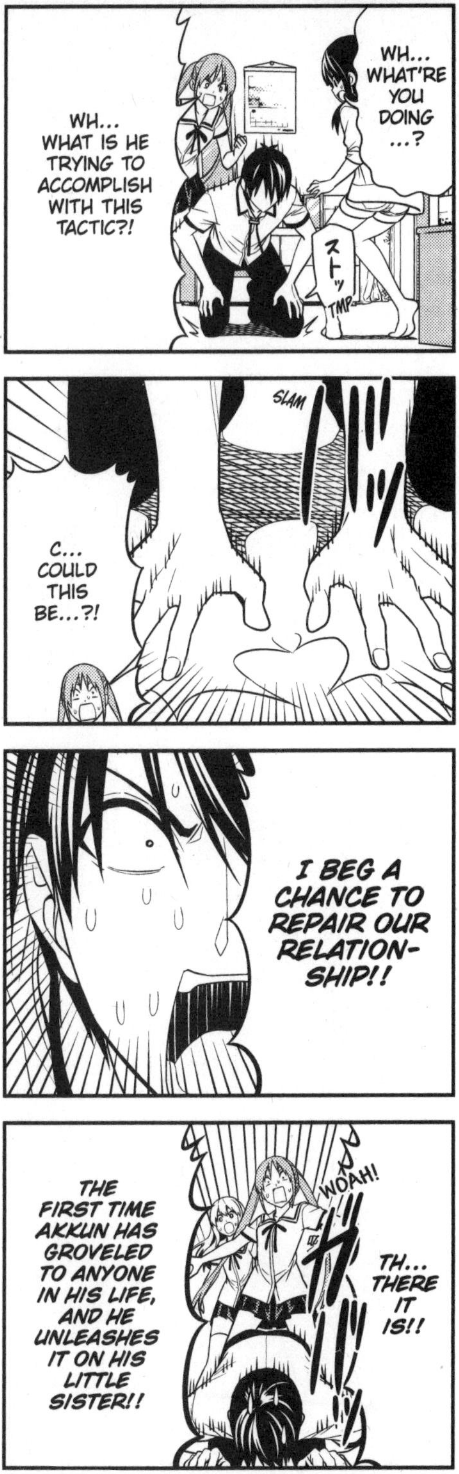
WH... WHAT'RE YOU DOING ...?
WH... WHAT IS HE TRYING TO ACCOMPLISH WITH THIS TACTIC?!
TMP
SLAM
C... COULD THIS BE...?!
I BEG A CHANCE TO REPAIR OUR RELATION-SHIP!!
WOAH!
TH... THERE IT IS!!
THE FIRST TIME AKKUN HAS GROVELED TO ANYONE IN HIS LIFE, AND HE UNLEASHES IT ON HIS LITTLE SISTER!!

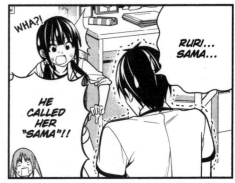

Thank Goodness

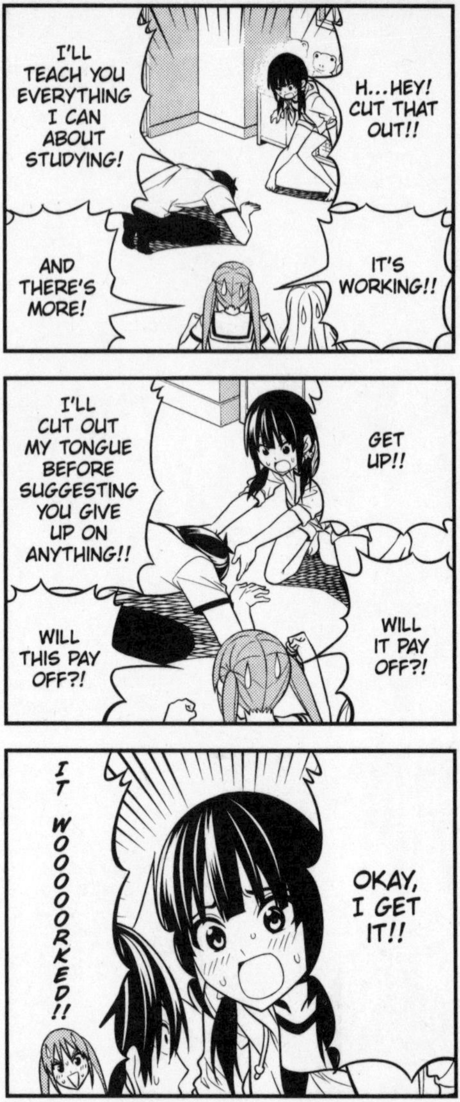
H...HEY! CUT THAT OUT!!
I'LL TEACH YOU EVERYTHING I CAN ABOUT STUDYING!
IT'S WORKING!!
AND THERE'S MORE!
GET UP!!
I'LL CUT OUT MY TONGUE BEFORE SUGGESTING YOU GIVE UP ON ANYTHING!!
WILL IT PAY OFF?!
WILL THIS PAY OFF?!
OKAY, I GET IT!!
IT WOOOOORKED!!
A VICTORY WON BY CASTING ASIDE PRIDE!
I... WASN'T VERY COMFORTABLE SEEING HIM LIKE THAT...
Your analysis, Sayaka-chan?!
THAT'S FOR SURE!!

Maybe Not

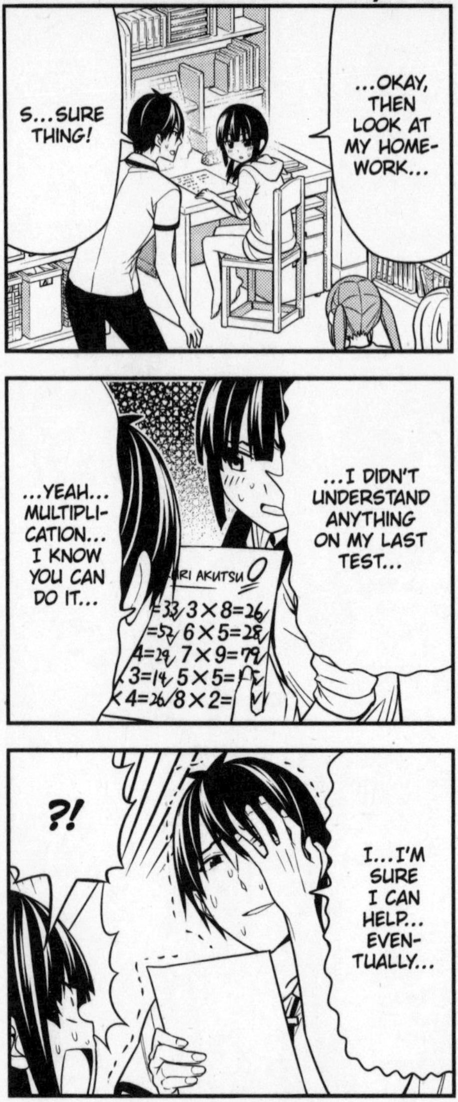
...OKAY, THEN LOOK AT MY HOME-WORK...
S...SURE THING!
...I DIDN'T UNDERSTAND ANYTHING ON MY LAST TEST...
...YEAH... MULTIPLI-CATION... I KNOW YOU CAN DO IT...
I...I'M SURE I CAN HELP... EVEN-TUALLY...
?!
FLING
I HATE IT WHEN YOU MAKE THAT FACE!!
THROW IN THE TOWEL!!
I CAN'T WATCH ANY MORE OF THIS!!

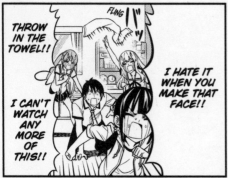

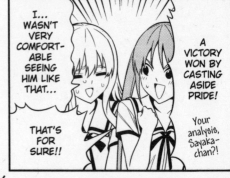

He Had to Flee Next Door

SIIIGH...
BAP
ポン…

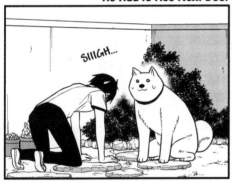

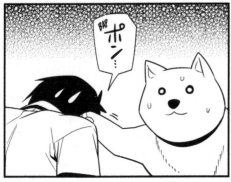

(The love that lives on in the time that we share makes me)

Aho-Girl

\ˈahô͵gərl \ *Japanese, noun.*
A clueless girl.

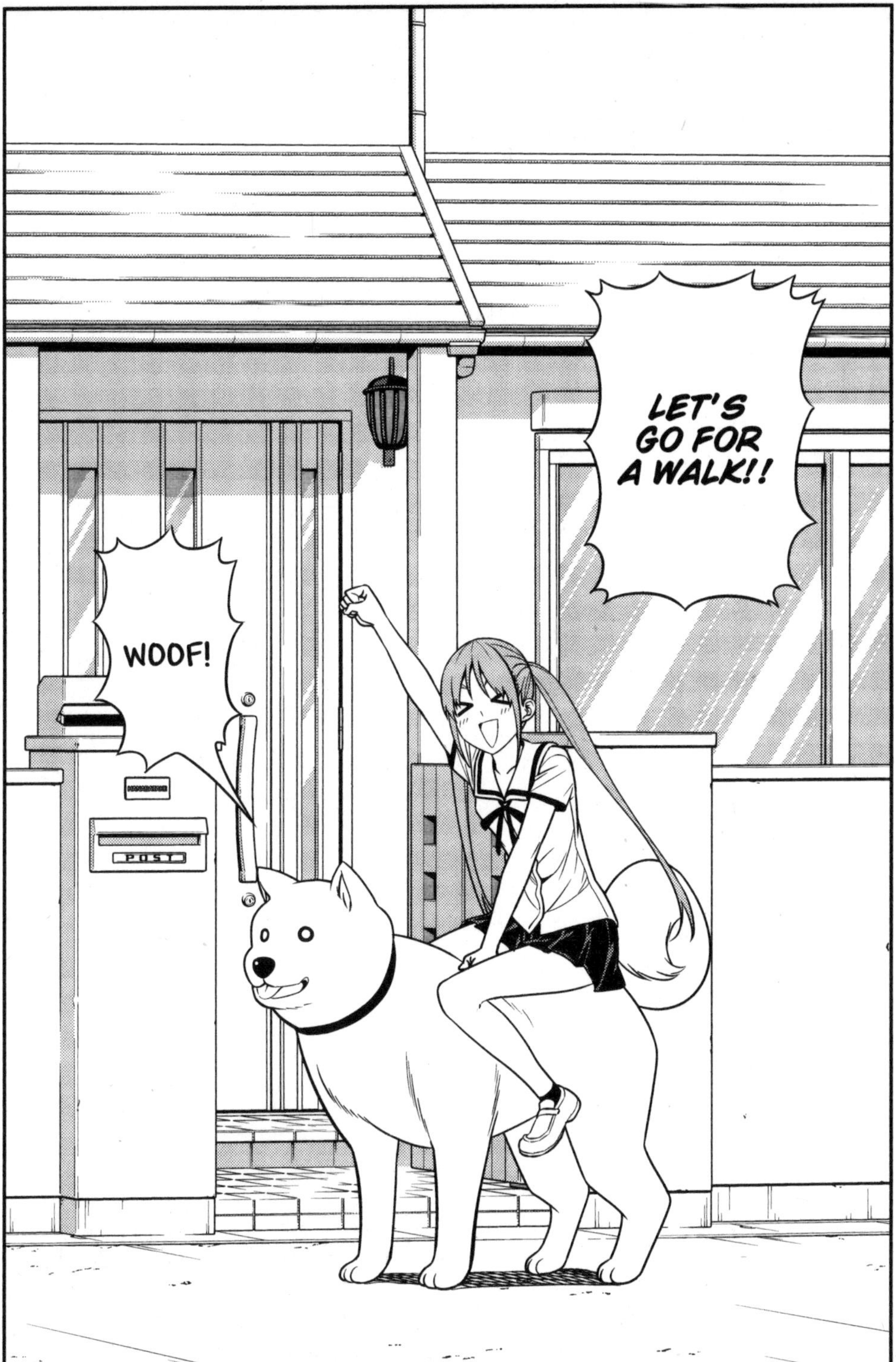
LET'S GO FOR A WALK!!
WOOF!
POST

Special Edition: Yoshiko & the Dog Go for a Walk

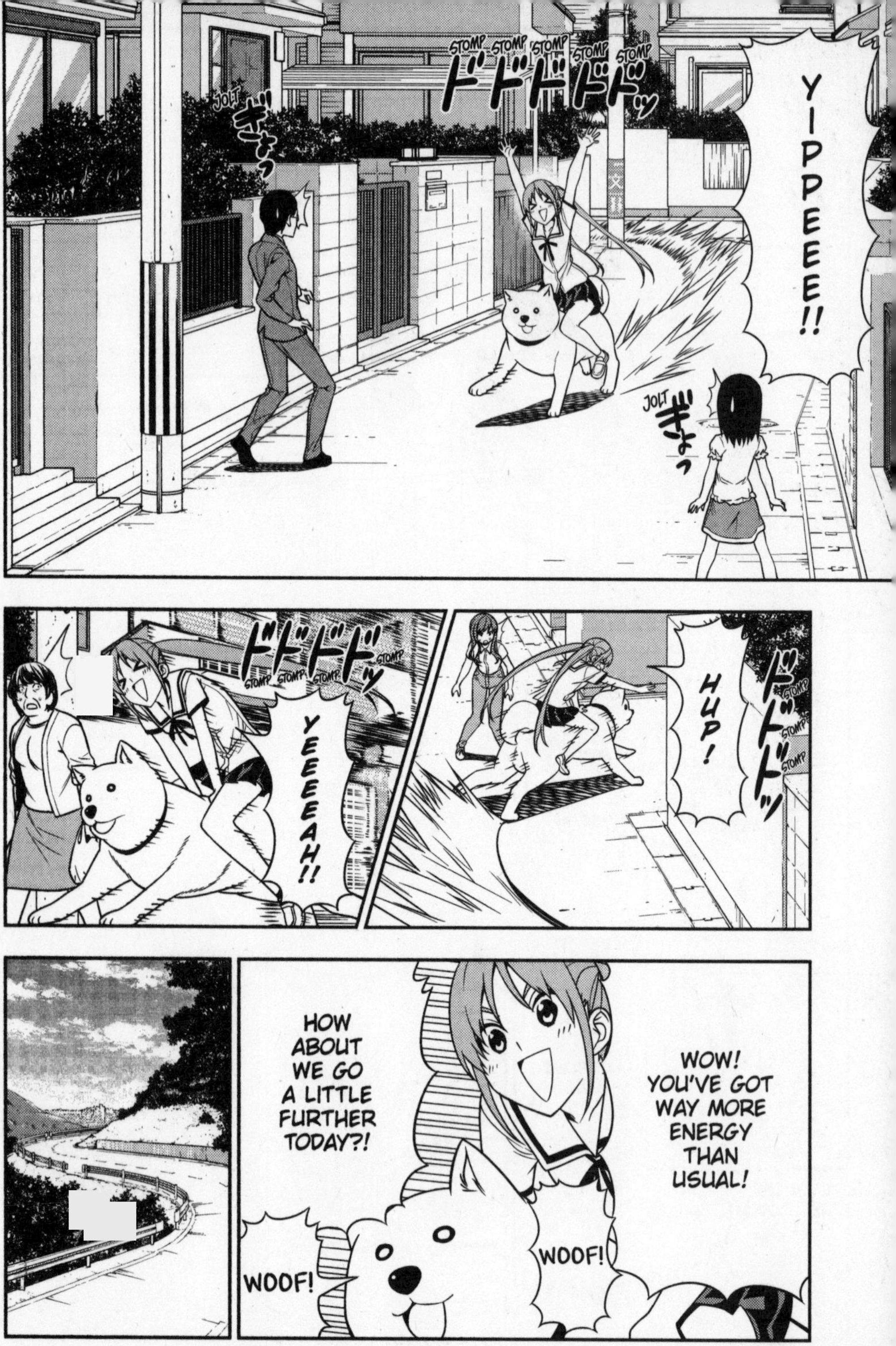

YIPPEEE!!
STOMP STOMP STOMP STOMP STOMP
ドドドドドッ
JOLT
ぎょっ
JOLT
ぎょっ
HUP!
STOMP STOMP STOMP
ドドドッ
ドドドドッ
STOMP STOMP STOMP STOMP
YEEEEEAH!!
WOW! YOU'VE GOT WAY MORE ENERGY THAN USUAL!
HOW ABOUT WE GO A LITTLE FURTHER TODAY?!
WOOF!
WOOF!

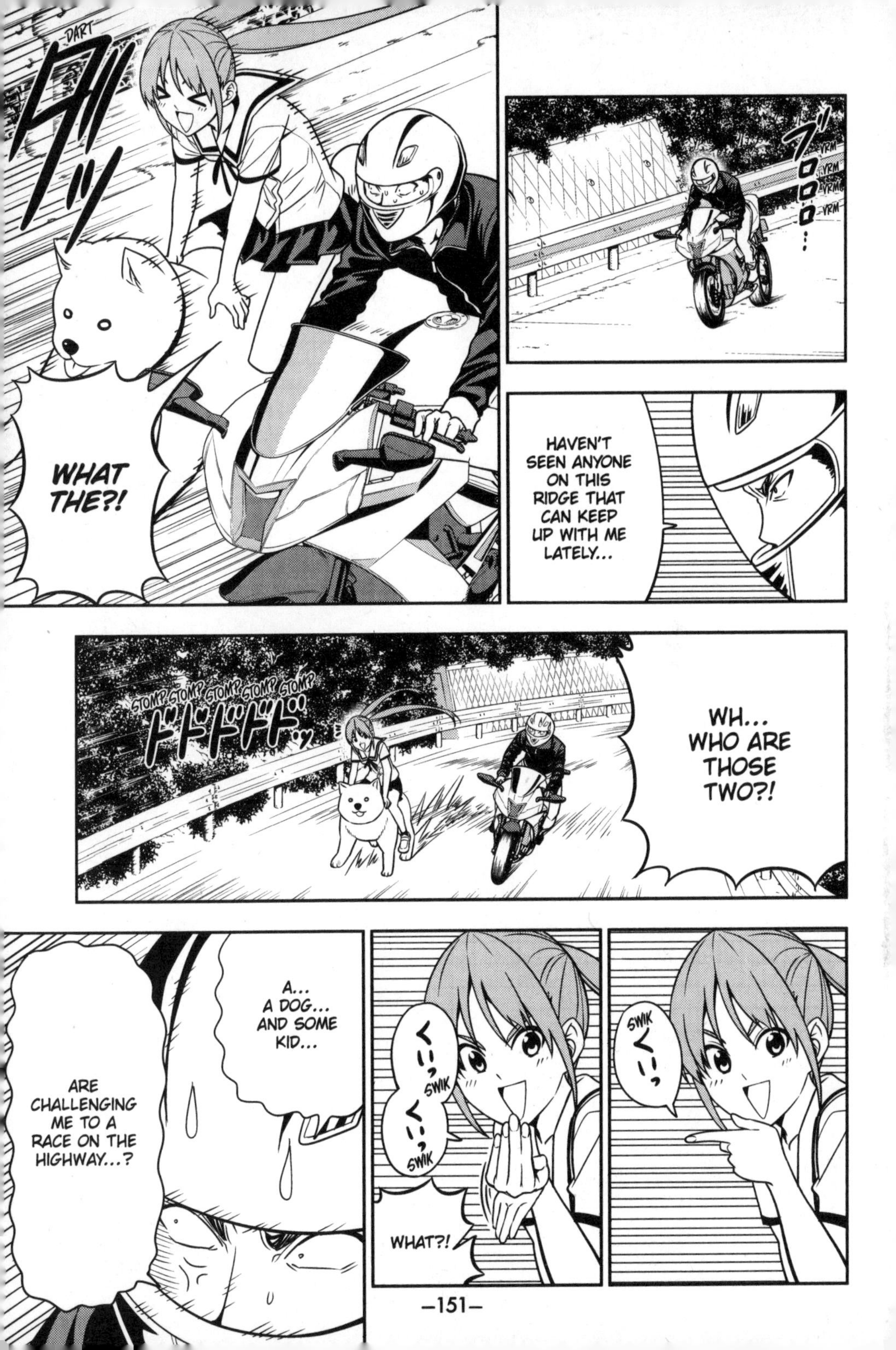
VRM VRM VRMG VRM
HAVEN'T SEEN ANYONE ON THIS RIDGE THAT CAN KEEP UP WITH ME LATELY...
DART
WHAT THE?!
WH... WHO ARE THOSE TWO?!
STOMP STOMP STOMP STOMP STOMP
SWIK
SWIK
SWIK
WHAT?!
A... A DOG... AND SOME KID...
ARE CHALLENGING ME TO A RACE ON THE HIGHWAY...?

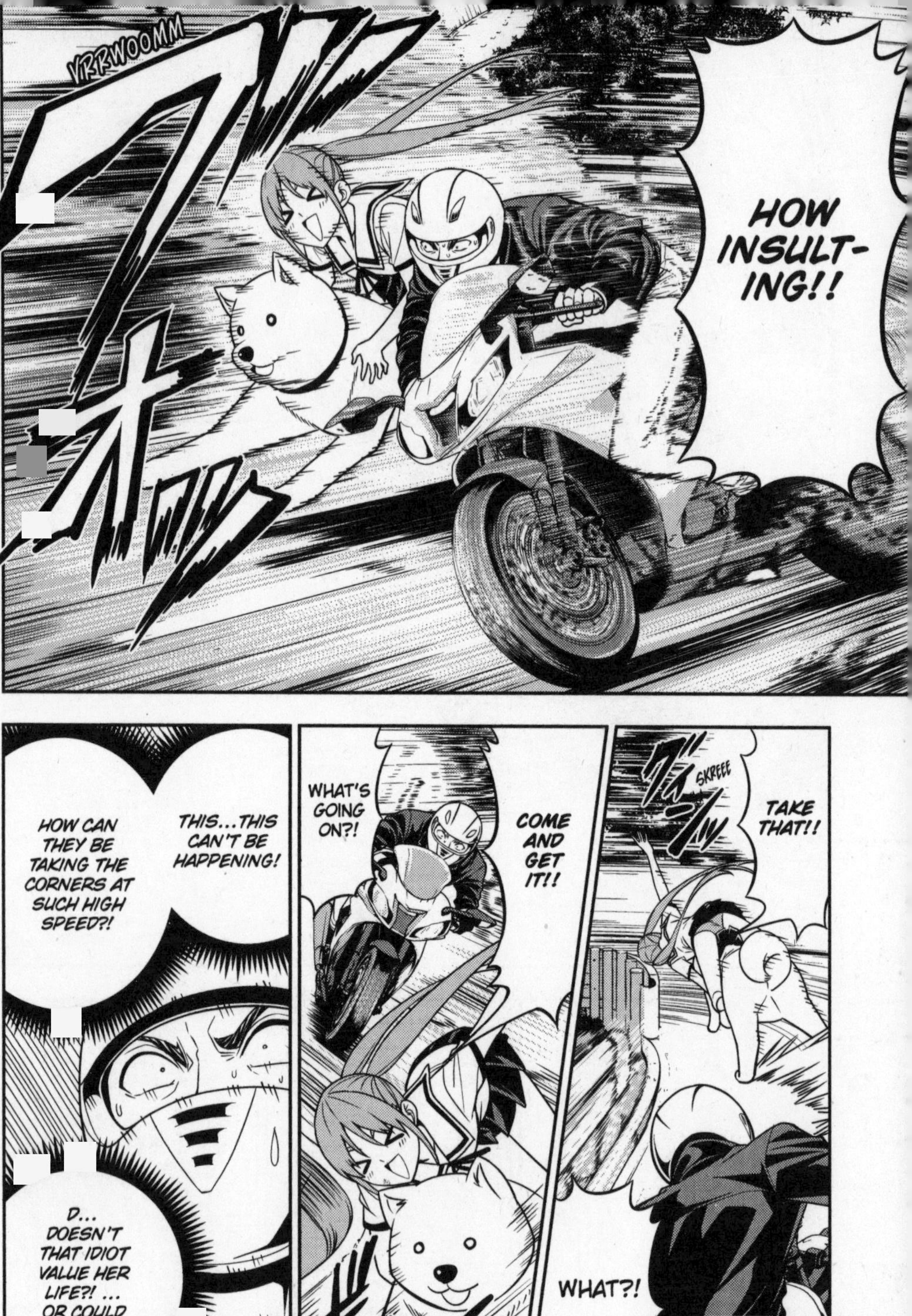
HOW INSULTING!!
VRRBWOOMM
SKREEE
TAKE THAT!!
WHAT?!
COME AND GET IT!!
WHAT'S GOING ON?!
SKREEE
THIS...THIS CAN'T BE HAPPENING!
HOW CAN THEY BE TAKING THE CORNERS AT SUCH HIGH SPEED?!
D... DOESN'T THAT IDIOT VALUE HER LIFE?! ... OR COULD IT BE...

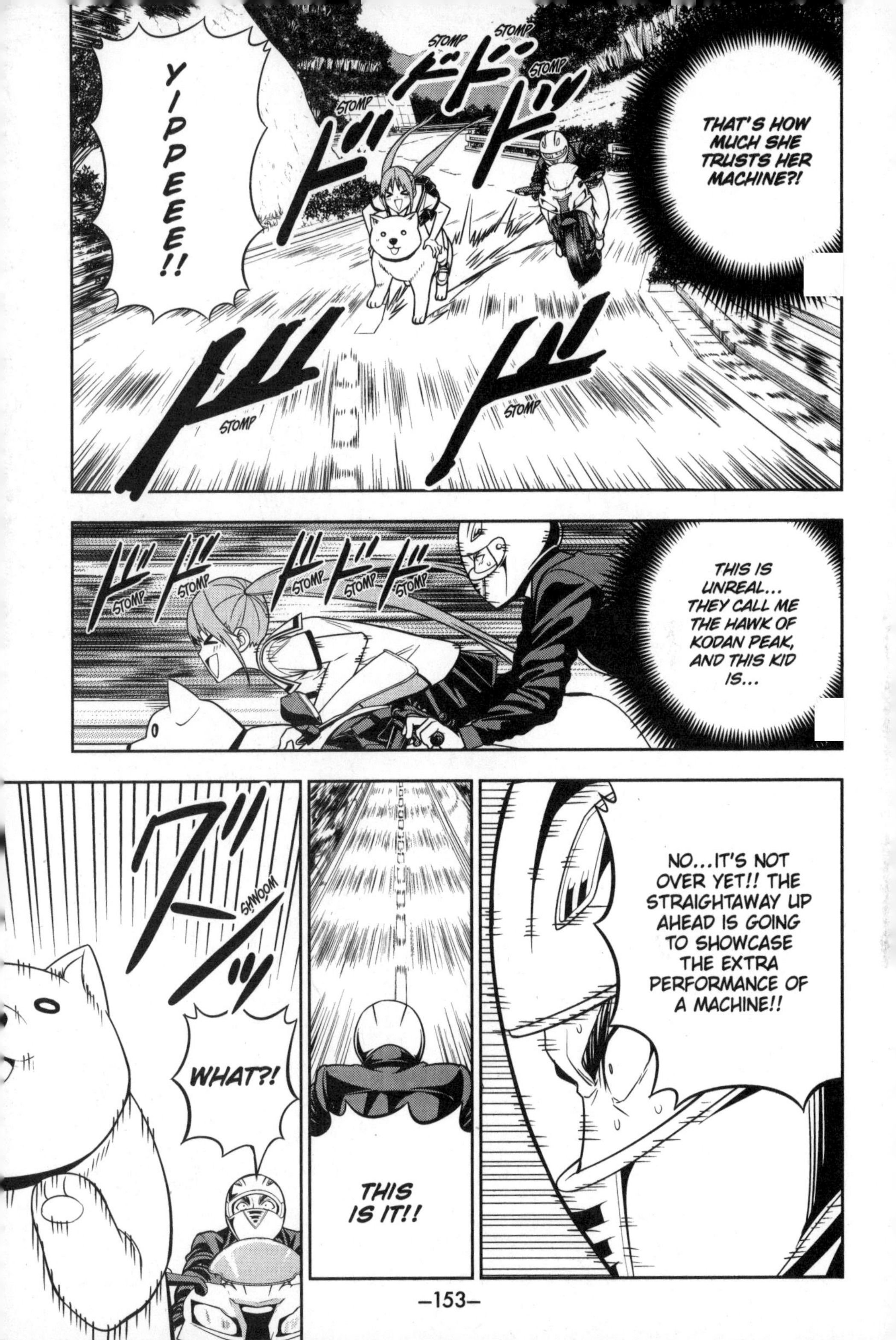
THAT'S HOW MUCH SHE TRUSTS HER MACHINE?!
STOMP
STOMP
STOMP
STOMP
YIPPEEEE!!
STOMP
STOMP
THIS IS UNREAL... THEY CALL ME THE HAWK OF KODAN PEAK, AND THIS KID IS...
STOMP
STOMP
STOMP
STOMP
STOMP
NO...IT'S NOT OVER YET!! THE STRAIGHTAWAY UP AHEAD IS GOING TO SHOWCASE THE EXTRA PERFORMANCE OF A MACHINE!!
THIS IS IT!!
SHVOOM
WHAT?!

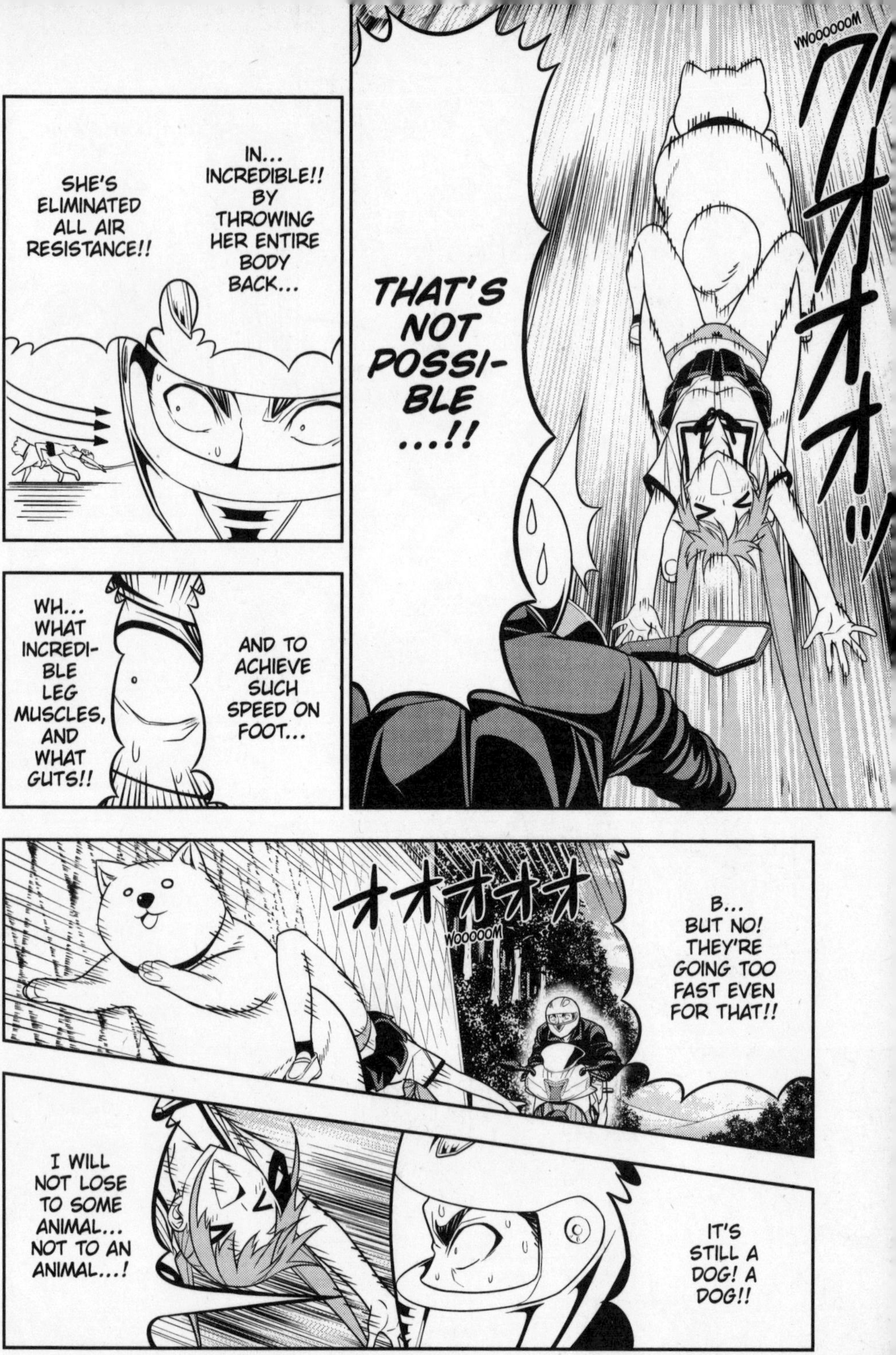
VWOOOOOOM
THAT'S NOT POSSIBLE...!!
IN... INCREDIBLE!! BY THROWING HER ENTIRE BODY BACK...
SHE'S ELIMINATED ALL AIR RESISTANCE!!
AND TO ACHIEVE SUCH SPEED ON FOOT...
WH... WHAT INCREDIBLE LEG MUSCLES, AND WHAT GUTS!!
B... BUT NO! THEY'RE GOING TOO FAST EVEN FOR THAT!!
オオオオオ
WOOOOOM
IT'S STILL A DOG! A DOG!!
I WILL NOT LOSE TO SOME ANIMAL... NOT TO AN ANIMAL...!

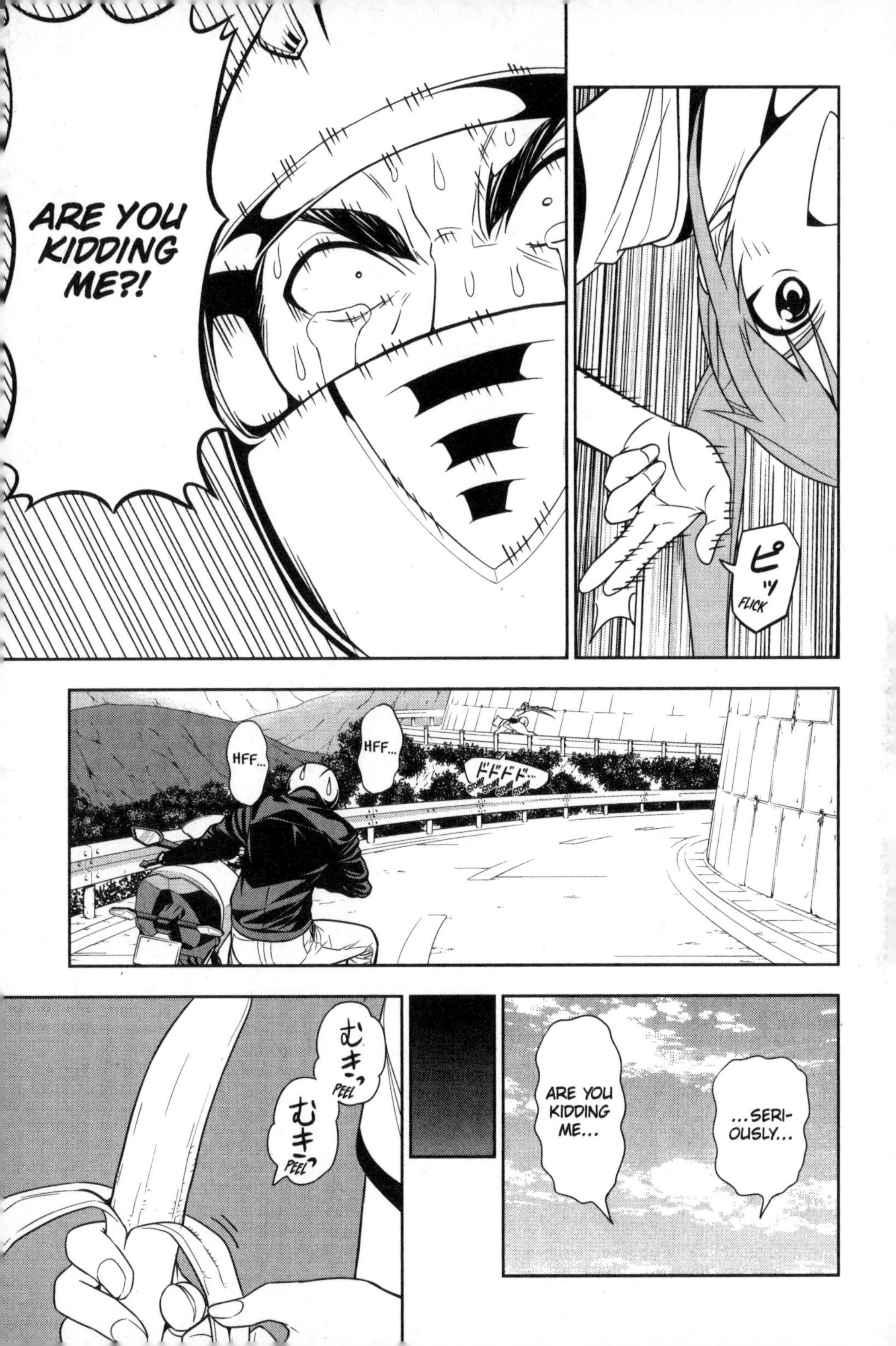
ピッ
FLICK
ARE YOU KIDDING ME?!
HFF...
HFF...
ドドドド…
STOMP STOMP STOMP STOMP
ARE YOU KIDDING ME...
...SERIOUSLY...
むきっ
PEEL
むきっ
PEEL

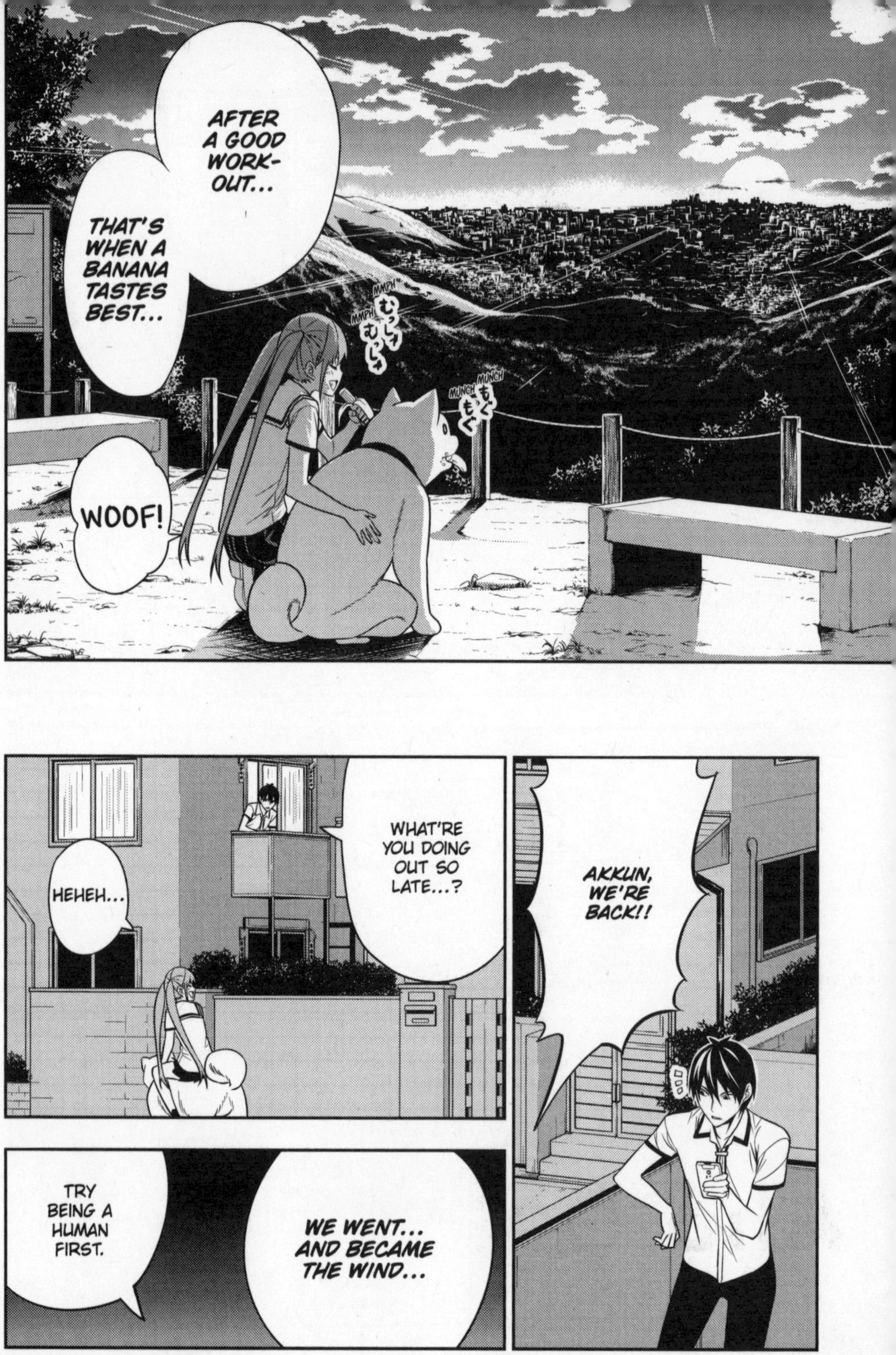
AFTER A GOOD WORK-OUT...
THAT'S WHEN A BANANA TASTES BEST...
MUNCH MUNCH
もぐもぐ
MMPH MMPH
むっしゃむっしゃ
WOOF!
AKKUN, WE'RE BACK!!
WHAT'RE YOU DOING OUT SO LATE...?
HEHEH...
WE WENT... AND BECAME THE WIND...
TRY BEING A HUMAN FIRST.

Continued in volume 4!

Aho-Girl

\\'ahô͵gərl\\ *Japanese, noun.*
A clueless girl.

The Drama of How Hiroyuki Became a Manga-Ka 2

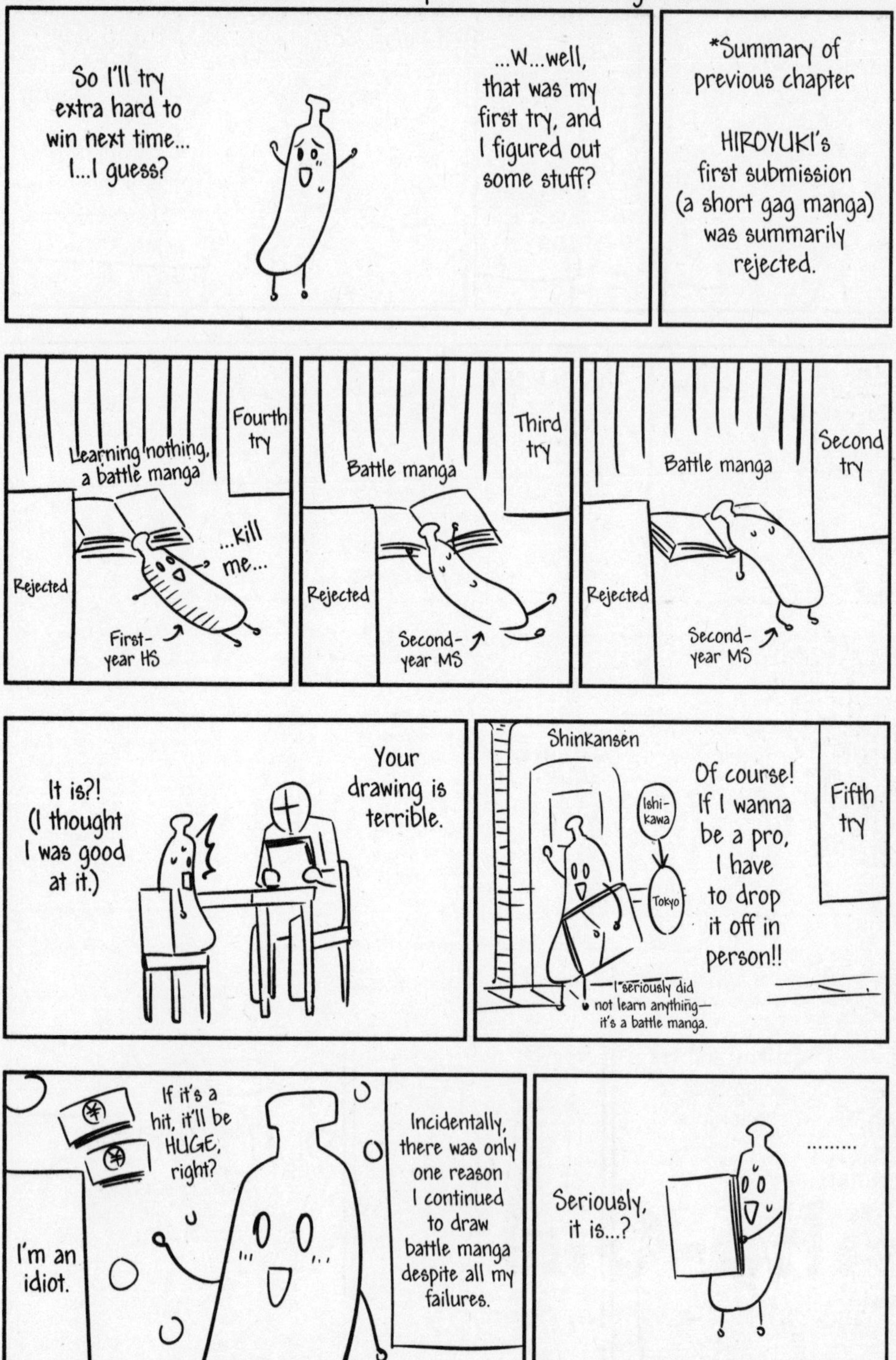
*Summary of previous chapter
HIROYUKI's first submission (a short gag manga) was summarily rejected.
...W...well, that was my first try, and I figured out some stuff?
So I'll try extra hard to win next time... I...I guess?
Second try
Battle manga
Rejected
Second-year MS
Third try
Battle manga
Rejected
Second-year MS
Fourth try
Learning nothing, a battle manga
...kill me...
Rejected
First-year HS
Fifth try
Of course! If I wanna be a pro, I have to drop it off in person!!
Shinkansen
Ishi-kawa
Tokyo
I seriously did not learn anything—it's a battle manga.
Your drawing is terrible.
It is?! (I thought I was good at it.)
....
Seriously, it is...?
Incidentally, there was only one reason I continued to draw battle manga despite all my failures.
If it's a hit, it'll be HUGE, right?
I'm an idiot.

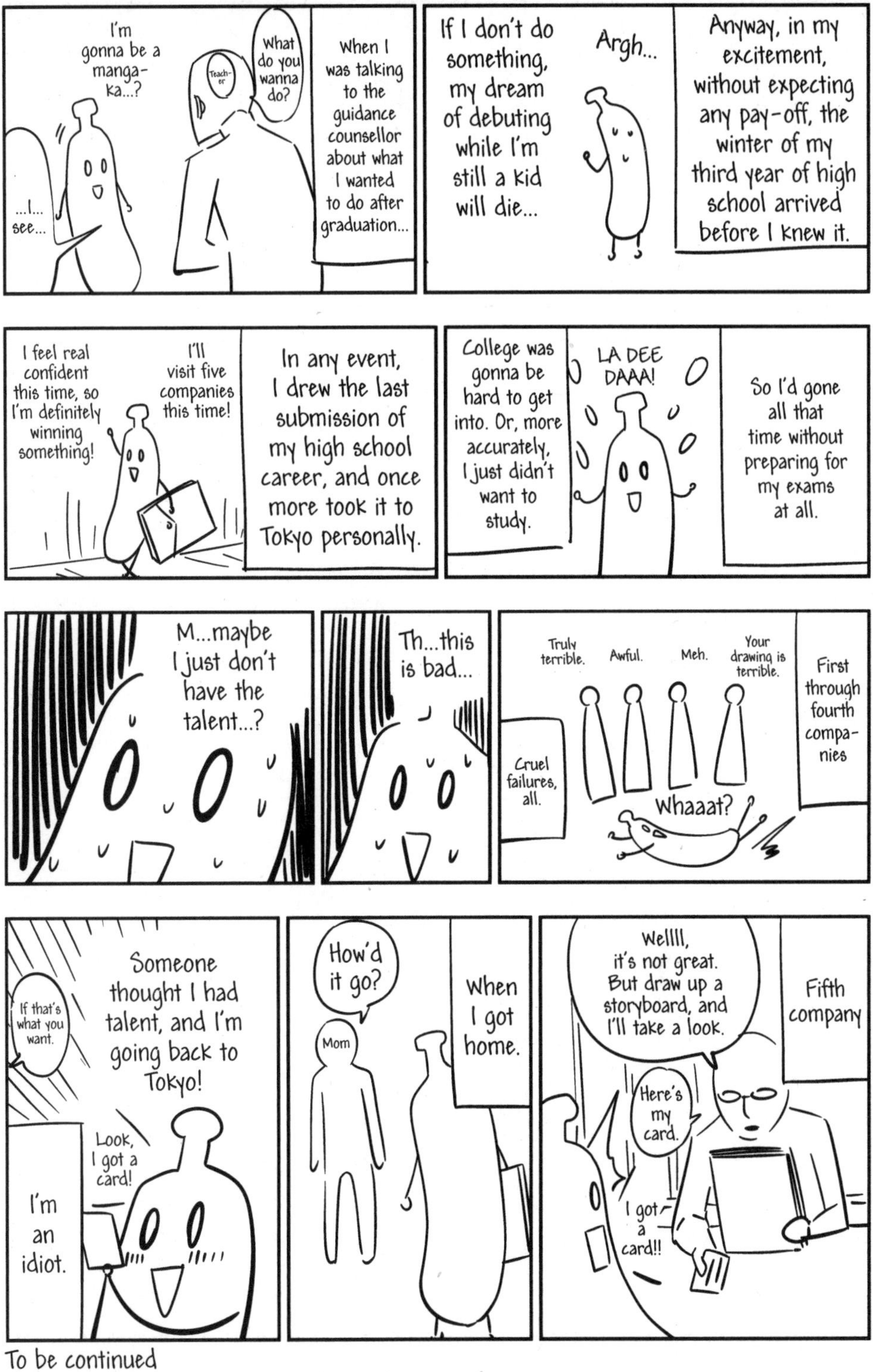
Anyway, in my excitement, without expecting any pay-off, the winter of my third year of high school arrived before I knew it.
Argh...
If I don't do something, my dream of debuting while I'm still a kid will die...
When I was talking to the guidance counsellor about what I wanted to do after graduation...
What do you wanna do?
Teach-er
I'm gonna be a manga-ka...?
...I... see...
So I'd gone all that time without preparing for my exams at all.
LA DEE DAAA!
College was gonna be hard to get into. Or, more accurately, I just didn't want to study.
In any event, I drew the last submission of my high school career, and once more took it to Tokyo personally.
I'll visit five companies this time!
I feel real confident this time, so I'm definitely winning something!
First through fourth compa-nies
Your drawing is terrible.
Meh.
Awful.
Truly terrible.
Whaaat?
Cruel failures, all.
Th...this is bad...
M...maybe I just don't have the talent...?
Fifth company
Wellll, it's not great. But draw up a storyboard, and I'll take a look.
Here's my card.
I got a card!!
When I got home.
How'd it go?
Mom
Someone thought I had talent, and I'm going back to Tokyo!
If that's what you want.
Look, I got a card!
I'm an idiot.

To be continued

Translation Notes

Page 2
"Aggravated straight man"
This is an explanatory gloss of the Japanese term "tsukkomi." The tsukkomi and boke duo are a common trope in manzai-style stand-up comedy routines. The boke, like Yoshiko, draws over-the-top and just plain stupid conclusions to the tsukkomi's set-ups. The tsukkomi tries to remain calm and reasonable during the act, but is invariably pushed into extreme and sometimes violent reactions out of his frustration.

Page 3
"Head Monitor"
The head monitor's title in Japanese includes the word fuuki, which roughly translates to "moral order" or "discipline." She would not be merely checking for hall passes the way a hall monitor in a Western school might, and would be more broadly responsible for reporting anything in violation of the moral standards of the institution.

"G Cup"
Going by Japanese bra sizing conventions, the head monitor's "G cup" would be roughly equivalent to an American DDD.

Page 12
"Today once again, we'll carry, fight, multiply and then be"
In the video game Pikmin, this line is featured as part of the refrain from the song "Ai no Uta" ("Song of Love"). The song was used in Japanese commercials for the game and expresses how the Pikmin feel towards the protagonist. In full, the refrain reads "Today once again, we'll carry, fight, multiply and then be consumed," quite thoroughly describing the role the Pikmin play.

Page 20
"We're messing around too much; we're children of summer"
This is a refrain in the song "Summer Nude" by the rock group the Magokoro Brothers, released in 1995. The song has been covered numerous times, and has inspired a TV drama and a manga series.

Page 21
Radio exercises
A series of light callisthenic exercises led by a radio broadcast. It is a nearly universal morning routine for school children and the elderly, and also famously for some Japanese businesses. As a student, Yoshiko receives an attendance stamp from the organizer each day she participates.

Page 22
"A new dawn has come"
This is the opening line to the song played during radio exercises. The vocal version signals that the exercises are about to begin, whereas a piano version without vocals is played during the exercise while instructions are given.

"She Sounds Like Hayashi-sensei"
Refers to a pop culture figure named Osamu Hayashi, who became a meme for his prep school commercials prioritizing kanji study with the slogan "When will you start? Right now, of course!"

Page 25
"Let's go, Cicadave!"
In the original Japanese version of this joke, Yoshiko names the cicada "Semitaro"—semi being the Japanese word for "cicada," and "Taro" being a common Japanese boys' name.

Page 28
"Swing your arms up, stretch as tall as you can"
This is part of the instructions given during the radio exercises.

Page 29
"Summer homework"
In Japan, the school year typically begins in the first week of April. Therefore, unlike the United States where summer break traditionally marks the end of the school year, summer break in Japan occurs in the middle of the school year (usually in the second half of July). So even though Japanese students are free to spend their summer days however they like, teachers will almost always assign homework to keep students sharp for their return to school in August.

Page 30
"Boss lady"
The term that was rendered here as "boss lady" is anego. Taken literally, anego is a respectful term of address for one's elder sister, but its more common connotation is as the term of address a low-ranking gangster would use for the boss's wife. This is appropriate given Ryuichi's criminal, ne'er-do-well affect.

Page 34
"Goodbye. Goodbye. Goodbye."
This is the title to a song by the visual kei air-rock band Golden Bomber (also known as Kinbaku) about trying to move on from a girl who broke up with the singer, even though he's still in love with her.

Ultimate Survivor Kaiji, which is a manga series by Nobuyuki Fukumoto about gambling. In the scene in question, the owner of a store hosting illegal gambling in his backroom suspects the protagonist Kaiji of stealing from him, and tries to physically attack Kaiji. One of Kaiji's friends pulls him out of the building and, once safely outside, Kaiji engages in some posturing smack talk like the above.

Page 76
"Standing in opposition to the mysterious white light, I am"
The "mysterious white light" refers to the whited-out anatomy in the preceding chapter.

Page 79
"Breaking disposable chopsticks with his butt"
This is a not-uncommon trope in slapstick comedies (both illustrated and live action), perhaps mocking the overly serious trope in martial arts movies of a character breaking a chopstick against the throat to demonstrate their incredible focus and physical training.

Page 80
"Her battle rating is off the charts!!"
This is another, non-specific reference to the Dragon Ball Z trope of battle ratings.

Page 82
"Farewell, Inn. I Return to My Faraway Home."
This is a play on the title of the final episode of the second season of the JoJo's Bizarre Adventure anime, which continued for six more seasons. The characters have been through a lot... and now that they've resolved some problems, they can relax for a bit. But there's so much more waiting...

Page 102
"Onigiri"
Yoshiko is asking for a traditional Japanese food of rice packed into a triangular shape around a salty or sour filling such as pickled plum, salted salmon, or roe, and usually wrapped in a sheet of dried seaweed. Onigiri are a staple pre-prepared "fast food" and are available in every convenience store and grocery store. But... sorry, Yoshiko... not in Western chain restaurants...

Page 109
"Bon Odori"
Dance performed at an Obon festival, which is an upbeat summer festival to commemorate the spirits of deceased family members and ancestors. Traditions vary by locale, but the dance is usually performed for

Page 36
"I don't give an"
This is a quote from the martial arts manga series Baki the Grappler, spoken by an underground kung fu master named Retsu Kaioh. When discussing how another fighter was taken down by someone using explosives in a fight, someone asks Retsu whether he finds that distasteful. Retsu replies that he couldn't care less, establishing his view that victory is the most important factor in a fight. The quote has become a minor meme.

Page 40
"My Feminine Power is 530,000"
In Dragon Ball Z, when Freeza (also rendered as Frieza) attacks a village that hides a Dragon Ball, he self-reports his battle power as 530,000 before defeating the strongest challenger the village has to offer.

Page 44
"Time for pajama"
This refers to a long-running segment on the children's television show With Mother (Okaasan to issho), with the sing-song name of "Pajama de Ojama" ("Time for Pajama Break"). The segment was intended to teach very young children how to get dressed on their own and showed children changing into pajamas to get ready for the next segment in the show.

Page 52
"A hat, a swimsuit, and"
This is the title of a 2003 song by JPOP star aiko, which appeared on the B-side of her single "Chouchou Musubi" ("Butterfly Knot"). The full title of this song is "A hat, a Swimsuit, and the Horizon" ("Boushi to Mizugi to Suiheisen").

Page 60
"You're my sun-bathed city"
This is a reference to a song by B'z released in 1990, titled "Taiyou no Komachi Angel" ("Sun-bathed City Angel").

Page 68
"Romance makes you put it on, love makes you"
This is an old but very well-remembered advertising slogan for the Isetan chain of department stores. The full slogan can be translated as "romance makes you put it on, love makes you take it off." This ties into the slogan's intention to sell high-fashion clothing.

Page 73
"Doubt Me? This Is War!"
This is a paraphrased quote from the manga series

bystanders by an official group that has been practicing for weeks ahead of time.

Page 111
"Yoyoi-no-yoi"
Yoshiko is doing an old-fashioned, upbeat nonsense chant that she can dance along to.

Page 116
"EZ Do"
"EZ Do Dance" is the name of a 1993 single by the group TRF.

Page 118
"Let's sleep until 6"
How could Yoshiko agree to this?! The radio exercises start at 6:30 AM!

Page 132
"Jaka jaka jan ☆ Jaka jaka jan ☆ Jaka jaka jaka jaka jan ken"
This is the not-at-all annoying song that plays during a segment of FujiTV's children's program Ponkickies, in which a cartoon girl plays rock-paper-scissors ("jan ken pon") with the viewers. The song ends on the line "jan ken PON!" and, after the result is revealed, the girl transitions back to the main show with "Pon pon Ponkickies!"

Page 140
"All too easy to hate"
A 1977 rock single by Kenji Sawada is titled "A Good-for-nothing All too Easy to Hate" ("Nikumi-kirenai roku de nashi").

Page 144
"I don't know what comes next!"
Yoshiko is at a loss here because she's chosen to do the count in English, rather than using Japanese numbers. Perhaps she's used to the counts in pro wrestling commentary ending sooner?

Page 145
"Ruri-sama"
Akkun typically does not use honorific (-san) or diminutive (-chan) suffixes when talking to Ruri. This is normal for family members (although someone more openly affectionate might call his little sister "Ruri-chan"). However, here he has switched to saying "Ruri-sama." This is an over-the-top expression of respect, putting Ruri on an almost god-like plane above Akkun.

Page 148
"The love that lives on in the time that we share makes me"
This is a lyric in the song "MELODY" featured in the dating sim Sister Princess. The premise of the game is for the player to take on the role of a brother to twelve sisters, who he must split his time between to provide "big brother" support such as walking a chosen sister to school in order to win her affection. The franchise began as a series of light novels before being adapted into several video games as well as anime series.

Page 157
"INITIAL"
This refers to the manga and anime series Initial D, which deals with illegal street racing, primarily taking place in precarious mountain passes.

Page 159
"Winter of my third year of high school"
In Japan, students graduate in late March or early April of their third year of high school.

Aho-Girl

\\'ahô͵gərl\\ *Japanese, noun.*
A clueless girl.

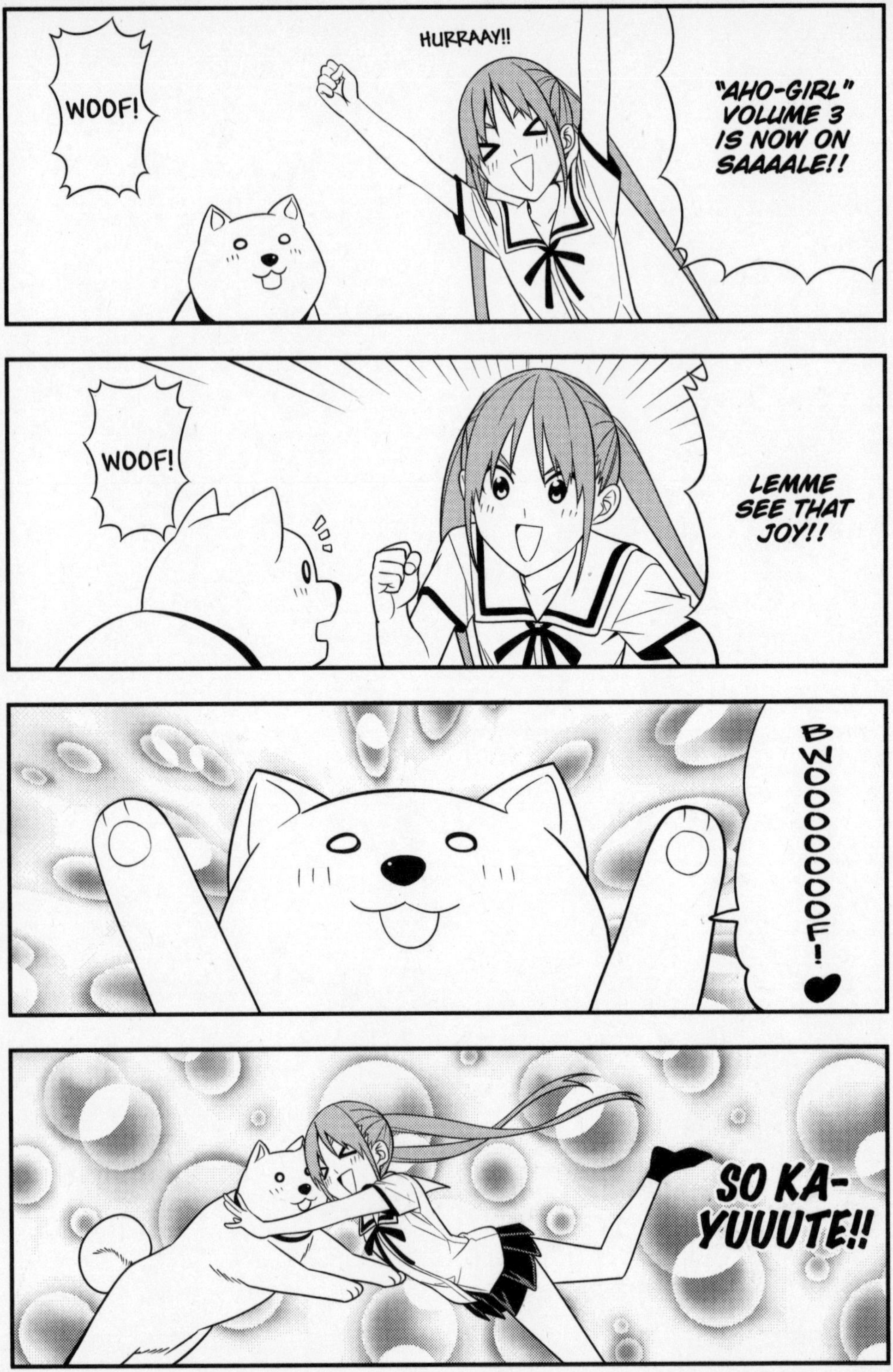
HURRAAY!!
"AHO-GIRL" VOLUME 3 IS NOW ON SAAAALE!!
WOOF!
LEMME SEE THAT JOY!!
WOOF!
BWOOOOOOOF!♥
SO KA-YUUUTE!!

HFF... HFF... HFF...

"An emotional and artistic tour de force! We see incredible triumph, and crushing defeat... each panel [is] a thrill!"
—Anitay

"A journey that's instantly compelling."
—Anime News Network

WELCOME TO THE BALLROOM

By Tomo Takeuchi

Feckless high school student Tatara Fujita wants to be good at something—anything. Unfortunately, he's about as average as a slouchy teen can be. The local bullies know this, and make it a habit to hit him up for cash, but all that changes when the debonair Kaname Sengoku sends them packing. Sengoku's not the neighborhood watch, though. He's a professional ballroom dancer. And once Tatara Fujita gets pulled into the world of ballroom, his life will never be the same.

KC
KODANSHA COMICS

The award-winning manga about what happens inside you!

"Far more entertaining than it ought to be... what kid doesn't want to think that every time they sneeze a torpedo shoots out their nose?"
–Anime News Network

Strep throat! Hay fever! Influenza! The world is a dangerous place for a red blood cell just trying to get her deliveries finished. Fortunately, she's not alone...she's got a whole human body's worth of cells ready to help out! The mysterious white blood cells, the buff and brash killer T cells, even the cute little platelets—everyone's got to come together if they want to keep you healthy!

Cells at Work!

はたらく細胞

By Akane Shimizu

KC/
KODANSHA
COMICS

A new
series
from the
creator
of *Soul
Eater*, the
megahit
manga and
anime seen
on Toonami!

"Fun and lively...
a great start!"
-Adventures in
Poor Taste

FIRE FORCE

By Atsushi Ohkubo

The city of Tokyo is plagued by a deadly phenomenon: spontaneous human combustion! Luckily, a special team is there to quench the inferno: The Fire Force! The fire soldiers at Special Fire Cathedral 8 are about to get a unique addition. Enter Shinra, a boy who possesses the power to run at the speed of a rocket, leaving behind the famous "devil's footprints" (and destroying his shoes in the process). Can Shinra and his colleagues discover the source of this strange epidemic before the city burns to ashes?

KC
KODANSHA COMICS

The Black Museum The Ghost and the Lady

By Kazuhiro Fujita

Deep in Scotland Yard in London sits an evidence room dedicated to the greatest mysteries of British history. In this "Black Museum" sits a misshapen hunk of lead—two bullets fused together—the key to a wartime encounter between Florence Nightingale, the mother of modern nursing, and a supernatural Man in Grey. This story is unknown to most scholars of history, but a special guest of the museum will tell the tale of The Ghost and the Lady...

Praise for Kazuhiro Fujita's *Ushio and Tora*

"A charming revival that combines a classic look with modern depth and pacing... **Essential viewing both for curmudgeons and new fans alike.**" — Anime News Network

"**GREAT!** The first episode of Ushio and Tora captures the essence of '90s anime." — IGN

Japan's most powerful spirit medium delves into the ghost world's greatest mysteries!

Story by Kyo Shirodaira, famed author of mystery fiction and creator of *Spiral*, *Blast of Tempest*, and *The Record of a Fallen Vampire*.

Both touched by spirits called yôkai, Kotoko and Kurô have gained unique superhuman powers. But to gain her powers Kotoko has given up an eye and a leg, and Kurô's personal life is in shambles. So when Kotoko suggests they team up to deal with renegades from the spirit world, Kurô doesn't have many other choices, but Kotoko might just have a few ulterior motives...

IN/SPECTRE

STORY BY **KYO SHIRODAIRA**
ART BY **CHASHIBA KATASE**

HAPPINESS

ハピネス

By Shuzo Oshimi

From the creator of *The Flowers of Evil*

Nothing interesting is happening in Makoto Ozaki's first year of high school. His life is a series of quiet humiliations: low-grade bullies, unreliable friends, and the constant frustration of his adolescent lust. But one night, a pale, thin girl knocks him to the ground in an alley and offers him a choice. Now everything is different. Daylight is searingly bright. Food tastes awful. And worse than anything is the terrible, consuming thirst...

Praise for Shuzo Oshimi's *The Flowers of Evil*

"A shockingly readable story that vividly—one might even say queasily—evokes the fear and confusion of discovering one's own sexuality. Recommended." —The Manga Critic

"A page-turning tale of sordid middle school blackmail." —Otaku USA Magazine

"A stunning new horror manga." —Third Eye Comics

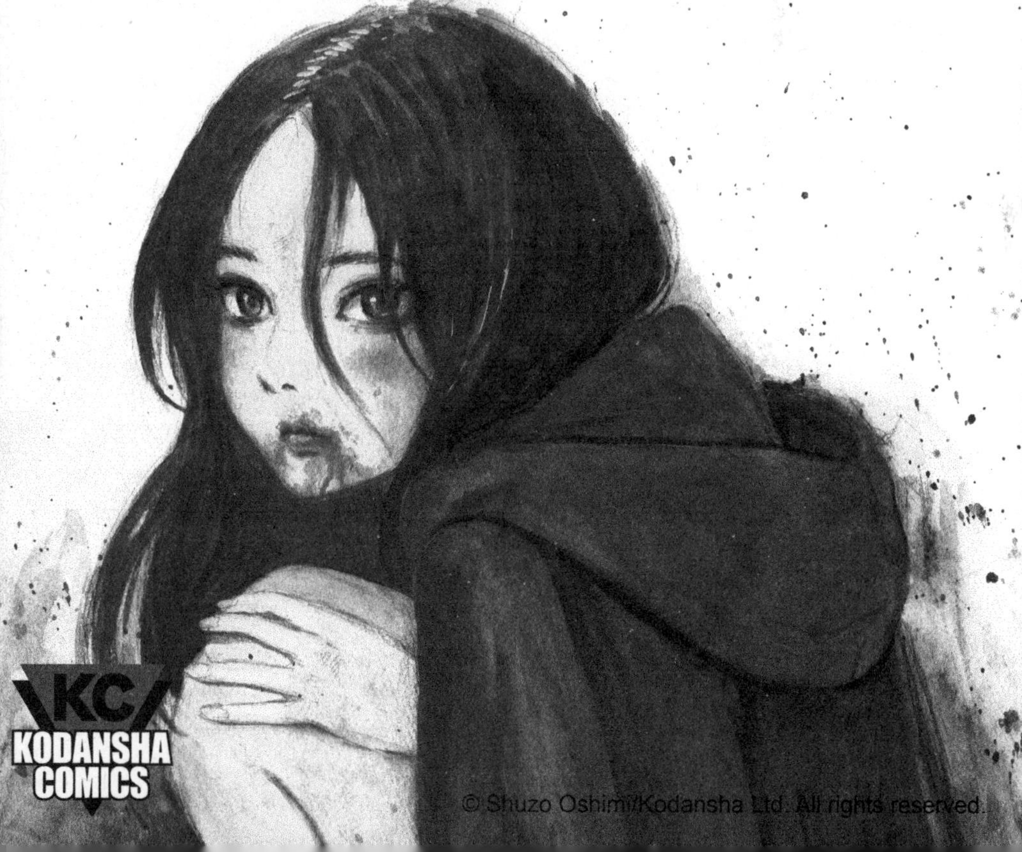

KC KODANSHA COMICS

Based on the critically acclaimed classic horror manga

The first new *Parasyte* manga in over 20 years!

NEO PARASYTE f

BY ASUMIKO NAKAMURA, EMA TOYAMA, MIKI RINNO, LALAKO KOJIMA, KAORI YUKI, BANKO KUZE, YUUKI OBATA, KASHIO, YUI KUROE, ASIA WATANABE, MIKIMAKI, HIKARU SURUGA, HAJIME SHINJO, RENJURO KINDAICHI, AND YURI NARUSHIMA

A collection of chilling new *Parasyte* stories from Japan's top shojo artists!

Parasites: shape-shifting aliens whose only purpose is to assimilate with and consume the human race... but do these monsters have a different side? A parasite becomes a prince to save his romance-obsessed female host from a dangerous stalker. Another hosts a cooking show, in which the real monsters are revealed. These and 13 more stories, from some of the greatest shojo manga artists alive today, together make up a chilling, funny, and entertaining tribute to one of manga's horror classics!

A Kodansha Comics Trade Paperback Original.

Published in the United States by Kodansha Comics, an imprint of Kodansha USA Publishing, LLC, New York.

Publication rights for this English edition arranged through Kodansha Ltd., Tokyo.
First published in Japan in 2014 by Kodansha Ltd., Tokyo, as Aho Gaaru volume 3.

ISBN 978-1-63236-459-3

Printed in the United States of America.

www.kodanshacomics.com

9 8 7 6 5 4 3 2 1

Translator: Karen McGillicuddy
Lettering: S. Lee
Editing: Paul Starr
Kodansha Comics edition cover design by Phil Balsman

The prince in his dark days

By **Hico Yamanaka**

A drunkard for a father, a household of poverty... For 17-year-old Atsuko, misfortune is all she knows and believes in. Until one day, a chance encounter with Itaru–the wealthy heir of a huge corporation–changes everything. The two look identical, uncannily so. When Itaru curiously goes missing, Atsuko is roped into being his stand-in. There, in his shoes, Atsuko must parade like a prince in a palace. She encounters many new experiences, but at what cost...?

Having lost his wife, high school teacher Kōhei Inuzuka is doing his best to raise his young daughter Tsumugi as a single father. He's pretty bad at cooking and doesn't have a huge appetite to begin with, but chance brings his little family together with one of his students, the lonely Kotori. The three of them are anything but comfortable in the kitchen, but the healing power of home cooking might just work on their grieving hearts.

"This season's number-one feel-good anime!" —Anime News Network

"A beautifully-drawn story about comfort food and family and grief. Recommended." —Otaku USA Magazine

sweetness & lightning

By Gido Amagakure

KC
KODANSHA
COMICS

New action series from Hiroyuki Takei, creator of the classic shonen franchise Shaman King!

In medieval Japan, a bell hanging on the collar is a sign that a cat has a master. Norachiyo's bell hangs from his katana sheath, but he is nonetheless a stray — a ronin. This one-eyed cat samurai travels across a dishonest world, cutting through pretense and deception with his blade.

STRAY CAT SAMURAI

By
Hiroyuki Takei